P9-CEN-064

PHILIPPINE ISLANDS

★ ★ ★

Pacific Ocean

130°   135°   140°

20°

15°

10°

5°

Luzon

↑ Cabanatuan

CLARK AIR FIELD ■

● San Fernando (Pampanga)

Olongapo ●

Subic Bay

Manila Bay

BILIBID PRISON
Manila

PASAY SCHOOL, Pasay ■

Cavite ●

CAVITE NAVAL BASE

Bataan Peninsula

Corregidor

South China Sea

Philippine Sea

0 Miles   50
0 Kilometers   50

POW/*ERIE MARU* route from
Luzon to Davao Gulf, Mindanao

THE
JERSEY
BROTHERS

A Missing Naval Officer in the Pacific and
His Family's Quest to Bring Him Home

★ ★ ★

SALLY MOTT FREEMAN

SIMON & SCHUSTER

New York London Toronto Sydney New Delhi

Simon & Schuster
1230 Avenue of the Americas
New York, NY 10020

Copyright © 2017 by SMF Productions, LLC

All rights reserved, including the right to reproduce this book or portions thereof in any form whatsoever. For information, address Simon & Schuster Subsidiary Rights Department, 1230 Avenue of the Americas, New York, NY 10020.

First Simon & Schuster hardcover edition May 2017

SIMON & SCHUSTER and colophon are registered trademarks of Simon & Schuster, Inc.

For information about special discounts for bulk purchases, please contact Simon & Schuster Special Sales at 1-866-506-1949 or business@simonandschuster.com.

The Simon & Schuster Speakers Bureau can bring authors to your live event. For more information or to book an event, contact the Simon & Schuster Speakers Bureau at 1-866-248-3049 or visit our website at www.simonspeakers.com.

Interior design by Ruth Lee-Mui

Manufactured in the United States of America

10   9   8   7   6   5   4   3   2   1

Library of Congress Cataloging-in-Publication Data is available.

ISBN 978-1-5011-0414-5
ISBN 978-1-5011-0417-6 (ebook)

Dedicated with love

to the First Siblings,

Adam Sutherland Mott and Jeannette Mott Fritz

Contents

PART TWO

PART THREE

On New Year's Eve of 1941, the American and Filipino army wounded at Manila's Sternberg Hospital were rushed from their wards to an awaiting hospital ship, the last vessel to depart Manila before it fell to the Japanese. Looking on in disbelief, navy nurse Bertha Evans asked, "What about the navy patients? What's supposed to happen to them?"

Preface

I have a clear memory of that moment when our innocence was fractured, perhaps because it was in such contrast to our blissful cousin-play. It was a midsummer night in the 1960s, and we were playing badminton on the south lawn of Lilac Hedges, our grandmother's home in New Jersey. The highlight of those summer visits was seeing our cousin there, whom we adored and rarely saw otherwise. I know it was dusk because that was when the bats started dive-bombing the birdie, our favorite part of the evening.

The adults—my father, mother, aunt, and grandmother—were having their cocktails on the front porch. Suddenly we heard Aunt Rosemary's voice rise up over the rest, after which she burst into tears. Then we heard a glass break, which is when we stopped our play, got dead quiet, and strained our ears. When I say *break*, I don't mean fall-off-the-table break; I mean throw-against-the-wall break. Then we heard our mother try to say something, and then *she* started crying.

My father was an admiral, and at the time serving as the navy's judge advocate general (JAG). He usually held the attention of the people around him—at work and at home. But his attempts to restore calm were in vain that evening, as apparently were my mother's attempts to assist him. We couldn't hear much, but without a doubt, the ever-charged topic was our mysterious Uncle Barton, a naval ensign who had been wounded and taken prisoner by the Japanese long before any of us was born.

We kids had never met Uncle Barton, but my siblings, cousin, and I all knew what he looked like. There were photos of him on every wall of every room at Lilac Hedges. You would hardly have known that our grandmother had three other children. I especially remember Barton's imposing oil portrait on the facing wall at the turn near the top of the front stairs. I was sure his smiling green eyes followed my every step as I walked up. We joked that he was winking at us, but whenever I reached that landing, I took those last two steps in a leap of terror, as though fleeing a ghost.

We left Lilac Hedges abruptly the next morning for the drive back to Washington, DC. A flimsy explanation for the early departure was offered as four glum kids took turns hugging our cousin, promising him unconvincingly that we'd be back, and then piling into our old Chevy wagon. I don't remember what reason was offered, just that none of us believed it.

One thing was certain: there was always tension when this Uncle Barton's name came up. Each time, I felt a familiar tingling at the back of my neck and then braced myself. *Here we go again.* What was going on here? As children, and then teens, and then young adults, we analyzed every syllable whenever the topic sprang from its dark corner, hoping to elicit conclusive details. But the mystery persisted long into our adulthood. Speculation on what had happened to him—and when—became a sort of a parlor game for us, and it never ended satisfactorily.

When I set out to unravel this family mystery, my objective was to uncover the facts that led to the anguished outburst that night—and which ended our traditional summer visits to Lilac Hedges. I was determined to learn more about this Uncle Barton, but what I uncovered would have stunned the adults on that porch.

PART

ONE

1

★ ★ ★

APRIL 1942, LUZON, THE PHILIPPINES

THEY HAD BEEN MARCHING at bayonet point when Barton Cross realized a fellow navy patient was dead. Neither Barton Cross nor Charles Armour—shouldering the other end of their friend's crude litter—slowed his pace, despite the dreadful truth that passed between them. They didn't dare stop. By this point in their imprisonment, they had learned that it was safer to proceed as silent pallbearers than call attention to themselves—risking a rifle butt in the rib, a bayonet in the back, or a shot in the head. Wordlessly, they moved in step with the grim prisoner procession through Manila's choking heat and rising red road dust.

Like Barton, the deceased had been wounded during the Japanese bombings of Cavite Navy Yard, the US naval installation near Manila. He was near death at the start of the march, but Barton and Charles had agreed not to let on if he were to die en route. They wanted to get him to a place where his name and death could be recorded. Hundreds before him had not been so lucky. As much as dying itself, all the prisoners feared being dumped into an unmarked grave, their fate forever untold.

Barton's own shrapnel wounds oozed with every step as he struggled under the corpse's sagging weight. The filthy, matted dressing had fallen away, exposing months-old gashes in his leg and foot that had never healed properly. Ahead of him, Charles stared at the road passing under his boots in a grim, trancelike state. His own wounds were deep, but invisible; it would do neither of them any good if Charles were to break down again.

Barton's gold watch had been taken from him when he was captured, but since then he had marked off the long days and nights on an old ten-peso bill. It had been just over a hundred days since he was taken prisoner from a hospital cot in Manila, the tip of a saber at his temple. As Barton worked to absorb the loss of yet another friend, he tried to make sense of all that had happened to him since those first moments as a prisoner of war.

IT SEEMED LIKE DAYS, not months, since Barton heard Don Bell's anxious voice over KZRH, Radio Manila, blaring from a nearby barrack. The carousing ensigns had returned to Cavite late the night before and were walking to the mess hall for Sunday-morning sausages and hotcakes. It was December 8 (December 7 in Hawaii). "Those dirty little bastards have struck Pearl Harbor!" Bell shouted between audible panting. "Reports remain sketchy, but there is no doubt! Oh my God!" Bell was actually crying, near hysteria. "Those yellow-bellied Japs hit our ships at anchor!"

The ensigns hurried on to the mess, which was in chaos over the news. All hands had been ordered to report to their commanding officers on the double. Captain Joel Newsom convened the crew of Barton's ship, submarine tender USS *Otus*, in the Yard's administrative building. Gathered, too, were the captains of submarines *Sculpin*, *Sealion*, *Salmon*, *Sailfish*, and *Seawolf*, all talking nervously among themselves and comparing notes on their clipboards. The room was abuzz with speculation but quieted instantly when Captain Newsom cleared his throat.

"Men, listen carefully. The following message was received from Admiral Hart this morning. 'To Asiatic Fleet . . . Urgent . . . Japan has commenced hostilities . . . the Pacific Fleet has been immobilized . . . govern yourselves accordingly.'" Admiral Thomas C. Hart was the Asiatic Fleet's commander in chief and the highest-ranking naval officer in the Philippines; they knew this meant they were likely the next target.

Captain Newsom proceeded to list a lengthy series of urgent tasks. They could come under attack at any time, and loading, camouflaging, and servicing the submarines were now time critical. Barton and *Otus*'s crew went straight to the docks following the briefing and ratcheted the work to a breakneck pace.

Later that same day, exactly nine hours after the decimation of the Pacific Fleet at Pearl Harbor, the Japanese began their assault on the Philippines. Their opening salvos went to the heart of the island's air defenses, which proved an easy mark. Despite Washington's urgent, repeated orders to General Douglas MacArthur—at the time the US Army Forces Commander in the Far East—to launch his planes and initiate air operations, beginning minutes after the start of the attack on Pearl Harbor, he did not respond. Nor did he ever issue the order. As a consequence, virtually every US plane at Luzon's primary airfields, Clark Field and Nichols Field, was bombed on the ground, wingtip to wingtip. The army's entire staple of bombers, their payloads full, was wiped out in a matter of hours.

The men at Cavite Naval Base reeled at the news. The loss was particularly alarming to the submariners, who relied heavily on army air reconnaissance to prevent enemy flyers from spotting them through some of the world's clearest coastal waters. With air protection gone, Admiral Hart was forced to change his strategy. For officers and crew of the USS *Otus*, one of the fleet's crucial submarine tenders, that meant preparing for immediate sortie into dangerous waters with the subs under their care. They would make for the relative safety of Darwin, Australia, and await further orders.

The slender Asiatic Fleet had a few vintage destroyers, but its signature strength was a large contingent of submarines—more than double that of the Pacific Fleet. Because of its miles of coastline, eddies, and deep harbors, the Philippines was deemed ideal for a submarine defense. The Asiatic Fleet's recent relocation from Shanghai to Manila was for the specific purpose of deterring a seaborne Japanese attack. The three tenders, *Otus*, *Holland*, and *Canopus*, were charged with keeping those subs, which required significant maintenance, action-ready and in uninterrupted service.

Inside the Yard, antiaircraft units were put on five-minute-alert cycles. Barton and his shipmates worked deep into the nights of December 8 and 9. First priority was to ensure that the subs were stocked, armed, and primed for launch. They filled *Otus*'s exposed fuel tanks with water to prevent incineration if hit and installed antiaircraft guns on her deck. Surplus machinery and ammunition were stored in casements and tunnels around the Yard, and as *Otus*'s paymaster, Barton rushed to secure the ship's funds and financial records.

At approximately 1100 hours on December 10, warning sirens pierced Cavite's soft tropical air. Following their wail came a stern broadcast over the Yard's loudspeakers: enemy formations were approaching from the northeast. Within minutes the assailants were visible—fifty-four planes in three tight Vs, the whole formation making one large V. The *Otus* crew looked up in surprise; they had never seen bombers fly so high.

Antiaircraft gunners squinted, aimed, and fired, but the planes were so far above the range of the 1918-vintage weapons that the shells burst in harmless black puffs less than halfway up to their targets. With air cover lost and only toylike antiaircraft guns for defense, the submarines had to get out to sea.

Two submarines with their hatches open lay astride *Otus*. Their crews were topside, scrambling to take on a last cache of supplies. Barton shouted to them to close their hatches and get under way as one enemy bomber after another opened its payload.

The first air group had barely cast a shadow on the east side of the Yard before ships, docks, men, and buildings started exploding in a line. The planes then flew at an almost leisurely pace to the other side of the Yard and discharged the rest of their payloads. The oil storage tanks erupted like geysers, and droplets of oily fire lit the surrounding ground. Corpses by the dozens flew into the air, their smoldering parts scattering down across the Yard.

The next air group set its sights on the congested center of the facility, where its bombs cut a glinting path of destruction. In minutes, fueling depots, machine houses, and storage facilities were ablaze, and plumes of black, choking smoke shot up across Cavite. That was the last thing Barton remembered before he too was struck down by branding-hot shrapnel. The explosion that snared him crippled *Sealion*, one of the two subs he'd been shouting at, and reduced the dock and pilings to splinters. When he awoke, he was lying on a stretcher in Cavite's base hospital intake area.

Men all around him were blackened from head to foot and lying in puddles of their own blood. Slashes of ripped khaki, soaked red, were all that remained of Barton's pant legs, and his shoes pooled with blood. Navy medics triaged among the wounded with surreal calm, applying tourniquets and giving morphine to some, and placing sheets over others.

By evening, the base hospital, named Canacao, was overwhelmed with casualties. Worse, since it was located next to a packed munitions depot, it was a prime future target. With air attacks expected to resume the next day, the facility had to be evacuated. By midnight, hospital staff had requisitioned a boat to move the Canacao patients across the bay to Manila's Sternberg Hospital.

IT SEEMED THAT ONLY bodies and body parts were left to be counted as the stretchered wounded were jostled in the smoky dark to Cavite's civilian docks. The stretcher bearers—an odd group of seventeen native musicians, none of whom Barton had seen before or since—struggled in the blackness to avoid stepping on some hideously burned arm or leg. Crews all around them gathered human remains to inter in bomb craters before the Japanese returned. The crews and stretcher bearers both had to sidestep frantic dogs, cats, chickens, and pigs tearing at the fallen flesh, already putrefying in the tropical heat. At the docks, a hastily appropriated pleasure cruiser named *Mary Anne* awaited.

The patients were quiet as the Filipino captain threw off *Mary Anne's* dock lines and steered toward Manila. The Cavite fireworks sliced up the night sky behind them, the Yard's molten carnage lighting the ghostly remains of the anchorage. Disoriented and morphine-dazed, the patients lay about the festively painted *Mary Anne*, muttering curses and such, making little sense. They periodically looked back at Cavite, shaking their heads. In front of them, Manila appeared relatively safe. They saw isolated columns of smoke over the city—but nothing like the conflagration at Cavite.

This was the night Barton met Ensign Charles Armour, who had been discharged from the USS *Louisville* at Cavite for "treatment" just weeks before. "Yeah, well, my timing's never been too good," Charles said in a dry Arkansas drawl. This was no time for laughing, but Barton was amused by Charles's quips in the midst of the madness all around them.

There was something strange about Charles that he couldn't pinpoint, though Barton felt grateful for the companionship under the circumstances. It was curious that his new friend was at Canacao in the first place. He had no obvious injuries.

At first light, the *Mary Anne* downshifted and drew up to the Manila pier. Corpsmen unloaded the patients in the spectral quiet and slipped them into waiting ambulances. It was about this time that Barton began to inquire what had happened to his shipmates. Dead? Wounded? And his ship? Sunk? But none of the medical staff knew that while he had been drifting in and out of consciousness at Canacao, *Otus* hastened out to sea after the *Sealion* blast, leaving Barton behind. With no time to spare, Captain Newsom had ordered an evasive zigzag toward Australia at flank speed.

By the time the navy patients got to Sternberg Hospital, Charles had fallen asleep. Barton's stretcher was placed along a wall off the entrance foyer, this time among a group of bleeding and weeping civilians, themselves waiting for treatment. One of the most seriously wounded, Ken Koenig, whom Barton also befriended on the *Mary Anne*, was taken to surgery right away. Ken's gurney disappeared through swinging doors, his attendants murmuring about blood loss and a weak pulse.

In retrospect, Barton realized that Sternberg had lulled him into a false sense of security. It was so orderly and lovely with its Spanish architecture, gardens, and large, gracious wards cooled by polished mahogany fans. On that first night, even in the chaos, he had believed that Sternberg, a US military hospital, was the first of many steps away from uncivil engagement. Supply Corps officers weren't supposed to be on the fighting front, were they? He hadn't even been issued a gun.

Barton's confidence ebbed as December wore on. He and his fellow navy patients listened nightly to KZRH as Don Bell somberly detailed the Manila-bound progress of tens of thousands of Japanese soldiers. Wave after wave of enemy troops had come ashore at Lingayen Gulf, 135 miles to the north. They were roaring toward the capital in trucks, on bicycles, and in marching columns, Bell reported in a tone so grave it required little interpretation.

On Christmas Eve, General MacArthur ordered a military evacuation of Manila and declared the Philippine capital an open city, meaning that all Allied defensive efforts had been abandoned there. The open city designation was intended to trigger the 1907 Hague Convention regulating land warfare that forbade attacks on undefended localities. But the designation was ignored by Japan, a Convention signatory; they continued to bomb Manila, including the city hall and other buildings close to the hospital.

By Christmas Day, MacArthur had completed his own retreat to the island fortress of Corregidor near the entrance of Manila Bay. The more than 70,000 American and Filipino troops had also evacuated—to either Corregidor or Luzon's Bataan Peninsula, which bordered the bay on one side and the South China Sea on the other. The evacuation was part of War Plan Orange-3, an emergency contingency plan developed before the war in the extremely unlikely event of a successful Japanese attack. WPO-3 also called for the prepositioning of a supply of food, fuel, medicine, and arms capable of sustaining the evacuated forces for a six-month defensive stand. This latter measure was not taken by General MacArthur.

By New Year's Eve, KZRH had gone off the air, and the sounds of sirens and frantic traffic exiting the city had faded. But the wounded at Sternberg had yet to be relocated to any safe haven. They were the only remaining US military contingent in Manila. Then the unimaginable took place.

Late on December 31, a brief but stunning order from MacArthur's Corregidor headquarters was delivered to the hospital: all army wounded were to be taken down to Pier 7 immediately. They were to be loaded onto a Red Cross ship, the SS *Mactan*, and transported to Australia. The ship must depart as soon as possible, it said, in order to evade Japanese forces, now hard by. Confused, nurses and doctors both responded to the order with the same question: "What about the navy patients?" MacArthur's order made no mention of the navy patients, the sentry said. Only the army patients.

As the senior-most military officer in the Philippines, MacArthur had the authority to include them, but unaccountably had not. Barton, Charles, and thirty other navy wounded at Sternberg Hospital now had no orders to anywhere, from anyone. Could their papers have been on the way, lost in the melee of civilian and military retreat? Could orders have failed to reach them due to blocked roads, cut power and phone lines? Or had this small navy contingent simply been forgotten?

The Filipino ambulance driver told the navy patients and skeletal Sternberg staff he would return for them if there was room aboard the *Mactan*.

They were encouraged, despite the nagging question of whether, absent specific orders, this constituted military disobedience.

Down at Pier 7, a total of 224 army wounded were loaded onto the Mactan—which had been hastily converted from an inter-island steamer into a hospital ship. Her dock lines were then hacked with a knife and tossed into the water. In the waning hours of 1941, amid pelting rain and high winds, the *Mactan's* Red Cross–painted funnel vanished into the mist. It was the last vessel to depart Manila before the city fell to the Japanese.

The navy patients had waited anxiously for the ambulance to return. Sternberg was darkened, and their ward was quiet as a tomb. Barton, Charles, Ken, and the others lay on their cots behind blackout curtains, listening, sifting through the noise of the pounding rain for sounds of a returning flatbed-truck-turned-ambulance.

Charles became increasingly agitated, and the other patients tried to placate him quietly. He had already been taken from their ward once, shortly after their arrival at Sternberg; he was reassigned to a mental ward with a diagnosis of manic-depressive psychosis. During his absence, Barton learned why Charles had been put off USS *Louisville* at Cavite. "Attempted suicide," reported the loose-lipped corpsman. "Japs can't do nothin' to him he ain't already tried to do to himself." When a somewhat withdrawn Charles rejoined his fellow patients, they took pains not to unravel him further.

The ward settled into an uncomfortable silence, but they knew they were trapped, and nobody slept. Over the years, Barton had developed an aptitude for getting out of tight spots—of which there had been many in his young life—but this time he came up empty-handed. As the night wore on, their sense of doom only intensified. When they heard loud banging on the hospital's front door and then what sounded like the door crashing on the foyer floor, they froze.

A nurse screamed. Dozens of footsteps, mingled with bursts of unintelligible Japanese, drew closer. They heard the double doors burst open and footsteps running up the first flight of stairs. Doors opened and slammed and glass shattered. Japanese soldiers chattered excitedly as they took the stairs by twos and threes.

The men lay stock-still. The footsteps were closer now—on *their* floor. The ward's wide doors finally swung open, slamming against the walls. Gripped with fear, their eyes closed, the navy patients lay helpless with fists clenched and hearts pounding, their bodies soaked with sweat.

OVER THE NEXT SEVERAL months, the patients were moved from one makeshift prison hold to another, none with even basic medical care, under steadily worsening conditions. Those that couldn't walk were carried. Ken, whose litter Barton and Charles had lifted through those long marches, did not survive. Every move of the prisoners began with their being paraded through the streets of Manila past a saddened citizenry. The macabre displays were intended to humiliate the captured Americans and brandish the new Japanese dominion over the Filipinos.

Their longest holding pen was at Santa Scholastica, a women's college seized by the Japanese to consolidate the navy wounded from Cavite that had been scattered around Manila for treatment. As the patients were being shuffled, meanwhile, the tens of thousands of soldiers and sailors on Bataan and Corregidor were putting up the fight of their lives against a Japanese onslaught. They were outnumbered, outgunned, and slowly starving on half rations, but they continued to hold out and inflict significant enemy casualties.

The longer Bataan and Corregidor held, however, the angrier the Japanese became over those casualties and their stalled seizure of the Philippines—and the worse it got for the navy patients. It was at Santa Scholastica that the patients and their medical attendants came to understand the depth of contempt the Japanese felt toward them.

They were viciously slapped, their food and medical supplies were confiscated, and they were forced to erect a vast stretch of barbed wire to cut them off from all but a tiny corner of the compound. Beds were removed, bathing curtailed sharply, and laundry facilities were declared off-limits. Perhaps worst of all, their precious supply of quinine, used to treat symptoms of rampant malaria—fever, chills, fatigue, vomiting—was seized.

As an officer, Barton was summoned repeatedly for questioning by a committee of Imperial military police, the Kempeitai. They inquired about the name and location of his ship and the submarines of the Asiatic Fleet, the number and layout of mines in the bays and harbors, and other surprisingly detailed questions. Barton replied that he had been wounded and unconscious early in the attack on Cavite and didn't know the answers.

But the interrogations continued. The Kempeitai eyed the navy patients and their medical staff warily, wondering why this single American contingent had stayed behind in Manila while all the others had evacuated to Bataan or Corregidor. The interrogators suspected that the group had been ordered to remain to conduct espionage and that the only thing their bandages concealed was their true identity as spies.

Barton offered little useful information because he had little, but he was also adept at appearing cooperative without being so. He was in the *Supply Corps*, he would tell the Kempeitai, suggesting a unique disinterest in warfare of any kind. The interrogations were a poignant reminder of others he had endured over time—at home, at the Citadel, and at the US Naval Academy—all of which had honed his ability to survive cross-examination without confessing much of anything. In fact Barton had built quite a reputation for his Huck Finn prowess at getting out of scrapes—and his success rate was nearly as high.

One set of facts was a concern, however: that Barton's two brothers *were* of meaningful rank, and, respectively, engaged in high-level naval combat and espionage. Would such a discovery by his interrogators make him a candidate for greater mistreatment, or worse, useful barter?

Benny and Bill—Barton's older brothers and lifelong protectors—were both Annapolis-minted officers. Biologically, they were half brothers, Barton being the only son of their mother Helen's second marriage. Benny, the oldest, was antiaircraft and gunnery officer on the carrier USS *Enterprise*, which was—or at least had been—stationed at Pearl Harbor. Barton had just visited Benny during his stopover at Pearl en route from New Jersey to Manila. That was barely three weeks before he was wounded. He'd had no contact with Benny since.

Bill, the middle brother, was a Naval Intelligence officer in Washington whose top secret work put him in regular contact with senior brass, not to mention with President Franklin Delano Roosevelt himself. Would Barton be guilty by association were the Japanese to make the connection?

BENNY AND BILL HAD been little boys when Barton, a premature baby, made his entry into the world in 1918. Whether or not it was due to his fragile early arrival, he could not recall a time when they had not looked out for him. If history was any guide, they were making every effort to find him now. In fact, Bill had pulled every imaginable string in Washington to help Barton get his officer's commission—no easy task, since Barton had bilged out of the Naval Academy after just two years. But Bill knew that his younger brother's subsequent business degree was just the expertise needed by incipient Supply Corps officers. And being the navy's business office, its mission was anything but dangerous, a winning card with their mother.

Helen's greatest fear had been that, without a commission, her youngest and favorite son would be drafted into the army and sent to God knows where. So she was most pleased with Bill's efforts. But the fleeting maternal approval ended when Barton's orders to the Philippines—over which Bill had zero influence—arrived. "Spitting distance from Japan!" lioness Helen groaned.

"She went on and on and on," Bill had vented to Benny. His brother simply listened, knowing a reply was not necessary. "She said, 'There you are, Billy, at Roosevelt's elbow. Can't you do something?'" Calling Bill by his affectionate childhood nickname always had its effect. On the other hand, her loathing of all things Franklin Roosevelt was a long-standing fact, and the possibility of the president's doing something that might please her was remote.

But reflexively, Bill and Benny sought to safeguard Barton when his orders came through. Bill arranged his accommodations at Manila's posh Army and Navy Club and they both contacted officer friends in Manila who promised to keep an eye on him. This had long been the family pattern: by cultivating their shared role as Barton's elders, they were assured their mother's sparing affection. If Benny and Bill were aware of the sad irony—that they always seemed to be seeking her attention and that Barton was always trying to break free of it—they kept it to themselves.

ONE THING WAS CERTAIN, Barton didn't want his brothers to pull strings and try to bail him out—not this time. He had *wanted* to go to the Philippines precisely for this reason: to break his family's stubborn tether. At twenty-three years old, surely he could now manage matters himself. That's exactly why he had asked one of the nurses at Sternberg to send a telegram to Lilac Hedges, the family keep in New Jersey, from Manila's Army and Navy Club on Christmas Eve—not from the hospital. He didn't want his family to know he'd been wounded and then try to pull strings and extract him like a child from the war zone.

"Quite well," he dictated. "Don't worry. Happy Xmas. Much love, Barton."

Nothing more.

The nurse expressed concern when Barton finished. Why wouldn't he give real information—quite possibly his last chance to do so? "Please," he'd said to her, "you don't know my mother. This is best for right now."

There was still a chance his luck would turn—that the promised reinforcements were on their way to repel the Japanese incursion. Optimism that his captivity might still be short-lived propelled him from day to day. He would finally get a chance to live up to his family's expectations—on his own terms and under his own power. He clung to this hope despite his mangled condition and the increasingly harsh Japanese treatment.

By March 1942, some two hundred navy wounded from Cavite had been consolidated at Santa Scholastica, at which point they were told to prepare for another move. The place, their doctors were told, was a well-equipped convalescence hospital where they would finally receive badly needed medical care. But when their transport trucks came to a halt at a place called Pasay, fear again replaced hope. A single order was announced as they filed into an abandoned, low-slung building surrounded by tufting weeds: obey all orders or be executed. The peeling sign over the front door of their new accommodation read "Pasay School."

The onetime elementary school was a small, rectangular building with a tiny courtyard at its center. Fifty men were quartered in each sixteen-by-twenty-foot classroom, which teemed with rats, mosquitoes, and green-headed flies. The dwarfish compound was bordered by open latrine trenches swarming with feasting flies. The courtyard, once the school's playground, was so small that the burgeoning prison population could not move about. Adding to the tension of perpetual restraint, the air was sickly hot and humid, and mingling latrine stench and smoke rising from burning garbage hung thick in the air. There were no beds, plumbing, or sanitation at Pasay.

Under these conditions, and with waning optimism that the Allies were coming to their rescue, the patients weakened further and also began to yield to a growing sense of hopelessness. Not only did Pasay claim men from gangrenous wounds, disease, and starvation, but also from sheer despair.

Though he had lost some twenty pounds from his modest frame, Barton had still not lost faith. Things were plenty grim, but so far the Japanese hadn't ordered him to dig a massive tree stump out of frozen ground with a pickax for punishment and "an opportunity for reflection," as he had endured many times at Christ School in Arden, North Carolina. Nor had they beaten him with a broom until he bled while balancing on billiard balls holding up heavy furniture as two Annapolis second classmen had done during his plebe indoctrination. He would weather this just as he had those and other early trials: with a persistent combination of optimism and imperturbable humor.

Barton was less concerned about his own predicament than he was about Charles's precarious emotional state, which was exacerbated by Pasay's miserable confines. A dark switch seemed to have been thrown permanently. Charles had an outsized hatred toward his captors, for whom he had various names, nearly always preceded by "those goddamn," including slopeheads, nips, yelluhs, and worse. He could often be heard saying to nobody in particular, "I'll tell you what, those goddamn —— can just shut the fuck up. Can't understand 'em anyway." The slurs may have been meant for dark amusement, but there was a growing fear that Charles's demonstrated disinterest in preserving his own life could bring harm to others.

Even when he wasn't cursing, his badass southern boy strut back and forth across the tiny courtyard alone seemed capable of sparking an incident. It was a dangerous game. Barton was in constant fear that Charles might do something to place them all at risk. The savage slapping of patients who neglected to bow to passing guards especially enraged Charles, and he threatened privately to retaliate. So Barton focused on helping his friend contain his rage by both cajoling him and deploying creative tactics.

Tenko was the twice-daily prisoner roll call during which guards would count off the bowing prisoners in a process called *bango*. While walking together to *tenko* one evening, Barton suggested to Charles that they take a deep breath upon the guard's approach and exhale only after he had passed them. Refusing to breathe the same air fouled by the breath of their captors was an act of resistance and self-respect, but no slapping would result from it.

As the guard approached, counting prisoners and awaiting bows— *"Ichi, ni, san, shi, go, roku . . ."*—Charles and Barton drew their breaths and bowed deeply. When the guard had passed, continuing his count—*"hachi, kyuu, juu . . ."*—they raised their heads, exhaling slowly. With this, Barton coaxed a rare satisfied smile out of Charles. Their developing partnership helped distract Charles from his self-defeating propensities and both of them from gnawing hunger and fear.

Despite the vitiated air, they would venture into the courtyard to the "shower": a hose fastened to a large punctured tomato can poised over a wooden grate. Since the water was turned on only at certain times, groups of twenty men would disrobe en masse and take turns stepping under the shower head. They would then step back and make way for the next group to do the same. Men given the job of manually emptying the cesspools were allowed to go first, a humane gesture but one that rendered the shower an even more dubious source of hygiene.

AND SO THE PRISONER patients felt a glimmer of hope when told they were to be moved again, this time to Bilibid Prison back in central Manila. As with Pasay, the Japanese told the prisoners that Bilibid had a clean, well-supplied medical facility with beds, medicine, and plenty of food and water. But when they passed through the prison's gates at nightfall, their hearts sank once again. The penitentiary, built by Spanish occupiers a century earlier, had been deemed unfit for criminals and closed by the Filipinos. The Japanese reopened the jail to use as a way station from which captured prisoners would either be dispatched to prison camps around the Philippines or shipped to Japan.

Bilibid stood at the corner of Azcarraga Street and Quezon Boulevard, a familiar intersection to Barton. He had clipped by it often in those early weeks, tanned and khaki clad, on his way to one of the area's many shopping destinations or lively nightspots. Now, under the watchful eye of the Bilibid guards, he could only gaze beyond the prison gates and recall his early infatuation with the city.

Manila's narrow streets, mix of architecture, and overlays of culture from foreign dominions had mesmerized him. Seventeenth-century Spanishbaroque buildings stood next to native huts of bamboo, nipa palm leaves, or grass, and they, next to shuttered stucco buildings with balustrades. There had been fresh fruit stands everywhere, piled high with pineapples, sweet mangoes, and neat lines of amber-streaked papayas, so fresh the stems were still damp from the picking. Tart calamanci limes nestled beside his favorite: the small native bukos. Barton would buy all he could hold of the succulent baby coconuts with their soft, sweet insides, just like the vanilla pudding Nelly, his family's cook, had made for him as a child.

Women with crosses around their necks had walked in twos and threes balancing goods in woven baskets on their heads. Barton had darted between automobiles that crept among pedestrians and calesas, the ubiquitous Filipino horse-drawn carts. The locals, even the children, had always met his gaze, smiling and nodding as they passed.

The earth at the intersection of Azcarraga and Quezon was still brown as tamarind, but the mingling aromas of tropical foliage and mashed peppers simmering in vinegar were gone. Cars were burned and turned on their sides, and calesa carts were smashed alongside bloating animal carcasses. Air attacks had left the streets pitted and impassable, and during the nighttime blackouts, looters finished the destruction the Japanese had started. Sandbags barricaded shops and buildings, and glass from shattered windows glittered on the sidewalk.

The Yangco Market, once a bustling bazaar of native products, stood cratered and vacant across the street. Barton had shopped for Christmas presents for his mother in its small, colorful booths. He had never mailed the bright hats, slippers, and linens he'd bought, nor even his first letters home. Were the packages still perched proudly on his dresser at Manila's Army and Navy Club—so close to where he stood now? Were the letters to his parents in New Jersey and to Benny, Bill, and Eve, the enchanting girl he'd met at Pearl Harbor, still sitting atop them?

When the sorry band of prisoners approached Bilibid's forbidding iron gates, sympathetic Filipinos along the route had been downcast, some tearful. A few daring young boys flashed their signature V signs before the gates slammed and locked behind the last prisoner. The Japanese had failed to calculate the degree of loyalty the Filipinos felt for the Americans, who had set up health clinics and new schools and established a representative government. The United States had also promised the Philippines its complete independence by 1946.

By contrast, the Japanese viewed Filipinos as impure Malayan inferiors and treated them brutally. In the short months since their occupation, the Japanese military had bullied and slaughtered thousands of citizens, ignoring the lessons of the revered ancient Chinese samurai Sun Tsu. In his treatise *The Art of War*, Sun Tsu instructed samurai warriors to "treat . . . captives well and care for them . . . By these means [the samurai] make their governments invincible." Sun Tsu might have predicted the result of Japanese cruelty toward the Filipinos: a heightened allegiance toward the Americans and mistrust of Japan's propagandist assurance of a united, prosperous Asia. Thus far, the Greater East Asia Co-Prosperity Sphere the Japanese had touted equaled only barbaric subordination, bloodshed, and starvation.

When Barton wasn't daydreaming about his peacetime life, he would join his expanding group of friends, usually huddled in the cool shadow of the prison's twelve-foot-high perimeter wall. In the evenings, from their crumbling cells, they would sit together and listen to the bombing and battering of the besieged Bataan Peninsula. And they continued to strain their ears for evidence of approaching reinforcements. Just one week earlier, in a surge of optimism, they had gathered for Easter worship and prayed that Bataan's defenders would hold on until the reinforcements could reach them.

They were sure that they'd heard the distinct *wrrrhh* of an American plane versus the *buzzzz* of the Japanese Zero airplane engine the evening before. At such times they'd laugh, maybe slap one another's backs, and then listen some more. Their fervent prayer on Easter Sunday had been to a common nondenominational God that surely loved them and would show

His mercy. Defiant church bells stung the air in the streets beyond, seeming to confirm that their solemn entreaties would soon be answered.

So when the news of Bataan's surrender hit Bilibid four days later, it shook the prisoners as hard as the earthquake that hit Manila that same morning. Many despaired that they'd been betrayed twice: first by MacArthur and then by God.

WITHIN DAYS OF THAT bitter news, the prisoners were ordered to prepare for another move, this time to a place called Cabanatuan, sixty kilometers (thirty-seven miles) north of Manila. Their misanthropic guards once again shoved the prisoners in line for another march past queues of long-faced Manilans.

The guards were hot, tired, and full of loathing for their charges, a sentiment that had only intensified during the long siege of Bataan. The best Japanese soldiers were reserved to fight the war; those put in charge of prisoners were either disgruntled conscripts or minimally trained third-tier recruits who were all too ready to turn their wrath on the prisoners.

Under the Bushido code—the ancient samurai code of conduct taught to every Japanese boy from an early age—surrender was among the most dishonorable of acts. For a soldier to allow himself to be taken alive or, worse, to surrender, was unthinkable; either brought permanent shame to the individual, his family, and his country. In fact, Japan had declined to ratify the 1929 Geneva Convention because of its opposition to the clause condoning the notification of relatives upon a soldier's surrender. This would not only bring permanent shame upon the soldier, but disgrace to his family as well. Perhaps Ashihei Hino, the Japanese wartime reporter, best described his country's view on this subject in his account of the surrendered men on Bataan: "I feel like I am watching filthy water running from the sewage of a nation . . . which has lost its pride of race."

Thus, by their way of thinking, all prisoners of war deserved only disgrace and hardship. The prisoners were well aware of their captors' disposition as they set out for Cabanatuan. Despite sore temptation, they dared not scavenge discarded American rations scattered among the war debris littering the roadside.

Barton had quickly learned to avoid all but necessary eye contact with his captors. Looking down was the best way to fend off fear—and to hide it. On these brutal marches, designed to weaken, demean, and humiliate, he would lock his eyes on the footsteps in front of him and follow their pattern hypnotically. And like so many of the prisoners, he would fixate on memories of home: of Lilac Hedges, of family, of the Jersey Shore and hours of diving into Atlantic waves and happy picnicking afterward.

Conjuring these images of life when it was whole and full of possibilities renewed his strength. There were the fragrant lilacs, cicada orchestras, postcard images of rolling farmland, summer orchards weighted with ripening fruit, and roadside stands piled high with tomatoes and sweet corn. And there were the family images, too: of Benny, Bill, his little sister, Rosemary, and, of course, his parents. But he lingered most on his mother, though this also brought stabs of pain.

His mother had come to represent everything he had wanted to escape, and only now, in his first experience of deprivation, could he see how much his efforts to distance himself from her had hurt her. Yet these regrets also impelled Barton. He wanted desperately to make amends; for her to know that he loved and appreciated her. He also wanted to make her proud, which he was sure he had long failed to do. If he were lucky enough to see her again, he would run to her, not away from her, and show her the gratitude and affection she had so persistently been denied.

2

★ ★ ★

BENNY

IN LATE NOVEMBER 1941, barely two weeks after Barton sailed for Manila, Benny and the crew of the USS *Enterprise* received abrupt orders from their commanding officer. Admiral William "Bull" Halsey's curt directive to sortie from Pearl Harbor for an undisclosed location "as soon as possible" was unprecedented. Benny could not recall a single instance in the past eleven years when shore leave had been cut without notice.

Even more curious were the twelve F4F Wildcat fighter planes being towed to *Enterprise*'s F-9 berth. The propeller-driven aircraft were hoisted onto the flight deck, after which a dozen marine pilots boarded with hastily packed luggage and very recent orders of their own. Why were these planes being loaded in addition to *Enterprise*'s own 140 dive bombers, fighters, and torpedo planes?

There was good reason for apprehension. Negotiations between Japan's ambassadors and officials in Washington had dragged on fruitlessly for months and tensions were rising fast. Prime Minister Tojo had ticked off a long list of demands—including that Japan be given a free hand in its oc-cupation of China and Indochina and that the United States cut diplomatic ties with Chiang Kai-shek, China's leader-in-exile. In addition, Japan had demanded President Roosevelt reverse his recent order freezing Japanese assets and restore the flow of American gasoline to its fuel-starved ports, not to mention halt the buildup of American forces in the South Pacific. As near as Benny could tell, little had been offered US negotiators in exchange.

Given the worsening standoff with Japan, Admiral Halsey's order un-leashed a torrent of questions from the air and gunnery crews. But duty-bound Benny was not one to second-guess Halsey or any other naval superior. They needed to do as instructed and fast, he told them. Benny had quite a few things of his own to do before departure. No telling how long they would be at sea, and he had to get a letter off to his mother. He knew she would be anxious about his visit with Barton before he pushed off for Manila, and there was much to tell.

November 27, 1941

USS Enterprise

Dear Mother,

Barton has come and gone--this is the first chance I've had to write you about it and I don't know when I'll have a chance to write again. I was on the dock to meet him as he came in. He looked healthy, he was smiling, and happy to be in that uniform!

I had the ship's station wagon for the day and took him sightseeing. Together with two friends of mine, we made a party of it. First we took him to the Pali overlook, then to the other side of the island for a cocktail party at

the home of Webley Edwards, the local radio announcer for
Hawaii Calls. The daughter of the family took Bart for a
swim at the Outrigger and Canoe Club at Waikiki beach and
he enjoyed himself hugely.

The Moanna [sic] Hotel is just next door and I took him
over there for a drink. I couldn't raise a bit of sympathy
from Bart about the loneliness in my life. He laughed and
said that crocodile tears were streaming down his face!

Later I called up a young lady friend, Eve, and we
went out to a local night spot, the South Seas, saw the Hula
shows and they danced and danced right up until it was
time for Bart's ship to leave. But when we took him back to
his ship we waited and waited and nothing happened. It
seemed that things had worsened in the Pacific and his
route had to be rearranged. I doubt now they called at
Shanghai or Hong Kong, which is too bad.

We finally left the dock around 3 a.m. after Eve had
collected about 20 flower leis that Barton and the boys
threw her from the ship. She liked Bart a lot, and went
down to the dock again the next day. She works at an office
downtown and saw that his ship was still there and got time
off to go see him again. Bart seems to have all the ladies
eating out of his palms. He had 3 of them running circles
around him here. All the way from 18 to 40.

Mother, I gave him the best advice I could. He isn't
in the best spot in the world right now, but he is young
and has his whole life before him--two years or so there
should be a great experience, providing he keeps a grip on
himself. Bill gave him the best advice of all--to do a good
job and guard his health and his money. If he does that he
will be o.k.

He should be there by now, and I really believe that he
will be fairly safe. He'll be on shore duty, from the gist
of his orders. That is far better and safer if anything
breaks in the Pacific. The Japs won't take the Philippines
easily, even if they send an invading force. Remember
Mother, Manila is protected by the guns of Corregidor,
plus the Army's Air Force, plus the Asiatic Fleet, plus
a half million men in the Filipino army, plus our own
forces. They will find the Filipino army trained by General
MacArthur--a pretty crack outfit and a tough one.

And remember, meanwhile, while they are doing that,
we aren't here in Pearl for nothing. Anyway, the next few
weeks will tell the story. They may back down completely
if we stand firm, in spite of the terrible loss of face they
would sustain. The Japanese man in the street is sick of
war. They've had severe restrictions now for years, and they
don't like it. Of course the Big Boys may decide on national
hari kari [sic] and take the big chance. There's always
that angle with those people.

I told Bart what it would be like out there in paradise
and not to throw pesos around just because there are two of
them for a dollar. I advised him to get up with a couple of
the boys and get a house in Cavite. Then they could hire a
cook and a house boy so they wouldn't have to worry about
food.

I agree with what you said about the rest being up to
Bart. I warned him to guard his values and judge those
around him carefully.

Your loving son,

Benny

P.S. I also told him to remember that it's only 8 or 9 days by
Pan Am Clipper to New York--and to write you often.

Benny had been the first of the three brothers to leave Lilac Hedges for Annapolis. That was in 1926, and he was one of the lucky 1930 graduates to receive an officer's commission. The Naval Academy was not immune to the economic reversals of the Depression, and peacetime commissions for rising ensigns were no longer automatic. He departed for Norfolk, Virginia, that June for duty on the aircraft carrier USS *Lexington*.

When the schedule of orders was posted at graduation, Benny had been disappointed to draw an aircraft carrier. In most navy circles, the battleship was the peerless ruler of the seas. The then-prevailing view was that a carrier's best use was to support battleships by scouting, range finding, and providing defensive air cover. Still, to Benny, a shipboard gunnery assignment was a dream come true.

The joke at Annapolis was that salt water, not blood, coursed through his veins, and there was more than a little truth to that. Benny could predict a change in weather long before it was announced on a barometer and seemed to thrive on a mixed aroma of salt air, gun grease, and a naval officer's mainstay of strong, scalded coffee. He was, as the saying goes, a real sea dog.

After a following stint at the navy's ordnance testing lab in Washington, DC, Benny was noted in his performance review as "cheerful, enthusiastic, cooperative, and honest" and recommended for promotion. It was a happy time for him and his new bride, Jeannette, whom he married in 1933. In 1934 they welcomed a baby girl, Jeanne Marie. But Benny's promotion came with new orders that uprooted the young family and sent them across the country, first to Bremerton in Washington State and then to the naval port at San Diego. The moves with a small child took an increasing toll on Jeannette, who had not wanted to leave the heady social swirl of Washington, DC in the first place. Benny's lengthening sea deployments strained the marriage further.

In 1940 the entire Pacific Fleet, including his new ship, USS *Enterprise*, was transferred to the US naval base in Hawaii. The move was intended to curb Japan's expansionist zeal, but it only infuriated Japanese leaders. Mutual mistrust had only intensified since. Worse for Benny, Jeannette announced that she and Jeanne Marie, now in kindergarten, would not pull up stakes again; they were going to stay put in San Diego with her mother. It was the first overt sign that the marriage was in trouble. Reluctantly, in May 1940, Benny shipped off to Pearl Harbor alone.

From Pearl, *Enterprise*'s primary role was to patrol the vast seas between Hawaii and California. The two other carriers available to relieve her, *Saratoga* and *Lexington*, were older and frequently in drydock for repairs. *Enterprise* filled the gap time and again. Perhaps it was just as well that lonely Benny and *Enterprise* had been on nearly continuous deployment since moving to Hawaii. At sea, his fellow crew had become an increasingly important source of ready companionship.

Since Annapolis, Benny had learned a great deal about gunnery and fleet practices and his views had evolved considerably. By 1940, he was part of a growing contingent of officers that saw carriers as the navy's primary offensive weapon, even though only a handful of them were in operation. These powerful and self-sufficient floating airports with their multiple air squadrons had many times the offensive reach of battleships. That view, however, had yet to be adopted by top brass.

AS *ENTERPRISE* EXITED PEARL Harbor Channel on November 28, 1941, and hove into the open sea, Benny was at the rail in Sky Control, his command station, scanning the water's surface through his ever-present field glasses. Rising not quite six feet from the steel deck, his eyes were deeply creased for a man of thirty-three, and he was as stout as navy regulations would allow. But his visual acuity of 20/15 was better than perfect, and he had yet to miss an errant ripple on patrol. "His eyes burn brightly, scorching the dainty wings of fair moths that fly his way," quipped the 1930 Naval Academy yearbook, *Lucky Bag*, beneath his photograph.

Sky Control was a partially enclosed platform on the tripod mast. At 110 feet above the waterline it was the best vantage point on the ship. Benny had a commanding view of the southwest corner of Oahu as *Enterprise* cleared Barbers Point. Shortly thereafter, an escort group of three cruisers and nine destroyers joined the carrier. Once in formation, all bows pointed due west.

Compounding the mystery of *Enterprise*'s present mission was the mimeographed order that was handed Benny next: to supply all aircraft with war-ready torpedoes and live ammunition. It also directed him to arm the ship's mounted guns and antiaircraft batteries with the same. Benny sent a message back to *Enterprise*'s captain, George Murray. If they prepared the torpedoes for war shots, they wouldn't be able to participate in the scheduled battle exercises on their return to Pearl. Word came back promptly: "Prepare torpedoes for war shots."

Such preparation took scores of men hundreds of hours. Stored ammunition was loose, and a million rounds had to be belted, clipped, and installed on all the guns on the ship. Torpedo gangs had to attach TNT warheads to the carefully stored bombs. At the same time, the ship's mechanics worked around the clock to put the marine planes in top-notch condition; there were no servicing facilities wherever they were going.

When the flotilla was safely at sea, the mission was announced at last: transport the twelve fighter planes and their pilots two thousand miles to Wake Island. The strategic mid-Pacific American base, with no fresh water source and only one known mammal—the rat—needed immediate fortification. After the 2,800-strong *Enterprise* crew and pilots were notified, yet another startling order circulated the ship and, by signal, transmitted to all escort vessels. The announcement was signed by both Captain Murray and Admiral Halsey, *Enterprise*'s flag officer:

CV6/A16-5(10-11t)

USS Enterprise

At Sea

November 28, 1941

BATTLE ORDER NUMBER ONE

1. The Enterprise is now operating under war conditions.
2. At any time, day or night, we must be ready for instant action.
3. Hostile submarines may be encountered.
4. The importance of every officer and man being especially alert and vigilant while on watch at his battle station must be fully realized by all hands.
5. The failure of one man to carry out his assigned task promptly, particularly the lookouts, those manning the batteries, and all those on watch on deck might result in great loss of life and even the loss of the ship.
6. The Captain is confident all hands will prove equal to any emergency that may develop.
7. It is part of the tradition of our Navy that, when put to the test, all hands keep cool, keep our heads, and fight.
8. Steady nerves and stout hearts are needed now.

G. D. Murray (signed)

Captain, US Navy,

Commanding

Approved, November 28, 1941

W. F. Halsey

Vice Admiral, US Navy

Commander Aircraft,

Battle Force

Enterprise at war? Scuttlebutt regarding the strongly worded memo shot from one end of the ship to the other. The crew shifted to an unfamiliar state of high alert, and more than one school of fish drew torpedo fire along the way. But the convoy's crinoline wakes were the only visible disturbance on the water's surface all the way to its destination.

On November 30 *Enterprise* crossed the International Date Line, and the calendar skipped to December 2. At daylight the next morning, the marine pilots boarded their planes, took off in a line, and lowered onto the largest of Wake's three tiny spits of coral, sand, and scrub.

On December 3, under blackout orders and radio silence, *Enterprise* and her escorts swung around and immediately began the trek back to Pearl. Having regained a day at the 180th meridian, they sailed through two December fifths. On the first of these, a young flyer named Ensign John H. Vogt returned from his patrol and reported seeing ships' masts through the haze at the outer perimeter of his search; the information was logged but not acted upon.

On the second December fifth, the convoy ran into a tremendous squall. High winds lashed and battered the convoy. Thirty-foot waves broke high over *Enterprise*'s bow as the carrier rose and fell in heaving seas. Benny lurched along slippery, crazily slanted walkways as he moved from gun emplacement to gun emplacement. He was not alone in wondering whether getting to Pearl on December 6 as scheduled was more important than getting there in one piece. Benny's concern was that pelting rain was blinding his already raw-nerved gunners, not to mention challenging their tenuous holds on the gun mounts.

Only when powerful trade winds collided with the mountainous seas and threatened to crack the bows of two destroyers did a reluctant Admiral Halsey order reduced speed. The convoy's scheduled arrival at Pearl Harbor was thus postponed to Sunday morning, December 7.

Benny and the crew were as relieved as they were disappointed. The slowdown eased their nerves, but after nine grueling days at sea, the delay also meant no Saturday-night dissipating at the Moana Hotel or Sunday on the links. Adjusting to the news, the men going off rotation gravitated to the gymnasium-like hangar deck to watch Gary Cooper in *Sergeant York*, a movie about a draftee-turned-World War I hero who saved hundreds of his comrades' lives while braving a hailstorm of enemy fire.

As the men settled into the film, *Enterprise* and her escorts slowed their eastward pace but remained on a near-convergence course with another convoy, *Kido Butai*, a mammoth six-carrier Japanese armada complete with 414 planes and 49 support vessels pounding southeast from its own late-November sortie, a remote anchorage in the Kurile Islands. The Japanese convoy was traveling under radio silence outside normal shipping lanes to avoid detection.

At dusk on December 6, scout planes again returned to the ship after their customary two-hundred-mile scan in all directions. Flyer D. W. Halsey (no relation to the admiral) jumped from his dive bomber, still zipped in his orange jumpsuit. He had an urgent report. Young Halsey felt sure he had observed the top of ships' masts on the horizon at the end of his northwest search. The admiral questioned sternly why he didn't investigate further. He quietly responded that he would not have had enough fuel to return to the ship. Because the pilot was relatively inexperienced, Captain Murray and Admiral Halsey decided to disregard the uncorroborated report.

In the predawn hours of December 7, Benny was on the "dog watch," which ran from 0400 to 0800. Damp cold and edgy nerves had him on full alert that morning. He paced back and forth in Sky Control, alternately raising his field glasses to scan the obsidian sea and swilling from a bottomless cup of coal-black coffee. At 0500 the day's first general quarters ("man your battle stations") sounded. Flight quarters ("pilots, man your aircraft") then blared from the loudspeakers.

It was customary to send one air squadron to Pearl Harbor ahead of the ship on the day of its arrival. This duty was sort of a rotating perk among the flight squadrons. Leaving *Enterprise* several hours early to arrange for the convoy's berthing allowed the pilots to greet anxious wives and girl-friends in two short hours instead of the five or six it took *Enterprise* to get there. On this particular morning, the honor went to Scouting Squadron Six, led by Commander Brigham Young.

As the pilots assembled, Benny sent an inquiry to the flag bridge as to whether the live bombs and antiaircraft ammunition were to be removed from Scouting Six's planes. After some delay, a runner brought word back from flag staff: remove the bombs but leave the ammunition. Benny nodded and transmitted the message. After Battle Order Number One, why should this surprise him?

Out on the Sky Bridge, he could see the pilots suiting up and preparing for takeoff. Crewmen huddled around them, asking the flyers to notify loved ones of the ship's impending arrival. *Enterprise* had departed so suddenly that many of them hadn't had the chance to explain that they might be gone longer than a routine weekend of maneuvers. Benny always felt a quiet pang overhearing the men chattering about wives and families waiting for them. Once again, nobody would be waiting for Benny.

Benny had already said his good-byes to Scouting Six pilots Vogt and Roger Miller, the men who had joined him for a day of revelry during Barton's stopover. They made a fast plan to go to Waikiki the following week when they all had leave. At 0615 the flight deck was finally cleared, and Squadron Six's eighteen planes took off and set a due east course. They would do a 180-degree sector sweep ahead of the ship, then land at Ford Island, the islet in the center of Pearl Harbor, by morning colors.

TWO HUNDRED AND FIFTY miles north of Oahu, nearly the same distance that the *Enterprise* now stood west of her port, the Imperial Japanese fleet pressed southeast at flank speed. Its twenty-seven submarines were already well ahead of the fleet. At 0550 the Japanese Imperial Navy's six aircraft carriers and escorts had commenced the launch of 184 Zero fighters.

★ ★ ★

AFTER THE *ENTERPRISE* PLANES took off, Benny fiddled with the radio dial until he found the squadron's flight frequency. This had become a habit in Sky Control on approach to Pearl, often just to relieve the boredom. The bravado chitchat among the pilots, usually on the bawdy side, was always a source of amusement.

About 0745, through the crackle and buzz of interference, Benny was jolted by the pilots' voices rising with alarm over the radio transmitter. They were shouting to one another.

"Hey, did you see that army plane shooting at me?"

"That's no army plane! That's a Japanese plane! Look at the red circles on his wings!"

"That bastard! I'm going to shoot back!" The charged back-and-forth continued as Squadron Six and the equally surprised Japanese pilots tangled in view of Pearl Harbor.

Relieved of his watch, Benny raced past the duty bugler and the officer of the deck, then past the quartermaster and the helmsman. He was heading for the secret radar console between the flag bridge and the ship's bridge. Benny found Jack Baumeister, *Enterprise* radar officer, hidden behind a long black curtain. Heart at a gallop, Benny told Jack what he'd heard on the pilot's frequency. "Can we get anything on radar?"

Perspiring, Jack leaned forward in his chair and peered at a cluster of echoing blips of unknown origin making their way across the screen of the ship's new radar machine. "It's strange," he said. "I've got a lot of bogies, but I shouldn't be getting any. We're a hundred and forty-four miles away, so they have to be flying really high for me to even get them on radar—I mean at least twenty thousand feet."

"Have you reported this?" Benny asked, incredulous. Jack replied that he had, but his tone betrayed a lack of confidence in the new radar technology. By then, however, numerous planes had sent messages back to

Enterprise confirming the worst. Benny and Jack stood together staring at the screen, the top half seeming to crawl with ants. Within seconds, the ship's sirens screamed. The radioman had received an official coded message: "Enemy air raid on Pearl Harbor X This no drill."

The quartermaster pulled the general quarters alarm, triggering its seventeen spine-chilling buzzes. The message blared repeatedly over the ship's loudspeakers as men scrambled to their battle stations. Back in Sky Control, Benny issued rapid but succinct instructions in preparation for a possible attack on *Enterprise* itself, first to the men on the large five-inch antiaircraft mounts and on down the line to the machine gunners amidships.

As Benny barked orders to his gunners, Halsey issued his own from the flag bridge. After sending up a combat air patrol (CAP) to search for enemy ships, the admiral motioned to the signalmen. In a finger snap, a new set of multicolored flags were yanked from their flag bag and hoisted up the yardarm. The message to the fleet: "Prepare for battle." With *Enterprise*'s battle flags now flying from her forepeak, the signal went out to the ships in the convoy to do the same. Wordless, from the ship's highest perch, Benny watched the opening scenes of *Enterprise* at war.

OVER THE NEXT TWO hours, the enemy force, commanded by Japanese admiral Isoroku Yamamoto, leveled the American fleet at Pearl Harbor. *Enterprise*'s Squadron Six, outnumbered ten to one, fought the swarming Zeros with everything it had. The pilots' voices through the crackling radio static rang in Benny's ears for days, especially that of Ensign Manuel Gonzales. "Please don't shoot! This is Six-Baker-Three, an American plane!" Next came Gonzales's urgent command to his rear gunner, "We are on fire—bail out!" The transmission went silent after that. They disappeared without a trace.

Brigham Young carried Admiral Halsey's staff officer, Lieutenant Commander Bromfield Nichols, in the rear of his plane. Nichols was carrying the classified report on *Enterprise*'s delivery of the fighter planes to Wake. Through the wind and static, Benny heard Young say something about antiaircraft puffs over the harbor and army planes over the marines' aviation hub, Ewa Air Station.

Next, Nichols shouted that bits of their left wing were gone. The next thing Benny heard was a long series of invectives, and then nothing. He later learned that Young barely made his landing on Ford—after taking more fire from confused US gunners on the tarmac than the Japanese pilots in the air.

News of the rest of Squadron Six trickled in. Lieutenant Clarence Dickinson and Ensign Bud McCarthy had been lucky. Under attack by six Zeros, they shot down one but were no match for the rest. Both their planes were riddled, but the men bailed out at low altitude and survived to tread water off Battleship Row, witnessing firsthand the entire horrific show. Ensign Edward Deacon landed in the water short of the runway. Holding his wounded gunner, he grabbed his raft from the sinking plane and paddled ashore.

Squadron Six leader Earl Gallagher miraculously avoided the enemy planes by flying back out to sea, low above the water. He felt sure the enemy ships had retired to the northwest. He then landed on Ford Island amid more confused American gunfire. After refueling, Gallagher flew 175 miles in the direction of the retreating planes but found nothing but empty seas. When the worst of it was over, Benny asked around for news of Ensigns Vogt and Miller.

Vogt's Dauntless dive bomber was last seen by marines at Ewa Station in a dogfight with three Zeros, firing his fixed and free guns with everything he had. Then he got on the tail of one of them and poured tracers into it, but it pulled up so sharply that Vogt collided with it. He was able to bail out but his parachute failed to deploy, and he died after slamming into a tree. Roger Miller managed to take out a Zero also, but he, too, was killed. Benny's two good friends had been struck down within minutes of each other in the first hour of the war.

STILL A RELATIVELY SAFE distance from Pearl, *Enterprise* searched for the retreating Japanese fleet for the next twenty-four hours. The Pacific

Ocean had become a vast hiding place for an invisible foe, however, and the attackers were nowhere to be found.

The search was abandoned late on Monday afternoon, December 8. At sunset, *Enterprise* and her convoy nosed up the channel and into Pearl Harbor. It was a silent, ghoulish glide through thousands of feet of smoldering wreckage and floating bodies. Soot-smudged soldiers manning antiaircraft guns lined the docks. "Hey, you better get out, or they'll get you too!" yelled one shell-shocked sailor. Another cried, "Where the hell were *you*?"

A dumbstruck Benny surveyed the devastation from the ship's superstructure. Grim-faced sailors lined the ship's rails, and thousands of faces fastened on the horror from every gun mount, hatch, and portal. *Nevada* was overturned and aground, *Utah* blown to pieces, its remains slouched in harbor mud. The capsized *Oklahoma* had rolled 150 degrees, her tripod mast jammed deep into the sludge.

Only the bottom of *Oklahoma*'s hull was visible. As the *Enterprise* crew gawked helplessly, word traveled that hundreds of *Oklahoma*'s sailors were trapped alive inside. Men huddled on and around her hull, frantically working pneumatic drills to free them before their oxygen expired.

The spit-and-polish harbor *Enterprise* had departed nine days earlier was aflame and clogged with charred ship remains and floating death. A pall of black smoke fed by the still-burning *Arizona* hung heavy and low over the entire anchorage. For *Arizona*, it was too late for heroics. Four Japanese bombs found their mark on the ship, and 1,700 men perished, among them 23 sets of brothers. By Benny's count, at least twenty ships had been sunk or damaged. He wondered with dread how many of the dead he knew.

Enterprise put in at a new berth, F-2, just astern of the stricken battleships. *Utah* sat capsized and burning at her usual slot, F-9; she had docked there only after *Enterprise*'s sudden departure for Wake Island. The torpedo that felled *Utah* was no doubt intended for the larger spoils of flattop *Enterprise*. Thanks to the diligent surveillance of the spy Takeo Yoshikawa, a Japanese ensign disguised at one point as a Filipino dishwasher in the harbor's navy mess, the enemy had been well apprised of the harbor layout. Yoshikawa's last communiqué to Japan in late November had noted *Enterprise*'s abrupt departure, but it was received too late for Admiral Yamamoto to alter his attack plan.

Once the lines were secured, the *Enterprise* crew promptly shifted gears to reprovision the carrier for immediate redeployment to a hostile sea. By the light of the burning *Arizona*, Benny set about his next exhausting task: rearming the ship. The work had to be done faster and to a greater capacity than ever before. And while the antiaircraft magazines were packed to the brim, millions of gallons of fuel oil gushed into the ship's tanks, and storerooms were crammed with a myriad of supplies.

Hundreds of thousands of pounds of potatoes, flour, eggs, chicken, wrenches, gun grease, bacon, cooking oil, soap, paper, pens, bandages, toothpaste, aspirin, and shoes were hauled aboard and stowed. Coffee stores alone for 2,700 measured in the tons. Instructions were shouted up and down long lines of sweating sailors pitching in from the docks. During rare pauses for rest, the *Enterprise* crew could hear the agonizing tapping on *Oklahoma*'s overturned hull by the oxygen-deprived men trapped inside. By the time *Enterprise* loosed her lines, the voiceless *tink, tink, tink* had stopped—and 429 sailors had presumably suffocated to death.

Benny's good friend Webley Edwards, KGMB's popular *Hawaii Calls* radio announcer, came down to the docks to see him off. The last time they had seen each other was at Webley's house—laughing and talking over rum punches with Barton and Ensigns Miller and Vogt. The flickering *Arizona* lit their faces.

"It's up to you carrier boys now," Webley said, clasping Benny's hand in a farewell handshake. "You're all we've got left."

At 0400 on December 9, barely a dozen grueling and traumatic hours since arriving, *Enterprise* and her escorts pushed back through the wreckage and headed northwest. With the harbor under blackout orders, their departure was illuminated only by oily water, still aflame. Her orders were to clear local seas of enemy submarines and repel subsequent attacks.

Swinging west to east and back again, they scrutinized Oahu's every seaborne approach, searching for a killer fleet that not a single pair of American eyes had seen. The lookouts reported so many sightings of Japanese submarines that dozens of depth charges were dropped and hundreds of gallons of precious fuel were expended in pursuit. An exasperated Admiral Halsey finally signaled to his task force: "If all the torpedo wakes reported are factual, Japanese submarines will soon have to report home to reload, and we have nothing to fear. We are wasting too many depth charges on neutral fish. Take action accordingly."

After breakfast on December 11, Benny picked up the ship's newspaper on his way back to Sky Control. He glanced down at the headline and stopped dead in his tracks to reread the headline splayed across the top of the typed mimeographed sheet: "Cavite Navy Yard Smashed." Casualties were estimated in the hundreds, with more feared.

Whether it was the instant remorse over the confident assurances he had just sent his mother or fear for Barton's life, Benny felt his knees go weak. There was no denying any longer that Barton was in the bull's-eye of a dangerous war zone. Benny's next call would be to Bill in Washington to see whether Barton had survived the attack and, if so, where he was now. If anyone could find out, it would be Bill.

3

★　★　★

HELEN

AT LILAC HEDGES ON Sunday night, December 7, Helen and Arthur Cross settled gloomily by the fire after turning off the Victrola. They had been fastened to the newscasts for hours while their dinner sat cold and untouched. They had been trying to reach Bill in Washington since hearing the news, assuming that he had more information than had been broadcast, or could get it.

But all of Washington was reeling, too. Even Bill could not supplement their meager information stores by bedtime, though he promised to do everything in his power to find out. Before retiring to a sleepless night, Helen unscrewed her fountain pen and took a long draught of blue-black ink from a porcelain inkwell. She opened her black leather diary with "1941" stamped in green on the cover and leafed to the seventh page of the last month.

Blackest of all Sundays! At 2 today, we got word that Japan foully attacked Hawaii while her 'ambassadors' talked peace in Washington.

Poor laddie Bart at Manila, getting his baptism by fire, he who never had a thought of hate for any man. Poor Benny on the Enterprise in Pearl Harbor! God be at their side.

After listening to President Roosevelt's declaration of war and address to Congress the next day, she wrote:

Let the Philippines not become another Dunkirk! The Japs according to radio are swarming like locusts. Have we got proper air protection? And Benny, on those boundless waters, looking for death from above and below! What have mothers done to deserve such grief? I stare numbly at my Christmas cards and packages, longing to stow away the gaudy reminders.

To her British-born husband, Helen revealed a stalwart and pragmatic side, but to her diary, she indulged fiery opinions, fierce indignation, and withering insights. Her entries the preceding several months had amounted to a dread-filled countdown to the hour of Barton's departure for the Philippines: the cholera shots, the farewells to friends and neighbors, and the final family dinner at the Russian Tea Room before the mournful trek to Grand Central Station to meet Barton's transcontinental train.

On his last evening at home, she wrote, "I must steel myself for the hour when dread imaginings give place to reality and he is gone. Every moment of his life has blessed me and I am truly grateful—and ashamed of my weakness."

Her emotions were not just those of an anxious mother relinquishing a grown child to a dangerous world—painful enough, any mother knows. Barton was much more than a son to Helen Cross. He was the very symbol of her own reincarnation in a promising second marriage. As if to cement that success, she had insisted on naming him after her new husband: Arthur

Barton Cross—Jr. With this, Helen had permanently cast off the forsaken image of failed wife and mother. Her apparent preference for this youngest of her three sons may have read as favoritism, but it was, more accurately, a mantle of gratitude for the miraculous second chance his arrival signified.

HELEN ESTELLE CHAMBERLAIN WAS born in New York City in 1883 of recently emigrated parents. Respectively, her father and mother were of English and Irish descent. Soon after Helen's birth, the young family moved to the historic and progressive township of Framingham, Massachusetts. By all accounts, Helen was focused and determined from an early age. She was an industrious child who excelled in school and spent after-school hours developing a mastery with the needle and thread. This was likely due to the County Cork needlecraft talents conferred by her mother, née Annie Lynch.

According to family lore, Helen's father, William Lincoln Chamberlain, was one in a continuum of prosperous enough English merchants. Though he supported the family well, Helen and Annie formed an alliance familiar among Irish American women in the late nineteenth century and one that supplemented their household incomes: fine embroidery and skilled needlework. For Helen and Annie, there was never a shortage of orders for their handiwork, particularly around Christmas.

Whether or not the independence gained from that experience was the reason, Helen joined the slim 3 percent of American women at the turn of the century who pursued a college degree. Triumphantly, at age seventeen, she made the brief but seminal journey from Framingham to nearby Wellesley College in September 1900.

Helen double majored in German and Latin, perhaps believing that mastery of Goethe, Virgil, and Horace gave her a certain gravitas that widened the distance from a relatively unremarkable childhood. Her superior showing in Wellesley's elocution classes completed Helen's transformation from ambitious student to a refined and elegant—if strong-minded—young woman.

The first decade of the new century was a time of expanding opportunity for American women, and Helen approached her 1904 graduation with optimism and self-assurance. Soon after her commencement, she was thrilled with the offer to teach Latin at a high school in a small New Jersey borough. But the social dictates of the time also stressed that young women should marry, and in the borough of Rockaway, Helen Estelle Chamberlain fell in love and did just that.

In the young and attractive Dr. Raymond Mott, Helen saw a promising future. Raymond in turn was delighted to have drawn such a prize. The town dentist, Dr. Mott descended from a long line of Motts, dating back to their arrival on Long Island from Saffron Walden, Essex, England, in the early 1700s. Rockaway Township, named after a historic Indian tribe that roamed its hills and fished its streams long before the American Revolution, was a close-knit community with a strong social fabric, and the surrounding Jersey countryside was an idyllic tapestry of stone mills, fields, streams, and woods threaded with old Indian paths.

Born into this stable and secure world were two Mott sons, Elias Bertram and William Chamberlain—Benny and Bill—in 1908 and 1911, respectively. The family lived in a white frame house with dark-green shutters a short distance from Mott Hollow, a once-thriving hive of mills and other business concerns settled by Dr. Mott's Quaker ancestors more than a century earlier. The young boys ran free with friends whose families had been neighbors for generations. Rockaway's general store, barbershop, soda fountain, and five-and-dime were all run by merchants who knew Benny and Bill by name. They also enjoyed a close circle of grandparents, aunts, uncles, and cousins.

Their grandfather, Elias Briant Mott, was Rockaway's grand patron. His large personality won him local adoration, and his civic and community activities were legion. Elias held the august position of Morris County clerk, was a patriarch of the Independent Order of Odd Fellows, and served as a standing member of the Improved Order of Red Men. The

Red Men were said to have descended from the Sons of Liberty, who, famously disguised as Mohawk Indians, boarded three East India Company ships and tossed ninety-two thousand pounds of English tea into Boston Harbor. Being grandsons of Elias Mott was the closest thing to royalty that little Rockaway had.

Raymond, the youngest of Elias Mott's four children, was overshadowed by his eldest brother, Bert. The most successful of the siblings and heir apparent to their father's revered community role, Bert became a bright and gregarious lawyer and founded many of the town mainstays, including First National Bank of Rockaway and the Rockaway Building and Loan Association. He succeeded his father as clerk of the conservative Morris County and rose to state Republican Party chairman. Under Bert's tutelage, the county GOP maintained consistent majorities of twenty thousand votes over Democrat opposition, a statistic of which he was very fond.

Raymond, a quiet man by comparison, chose dentistry as a solid if less prominent profession than his brother's. From a young age, he was deeply affected by his father's preference for Bert, and his early insecurities metastasized into overwhelming melancholia when he became an adult. Raymond's family life and marriage to Helen came to suffer as a result. Perhaps for fear of falling short of his wife's expectations in the same way he felt he had his father's, he sought refuge in the quiet world of his dental office and possibly relief from anxiety in his supply of the calmative ether.

While Raymond saw to his dental patients, the diminutive Helen rose in stature at the local American Association of University Women chapter as well as at Wellesley's local alumnae chapter. She became friends with the well known and well respected, including fellow Wellesley graduate Madame Chiang Kai-shek, the future first lady of the Republic of China. Helen also aspired to the intellectual and social world of nearby New York City and relished her Wellesley Club teas and lectures in the city. When Benny and Bill came along, she proved a caring, if emotionally contained, mother.

Then something went terribly wrong, though accounts vary. Did Dr. Mott's melancholia tear at the fabric of the marriage? Did the former Quaker village of Rockaway become too limiting for his ambitious and intellectually curious wife? Whatever the truest answer, Dr. and Mrs. Mott's marriage ceased to flourish in that environment. At first, young Benny and Bill were only vaguely aware of the growing distance between their parents, but the boys grew anxious as their mother spent more and more time away from them. Rumors spread that the marriage was on the brink.

In an era when divorce was rare, Helen and Raymond parted ways in 1915. Helen returned to teaching and relied on family to care for her young boys, now seven and four, when she was at work. Society of the day looked unkindly on divorced mothers, and Helen wanted nothing more than to be released from that stigma and a second chance at a respectable and respected life.

In 1916 she met a prosperous British textile merchant, Arthur Barton Cross. Arthur was handsome, well dressed, and worldly. She was captivated from their first meeting while on an outing to New York City. He had attended the Citadel in Charleston, South Carolina, and then returned to England for university in the renowned textile city of Leeds. Within five years of his graduation, he had achieved high professional regard in the burgeoning international textile and cloth-making industry.

Arthur had offices in both New York and the textile-rich town of Rock Hill, South Carolina. With a casual, high-born manner, he smoked Chesterfields and drove a Model 30 Cadillac. He was interested in observing the birds of America and in purchasing good art, and had the time and money to indulge in both. Within six months, Helen and Arthur became engaged.

At Arthur's insistence, they traveled to England to wed, leaving Benny and Bill behind in the care of relatives. After the nuptials, they took an extended honeymoon trip throughout the British Isles. When they returned to New Jersey, the newlyweds launched their new lives with enthusiasm.

They collected Benny and Bill and moved to an old farm estate in the afflu-
ent borough of Eatontown in Monmouth County.

The main house was a large, gabled Victorian with scalloped cedar shin-
gles and green-striped awnings that stretched over a broad span of south-
facing windows. Its ample, manicured grounds met an acres-wide nursery
of English boxwoods in the rear, beyond which was an apple orchard and
a broad expanse of farmland on the western border. But the estate's most
prized feature was a full surround of mature, brilliantly purple lilac bushes
that passersby would famously stop and admire every spring. The property
was named Lilac Hedges.

Despite her newfound happiness, Helen had been shaken by the failure
of her first marriage and occasionally fretted that she couldn't live up to
Arthur's idealized image of her. She confided to her diary:

> Ah me! I can only give Arthur what life gave me . . . what my good
> blood called for and which life nearly squeezed out of me. Is there not
> virtue in struggle, in attainment through one's own effort, in the simple
> joys of love and work well done, even if spent by the effort?

Arthur was a decent enough stepfather, easing Helen's concerns over
the marital transition's effect on Benny and Bill. But the new family arrangement had not eased the boys' anxiety. Though they had been quite young,
their parents' divorce made them freshly aware of hidden messages in adult
behavior that before had eluded them. Benny and Bill also became highly
sensitive to their mother's priorities, even before they knew what those really were. Her behavior toward them had always been more matter-of-fact
than affectionate. Occasionally, however, her habitual coolness was interrupted by spells of genuine warmth and interest in them, and the two responded hungrily to such moods. They worked fervently to maintain her
approval and win what affection might be granted under these new circumstances.

Most afflicted by the sudden change in family life was Bill. In neither parent, it seemed, could he find reliable emotional sustenance. His mother's remarriage compounded by irregular contact with his father ultimately pushed him toward his schoolwork, at which he excelled. The kindness and positive reinforcement of his teachers and, later, his professors and professional superiors seemed to compensate for the early parental shortfalls. The consequence of Bill's early childhood was a hyper-self-reliance fueled by a determination to excel.

Though Dr. Mott never remarried, he overcame his difficulties with the loving help of the extended Mott family and local community. But his ongoing emotional frailty made being around him increasingly awkward for his young sons. Their grandparents Elias and Lauretta Mott stepped in and filled this gap admirably.

They performed all the requisite parental duties, from bathing and feeding to nightly reading, and, with the help of their great-aunt, Mathilda, taught them the family art of making bread with scalded milk. Lauretta nursed Bill back to health during an early battle with typhoid fever when neither parent could minister to the bedridden boy. But after Helen and Arthur returned from England, Bill and Benny made the permanent move to Lilac Hedges.

One year after Helen and Arthur married, two brothers became three. In April 1918, with the lilacs in full bloom, Arthur Barton Cross Jr. was born. He came into the world the same joyful year that saw the end of the Great War, which President Woodrow Wilson declared would be the "war to end all wars."

Barton was born a month premature, and Benny and Bill were protective from the start. That Barton was their half brother was no more than a biographical detail to the older boys. In fact, the ensuing years were happy ones for Helen and Arthur and Benny, Bill, and Barton.

They spent long summer days at the Jersey Shore, where the boys played endlessly in the waves. Their painted woven beach basket was always filled with the family's summertime favorites: cold shrimp and potato salad, sandwiches, shortbread cookies, and a jug of freshly squeezed lemonade. After hours of play in the cold water, the boys would rejoin Helen and Arthur to picnic on the beach, she always under a broad-brimmed, brightly colored hat, and never without a book in hand.

When they returned home from these outings, siblings William and Nelly, their southern black live-in housekeepers, would have the chores done and dinner under way, the house full of aromas drifting from the large, well-stocked kitchen. The antique dining table was set nightly for five. When their new baby sister, Rosemary, arrived, a mahogany-and-cane high chair was added in the corner.

Arthur presided over these meals, tapping the butler's button under his foot from time to time should they lack for anything. He was always the initiator of well-chosen conversation, in keeping with his orderly British upbringing. Helen's place at the long, polished table was across from Arthur. Barton sat by himself to his mother's right, freeing his right hand to toy with his food or to slip minty chops, scraps of tenderloin, or fresh cherry pie to his cocker spaniels. Benny and Bill always sat together, across from the favorite young son and to their mother's left.

The older brothers were delighted with their new siblings—first Barton, and then fiery and quick-witted Rosemary, nicknamed Muff for reasons lost to history. They did not seem to care or notice that Barton and Rosemary had nicer clothes, more toys, and the majority of their mother's and stepfather's attention. The older brothers attended public schools and worked paper routes to earn their spending money, while Barton and Rosemary were privately educated and flush with pocket money from their parents, who seemed to not want them to take on odd jobs.

AS BARTON GREW, THE older boys welcomed him into their lives with open enthusiasm. They taught him how to fish, catch lizards, race across the millpond, and both impress and spy on girls. They also vigorously defended the undersized Barton against countless would-be bullies. One eleven-year-old neighbor in particular taunted him mercilessly, calling Barton a runt and—slamming him in his Achilles' heel—repeatedly jeering "Mama's boy!"

Bill famously picked the young fellow up by his hair one afternoon, ignoring his screams for mercy. The alternately crying and whimpering miscreant begged to be let go. Even Barton was beginning to feel sorry for him. When Bill finally released the boy on condition he keep away from Barton and Lilac Hedges or else, he ran as fast as his eleven-year-old legs would carry him, not once looking back.

When Barton was finally big enough, Benny and Bill introduced him to touch football. They gave him tips and took him to high school games. The school football team had long been the star of the surrounding boroughs. Every boy between eight and eighteen dreamed of someday being its quarterback.

But Barton never developed an appetite for the primal aggressions of gridiron warfare. It was baseball that became his favorite activity with Benny and Bill. The three brothers spent hours each night after dinner on the broad south lawn of Lilac Hedges, playing their improvised game with one pitcher, one hitter, and one outfielder. They made bases out of anything they could get their hands on, including the dried hide of an unfortunate squirrel. Barton was neither fast nor much of a hitter, but he loved the game just the same. Unusually tall for their adolescent ages, Benny and Bill towered over him. Their height endowed them with that much more star quality to Barton, ever undersized for his age.

They taught him what they knew without a trace of older-brother bravado. They only smiled when he took up the bat with his left hand, and frequently slowed the action in the outfield to let Barton score. Barton grew accustomed to this preferential treatment over the years, which later made it difficult for him to survive, not to mention realize his full potential, outside a system not specifically calibrated to optimize his chances.

Nonetheless, their mother was as pleased by the brothers' bond as they were themselves. On summer nights, she and Arthur sat on the wide, covered porch watching them play until circling bats began their nosedives toward the airborne ball and the long shadows of twilight reached the fields beyond. Helen would call to Barton to come in for a bath and bed while the two older brothers routinely stayed behind, gathering up the tools of their play. Then they walked together in the gathering darkness toward the house.

Benny and Bill would do as she expected, and that was good enough for them, it seemed. Their twin imperatives were to cultivate their shared role as Barton's elders, ensuring at least sparing maternal affection, and to prepare for a life in which they would almost certainly be expected to take care of themselves.

4

★ ★ ★

BILL

AT THE OFFICE OF Naval Intelligence (ONI) in Washington, DC, Bill Mott had worked forty-one straight days since Pearl Harbor was bombed and war declared. By mid-January 1942, the Navy Department was running on a twenty-four-hour schedule and still struggling to keep pace. With two brothers in the Pacific—Barton listed as missing in action and Benny facing mortal danger by the hour—Bill needed no reminder that superior intelligence was the Navy Department's top priority. But shortages of naval officers schooled in codes and ciphers were acute, even as blame for the mishandling of pre–Pearl Harbor intelligence was cast and recast in the daily newspapers.

Bill retrieved the *Washington Times-Herald* from his icy Chevy Chase walk each morning to read of the Roberts Commission, a formal government panel assembled to "report the facts" leading to the disaster. To the navy, its mission seemed more a search for scapegoats rather than facts and answers. Like many divisions within ONI, the one in Bill's charge—Secret

Dispatches, Letters, and Documents Branch—had been besieged with inquiries and subpoenas, even as it sought to run a world war around the clock.

Washington's naval leaders felt the hot glare of a global spotlight and an enraged citizenry. The American public viewed the Pacific War as the navy's war and the unspeakable losses at Pearl Harbor theirs to explain. These woes were compounded by daily reports pouring into the Navy Department of American tankers being sunk much closer to home—by German U-boats off the Atlantic beaches of New York, New Jersey, Delaware, and other East Coast states. Germany, Japan's ally, had declared war on the United States four days after Pearl Harbor.

The Germans' race to sink more US ships aiding Britain than the latter could buy, build, or borrow had continued unabated since. More than thirty were lost in January 1942 alone, eight on a single night within sight of New York Harbor. Burned bodies and thousands of ship remnants were washing up on coastal beaches all along the Eastern Seaboard. It appeared that the US Navy couldn't even protect American shipping within swimming distance of its own shores.

Washington's ordered society and stolid military establishment had been slapped awake on December 7, 1941. By mid-January, a world had turned. The nation's capital, long accustomed to its southern-leaning traditions and unhurried pace, was now in a chaotic struggle to ramp up and run a war that suddenly spanned the globe. Hastily minted reserve officers descended from Pullman cars at Union Station only to form long queues and crowd the city's rickety trolleys and small pool of taxis.

They headed for all manner of temporary lodging in boardinghouses, barracks, hotels, and apartment buildings, most of which were already overbooked with long waiting lists. Nearly seventy thousand Washington initiates—from fresh inductees, to eager purveyors of war goods, to stenographers and government workers of all ranks—swelled the city's population to overcapacity in no time. In less than six weeks, the district government had issued more than 1,500 new building permits and still couldn't keep pace with the soaring demand—the housing bottleneck just one small piece of the shocking transition to a previously unimaginable second world war.

Upgrading the security at Washington's military departments and the White House was another major undertaking. Machine guns were mounted on the bridge leading to the Lincoln Memorial, and guards with tin hats were posted outside the State and War Departments. The White House had installed bulletproof glass in the three south windows of the Oval Office, and a bomb barrier was poured along the west wall. General Electric was commissioned to design special outdoor lighting to dimly illuminate the grounds without casting light on the house itself. An air raid shelter was built under the newly constructed East Wing.

The lights at Naval Intelligence burned nightly as the bitter struggle for control of the world's oceans intensified. All eyes were on the men who could read the codes and divine new threats before a widely dispersed enemy could strike again. Recruiting and detailing of naval intelligence officers had reached a frenzy by January 1942. Desperate to crack the Japanese naval codes and keep abreast of the Germans' changing ones, senior officers routinely pulled rank to detail personnel from one office to another according to which intelligence functions were deemed most critical.

Around this same time, President Roosevelt decided to set up an intelligence center of his own in the West Wing of the White House. He had come up with the idea after Winston Churchill's White House visit in late December. To command Britain's war with Germany, the prime minister maintained an underground headquarters in London full of maps; when traveling, he carried with him a matching set on which staff continuously updated enemy movements. During his December 1941 visit to the White House, he had set up the vivid portable display in the room across the hall from his quarters, the Queens' bedroom, on the second floor.

"Franklin, you must have a map room of your own," Churchill effused, and even temporarily loaned him the aide traveling with him at the time, one Sublieutenant Cox, to get the project under way. Roosevelt needed no convincing; he immediately ordered his naval aide to "Fix up a room for me like Churchill's." A ladies' coatroom on the ground floor, located between the Diplomatic Reception Room and the president's physician's office, was thus hastily converted into the new chart room.

Cox was also charged with training Lieutenant Robert Montgomery, an American naval reserve officer and well-known actor who was also familiar with Churchill's London map room, having recently worked for the US naval attaché in England. Montgomery built on Cox's preliminary work setting up the new White House Map Room, but within weeks, he requested a reassignment to join the hunt for German U-boats in the Atlantic. A replacement was needed in short order, preferably someone who would not also be tempted to depart for the war front.

The search for Lieutenant Montgomery's successor was intense, and speculation was thick in the staff-strapped Navy Department on who might ascend to the position. There was no application process for Roosevelt's military aides; the president's men did their own scouting. Their scrutiny of potential naval aides was particularly focused. As a onetime assistant secretary of the navy, Roosevelt had a strong preference for his naval representatives over other military aides.

Officially, naval aides served as the formal liaison between the White House and anything relating to the US Navy, but under FDR, the position entailed much more. They were the president's intelligence officers, chargés d'affaires for heads of state visiting the White House, unofficial executors of special requests from Mrs. Roosevelt, and now, overseers of the Map Room. Intellect, personality, and discretion were essential qualities, as well as one's ability to work long and unpredictable hours.

Captain John McCrea, Roosevelt's senior naval aide, told the president, "I have my eye on a chap named Mott—an Academy graduate and naval reserve lieutenant. I want to bring him over here to take over from Montgomery as executive of this operation . . . I like the cut of Mott's jib. He's intelligent, quick witted, and a take-charge doer . . . Since I spend so much of my time at the Navy Department, I need my Map Room deputy to be a 'take-charge guy.'" McCrea further stipulated that the Map Room was to be a primarily "naval operation," although all theaters of war would be covered. And he wanted its executive to remain in the position for the war's duration. Mott's nearsightedness, he surmised, would permanently disqualify him for sea duty.

BILL'S 1929 NAVAL ACADEMY appointment came three years after Benny's. Unlike Benny, however, who was happy enough to do well, Bill had stood at the top of his high school class and undertook every academic task with near-fanatical intensity. Beneath his senior yearbook picture was the quote "Some are born great, some achieve greatness, and some have greatness thrust upon them." Under it, his English teacher, Mrs. Carpenter, had written, "To Bill, the best English student I have ever had."

The prolonged economic depression following the stock market crash his plebe year had a near-catastrophic effect on Arthur's business. As he struggled to recover, Bill's Annapolis appointment was not only a goal attained, but also an economic necessity. The fact that Uncle Sam covered the cost of a midshipman's education was a luxury-turned-saving-grace.

Budgetary cutbacks forced on the navy by the Depression, however, had an even worse effect on Bill's graduating class than it had on Benny's three years earlier. Only half of the 1933 graduates received officer commissions; the rest were honorably discharged and offered a place in the naval reserves. Any shortcoming among classmates competing for commissions was grounds for the dreaded cut. In the spring of 1933, as Bill's June graduation approached, he was met with an obstacle that prevented him from taking the same coveted course as Benny.

Each midshipman had to undergo a rigorous physical examination prior to receiving any postgraduation orders, and among the most dreaded of the compulsory tests was the vision exam. Perfect eyesight was an absolute prerequisite for a naval officer, particularly for sea duty. Failure to observe the slightest threat—a light, a periscope through the mist, a critical guiding star—could jeopardize the ship, not to mention the lives of thousands. The eye test was therefore especially exacting.

Replacing the familiar reading charts that hung in eye doctors' offices everywhere (because they could be memorized) was the Snellen tester, which was manipulated by the examiner to make letters of various sizes slide into view horizontally and pop up vertically in constantly changing order. The eyes were dilated beforehand, then refracted with a homatropine solution that was applied every ten minutes, several times in a row. A retinoscope then threw light on the pupil at a distance of one meter to determine if the eye was myopic or near- or far-sighted, and if so, by how much. These refractions were conducted on each midshipman by four naval eye specialists.

"Son," the Academy physician said to Bill after his exam, "you're a fine midshipman. But you can't go active with those eyes, eyeglasses or not."

Bill was stunned. When he entered the Academy, his vision had been 20/15 in both eyes. The shock that his less than perfect vision was enough to bar him from the navy career he'd been planning as far back as he could remember rocked him to the core. He was crushed, not accustomed to the sort of setback he couldn't overcome with tenacity and hard work. After receiving sunglasses to protect his dilated eyes from sunlight, he pulled his cap down low over his watering eyes and began formulating the unimaginable: an alternate life course.

If the career of a naval officer was not to be his, Bill concluded, he would not join the Reserves, at least not right away. He loathed the idea of civilian life, but with few other choices in view, he moved directly from Annapolis to Washington, DC, and began searching for a job. His first stop was the northwest gate of the White House on Pennsylvania Avenue.

In hand was an article Bill had obtained from the stacks at the *Washington Times-Herald* summarizing the commencement speech that President

Roosevelt had just delivered at his Annapolis graduation. Bill politely asked the gate guard if he could speak with the president. When the surprised guard queried further, Bill explained patiently that the chief executive had offered to help any of the noncommissioned Academy graduates—and pointed to a passage in the accompanying news article: "Now, I can't promise you anything," Roosevelt said, "but if any of you boys who are not commissioned need help, well, you know you have a friend in Washington."

Bill waited for some time as the message was carried inside the White House and debated. Finally, a man came out and introduced himself as Steve Early, FDR's press secretary. Trying to conceal his irritation, Early smiled and, with a southern drawl, said, "Well, it's nice that you came by, but I'm sure you know the president's comment was, well, you know, rhetorical."

Bill said, "Well, I took him at his word, and I need a job."

Early sighed, exasperated. "Okay, I'll tell you what," he said. "Give me your telephone number, and I'll look into it."

The next morning at about seven thirty, Bill received a call at his boardinghouse. He was to report to the Washington Navy Yard as an ordnance inspector, charged with examining lead castings eight hours a day. The work was stunningly boring, but he endured it long enough to gain acceptance to George Washington Law School (which he attended at night) and get a job as a patent examiner for the US Patent Office.

Bill worked at the Patent Office by day to pay for law school and living expenses. In the evenings were classes and many a solitary dinner at Ford's or Child's, local counter-and-stool eateries where he could study his law books and, for forty cents, fill up on specials such as pot roast, mashed potatoes, string beans, and coffee. Despite late-night classes, studying, and the tedium of patent work, Bill excelled academically and moved up in professional rank. By the time he was admitted to the DC bar, he was a senior patent examiner in the General Counsel's Office and confident that a lucrative career in patent law lay ahead.

Despite the promise of fame and fortune the US Patent Office offered to eager young inventors, it was a classic federal bureaucracy, slow and leaden. Bill battled daily stacks of applications and rote procedures but greatly enjoyed the dogged energy of the entrepreneurs who streamed in and out of his office. As the son of a dentist, he had more than a passing knowledge of that profession and unwittingly became the resident expert on patent applications for fluoride removal from drinking water. Fluoride was thought to be the cause of brown spots on children's teeth. Dental scientists discovered subsequently that fluoride actually protected tooth enamel from decay and might even have tooth-hardening properties. Two years later, Bill oversaw the patent process for *adding* it to municipal water and toothpaste.

This wasn't the military career that Bill once dreamed of, but it was a secure and respectable profession during grim economic times. Meanwhile, his affinity for the navy never extinguished, he sought every opportunity to stay involved with his Annapolis classmates and colleagues. He was an officer in the US Naval Academy Alumni Association, a position that gave him considerable control over local distribution of army-navy football game tickets, a source of stature regardless of rank. He visited Annapolis often for alumni meetings, and befriended Academy football coach Rip Miller. Bill always brought Rip fresh intelligence on promising high school football players with the academic potential to enter the Academy.

In 1938, he organized the first of what would become an annual army-navy-game rally at Washington's Ambassador Hotel, smartly securing the attendance of the secretary of the navy, the secretary of commerce, the postmaster general, the chairman of the Maritime Commission, the chief of naval operations, the Marine Corps commandant, and the coaching staffs from West Point and Annapolis. Bill also arranged for starlet Linda Darnell, one of Hollywood's loveliest, to lead off the event with the help of an NBC radio commentator. Cocktails were generously served. A popular and patriotic event, the rally was broadcast throughout the country.

Such good-natured and high-spirited gestures earned Bill respect and fellowship among Washington's political and navy elite. Further, his 1938 marriage to witty and astute Rosemary "Romie" Baker, a Madeira School and Sarah Lawrence College graduate, was considered a union of one rising star to another. The couple became regulars at the right parties and weekly tennis matches at the exclusive Chevy Chase Club.

One cool afternoon in September 1939, Admiral Walter Anderson, chief of Naval Intelligence, introduced himself to Bill Mott in the Chevy Chase Club men's locker room. The admiral had noticed the young man's Naval Academy ring. Both half clad, they struck up a conversation. The only other person in the locker room was the club's bootblack, busy spit polishing Admiral Anderson's shoes. After chatting at length about tennis, the court conditions, and a brief game of navy who's who, Admiral Anderson's demeanor grew serious. At once the world's democracies seemed under siege and daily war headlines were on everyone's mind.

Nazi Germany had just invaded Poland, prompting declarations of war against the Germans by Polish allies Britain and France. And Japan's slaughter of Chinese civilians and unceasing incursions across Southeast Asia had prompted US cancellation of its commercial treaty with that country, removing all obstacles to an outright trade embargo against the import-dependent Japanese.

"So when did you graduate the Academy, son?" Anderson asked, pulling on a white athletic shirt marked with the club's red-and-black crest.

"Class of thirty-three, sir, but I wasn't commissioned because I'm nearsighted. Now I'm a patent lawyer. Not my first choice, of course, but it's a good job."

Admiral Anderson listened quietly, then continued. "Are you in the Reserves? There's going to be a war, you know, and I could use you down on Constitution Avenue. If I get the paperwork drawn up, would you accept a commission in Naval Intelligence? I happen to run the place."

Surprised but not displeased, Bill hesitated.

"Well, thank you, sir, but no, I'm actually not in the Reserves right now.

With all due respect, I hear they treat reserve officers like shit down at the department."

The bootblack raised one eyebrow without looking up.

Amused by Mott's candor, Admiral Anderson replied with a chuckle, "You let me worry about that, Mott. You may be sure that if you fit the bill for what I have in mind, nobody's going to treat you like shit, as you would say. Can you be at my office at 0800 Monday morning?"

"Yes, sir, I can," Bill replied, smiling.

A flurry of letters followed, waiving Bill Mott's vision disability, and in 1940 he was back in the navy, as a lieutenant. By restarting his military career as a Naval Intelligence officer, Bill became an expert at the incipient enemies' military codes, as well as deciphering the department's byzantine protocols of power, rank, and advancement. He was placed in charge of the office that received, circulated, and stored top secret correspondence at the Office of Naval Intelligence.

The Secret Dispatches, Letters, and Documents Branch ("Office A-3-c") had custody of the most highly classified telegrams and intercepts (diplomatic and military) coming into ONI. With the recent and top secret breaking of the complex Japanese cipher system (code-named Purple) used to transmit that country's diplomatic cables (decryptions were code-named Magic), Bill came to understand the looming war threat better than most.

He was frequently called on to summarize the essence and import of these communications for both the director of naval intelligence (DNI) and the chief of naval operations (CNO). The intercepts were selectively shared on an "eyes only" basis and were never to be copied. They were hand carried to a handful of designated recipients who read them on the spot and handed them back. After circulating in this manner, they were returned to A-3-c, where they were filed and placed under lock and key.

Bill also became familiar with Ultra, the code name for British decryptions of German military signal intelligence but which eventually expanded to include those of the Japanese and Italian military as well. These decryptions were challenging to paraphrase, but he developed a reputation for synthesizing them without sacrificing accuracy.

By early 1942, Bill's unusual combination of talents were increasingly sought after. When ONI's Admiral Frederick Horne declined Captain McCrea's request for Mott to report to the White House, he offered alternative officers—all discreet and versed in the communications and cartography (the science of creating maps). But McCrea turned them down. The White House was superior to Horne and all the other navy admirals combined, and McCrea, not accustomed to negotiating for personnel, simply ordered Bill Mott to 1600 Pennsylvania Avenue. With this, he became the full-time overseer of the new White House Map Room.

DESPITE THE TORMENT BILL felt over Barton and his failure to locate him, his demeanor gave little away on his first day at the White House. Captain McCrea introduced his new recruit to the president, his family, and the close-knit White House staff.

Bill was gregarious and smiling as he was ushered around the West Wing's rarified environs, shaking hands, exchanging pleasantries, and generally endearing himself. Roosevelt clearly enjoyed the banter with his new aide, particularly when conversation digressed to navy football. FDR also took a keen interest in Bill's family, empathizing as a parent might over Barton's disappearance in the Philippines and the constant perils Benny faced. It marked the beginning of a friendship that would last until the end of the president's life.

In March 1942 Bill wrote Benny from the White House:

> My new job is quite interesting, and even with my Republican background I can't help but like and admire the man. He certainly is interested in the Navy, as well

```
as being very human personally. I have talked with him
many times about you and Barton and he asks me after every
Pacific engagement if you are alright . . .

    I'm glad to see your luck is holding out and that the
good work carries on. Believe me I follow your movements
with an anxious eye. I am always immensely relieved each
time you come through.
```

The Map Room was twenty-seven and a half by twenty-two and a half feet, but it had a close feel to it, with its low-slung ceiling, blacked-out single window, and unusual furniture arrangement. Desks and file cabinets formed an island in the center of the room and the walls were overlaid with fiberboard on which large-scale charts, covering all theaters of the war, were hung. The room's design and the height of the maps allowed Roosevelt to navigate around in his wheelchair to study them at close range—and occasionally confirm the remote location of a postage stamp from his collection—without having to stand.

Battle areas were covered with clear plastic and continuously updated with grease pencils to reflect the ever-changing locations of Axis and Allied forces. The ocean areas were sprinkled with different-colored pushpins to identify ships by country—blue for American vessels, red for British, black for German, and so forth. An impressed War Secretary Henry Stimson confided to his diary, "Every task force, every convoy, virtually every ship is traced and followed in its course . . . as well as the position of the enemy ships and enemy submarines, so far as they can be located." Pins of various shapes denoted types of military vessels: round heads for destroyers, square heads for heavy cruisers, etc. . . . Different pins indicated the location of the Allies' Big Three: a cigar for Winston Churchill, a cigarette holder for FDR, and a pipe for the Soviet Union's leader, Joseph Stalin.

The president visited the room twice daily, usually on his way to his office in the morning and again in the afternoon after visiting the doctor's office across the hall where he had his polio-withered legs massaged or his congested sinuses packed. Roosevelt's closest aide, Harry Hopkins, and CNO Admiral Ernest King were also regular visitors, as was the army chief of staff, General George C. Marshall, and War Secretary Stimson.

Under Bill's tutelage, the Map Room—which was also the sole repository of Roosevelt's diplomatic correspondence—quickly assumed an aura of permanence. He took what had been started under Cox and Montgomery and refined systems for receiving, distilling, and securing top secret information. Within weeks of Bill's takeover, a decimal filing system for classified documents was established and a codification manual was created to ensure that critical documents could be retrieved in short order.

New practices simplifying the charting and recharting of Japanese, German, and Italian military forces and their estimated aircraft distribution were also put in place, as well as an improved system for monitoring merchant ship and submarine activity. He also improved upon the system for charting and recharting orders of battle and supply line threads that, literally, stretched around the globe.

Locked leather pouches containing classified cables, military memoranda, and other Top Secret and Most Secret documents were delivered around the clock to the heavily guarded room. The deliveries were logged, studied, and summarized, and then relevant updates were applied to respective war theater wall charts. Subject files were created so that the president could draw on them easily to formulate policy and draft correspondence. Bill also set up a system for logging, distilling, and distributing situation reports from all theaters of war, as well as daily intelligence summaries gleaned from translated Ultra and Magic enemy intercepts.

While the Map Room started as a center for naval war information, it expanded quickly to cover all theaters of war. Bill had a staff of six: three army and three navy watch officers, all members of the Reserves. He required that all watch officers memorize the secret center's critical priorities and protocols. For example, whatever important news might be breaking,

all communications between Roosevelt and Winston Churchill, followed
by his communications with Generalissimo Chiang Kai-shek and Joseph
Stalin, took absolute precedence. Either Bill or Captain McCrea walked intelligence summaries and these priority cables straight to the Oval Office
or, depending on the hour and urgency, to Roosevelt's private quarters.

Reliable and discreet staff were critical, and Bill held his watch officers to the same standards he expected of himself. Ensign George Elsey, a
Princeton-educated naval reserve officer whom Bill had hired back at Naval
Intelligence, was his first recruit. When Elsey and Bill's subsequent hires
first entered the Map Room, Bill would close the door and point to a "three
monkeys" cartoon taped to the back. Under the first monkey, whose eyes
were wide open, was printed "sees everything." Below, in pencil, was written "something." Under the second monkey, holding a hand behind one ear,
was printed "hears everything"—the penciled note below: "a little." The
third monkey, hand over his mouth, "tells nothing." Below, in pencil: "less."

Bill would then disclose that the penciled annotations were the work
of Secretary of War Stimson, as dictated to him one evening in the Map
Room by FDR himself. This made the point that Bill's imperative of extreme discretion was dictated straight from the top. He would then simplify
his expectations: "I explain a task or clarify a complex matter to you once,
and from that point forward, I expect you to act promptly and precisely
with respect to it." Their boss was a stern taskmaster, but both the army
and navy watch officers felt a strong loyalty toward him. Confidentiality,
accuracy, and speedy access were the three imperatives of Bill Mott's operation, and they were all enhanced by that loyalty and seamless teamwork. By
the spring of 1942, the White House Map Room had become the de facto
epicenter of Allied war planning.

Both the president and his closest advisor, Harry Hopkins, were impressed, as well as with Bill's deft handling of non–Map Room matters,
including quick and charming responsiveness to requests from Eleanor

Roosevelt. His temporary detail from Naval Intelligence to the White House was soon made permanent, and a promotion to lieutenant commander came with it.

Throughout the exacting early months in his new job, Bill found time each day to pen inquiries about Barton. His search had been a roller coaster from the start. Though "Casualty and Missing-in-Action" manifests were infrequent and error-ridden, he reviewed every single one; Barton was not listed on any of them. He wrote Captain Joel Newsom, commanding officer of Barton's ship, now docked at Port Darwin, Australia. Replies to his urgent missives yielded a few answers, but each generated new questions in turn. He learned that Barton had been wounded during the bombing at Cavite. He had survived and was hospitalized at Sternberg. But then what?

Bill had felt a surge of confidence when he learned that MacArthur had commissioned a hospital ship to ferry Sternberg's wounded to Port Darwin. The ship had departed within hours of the fall of Manila. There was no manifest to examine, but Bill contacted Australian naval authorities and requested that Barton be tracked down and instructed to call him. White House operators were placed on full alert: "Put Barton's call through no matter what time, day or night." The head operator, Louise "Hacky" Hackmeister, had been on duty that day. She swiveled away from the switchboard's gnarled panel of wires and insistent beeping to face him. She was calm and sympathetic despite her tether to the humming board. "Believe me, son," Hacky said, "I'll call you at once if anything comes through."

But weeks stretched into months with no call from Australia.

Helen peppered Bill week after week with fresh rounds of questions to which there were no immediate answers. His mother had scant idea how much effort he was expending to learn Barton's fate or how troubling what little information he had secured was. But the family continued to hold out hope for Barton's survival, in no small part because Bill projected confidence—real or forced—that Barton had surely pulled through. He would make every effort to perform on that assurance. The unrelenting pressure he was putting on himself was not just because he loved his brother and was worried about his mother. It was because, despite the purest of intentions in helping Barton attain his commission, Bill felt fully responsible for thrusting him in harm's way.

5

★ ★ ★

CABANATUAN, SPRING 1942

AFTER MARCHING FOR HOURS in the midday sun, the navy patients and other Cabanatuan-bound prisoners arrived at the Manila train depot. A north-facing freight engine hitched to a dozen boxcars awaited them. The men were ordered to disperse along the platform and climb aboard. After medics took over the deceased patient, Barton stepped onto the black, heat-buckled floor of the second boxcar. It quickly became impossible to see any activity on the platform as he was forced to the rear of the car by continuously boarding prisoners. Barton's uneasiness grew in the new surroundings: a dark, ten-by-six-foot, furnace-hot steel crypt. Worse, Charles had boarded a different car, either by mistake or by force.

What happened next was unimaginable. Yelling from the direction of the engine, a Japanese soldier signaled to the guards standing at each boxcar door. Impervious to protests from the prisoners, the guard at the second boxcar shouldered the creaking metal door closed. The men heard the exterior latch slammed down and hit twice, as though barely able to contain its cargo.

Pinned between the car's back wall and a wall of sweating flesh so close to his face that he struggled to breathe, Barton felt a wave of panic. Even before the train lurched forward, men began to gasp for air. Little could be heard above the moaning, the helpless splattering of defecation from the dysentery-ridden, and knees thudding to the floor by those losing consciousness. Those that remained conscious endured something potentially worse, an hours-long terror that they would die before the journey's end. Barton struggled to contain his own rising claustrophobia, possibly remembering he had survived it once before.

In 1930, when he was twelve years old, his parents took him on a very special outing into New York City to take in the view from the top of the brand-new Chrysler Building. At 1,050 feet, it was the tallest building in the world and its gleaming steel spire seemed to reach the heavens. The opening-day tickets were to its viewing gallery on the top floor. One by one, the guests filed into the building's thirty-two gearless electric elevators, among its many modern inventions. Their elevator car was dimly lit, with polished wood panels, and there was an operator wearing a uniform and cap with shiny gold buttons. But with so many people eager to get to the gallery, the car quickly overfilled.

When the operator cranked the brass doors shut, Barton felt a fear he had never experienced before and began perspiring heavily. The second the doors opened, he burst past the exiting guests into the viewing gallery. When his bewildered mother finally found him, he dismissed her concerns and moved toward one of the enormous triangular windows to take in the view. It was never formally diagnosed, but Barton's established fear of tight, enclosed spaces was for him at least as powerful as any triggered by armed Japanese.

THE FREIGHT TRAIN'S RUSTED black cars came to a merciful halt in the late afternoon at Cabanatuan City, the north central terminus of the Manila railroad. While unconscious prisoners were dragged out of the boxcars, Barton and the others staggered onto the train platform, gulping fresh air. As more and more dazed men stumbled into the blinding sunlight, small groups of Filipinos and their children began materializing from side streets and alleyways near the tracks.

Nervously shuffling bare or sandaled feet, they gawked silently at the pitiful scene of the prisoners exiting the boxcars and bodies being laid out on the platform. While Barton scanned this mixed sea of faces in search of Charles, Filipino boys began darting toward the men and thrusting pieces of sugarcane into their hands. Encouraged by the boys' success, others approached the prisoners with bananas, panocha (a Filipino sweet made with peanuts), and cane candy. Some offered cassava cakes or balls of rice wrapped in banana leaves, while still others set down cups of water as close to the prisoners as they dared.

Suddenly aware, the head Japanese guard shouted an angry command. His comrades immediately turned on the crowd, pushing and striking at will. They withdrew, but defiantly hurled their remaining goods over the picket of guards to the prisoners. Men all around Barton reached up desperately, like spinsters for a bride's bouquet. In this sudden display of hands and arms, there was a familiar one, long and freckled.

The combination of the edibles and relief at finding one another revived both Charles and Barton, whose crisis-born friendship seemed to strengthen by the day. In fact Charles seemed to be improving, perhaps because of it; he was unusually resilient after the train ordeal. And while captivity seemed to bring out the worst in him, it also had given him a reason to live. "Not gonna let a bunch of goddamn Japs decide whether I live or die," he declared, and not for the last time.

No food or water had been issued the prisoners since morning, and little then, but none was offered by their captors after they exited the boxcars. Instead, the guards ordered the men to reassemble in four-abreast columns. Minutes later, the prisoners set out again, first dragging through the heart of Cabanatuan City and then turning east onto a rutted dirt road.

It was near the end of the dry season in the Philippines, the hot and windless stretch of months that precede the drenching monsoons. While acacia, papaya, and banana trees lushed the distant landscape, the shadeless road was inches deep in dust. The powdery soot exacerbated the men's thirst, settling onto their swollen tongues, between their teeth, and in the rims and corners of their eyes. Several prisoners staggered out of the columns from heat prostration and were loaded onto trucks trailing the marchers. Others passed out completely and were tossed like cordwood onto the truck beds.

While these horrors demoralized many of the prisoners, it had the reverse effect on others, including Barton. It tapped in him a wellspring of desire to live. In fact, this difference marked an early divide in the burgeoning prisoner population. Mistreatment and deprivation destroyed the wills of some, eventually killing them. But it strengthened the resolve of others. Strong religious faith and a positive personality were predictors, but the galvanizing power of anger can also be credited. Whatever their motivating muse, Barton and these others seemed to intuit that making the simple mental choice to live could make all the difference in their survival.

At dusk, the marchers came to a halt in front of a squarish barbed wire stockade. The entrance faced the road on one side; the other three abutted open land. The prison camp's interior was flat, barren, and chalk dry. Bamboo barracks with roofs of thatched nipa palm leaves were its only adornments other than the manned, forty-foot-high machine gun emplacements marking each corner of the compound.

Ordered to stand at attention, the exhausted prisoners waited forty-five minutes for their "welcome" instructions from the camp commandant. Their legs trembled, and they swayed almost drunkenly in the searing heat. Finally, a dwarfish man in an immaculate uniform emerged from his makeshift headquarters. Lieutenant Commander Masao Mori had a coiffed, bristling moustache and was wearing knee-high boots polished to a high shine. He puffed out his chest, folded his arms, and gave his new charges a long, contemptuous look. He then addressed the prisoners through an interpreter.

The Cavite-based ensigns were in collective dismay. Like Takeo Yoshikawa in Pearl Harbor, "Lieutenant Commander" Mori's prewar occupation—running a bicycle shop in Cavite City—had been an apparent cover for a higher calling: assessing the layout of Cavite Navy Yard for its incipient attackers.

It was a reminder of the unflattering saying the Filipinos had for the thousands of Japanese domiciled in the islands, disliked for their arrogance and airs of superiority over them. In Tagalog, their native tongue, the phrase was *"Pasukab kung tumingin, parang Hapon,"* meaning, "He eyes you in a treacherous manner, like a Jap."

The Cabanatuan commandant's manner had changed since his tip-seeking bicycle repair days. Mori's speech was terse and harsh. Punishment for violation of any of the camp rules was death. Prisoners would be put in groups of ten. If there was an escape by one in the group, the remaining nine would be executed. He then reversed direction with a flourish and returned to his headquarters.

At Mori's exit, the ravenous and desperately thirsty men were each given a ball of rice and a canteen cup of water, after which they were assigned to barracks according to rank and branch of service. Work orders would be issued in the morning after *tenko*. Barton and Charles were familiar with that drill and knew exactly how they would handle it.

The interior of their barrack, where they were quartered with other naval officers, consisted of two long, wooden planks divided by a dirt aisle. Each platform was split into five sleeping bays. Prisoner discouragement over their new home was palpable, but on that first night at Cabanatuan they could only collapse on the hard wooden bays. Some drifted to sleep mulling escape, others contemplating how they would survive, and others, their souls already crushed beyond repair, hoping only for death's merciful release.

★   ★   ★

SOON AFTER BARTON'S GROUP arrived at Cabanatuan came the defeated Corregidor defenders, and soon after that the defenders of Bataan—all prisoners now. The state of the Bataan prisoners shocked the Cabanatuan residents, even in the context of their drastically altered living standards. They horrified all who heard their tale of a brutal hundred-kilometer (sixty-two mile) march from the Bataan Peninsula to their first prison hold, a place called Camp O'Donnell, where thousands, they learned, had died already.

One Bataan survivor told of not only impossible thirst, starvation, and beatings, but of Japanese guards driving American trucks over fallen prisoners and then sticking out rifle bayonets to slit the throats of lines of marching men. Others that fell out of the marching columns were shot by rear-guard "buzzard squads." But the horrors of Cabanatuan were plentiful, too.

Without sanitation, clean water, and adequate food, an average of thirty men a day died during Barton's first months there, not counting executions. The most common causes were malaria, beriberi, diphtheria, and dysentery—and despair, too, though despair was not formally listed as a cause of death. The Japanese kept their distance from the prisoner hordes, wearing masks when near them and throwing food into their barbed wire enclosures.

With the majority of prisoners weakened or sick, their dependence on one another became primal. It was in this context that Barton began to see a role for himself. He started small by organizing groups on work details while they chopped wood or buried their dead. His idea—and that of a growing number of prisoners—was to pool their resources and restore the weakest among them to at least a functional state. This would be accomplished by giving the most infirm larger rations and, if they could get their hands on them, medicines such as quinine. Such supplements could be obtained through Cabanatuan's emerging black market, where medicines and food could be purchased from Japanese guards who had procured them to sell to their captives at a fat profit or as barter for gold watches or rings. That such a market existed at all, however, infused a measure of hope among the prisoners, a precious commodity at Cabanatuan. Even the strongest among them knew they could become the next needy patient.

Such brotherly acts forged powerful bonds among the men and spawned a determination to pull one another through. Barton understood, either consciously or unconsciously, that he had been mostly a recipient in his life, and that this one-way generosity had diminished him. That he had the physical and emotional capacity at Cabanatuan to help others survive was more satisfying than all the times in his life he'd been singled out for special treatment. He couldn't help but reflect whether his family might recognize him less and less as his imprisonment lengthened, and not just because he was dirty, unshaven, and underweight.

6

★ ★ ★

WHITE HOUSE MAP
ROOM, APRIL 1942

WITH WAR EXPLODING ON every ocean and continent, Bill Mott worked late again on April 17. At seven o'clock, the Map Room was in a rare lull. The radiator under the blacked-out window hissed and clanked as Bill examined the pins and grease pencil markings on the Pacific-plotting map. At thirty years old, Bill stood nearly six feet and was fighting trim. He had the bearing of a military man: high cheekbones, a thicket of jet-black hair combed straight back, gilt collar leaves reflecting his recent promotion, uniform crisp, and shoes shining like mirrors. But anxiety roiled under that polished exterior.

Crossing parabolas of tacks plotting Allied and Axis movements across a seventy-million-square-mile Pacific war front were measured in degrees and centimeters. To the middle left was Cavite, where Barton had been wounded during the Japanese air attacks in December.

A few centimeters to its right was the Bataan Peninsula, where the largest-ever defeat of American forces had occurred the previous week.

A thumbnail beyond it was Corregidor, which, Bill knew, would also be forced to capitulate. Somewhere between those three hot spots, Barton had disappeared without a trace.

Long before it was public, Bill knew of the decision not to reinforce the flagging garrisons in the Philippines. The die had been cast in December 1941 during Winston Churchill's emotional Christmas visit to the White House. The prime minister made the lengthy trip shortly after the US declaration of war on Japan to ensure Roosevelt's commitment to a "Europe First" strategy. Churchill understood the rage the American public felt toward the Japanese and wanted to prevent emotional diversion of American resources from Britain's defense against the Nazis to the Pacific.

Available Allied resources to wage global war were stretched to the limit and had to be prioritized. Churchill's Yuletide mission and persuasive charms ensured that helping Britain defeat Nazi Germany would take precedence. War Secretary Stimson's reluctant entry regarding the Philippines, which he confided to his diary during Churchill's visit—"There are times when men have to die"—was the cruel verdict.

Within the context of other threatened Pacific bases, the consensus that the Philippines could not be won back quickly or easily—and that Allied troops there would be abandoned—had been reached thanks to cold military math. By that same calculation, Australia, still in Allied hands, had to be held. Otherwise supply-and-communication lines would be severed and Allied access to the entire Southwest Pacific lost. Australia was also the only Allied base left in the region for staging countermoves against Japan.

It was an open secret that Roosevelt had little affection for Douglas MacArthur—and was wary of the Republican general's presidential aspirations. But he agreed well before the fall of Bataan that MacArthur should be evacuated to Australia both to protect it from Japanese seizure and to prepare counteroffensives against Japan. The decision took a number of factors into account. There were no other generals in the region to put in charge, and Roosevelt could not afford the political fallout of General MacArthur falling into enemy hands. Home front public opinion played a role in the president's decision.

MacArthur and his public relations team had released more than a hundred press communiqués from besieged Corregidor, which were picked up by every newspaper in the country. They touted the general's bravery, genius, and leadership in the face of a scurrilous enemy. Reeling from serial reversals on the world stage, the American public gobbled up the flowing heroic narrative; babies were named after MacArthur and streets renamed after him.

So there would be no outcry or even a congressional inquiry into why all the general's planes in the Philippines were destroyed on the ground, wingtip to wingtip, despite repeated pre-attack directives ordering him to launch them. Nor would there be an investigation into his inexplicable nonresponse to the War Department's advance war warnings. Bill had been at the War Department that entire night, waiting tensely with others far senior to him for MacArthur to acknowledge receipt of the warnings and to confirm that defensive air measures had been taken.

The first cablegram, sent seven minutes after the bombs began dropping on Pearl Harbor, warned specifically that Manila and greater Luzon were Japan's next likely targets. MacArthur neither replied nor commenced air operations, with tragic results. With American airpower destroyed, Cavite Navy Yard was the obvious next target—easy pickings without air protection. Bill was not the only naval officer to question MacArthur's reckless military judgment in the Philippines.

He then ordered over seventy-five thousand American and Filipino soldiers to the Bataan Peninsula in compliance with a pre-war defense contingency plan. Yet inexplicably, all but minimal stocks of food, ammunition, and medicine were left behind. These errors appeared grossly shortsighted to navy brass, who were further incensed that MacArthur *blamed* the navy for defeat in the Philippines by not heeding his demand to send ships to rescue the very men he put in harm's way.

The two-inch circle on the Pacific plotting map marked the widening Japanese-controlled perimeter around everything north of Australia, making it increasingly difficult to get reliable information on those men left behind. Thus far the Japanese, not a signatory of the 1929 Geneva Convention, had refused to discuss adherence to its provisions on prisoners of war. Requests for updated casualty lists were also proving futile. Unconfirmed reports indicated that quiet exchanges of noncombatants, mostly Filipinos, had taken place, but not military men.

Barton's whereabouts was not Bill's only concern in the Map Room that evening. A quick calculation of speed, distance, and a glance at the clock meant that the top secret convoy stealing across the Pacific to bomb Tokyo had reached its rendezvous point. With *Enterprise* leading the covert task force, no doubt Benny was on high alert up in Sky Control at the moment. Backed by steely determination and burning revenge, the covert plan had been approved unanimously by top brass, despite the severely handicapped state of the US Navy.

Shortly after Pearl Harbor was bombed, President Roosevelt asked his military planners to find a way to strike Tokyo. America desperately needed a win to stem sinking public and military morale. FDR understood the importance of bolstering outgunned soldiers on every front, not to mention rationed citizens who were also being asked to build a massive war arsenal.

The December 7 losses had been staggering: 2,400 killed, another 1,200 wounded, 18 warships and 188 aircraft destroyed, and an additional 159 damaged. And bad news had piled up ever since. Guam, Hong Kong, Singapore, Burma, Sumatra, and the East Indies had all fallen to the Japanese in the following four months. And now the Philippines were lost; Americans were in a vengeful, morose free fall.

In February 1942, partly in response to the national mood, Roosevelt had ordered the sequestration of more than a hundred thousand Nisei—US residents of Japanese ancestry—at internment camps across the United States (including Pearl Harbor spy Takeo Yoshikawa, to an Arizona camp, though his misdeeds had not yet been discovered). Even this action failed to shake Americans out of their malaise, but Roosevelt knew what would: bombing Tokyo. Such a bold and aggressive initiative, he believed, would unify the country, restore confidence, and offer Japan a taste of US resolve. The logistics, however, were formidable.

An aircraft carrier would have to get within two hundred to three hundred miles of mainland Japan for its small F6F Hellcat bombers to strike Tokyo and have enough fuel to return to the ship. But it was far too risky to send the few remaining ships in the Pacific Fleet that close to Japan. Only the army's burly B-25 bomber had the size and range necessary for such a mission. But B-25s had never taken off from an aircraft carrier, and it was physically impossible for them to land on one. So the president ordered the army and navy to work together on a solution to that problem, and fast.

Bill had known about this mission for months and had been long preoccupied with its high risk and poor odds—the worst so far for Benny. In fact, Bill knew to a footnote the scope and perils of every *Enterprise* mission well in advance of Benny. Though they wrote each other often, wartime censorship prevented Bill from sharing such classified details, including any mention of this daring operation. Understanding the dangers Benny faced yet unable to warn him was an acute source of anxiety for Bill.

The state of the floating navy, moreover, was deplorable. To lose the slim surviving strength of the Pacific Fleet would be to virtually relinquish US naval presence in the entire region. The recent dispatch from Admiral Chester Nimitz, CINCPAC (Commander in Chief Pacific Fleet), that Bill had distributed, eyes only, offered no comfort:

```
                     TOP SECRET
Pacific Fleet markedly inferior in all types to enemy. Can-
not conduct aggressive action in Pacific except raids of hit
and run character which are unlikely to reduce pressure on
Southwest Pacific. Logistical problems far surpass peacetime
conception and always precarious due to fueling at sea and
weather . . . Unless this fleet is strengthened, it is in un-
precedented danger and its effectiveness . . . is limited.
                                                   Nimitz
```

According to the punctilious Map Room clocks, it was 0700, Saturday, April 18, 1942, on the other side of the international date line. They should have executed by now, if indeed *Enterprise, Hornet,* and their escorts had made it to the launch point where Colonel Jimmy Doolittle and his B-25 squadron were to take off. All there was to do now was wait. The bank of clocks on the far wall ticked away the seconds in every time zone, and the teletype taunted from the corner, its incessant repetition as ominous as it was monotonous: *click, reset; click, reset; click, reset.*

Bill had learned to display grace under pressure at a young age, thanks to tumultuous family circumstances, but that day tested him. The Pacific map's vast watery expanse off mainland Japan's coast offered no consolation. Were he to press his whole hand over the convoy's route, it would touch no land relief at all—only enemy-infested waters; an enemy that was superior in size, strength, and sea power. Another worry roiled also. If the Tokyo bombing mission was successful, would the resulting Japanese rage further endanger Barton, who, under the best of circumstances, had been taken prisoner?

His mother's letter, delivered to the White House that same afternoon, throbbed in Bill's ears. "My mind," she wrote, "swings like a pendulum, Barton, Benny, Benny, Barton . . ."

Bill stepped over to a typewriter, scrolled in a blank sheet of paper, and began typing.

```
                                    The White House
                                    Washington


To: Lt. Comdr. X. B. Taylor
Bureau of Navigation


    If the Regulations permit, I should like to be notified
first in the event of the death of either of my brothers,
Lt. Elias Bertram Mott, II, at present serving on the USS
Enterprise, and Ensign A. B. Cross Jr., missing after the
bombing at Cavite in Manila. I feel that I could more easily
break the news to our mother, Mrs. A. B. Cross, than could a
stranger should either such unhappy events come to pass.


                                    Lt. Cdr. W. C. Mott
```

7

★ ★ ★

"THIS FORCE IS BOUND
FOR TOKYO"

JUST HOURS BEFORE SEVENTY-FIVE thousand troops on Bataan surrendered to the Japanese, the USS *Enterprise* and her escorts once again nosed out of the ships' channel at Pearl Harbor in single file. After clearing the channel, the task force's heavy cruisers and destroyers fanned out into protective positions. Admiral Halsey then issued the order to head northwest, and *Enterprise* signalmen relayed the directive to the rest of the convoy.

Three long days and nights passed, with the crews in the task force still unaware of their destination. They pressed inexorably north and west into cooler and cooler latitudes. The goose-bumped crew finally changed out of their tropical uniforms into long-unused cold-weather gear.

On Sunday, April 12, Benny Mott was once again on the watch in Sky Control, discerning what he could through the filmy morning mist. Down on the flag bridge, thirty-five feet below, Admiral Halsey was locked in his familiar pugilistic stance, his cap down low over his face, obscuring a set jaw, beetle brows, and unruly silver hair. Benny didn't like not knowing their destination or mission but just then it didn't matter. He believed to his core this man would get them there and back, recalling the fear, admiration, and camaraderie Halsey inspired during his midshipman years.

BACK THEN, CAPTAIN HALSEY had been commanding officer of the Academy's Annapolis station ship, the USS *Reina Mercedes*, a former cruiser captured during the Spanish-American War. Among its functions was to imprison transgressing midshipmen. Benny was glad he'd never met Halsey under those circumstances; their interactions had only been at pleasant social gatherings the Halseys hosted for upperclassmen, whom the couple treated with emphatic warmth. During these more relaxed affairs, Benny and Captain Halsey often discussed navy football and another common passion: the underappreciated virtues of their shared home state of New Jersey.

Halsey had relished these chest-beating interludes about the state: "The home of Alexander Hamilton, Thomas Edison, and Albert Einstein!" he would crow in mock exasperation, drawing wide grins from Benny every time. At Annapolis, Benny and Bill were both known for their proud defense of the Garden State—against routine mockery. They even embraced their nickname, "the Jersey Brothers," despite its implicit derision. Was it Halsey who started that? Benny couldn't remember, but it stuck.

The feisty *Reina Mercedes* captain enjoyed his own Jersey-native spiel— he was the product of generations from the august town of Elizabeth, one-time state capital, founded in the seventeenth century by English settlers. He groused that it was now known less for its critical submarine industry or as the birthplace of the electric car than for being the base of the notorious "Jersey family," the oldest US Mafia syndicate in La Cosa Nostra (Sicilian) and the only one indigenous to New Jersey. The persistent media spotlight on the Mob irritated the state's proud and long-established natives, including Captain Halsey and Midshipman Benny Mott.

Benny would chime in with his own New Jersey yarns. "Well, sir, we love a spirited defense of our much-maligned state. You see, the Motts arrived with the Quakers back in the seventeen hundreds, but they didn't just sit around pritheeing this and pritheeing that!" Halsey always appreciated Benny's family high notes, including the Motts' ancestral link to members of the iconic fraternal order that boarded the tea-laden vessels *Dartmouth*, *Eleanor*, and *Beaver* in Boston Harbor in 1773. The rest of the story is textbook history, but rebel-hearted Halsey would laugh and clap Benny on the back every time. Between the two of them, New Jersey's reputation was restored every time.

The whole *Enterprise* crew felt Benny's combination of awe and affection for Bull Halsey. Before every mission, Halsey reveled in his anti-Japanese epithets and scowling, serial invectives, like a football coach before the big game. The men loved his bellicose quips, including "Hit hard, hit fast, hit often," and his "perfect willingness" to divide the Pacific Ocean with Japan: "We'll take the top half, and they can take the bottom." And they reliably whistled and clapped when he staked claim to Emperor Hirohito's white horse when it was all over. Halsey would trot it right through Tokyo, he declared, and the Japanese language would only be spoken in hell when he was done with them.

Never mind that Halsey was a late admit and graduated near the bottom of his 1904 Academy class. Nobody cared. The man they knew was a trained pilot, schooled in intelligence, and knew aircraft carriers like the back of his hand. "He can calculate to a cat's whisker the risk of an operation" was the oft repeated quote among *Enterprise*'s 2,700-strong crew.

That faith was needed more than ever right then. While they didn't know their destination or the purpose of this mission, they did know that the odds were stacked against them. Two months earlier, a triumphant *Enterprise* had returned to Pearl after its first enemy offensives in the Gilbert and Marshall Islands. They had damaged or sunk a dozen or more Japanese vessels and downed more than forty planes. When *Enterprise* entered the channel, slid through the torpedo nets, and returned to port, every sailor in Pearl Harbor had lined the rails, cheering and shouting. Ships blew sirens and horns, and men of every rank whistled and hooted. Admiral Halsey was grinning from ear to ear on the flag bridge, taking it all in.

In those early raids, *Enterprise* had been outnumbered but not outwitted, giving its sailors—and the country—a needed shot of good news. Still, it had come at a price. Though *Enterprise* had brought home the war's first victory, the Gilberts and the Marshalls had been a trial by fire for its untested crew.

While retiring from the engagement, *Enterprise* came under surprise attack by enemy bombers. Benny's machine gunner on the port catwalk, George Smith, was killed, becoming the carrier's first gunnery casualty of the war. An enemy plane had dropped out of formation and aimed straight for *Enterprise*'s deck. Its right wing hit the ship, killing Smith before skidding into the sea. Fuel from the plane's ruptured tanks drenched half the carrier, all the way up to the superstructure. This first-known airborne suicide attack had stunned Benny and his men. None of them had even considered the possibility of an enemy plane flying directly into their ship.

George Smith's funeral gave the *Enterprise* crew their first taste of burial at sea. They'd stood at attention on the fantail while an honor platoon came to parade rest before them. The men bowed their heads and prayed as gun salutes and the trumpeting of taps competed to be heard above the rushing, high-seas wind. The body bag—weighted with lead shells so that it would sink quickly—was placed beneath an American flag on a stand, angled feet-first toward the thrashing waters below. The draped figure was then released into the sea and disappeared beneath the ship's steady wake. Until then, this ritual had only been practiced, like so many other war exercises and drills, off sunny, peacetime Oahu.

ON THIS MISERABLY COLD April morning two months later, Benny turned his attention to the horizon. Tightening his plump fingers around the cylinders of his field glasses, he steadied his focus. With the weather stormy and foul and the rise and fall of the deck spanning 150 feet, he was not initially certain of what he'd just seen. Once assured that it was not the waters' pitch and hurl tricking his eyes, he motioned to *Enterprise*'s Captain Murray and pointed to an approaching vessel. Murray was out the door at once.

By the time Murray reached the wing of the flag bridge, a wraith-like outline of seven more ships—two cruisers, an oil tanker, and four destroyers—appeared through the mist; a dull series of gunmetal-gray silhouettes against graphite seas and cinder skies. Within minutes, an entire convoy was in view.

The lead vessel was an aircraft carrier, the spanking-new USS *Hornet*, and it was carrying a mother lode of unusual cargo. Atop her aft flight deck in two parallel rows sat sixteen dark-green Army Air Forces medium-range bombers. Were those B-25s? They were twice the size of an aircraft carrier's elevators, which were used to raise and lower aircraft between the flight and hangar decks. "What in *theeee* hell?" Benny said aloud.

He wasn't the only one gawking. Speculation swept *Enterprise*, and within minutes, there were multiple theories about the force's mission: The bombers were being delivered to reinforce a base in the Aleutian Island chain that stretched westward from Alaska to Russia, just as *Enterprise* had done with the bombers to Wake Island in what seemed an eternity ago. Others speculated they were destined for a Russian airfield on the Kamchatka Peninsula. "Only God and Halsey know for sure," mused Benny.

But speculation ended minutes later when they heard the admiral clear his throat over the ship's loudspeaker. The men were quiet, expectant.

"This force is bound for Tokyo!" Halsey bellowed.

Wild cheers erupted from every one of the ship's steel compartments. Benny shivered with excitement and disbelief. Down on the flag bridge, Admiral Halsey reacted to the elated chorus with a broad, satisfied smile.

"This force is bound for Tokyo" was flashed in code to all the other ships. The *Hornet* and *Enterprise* convoys then maneuvered into a single force, named Task Force 16. It was composed of the two carriers, four cruisers, eight destroyers, two tankers, and two submarines. All bows of the largest assembly of American warships since Pearl Harbor pointed west at a determined twenty-three knots.

Benny felt a surge of pride being part of the USS *Enterprise*. Despite the chronic fatigue and persistent anxiety over his troubled marriage and the well-being of his baby girl, his powerful bond to his shipmates was as inextricable as that of any family. Benny would do anything for this crew, and the feeling was mutual.

While docked at Pearl, he had overseen the installation of state-of-the-art Oerlikon 20-millimeter antiaircraft guns throughout the ship, a vital upgrade ordered by Halsey after February's tactical air strikes in the Gilbert and Marshall Islands. The old water-cooled cannons were removed, and potent new guns with unprecedented range and precision were positioned on catwalks and walkways on every level. Word traveled quickly regarding the powerful new artillery, and he'd gotten several heartfelt kudos and shoulder claps since their departure. *Enterprise* and her crew was his entire world now, and these gestures of confidence had come to mean everything.

All too often, Benny lay awake during the brief intervals he was supposed to be resting on his hard, narrow sleeping rack. Before their departure, Jeannette had not only informed him that she wouldn't ever be visiting at Pearl but also that her lawyer would be in touch. He was still reeling from it. A thousand times, he had sworn to himself that no child of his would ever endure what he had endured as a child. Now the full weight of her leaving him and taking their little girl was upon him, and he was powerless to alter her plans—especially from out here in the middle of the Pacific Ocean.

He careened from despondence over his own troubles to wrenching anxiety over what had become of Barton. Was he alive, or had he been bayoneted and cast aside, never to be found? Had he been taken prisoner? This night, even steaming toward Tokyo, was no different for Benny. He needed the rest—desperately—but he had received no mail from home in weeks and was endlessly anxious for news. He watched for letters like a perched falcon, especially for those carrying a White House or Lilac Hedges return address—anything.

After tossing, turning, and staring at the blank metal ceiling for what seemed like hours, he switched on the tiny light over his bunk and pulled out a piece of onionskin letterhead proudly embossed with a sketch of his ship. He needed to shake off the miserable scenarios gathering strength in the dark.

USS Enterprise

At Sea

April 12, 1942

Dearest Mother,

I don't know when I shall have another letter from you but I hope it will be soon. I enjoyed reading the diary entry that you sent about your trip to the shore. Guess I've read it through three times and each time it is like going home for awhile. It is so much you and conjures memories of our early days, of Sea Bright, Ocean Grove, Red Bank, the grand Atlantic and its wonderful swimming. If I could only have a little bit of that now I'd be rested and ready for anything. I guess that is not to be my lot for a while though.

Bill has written me all about his new job. One of grave responsibility and trust. I hope he believes now that he can serve much more usefully there than at sea. Also, I've had a couple of letters from Dad. His letters were interesting and he seems quite proud of both Bill and me.

Mother, I want to do something nice for you. I can afford it and I want to. The money is rolling in now and frankly I have no opportunity to spend it. So while I am saving (I am anxious to know if you received the bond I sent for safekeeping by the way) I feel there will be plenty of time left to buy and pay for war bonds.

I want you to take the enclosed check and get yourself something nice. The time may soon come when you will no longer be able to obtain many things, if indeed it is not already here. You deserve it Mother, and don't worry, we'll still be buying bonds.

I had in mind a nice coat for next winter, and I mean a really nice one--please go do this while the getting is good!

Know that I love you Mother, and <u>know</u> that I will press on until I reach Barton. It keeps me going even on the worst of days.

Please write and be brave.

> Your loving son,
> Benny

p.s. I am enclosing some pictures of me with several war correspondents. Am not sure if they can be sent but if they are not at least one can try. Anyway, they will be in many newspapers so perhaps you can see them there.

Benny was mindful that it was April 12, Barton's birthday, and it was sure to be a bad day for her, particularly with the fresh crop of bad news coming out of the Philippines. After rereading the letter, he placed it and his signed-over allotment check in an envelope. He reached up and switched off the light; perhaps sleep would be his reward before the midwatch.

TASK FORCE 16 CONTINUED its strong westerly course, covering three hundred to four hundred miles each day. With *Hornet*'s flight deck unusable thanks to the tightly parked B-25s, *Enterprise* search planes scouted two hundred miles out on both flanks while her fighter pilots patrolled protectively above. April 17 dawned raw and cold and the seas were rough. Still a thousand miles east of Tokyo, the carriers and cruisers fueled one last time before they left the tankers and destroyers behind for the final dash to the launch point. Throughout the afternoon and night, they rolled and pounded through the heavy seas. The screening ships were barely visible through a steady drizzle and low, pumice-colored skies.

At 0315 on the morning of April 18, for the first time in six weeks, the insistent electrical clambering of the general quarters alarm ripped through the ship. Benny was standing the midwatch. He scanned the horizon through his binoculars—back and forth, over and over, without pausing as he awaited the next set of signals. Nothing.

Then *Enterprise* jerked so sharply to starboard it nearly knocked Benny over. Seconds later, Captain Carey Randall, the marine commanding officer aboard, burst through Sky Control's door. Jack Baumeister's radar had picked up two surface contacts ten miles ahead, he reported; the task force was turning to avoid detection from the suspected Japanese patrol vessels. Together they waited, studying the horizon for forty-five minutes. Finally, the task force turned back, resuming its westerly course. They were still seven hundred miles from Tokyo; hundreds of miles from launch point.

At 0500, an *Enterprise* scout bomber flew low over the deck. The pilot reached out and dropped an orange beanbag with a scribbled message attached. He had sighted another patrol vessel, fifty miles ahead. Worse, he was sure he'd been spotted. Even with that news, gutsy Halsey pushed on for thirty more minutes, gaining another eleven miles that the fuel-strapped B-25s wouldn't have to fly to gain safety after their raid.

Suddenly, through the fog and rain, Benny made out two ships' masts and a low black hull, about a hundred feet long, off the port bow. He immediately reported it via *Enterprise*'s sound-operated telephone. "We have a setup on enemy vessel. Request permission to fire five-inchers [guns]." He waited an interminable three minutes for a reply. But Admiral Halsey said no and instead dispatched the cruiser *Nashville* to sink it. The Japanese vessel fought back with its single gun until its rounds finally fell short, and the ship started sinking fast. Heart pounding, Benny picked up another patrol vessel in his field glasses. *Enterprise*'s fighter planes began to strafe it, but soon it too was sunk by the *Nashville*.

Halsey wasted no time with his next order. There was no longer any doubt that they had been reported to the Japanese military by at least one of these civilian-manned "picket boats" surveilling the distant waters arcing around the home islands. At 0800, 650 miles from Tokyo and 150 miles short of the objective point, Halsey sent a signal to *Hornet* telling Lieutenant Colonel Jimmy Doolittle to launch his planes:

```
To Col. Doolittle And His Gallant Command


              Good Luck And God Bless You--



                                                   Halsey
```

Benny watched *Hornet* turn into the wind and speed up for the launch. Between the forward velocity of the carrier and the winds churned up by the stormy weather, the pilots had the benefit of a forty-six-knot (approximately fifty-five-mile-per-hour) headwind. The plane directors on *Hornet*'s deck also tried to time the launches so that the heavy bombers could take off on the up-pitch of the bow.

Hornet's bow lifted and plunged violently as Jimmy Doolittle's plane was the first to race across the carrier deck, catching the bow as it rose on a wave crest. The crew from the *Enterprise* cheered wildly into the howling wind. There was a split-second pause before the second plane was released from the flight deck's trip wire. Benny watched, relieved one second and horrified the next, as the plane took off on the down-pitch of the bow. He closed his eyes as it slanted toward the sea and hung precariously low over the water for hundreds of yards, straining to become airborne before finally gaining altitude.

When Benny reopened his eyes, the plane was still struggling to pull up; it was no more than a foot or two above the water. For more than half a mile, it hung so close to the heaving sea that it seemed certain the plane would crash. Benny and Captain Randall stood together in the tower chanting over and over, "Pull up, goddamn it! Pull up! Pull up!"

And the next fourteen planes—"in a nicely judged bit of timing," Benny would later regale his audience in the officers' wardroom—"observed first-hand the advantages of taking off on the bow's *up* pitch."

Despite the difficulty gaining altitude, all sixteen planes finally lifted skyward and disappeared single file into low, fast-moving clouds. They headed due west in the direction of mainland Japan even as *Hornet's* and *Enterprise's* scout bombers reported fifteen more patrol vessels, several of which they sank. With no time to waste, Task Force 16 immediately reversed course and boiled their wakes to a high froth in a breakneck twenty-five-knot race for safety.

Benny and a gaggle of other officers gathered in the wardroom annex to relieve excited anxiety and speculate on the raid's success. Estimating that Colonel Doolittle was nearing his target about that time, they tuned the dial to Radio Tokyo, which happened to be broadcasting an English-language propaganda program.

A little after 1400 hours—noon Tokyo time—the announcer, in stilted, heavily accented English, laughingly read a Reuters News Agency report—strictly embargoed but inexplicably released—that Tokyo had been bombed. The broadcaster went on at length about how this was a ridiculous joke played on the Japanese people: no foreign bomb or shell had ever landed on Imperial soil. As he looked around him on that lovely spring day in Tokyo, he said he saw nothing but calm, serenity, and cherry blossoms.

Suddenly sirens sounded in the background, and his voice gave way to frantic Japanese—then he abruptly went off the air. Benny turned and smiled at Captain Randall and slapped his knee; it was the best he'd felt in months.

8

★ ★ ★

BARTON, 1930–1941

GROWING UP, BARTON HAD not approached academics or any of life's other responsibilities the way his older brothers had. Nor had he adopted their relentless imperative for self-improvement. Instead, friends and social activities had been at the center of Barton's early life. A happy-go-lucky boy with a seemingly endless reserve of goodwill, he took an unusually genuine interest in others. Peers and adults alike were drawn to his warmth, puckish wit, mischievous sense of humor, and amusing collection of arcane facts, sports-related and otherwise.

Yet Barton always seemed to fall short of his father's expectations; in academics, sports, even in his height. Helen did what she could to bring her husband's lofty goals for Barton to fruition. She alternately prodded and upbraided him about his lessons, particularly math and science, two basic assets of any Annapolis candidate, which they were determined he would be. He actually did well in literature and poetry studies and had a perfect ear for music, but these strengths were not encouraged. Barton handled the strain by appearing not to care, and his mother's expectations by appearing not to try.

Things got worse after Benny and Bill departed for the Naval Academy. Only eleven when the second of the brothers left home, Barton soon found life at Lilac Hedges quiet, lonely, and uncomfortable. While he adored his young sister, Rosemary, she couldn't replace the loss of his brothers. What had once been the epicenter of fun and boisterous camaraderie suddenly felt all wrong, and his parents' angst over his studies only exacerbated his unhappiness. To Barton, all their gestures equaled reproof, and he became increasingly restive and brash. Disciplinary issues both at home and school spiked.

The town movie theater offered refuge, all the better if the occasional girl was involved. The fairer sex was apparently beginning to find Barton Cross quite attractive and witty. He also developed a taste for good tobacco at a young age, and for the occasional beer. When Helen reproached him for these transgressions, he replied that it was her own liking for Benson & Hedges that sparked his interest in the first place, and she could hardly criticize him for a little beer considering his parents' not infrequent scotches with a dash of soda. This left her stammering for the appropriate response to the little scamp, which never seemed to occur to her in time to do any good.

Beset by business crises, Arthur was rarely available to help. The textile business, already wobbling from labor strikes, was on its knees after the stock market collapse. Mills and plants were shuttering, and ships carrying cloth sat idle at coastal docks. It was growing ever clearer that Helen could not cope with Barton's burgeoning adolescence by herself. She hoped that at least one of the older boys might return home before the launch of their careers, but it was not to be.

And so it went until one evening in 1932 when an exasperated Arthur had finally had enough. Barton was fourteen years old, and "Little Lord Fauntleroy," as he sputtered to his wife, needed a paradigm shift. Arthur turned to his longtime friend David Page Harris, headmaster of Christ School for Boys in Arden, North Carolina. With its motto "The school that makes manly boys," Christ School seemed the perfect antidote to Barton's persistent lassitude.

No one was more surprised than Helen by how well her coddled son took to his new environs that fall. She both feared and hoped he might return to Lilac Hedges after a disastrous first week or two. Yet daily chapel, classes, and chores—making beds, waiting tables, cutting wood, and feeding chickens—all, as it happened, delighted Barton. Even digging up tree stumps, so arduous its assignment was reserved for repeat rule breakers, gave Barton a sense of satisfaction. His droll humor and high-spirited bonhomie won him fast friends, and his quick-wittedness snagged him a spot on the *Warrior*, the school newspaper.

After expecting the worst, Barton not only adapted to life at Christ School but also thrived on its structure and the constant companionship of fellow boarders. He performed surprisingly well in academics, too, even in the once-dreaded subjects of math and science.

Barton was also intrigued by the morning services in St. Joseph's Chapel, the spiritual center of Christ School life. At home, the Episcopal Church equaled monotone sermons followed by droning bids for contributions and coffee hours that bored him to despair. At Christ School, the daily sounding of the chapel carillon, known as the Angelus bells, called students to worship but also to hear homilies on such topics as "Failure is a chance at a new start, not a measure of self-worth" or "When we work together, we cannot fail." The effect on Barton of these daily sermonettes—simple but profound guideposts—was like spring rain to a dormant garden. Almost subconsciously, he began applying their lessons.

But perhaps best of all, the school's top sport was baseball. Unlike other secondary schools where football reigned supreme, baseball had been Christ School's athletic mainstay since its founding in 1901. Barton had never been on a real baseball team before. Likely due more to his knowledge of the game and his unmatched command of professional base-ball statistics, he was given a spot on the school's second team. He would always remember the day he became a "Greenie," even the weather—a cool spring afternoon—when he returned to his log cabin and laid out the uniform—crisp and white, bearing Christ School's green insignia—on the simple woolen blanket that stretched across his bunk.

The chores at Christ School did as much to educate Barton as the hom-ilies and classes, but so also did the presence of a different society of boys than he had known near Lilac Hedges. While some were of the same back-ground as he, a number of others were on scholarship. Some had no moth-ers, some no fathers, and still others were orphaned entirely.

Such circumstances seemed unimaginable to Barton. These particu-lar boys often worked the hardest to succeed—and succeed they did, aca-demically, athletically, and socially. He pulled himself up on this developing wisdom, and it gave rise to self-confidence, a previously unfamiliar feeling. By graduation, Barton had a reputation as one of the smartest, if nearly the smallest, in his class. And while his inner prankster put him at the top of the penalty work list (and claim to the most excavated tree stumps), he finished Christ School with the second-highest GPA in the class of 1934.

Arthur was delighted when Barton gained acceptance to his alma mater, the Citadel, the Military College of South Carolina. The few coveted congressional appointments to the Naval Academy were taken that year and the Citadel had been Barton's next choice. He was also quite young for a high school graduate, having finished Christ School at age sixteen; a year of maturity in a military environment ahead of the Academy was a prudent move, his parents concluded. Helen was determined that her boy would try again for the Naval Academy the following year, but he was Charleston-bound for now and determined to make the best of it.

THE CITADEL'S STERN WHITE stucco buildings topped with medieval-style turrets accurately reflected its rigor. And while Barton may have thought his legacy status might shield him from the legendary hazing that cursed the life of a plebe cadet, or "knob," he was not so lucky. Barely an hour after passing through the Citadel's Lesesne Gateway that steamy August morning, he found himself at the start of Hell Week.

Fresh off a year of being on the receiving end of such treatment, the second classmen were spiteful; it had been done to them, and by God they would now have their turn inflicting the torture: ear-splitting shouting of orders and questions; slapping; food deprivation; marching knobs down to the low-country swamp to stand at attention, waist-high in muck, while swarms of mosquitoes feasted on them.

The first few days of this working-over broke more than a dozen of them; they simply packed up and went home. But Barton showed surprising pluck. Determined to survive the mistreatment (possibly motivated by the imagined disappointment on his father's face had he not), he urged on his new colleagues as well. With a spirit of defiance, humor, and an ever-present helping hand, he exhorted them to stick it out. "We're not going to let them beat us at this game!" he would say over and over.

Barton did everything he could think of to coax his miserable fellow knobs. He also vowed to himself and others that he would never engage in these black arts toward future initiates—if he got that far. "We'll show these bastards how officers are supposed to behave when we get the chance," he'd say. But Barton also learned at the Citadel how to avoid drawing unwanted attention.

Lesson One was to conceal that his father was a Citadel alumnus. Legacies, presumed to be overentitled braggarts, were traditionally given double the treatment. Lesson Two was to absolutely do what he was told, however absurd, however many times, whatever time of day. The fact that he was a legacy gave him additional fortitude in this, so anxious was he to not disappoint his father. By heeding these lessons, Barton survived knob year, if not happily.

Barton became popular in his company, less for drill proficiency than for wicked mimicry of his superiors, well-told jokes, and hilarious attempts at the distinctive Charleston drawl with New Jersey inflections. Dormitory pranks were another source of amusement. Painting slumbering colleagues' fingernails with pink enamel was a knob-barracks favorite, since polish remover was a scarce commodity on the Military College of South Carolina's campus.

Nonetheless, as the year progressed, the option of leaving Charleston for what Barton imagined to be the gentler Annapolis became a paramount goal. One year at the Citadel, he concluded, was plenty.

And so, at long last, Barton Cross was accepted into the Naval Academy's class of 1940. Delighted, Benny and Bill were full of counsel and stories. After all the halcyon tales from their own Annapolis days, Barton expected nothing less than a pleasant high-seas adventure. He was ordered to report to "latitude 38°58'53" N, longitude 76°29'08" W" (Annapolis) the first week of June. Barely returned from Charleston, he bade his parents farewell again, this time at the main entrance to the Naval Academy. With a mix of pride and anxiety, Helen and Arthur watched as Barton fell in line with another class of plebes to begin a fresh series of unremitting humiliations.

AFTER PASSING THROUGH THE Academy gate, Barton was directed by uniformed guards to the administration building. Turning right past a nest of mounted naval guns from the Spanish-American War, he walked up the steps of administration and took his place in a line of other would-be naval officers waiting to be processed by the chief clerk. Following receipt of a date-and-time-stamped instruction sheet, the inductees marched awkwardly across the Yard to that most hallowed of buildings, Bancroft Hall. There they were herded and hustled—from physical exam to haircut to supply store—right up to that momentous hour: their swearing in as midshipmen of the United States Navy.

The apprehensive assembly faced the great marble stairway leading to Memorial Hall and the Academy's most treasured relic: a dark-blue flag bearing the phrase "Don't Give Up the Ship." The revered banner, quoting the dying words of Captain James Lawrence, had been hoisted by a defiant then-Master Commandant Oliver Hazard Perry as the US Navy battled the British at Lake Erie during the War of 1812.

When the moment came, Barton raised a slightly trembling right hand and pledged: "I, Arthur Barton Cross Junior, of the state of New Jersey, aged eighteen years, having been appointed a midshipman of the United States Navy, do solemnly affirm that I will support and defend the Constitution of the United States against all enemies, foreign and domestic; that I will bear true allegiance to the same; that I take this obligation freely, without any mental reservations or purpose of evasion; and I will well and faithfully discharge the duties of the office on which I am about to enter: so help me God."

Following the ceremony, the orders came fast and furious. It did not dawn on Barton until it was too late that he would have to endure another year of plebe purgatory before things had any chance of improving for him.

As with the Citadel, it was the second classmen, or "youngsters," who were charged with conferring a range of cruelties on the entering class: Only walk down the center of corridors. Turn square corners and walk head up, shoulders squared, chest out. Fingers along the seams of your trousers. There was a new language to learn as well. Bancroft Hall walls were "bulkheads," floors were "decks," stairs were "ladders." Plebes were told when and where to form lines and how to march to and from them (double time, meaning at a run), where to sit for meals, and how to eat them. Endless instructions covered every minute of the day, from reveille to taps.

The midday meal became its own source of dread. Barton was ordered to eat many plebe-year lunches *under* the dining hall table, thanks to his failure to correctly answer a firestorm of questions on an array of arcane naval facts spat out by one especially unkind youngster. These included the birth and death dates of any number of navy greats and the width and length of the deck planking on a particular class of ship. The hazing worsened over time as others in the class above him sensed Barton's vulnerabilities. Unlike at the Citadel, he had a hard time staying below his Annapolis tormentors' radar.

Barton's sole extracurricular activity at Annapolis was the Academy Chapel Choir, where his rich and well-trained tenor voice was enthusiastically welcomed in a choir replete with baritones. In fact, his solo pieces gained some acclaim—a rarity for him at Annapolis.

As his difficult plebe year wore on, Barton began to develop a visceral dislike for the Naval Academy—for all things naval, in fact. Demerits were given for everything; by Christmas, he had more than forty, and the time and effort it took to work them off only yielded more deprivation and hard work. Daily room inspection required that floors (decks) be washed and waxed; blinds be dust free, at "half-mast," and opened; shower walls be clean, dry, and unspotted; and light fixtures be white-glove spotless both inside and out—among two dozen other requirements. Even on days when Barton managed to pass inspection, he frequently failed a second unannounced "spot" check, which could occur at any time during the day. He compiled dozens of demerits for violations of this particular banality alone.

Barton's distress was compounded by letters from friends who had gone off to "normal" colleges, an experience he increasingly desired. The creep of self-doubt was unstoppable. He had never been much interested in fighting or hurting other men. Why, then, had he landed in these places where learning to excel at that very thing was a core requirement? It simply wasn't his nature, any more than football's block and tackle. If his experiences at the Citadel and now Annapolis were any clue, the military life was not a promising line of work for him.

Sensing trouble, Helen traveled to Washington for a month to monitor Barton's progress. She insisted it was only to hear him perform with the Academy choir in Sunday chapel—among the rare times parents were allowed on campus. It wasn't long before she learned of Barton's hazing. Bill's wife, Romie, had told her of one particularly upsetting incident shared by a visiting midshipman at a Washington cocktail party. Bill would likely have taken Romie to task for leaking the tale to his mother, knowing full well how such matters tended to play out. After promising her daughter-in-law that her source would remain anonymous, Helen promptly wrote Barton inquiring if the rumor was true.

Surprised, he emphatically denied the incident had occurred and implored his mother to drop the subject. Her pursuit of the matter could only hurt him, he insisted. But unable to subdue her anxiety, Helen penned a letter to the Naval Academy's superintendent, David Foote Sellars:

My dear Admiral Sellars,

Against the advice of everyone, I should like to talk with you about my son, Arthur Barton Cross, now a midshipman in his plebe year. He is the third of my sons to enter Annapolis. . . .

To most civilians, you are simply the austere trainer of men, but I am presuming you also possess that trait of sympathy given the youthfulness of plebes. My son went into his recent examinations ill in body and I fear subnormal in spirit and mind. No boy was ever braver than he—he knows about hazing and expects it—he learned that at The Citadel, I can assure you.

Barton has not written or spoken a word of this to me or to his father, but a classmate of his mentioned the cruelties he is undergoing to his older brother in Washington. Through devious means unknown to either the older brother or the lad himself, news has reached me.

This "youngster" [3rd classman] has peculiar tendencies—almost sadistic one might think. To beat a boy until blood appears, to force him to hold heavy objects of furniture on his bare head while balanced on billiard balls—all to the breaking point. He was forced to crouch and do knee bends, and this youngster told him he will see to it he cannot study and will fail his examinations.

To continue torturing devices for two-hour periods—is this necessary to make officers? This youngster's name suggests Germanic extractions, I believe.

Both older sons, my husband, everyone, says, nothing can be done, and I would only hurt Barton by publicizing it. In fact, my husband says that even if he fails his examinations, he must never know that we know.

Naturally I would not go to my Senator who appointed Barton to report it, but surely there is some remedy for this. Will the Service lose this splendid young man because of petty, vicious, contemptuous persecution? I know you do not condone this.

Yours Sincerely,
Helen C. Cross

Barton would never tell his parents what really happened that terrible night—or on so many others nearly as bad. No good came of ratting out fellow mids, despite nominal rules against hazing. His suffering was all thanks to the intractable grudge of one Midshipman "R.," who had no family wealth or navy legacy to tout and resented those who did. His determination to settle the score with those more fortunate than himself was insatiable.

Returning from the showers to continue studying, Barton had been summoned by R. to his room once again—this time the evening before his Steam Enginery exam. But the hours-long torture that night left him physically and emotionally shattered. He stood on two billiard balls and, per orders, lifted and balanced R.'s desk while R. playfully jabbed him in the ribs with the business end of a wet broom, demanding answers to a string of obscure nautical questions. At some point, the towel dropped from Barton's waist and the torture continued while, wet and naked before a growing throng of revelers, he struggled to stay balanced. When it was over, his ribs were bruised and he was bleeding from the repeated jabbing.

In the end, Barton didn't cry; he didn't "break." But he could not return to his studies after R., in mock disgust, finally released him. Miserable, humiliated, pained, and exhausted, Barton collapsed on his hard, narrow bed and slept until morning bells. He awoke to a pounding head, every inch of his body aching. Completely unprepared, he dressed to face the dreaded Steam exam.

It was unclear whether Helen's comment regarding "my Senator" was a veiled threat, but Admiral Sellars responded to her letter promptly, assuring "drastic and summary" action. The admiral wasted no time broaching the topic with a much-surprised Midshipman Cross. Barton stood at attention in Admiral Sellars's office until he was gently told to stand at ease. Then, with a stunning degree of specificity, he inquired of Barton whether the incident had taken place. Barton never altered his facial expression; he just listened to the admiral describe his own nightmare in remarkable detail.

When allowed to speak, he said, "I'm sorry, sir. I've had it rough here and there, but no, sir. It never happened." He repeatedly denied the incident, refusing to rat out his tormentor. The commandant impressed upon Barton the importance of his obligation to tell the truth, but Barton responded evenly that he'd "been asked a few stern questions from time to time," but not physically abused. He was sure this was a case of mistaken identity, sir.

Admiral Sellars wrote Helen again, asking for the name(s) of the accused. He wanted to get to the bottom of it for his own reasons and was becoming insistent. At this, she balked, realizing that if Barton refused to cooperate, she stood alone. She wisely deduced that if she took the matter any further, she would bring her entire family down on her head. Midshipman R.'s identity would not be hers to reveal, she decided reluctantly.

To Admiral Sellars, she replied:

My dear Admiral Sellars,

I should hate you to think me a silly, hysterical mother. My only aim is that Barton should have had freedom of mind to pass that Steam examination . . . We have never been able to get corroboration from him except, "I am having it rough but I can take it." You see I must not hurt his pride and of course shall not mention our correspondence on the subject, EVER, to anyone.

In my eyes the Naval Academy can do no wrong, and I already have two fine sons to prove this. Therefore I have complete confidence in your wise handling for the situation. It has distressed me deeply—I think interfering mothers are most disagreeable.

In Sincere Appreciation,
Helen C. Cross

Barton could not figure out how Admiral Sellars had learned of the incident, but he held firm that he would not be a tattler. Helen retreated back to New Jersey, realizing that many a Naval Academy mother before her had tried and failed to gain exceptions for their sons. Perhaps Admiral Sellars had her in mind with his often-repeated response to the question of why barbed wire was strung atop the school's perimeter. It was not, he would reply, to keep midshipmen in, but meddling mothers out.

IN PREVIOUS ENVIRONMENTS, BARTON had survived on varying degrees of cleverness. He had done well in group dynamics, too, from which he had drawn personal strength. But he was finding it more and more difficult to get by on these assets at Annapolis. The atmosphere, in his view, was emphatically not collegiate.

Rather, it was designed to train and mold men to a specific shape and culture. While Bill and Benny had toughed it out—and became misty-eyed over Academy traditions and monuments—Barton was intimidated and irritated by them. Every building, every road, and every structure was named after one or another of the navy greats. Reverence for past naval icons was ubiquitous. Nowhere on the grounds were monuments to the likes of Barton Cross, overwhelmed and undersized.

The summer after his first year was spent on the midshipman cruise, a weeks-long training in practical seamanship. To Barton, the cruise mostly meant cold saltwater showers, bad food, and grueling chores. With trousers rolled, he scrubbed teak decks with sandstone by day and served endless midnight watches shivering on deck or in the suffocating boiler room. He studied marine engineering, turbines, boilers, and the ship's auxiliary machinery. He hated every minute of it and rejected the notion that some sort of hallowed bond would develop through a round-the-clock regime of punishing duties aboard a ship.

Nonetheless, Barton returned to Annapolis for a second year of personal and academic crucifixion, with the new perils of naval tactics, gunnery training, and increasingly rigorous mathematics. He made it through the fall semester, landing near the bottom of his class. But things got tougher in the spring. Barton failed the final mathematics examination; and though he was allowed a reexamination, for which he studied hard, he failed it, too—by seven-hundredths of a point.

If hazing was a factor in his fatal academic stumble, he never let on. No exceptions were made at the Naval Academy for those who failed a course, despite Barton's good standing in other subjects (particularly English literature and history) and his legendary voice in the Academy choir. He was compelled to withdraw, in shameful comparison with his two brothers. Helen and Arthur were crushed.

Helen poured her heart out afterward in a five-page letter to the Academy's new superintendent, Admiral Wilson Brown. Her tone had decidedly changed from her last letter to Admiral Sellars:

My dear Admiral Brown,

I realize that you are a very busy man and there is nothing to compel you to answer civilian criticism.

I do agree with your intimation that mathematics did not come easily to my son, Ex-Midshipman Barton Cross. However, he has a brother who fell to 1.9 percent on one occasion in the same subject at Annapolis. He got through by a fair reexamination or perhaps by virtue of his luck, drawing a particularly good instructor when he needed one. When he left the USS Lexington's engineering department, his Captain remarked, "I hope Annapolis will send us a few more like you!" Someone saw through his fractional mark and gave him a chance to develop speed and facility.

Unless of outstanding brilliance, getting through the Naval Academy is largely a matter of luck. Grant and Pershing [at West Point], and many Admirals at Annapolis, including William Halsey, were near or at the bottom of their classes, and the country is grateful for this element of luck, this avoidance of the fatal fraction!

Your methods appear unpedagogic. You permit enrollment of 740 or more Plebes, knowing that half of them have to be failed, rather than build up 370 good candidates with proper instruction. Some of those you fail go on to distinction in the very subjects you fail them in. One boy I know led his class in Mathematics at Brown University, another at Cornell. Are we to conclude that the great universities of this country are inferior or that your product is superior? Neither is true but the universities do have civilian instructors who can teach, not bewildered young lieutenants.

*In Barton, I believe you had a lad of considerable latent
ability, who stood number 12 in a Citadel class of 400, and whom
[Citadel's] General Summerall spoke of as "fine officer material with
exceptional ancestry and fine family naval tradition behind him." The
reexamination that he took failed 21 of the 28 who took it! Was this fair
or just an ouster to necessarily reduce your numbers? Barton's loyalty
and love of the Service, and good marks in other subjects counted for
naught against 7/100 of one point in one subject? Yet you have boys there
right now skimming in several subjects, and many more who intend to
quit the Service as soon as allowable and a free education obtained—I
know because I've heard them talk on many occasions.*

*For this, crushing humiliation has been brought on his two brothers
in the Service who wanted so to see him with them and who know
his abilities, a feeling of abasement, and a loss to the Service of one
worth keeping. Your Academic Board must be made conscious of the
unfairness of that reexamination.*

*Yours Sincerely,
Helen C. Cross*

Before filing away the letter—alphabetically under the letter U for
"Unpedagogic Methods"—Admiral Brown penned a note to his subordinate, ordinarily charged with responding to these sorts of letter: "We won't
answer this one," he wrote, "but the point of view is interesting."

A DEFEATED BARTON CROSS returned to Lilac Hedges, feeling
all the worse that his own wounded pride and humiliation extended to his
family. Unable to endure forced conversations with his shell-shocked parents, he made plans to go into New York. He said he might just quit school
altogether, damn it, and get a job in the city. At a rare loss for words, Helen
and Arthur raised no objection.

Barton felt awkward in the first civilian clothing he'd worn in some time, and it may have added to his discomfort with incipient manhood. In fact, he was still a struggling postadolescent. A bullet of a young man, Barton was now presumably full height at five feet nine inches. His face radiated a boyish pink hue and his cheekbones were high and prominent. Cropped brown hair went this way and that, as resistant to conventional taming methods as he himself had been growing up. A high, broad forehead gave him a likeness to his brothers, though his eyes were a playful green instead of blue.

He trudged out the front door, down the painted porch steps, and headed toward the train station. His parents were working in the vegetable garden that day, desperate to appear normal and busy. But the angst on their faces revealed that the alkaline balance for growing perfect tomatoes was the furthest thing from their minds.

From Grand Central Terminal, Barton walked the brief distance to Radio City Music Hall. He proceeded to fill out an application for a spot in their chorus, a fantasy he had quietly entertained for some time. The *Radio City Christmas Spectacular* had become an annual family highlight since the hall's opening in 1932—his mother especially loved it. Until now, Barton's young life had been defined by the expectations of others and by their criteria for success. Perhaps this offered a unique opportunity to please both his parents and himself.

Barton had shown considerable musical talent throughout his life, despite his parents' efforts to interest him in more "acceptable" pursuits. Maybe now they would see fit to let him chase his own dreams. That night, he followed up with a letter to Admiral Brown, requesting a reference. The Barton Cross letter file in the Academy superintendent's office would grow thicker still:

Dear Admiral Brown:

I have taken the liberty of referring a prospective employer to you, as a character witness, in order to help me

obtain a position in New York . . . Having had much choral
experience prior to Annapolis and also in the Academy
Chapel Choir, there is perhaps an opportunity for me at the
Radio City Music Hall.

Naturally I showed my prospective employer my Academy
resignation, feeling that he would not be concerned over
the fact that I fell just short of the required grade in
mathematics. As a reason for my resignation, I told him
that I was perhaps unsuited for a naval career. If this
particular is referred to, I trust that you will realize
that this was not my heartfelt sentiment, only an answer to
an interviewer's question. In view of the circumstances, I
feel you will do all in your power to help me get started in
civilian life.

Respectfully Yours,

A. B. Cross Jr.

The letter displayed a combination of determination to pursue a career
that matched his abilities and absence of guile in approaching the Naval
Academy commandant to recommend him for a singing career. It was both
courageous and refreshingly naïve. Before Admiral Brown received any
follow-up inquiries from Radio City Music Hall, however, Barton's parents
regained control of the situation.

A chagrined Arthur made a telephone call to the University of North
Carolina's president, Frank Porter Graham. It took only this gentlemanly
phone conversation to ensure Barton's acceptance and transfer to Chapel
Hill. Helen and Arthur were weary from the struggle and hoped that North
Carolina's southern graces would be a better fit. In any case, they were de-
termined to short-circuit any further talk of a singing career.

Barton did indeed take to the easier manner of Chapel Hill and flourished there. Ironically he declared a math-heavy major in business and commerce and did well. Helen savored that this richly proved her point about the Academy's "unpedagogic methods" versus other fine universities. Still, Barton's departure from Annapolis had stung and left her feeling rejected herself.

Bill wrote to Barton at Chapel Hill regularly with newsy discourses on his newlywed life, including the proud arrival of Adam Sutherland Mott, his firstborn child. He also ventured the occasional navy update—to the degree he thought it would be tolerated, if not appreciated. He ended each letter with the same refrain, which he knew would be unpopular but was increasingly urgent: despite his Annapolis experience, Barton must enter Chapel Hill's Naval ROTC program; war news threatened, and he wanted Barton poised for reentry into the military as an officer should the country go to war.

Benny wrote to Barton too, sharing lengthy news about his own navy man's life on the West Coast. But from Barton's pleasant perch at Chapel Hill—where he happened to be having the time of his life—Bill's domestic bliss and Washington career trajectory and Benny's colliding worlds of marriage and life at sea sounded more like weighty, joyless commitments.

So instead of NROTC, Barton joined a fraternity, Chi Phi, the oldest and most pedigreed order on campus. His pledging ceremony was far more gracious and refined than any experience during his Citadel or Naval Academy tenure. The Chi Phi creed—"So then let modesty and dignity go hand in hand with loyalty"—was much more to his liking. He was a Tar Heel now, and had taken well to Chapel Hill's southern charms. And, as ever, he had also attracted a broad and fun-loving group of friends. His father's respected business presence in the South spared him the dreaded Yankee label in a town where, even seventy-five years after the Civil War, northerners were not welcomed.

GRADUATING CHAPEL HILL IN June 1940, Barton prepared for a career in the mercantile world. By then, however, Britain, France, Poland,

and other European Allies were at war with Nazi Germany and its new ally, Fascist Italy, and his and every other young American male's future was clouded by it. Since derision of the army was a favorite pastime of his family's, that option was out of the question—but he didn't have the appetite for more torturous rejection by seeking a naval officer's commission. The matter was thus deferred again.

Instead, Barton chose to participate in the war effort on his own terms: as an iron and steel procurement officer at the British Purchasing Exchange, located just off Wall Street. His academic background had actually prepared him well for the position, and he quickly mastered the accounts amassing American scrap iron for Britain's fight against the Nazis.

Respected and well liked at BPE, Barton worked hard. Being in the city energized him and restored his sense of *potential*. He and his father took the train into Grand Central Station together each morning, and, after a brief walk down Madison Avenue, they turned toward Rockefeller Center and parted under the statue of Atlas on Fifth Avenue. The rest of Barton's route to Lower Manhattan was by subway, but he frequently exited several stops ahead of Broad Street station, preferring to walk the rest of the way.

Jaunty and distinguished looking, he clipped along the bustling streets of Manhattan threading among pedestrians, streetcars, and fresh fruit and flower stands setting up in the morning cool. His argyle socks were tucked neatly into polished cordovan shoes, and an open overcoat and scarf flapped in the breeze. Barton could usually be seen rounding the corner of Broad at 8:55 a.m. Ever genial, he greeted acquaintances and nodded to the Exchange doorman at 15 Broad before disappearing into the lobby. By 5:45 in the evening, he was headed back up to Midtown, usually to parties or clubs populated by New York's young cosmopolitan set.

Barton was the gin-and-tonic fellow with a pack of Luckies in his breast pocket and always seemed to have a pretty girl at his elbow. He was treated to more than a few overnight stays in the city when it was too late to return home by train. Different girls were invited to Lilac Hedges on weekend retreats as well. His mother scrutinized each and every one—but, both to her disappointment and relief, Barton never became steady with any of them.

Despite his earnest role at the Purchasing Exchange, heightening war news was making Barton ill at ease. News stories of battlefront horrors intensified daily. The miraculous rescue of some 200,000 British troops cornered by the Germans at Dunkirk, France, had a grip on the Cross household for days. Moreover, many of Arthur's English friends were being bombed out of their homes by the Luftwaffe's relentless London blitz.

Then one morning in September 1940, as the family sipped their coffee and waited for breakfast to be served, Arthur returned to the dining room with the damp morning paper. Barton's hair was in disarray, and his eyes betrayed another late night out. He barely noticed his father's reticence after reading the front page.

Arthur handed the paper to Helen, telegraphing his concern with a certain look. She scanned the headline and article, and then heaved a deep sigh. The news was that Roosevelt had signed the military draft bill into law, calling up the first nine hundred thousand men. It had been expected, but the reality of *mandatory* was something different, particularly when combined with the other news of the day—that Japan had joined Germany and Italy to sign the Tripartite Pact, which formed the Axis powers. Breakfast that morning ended with plenty of leavings for the dog. Barton was now a prime candidate for the draft.

Two months later, this family of avid Republicans was further disappointed by Roosevelt's besting of the GOP's Wendell Willkie to win a third presidential term. The Crosses despised Roosevelt's pervasive approach to boosting the economy, the so-called New Deal, which they viewed as aggressively antibusiness and fraught with ever-expanding government subsidies. Anglophile Arthur pointed out to whomever would listen that the real reason for the economic uptick since the Depression was not Roosevelt's

New Deal, but spiking textile and other war-materiel orders from his native Britain.

On the night of November 5, 1940, Helen wrote in her diary:

Election Day! Roosevelt, the glamour voiced lad, made the grade— elected by 24 million against 20 million for Wilkie. The Electoral College of course shows proportional representation—there one sees the fine hand of the bosses in the big cities. Let's hope that those 20 million protesting votes will curb him to some degree. We did not sit up for returns, feeling the results in our bones.

Barton began to feel sidelined as 1940 stretched into 1941. He returned home each night to Rosemary studying for her Waves exam [Women Accepted for Volunteer Emergency Service] and his mother's Bundles for Britain sewing circle. The women were gathered in the drawing room around the Victrola, listening to Edward R. Murrow's nightly broadcasts from London—ablaze from German bombing raids. "This . . . is London," Murrow would begin, as the spellbound women knitted away at scarves bound for Royal Air Force fighters battling the Luftwaffe.

Unable to escape the significance of events unfolding an ocean away, Barton began to yearn for a chance to reenter the navy. For a while, he had convinced himself that the British Purchasing Exchange *was* helping with the war effort, but with the mandatory draft, he knew he would be called up eventually. In the spring of 1941, Barton decided to swallow his pride and see if Bill could help.

Meanwhile, Bill had been formulating an idea of his own, one that matched the navy's needs with Barton's business degree and training. When the call came through from Lilac Hedges, he jumped at the chance to take responsibility for Barton's naval future—and an opportunity for maternal recognition for his mother's oft-overlooked middle son.

And so Barton's prestigious appointment to the Supply Corps, the navy's business managers, was Bill's doing. "I had planned to have you ordered down here as one of my assistants," Bill wrote Barton, "but I hesitate to do anything that would deprive you of a commission in the Supply Corps; it is the best opportunity offered any applicant these days. You have the right background, and the advantage of learning things that will be of great value to you in the business world, should you later leave the Navy."

Supply Corps commissions in 1941 were a hot commodity, but Bill knew how to maneuver along the navy's inside track to ensure that one of those coveted commissions went to Barton. After that, Bill pushed for his brother's acceptance into the Harvard Supply Corps training program, recently incorporated into its business school. At Harvard, Barton would master the rigors of the Supply Corps with FDR's son, young John Roosevelt. Bill followed his brother's progress with barely concealed pride and enthusiasm.

The new ensign's orders arrived quickly after his return from Boston that September. Congress had finally loosened its purse strings for an all-out fortification of an increasingly vulnerable American base in the Pacific: the Philippines.

It was a good opportunity, Bill assured Barton—although their mother was of a distinctly different mind. The evening his orders to the Philippines arrived, Barton joined Helen and Arthur for a glass of sherry on the porch. He tried to comfort his anxious parents and reminded them that this was the course they had long wanted for him. There was a clutch at Helen's heart when Barton raised his glass in mock celebration and toasted, "Here's hoping the Japs don't get me, Mother. I'd hate to give all this up!"

9

★ ★ ★

THE PERILS OF ESCAPE—
AND A LITTLE BASEBALL

THE POSSIBILITY OF ESCAPE crossed every prisoner's mind, but during the summer of 1942, Barton abandoned the fantasy for good. Men who had tried and failed were brought back to camp and beaten, mutilated, and tortured in public view. Nothing focused the mind on the perils of escape more than the particular return of three prisoners—two army colonels and a navy lieutenant—who were each summarily stripped naked, marched across the camp to the entrance, tied up, and flogged to insensibility.

They were then kicked to their feet, led out the front gate with their hands tied behind them, and strung up to hang from cross-pieces of wood several feet above their heads. A two-by-four was placed beside them, and when any Filipinos passed by on the road, they were summoned by the Japanese guards to pick up the timber and smash each of the hanging prisoners in the face. Then the guards would follow up and lay on their whips.

The beatings, whippings, and subsequent screams could be heard everywhere in the camp. Even in the middle of the night, the cracking whip sounded in the darkness. At the end of the third day, the other prisoners watched through the barbed wire as the three men, miraculously still alive, were loaded into a covered truck and driven away. Soon, two shots were heard from the direction of the retreating truck. The prisoners later learned that the third man had been beheaded.

Barton was as traumatized, enraged, and disgusted by this savagery as the rest of the prisoners. But it wasn't just this incident that permanently put the temptation of escape out of his mind. It was the grim story of ten men selected for execution in reprisal for another man's attempted escape from a bridge repair detail outside Cabanatuan. While the stunned men in his outfit looked on, the captured escapee was forced to join the nine other men in his ten-person shooting squad to dig a large hole, line up at its edge, and be shot at close range one by one. One of the unfortunate victims, Staunton Ross Betts, called out to his older brother Edwin, whom he called "Jack," standing among the horrified captive audience. "Take it easy, Jack," Ross said. "I'll be all right. And take care of Mother."

This Japanese deterrent to attempted escape—which came to be called, variously, "the ten-and-one-rule," "the blood-brother system," or, simply, "shooting squads"—had the desired effect, especially since none of the POWs knew who his fellow squad members were. This prevented them from conspiring to escape together. It would be one thing to escape and die trying, but quite another to bring down that kind of horror on others, Barton decided. He resolved then to survive by other means.

THOUGH MEASURABLY WEAKENED, BARTON had so far avoided contracting the serious tropical diseases that raged at Cabanatuan. Oddly, the larger and heavier men tended to fall ill and die more quickly than did those of smaller build like Barton. In fact, he was among the healthier prisoners, allowing him to continue in his quest to boost the morale of a growing group of friends, some teetering on the edge of despair. It wasn't uncommon for those whose mental, physical, and emotional health had become so bruised and degraded to simply decide to die.

Providing succor to these depleted and fragile men in this newly confined world became Barton's calling. Hopelessness was as fatal as any disease at Cabanatuan, and having visited its dark provinces a time or two himself in life, he knew when someone was on the brink. He might notice one friend drooping into apathy, offering little or no conversation, retreating into solitude. Another, frail as balsa wood, might be found lying in the scratchy cogon grass, eyes staring blankly ahead.

So Barton would return to the barrack and shake out his shoe on a dirty board, yielding maybe only a handful of rice, still in husks. With gusto, he and his friends would beat open the husks using the side of their canteens. Barton always drew laughs and groans with his constant refrain, "Cold Rheingold, anybody?" He'd then swill some tepid water, pretending it was a beer, and wipe his mouth with a dramatic swipe of his forearm. "Ah, that was *good!*"

The discovery that adversity has its upsides was one of the powerful lessons Barton had learned at Christ School. It is unknown how many frozen pine stumps and their notoriously long root systems he was forced to dig out with a pickax and shovel in the Smoky Mountain winters, but given that he held his class's record for total accumulated demerits, it was more than a few. Stump duty was the stiffest of punishments and difficult work, but completing those excavations in the quiet winter woods always offered Barton a measure of satisfaction. Cabanatuan's world of deprivation offered a certain sanctuary, too—and opportunities for fulfillment that had mostly eluded him in his former life.

At Annapolis, he had been drawn to the humanities, particularly the study of William Wordsworth. His favorite of Wordsworth's poems was "Lines Written a Few Miles Above Tintern Abbey." Concerning the poet's reflection on his younger self, it addressed the burden of self-doubt and how it sparked him to perform selfless acts:

> *In hours of weariness, sensations sweet,*
> *Felt in the blood, and felt along the heart,*
> *And passing even into my purer mind*
> *With tranquil restoration:—feelings too*
> *Of unremembered pleasure; such, perhaps,*
> *As may have had no trivial influence*
> *On that best portion of a good man's life;*
> *His little, nameless, unremembered acts*
> *Of kindness and of love.*

Not until Cabanatuan did Barton come to personify the principles of this well-loved verse. He organized card games and informal prayer, commanded ready audiences for his jokes and wickedly good stories, and contributed his tenor voice and eclectic musical repertoire to a group of singers who strolled the camp, crooning everything from Christian hymns to Broadway show tunes. As he had at the Citadel and Annapolis, he was also a willing participant in brainstorming nicknames for their various tormentors—in this case, the prison guards: Big Stoop, Little Speedo, Clark Gable, Air Raid, Laughing Boy, Donald Duck, Many Many, Beetle Brain, Fish Eyes, Web Foot, Hammer Head, Hog Jaw, and Slime. A latent thespian too, Barton always provoked precious, restorative laughter with his inimitable renditions of various camp guards' struts.

But he also recognized—astutely—that not all Japanese guards were cut from the same nasty cloth, and he developed something of a rapport with one of them. Lieutenant Oiagi, the camp's quartermaster and a Christian, was a quiet sort who had played on Japan's Davis Cup tennis team in the United States in the 1930s. He treated the American prisoners with fairness and relative restraint, particularly in contrast to his Cabanatuan colleagues. Barton's friendly banter with Oiagi had other benefits. When his friend and barrack mate Ensign Jack Ferguson was suffering from malaria, Oiagi found some quinine.

Jack was grateful beyond measure when Barton proudly produced and administered the quinine. As they sat together, talk of their respective homes and families ensued, as was so often the case at Cabanatuan. Ferguson, who was from Pennsylvania, talked mostly about his mother: how smart she was, how pretty, what a hell of a time he and his brother had given her when they were kids. Such topics formed the core of thousands of hours of conversation among the prisoners: peeling back layers of memory through countless recollections of home and childhood. Each man came to know the others' personal history totem—their towns, families, sweethearts, neighbors, favorite foods, best friends, and homes—inside and out.

Barton learned all about Charles Armour's upbringing in Little Rock—an American subculture as different from that of New Jersey as could be imagined within the borders of a single country. Like Barton, Charles was his father's namesake and the firstborn son of a second marriage. Charles, too, had chafed under outsized parental expectations; he felt in particular that he had never quite measured up in his father's eyes.

Before Mr. Armour died, he had been a soda-pop bottler representing the popular NuGrape brand. To help advertise the business, Charles's father had a car built in the shape of a NuGrape bottle: it was painted purple, and its exposed radiator was designed to resemble a bottle cap. Riding around town in that distinctive automobile afforded Charles a solid adolescent identity and made him feel like he *was* somebody—a schoolboy celebrity, to be sure. But all that vaporized with the 1929 stock market crash. Charles told the ensigns the story one evening as they crouched behind the barracks sharing a contraband cigarette.

Folks weren't spending money on soda pop when they could barely put dinner on the table, Charles said. When things in the Armour household seemed like they couldn't get any worse, he continued, his father had a heart attack while driving. The car slammed into a telephone pole after he slumped over the steering wheel. It wasn't long after his father's death that Charles joined the navy. "You know, get the hell outta the Wonder State. See the world. We see how that worked out."

Barton learned from Charles that being four inches taller might not buy happiness after all. Charles learned from Barton that lots of money and a fancy education were no guarantee of it, either. But of their respective homes, they were unequivocal in their proud recollections. They took turns drawing sketches of their houses in the dirt: Charles, of the unique Craftsman bungalow his family built at 501 Holly Street in Little Rock; and Barton, of his beloved Lilac Hedges.

The Armours had built 501 Holly with special attention to detail throughout. It had an L-shaped porch, the longer segment facing west toward beautiful sunsets, and the shorter part wrapping around to the south side. Charles explained that his parents designed the house so it could catch a breeze from every direction, a key attribute in a town where the thermometer could top 100 degrees on an August afternoon. Its wide eaves protected it, both from torrential summer downpours and the relentless sun that beat down from the south and west. French doors throughout the first floor not only gave the interior added grace, but also allowed for air circulation from one side of the house to the other.

In turn, Barton proudly described Lilac Hedges's white clapboard facade and classic Victorian gables, its green-striped awnings and painted porches, his mother's lovingly tended flower and vegetable gardens, the sprawl of English boxwoods, and, of course, the bursting surround of lilacs. He thought about the place all the time, he told Charles, and sometimes in his sleep he could hear the creak of the porch steps and whine of the old screen door opening and closing.

In their current state of wretchedness, some of the men found it easier to black out such emotional keepsakes than to conjure them up. For Barton, this might have included the sumptuous al fresco meals on the south lawn (and William's lemon cake); the rustle of his mother's favorite chiffon skirts in the breeze; the rich, earthy, cherry aroma of his father's pipe tobacco, and the lilacs, always the lilacs, glistening in the spring sun like a cache of amethysts. Their fragrance was so distinct and memorable, he might have broken down if he'd thought of it for too long.

Still, the occasional urge to share how their lives had once been, dignified and whole, was irresistible. The prisoners surely knew more about one another's lives than friends or even spouses or girlfriends might have learned back home. This was as true of Charles and Barton as it was of any other two men who'd been together since the start of this hellish odyssey.

WHEN IT CAME TO interacting with his captors, Barton's relatively small stature conferred a surprising natural advantage: he didn't tower over the diminutive Japanese guards as many other prisoners did—which often infuriated them and alone brought reprisals. Barton further disarmed them with another tactic he'd learned in his adolescence: projecting a distinctly nonthreatening manner. His ambassadorial role in persuading the prison guards to allow a game of baseball was one of its rewards. Baseball was not only the great American pastime, but a game much loved by the Japanese as well.

The prisoners carved bats out of native wood, and a softball was produced by the Japanese. A diamond was laid out on the camp's former inspection grounds, and two teams of players were drafted: one of army prisoners and the other navy. In the first game, the navy squad defeated the army team 3–1. The would-be blue-and-gold cheering section was as happy as the players.

Another game was scheduled, this time against a local team of Filipinos. Though the Americans lost 6–3, Barton hit his first-ever home run. A small Filipino band played "Onward Christian Soldiers" as he rounded third base and made it safely, incredibly, home, just seconds before the catcher tagged him. When Barton Cross crossed home plate he was as electrified as he was exhausted, hungry, and dirty. He laughed out loud and nearly burst into tears. The absurdity that this was actually one of the happiest moments of his life struck him full force.

The games lifted the spirits of all the players—even one they played against the Japanese guards themselves, which they elected wisely to lose. But playing ball burned precious additional calories not made up for at dinner afterward: a serving of rice and the occasional addition of a watery soup called *lugao*, with a few floating bits of yamlike *camote*. The games on top of their work details left the prisoner-players more famished than ever, and they realized with some sadness that the added energy playing ball required had to be factored into the cruel calorie math that determined survival. With a diet of fewer than 1,000 calories per day, they were all losing weight. Eventually, baseball at Cabanatuan was suspended for lack of participants.

10

★ ★ ★

A BROTHER'S BURDEN:
THE SEARCH

THE DEMANDS OF BILL'S White House job grew exponentially during the first half of 1942, as did those at home, with Romie and toddler Adam increasingly wanting of his time, attention, and company. Bill did the best he could to balance the dueling claims for his primacy, not to mention those imposed by his mother, whose almost daily letters and telephone calls about Barton regularly refreshed his sense of urgency and feelings of guilt.

But replies to Bill's persistent calls and letters about his missing brother arrived at their own unhurried pace. One came from an army nurse in Australia who had been evacuated from Sternberg Hospital just before Manila fell. Bill had recognized the old family friend's name on the evacuee list. His letter expressed relief that she was safe, and then asked about Barton. Had she seen him after the Japanese attack on Cavite? Did she know his whereabouts?

She replied that in fact she *had* seen Barton: he was a patient at

Sternberg! He had been wounded in the foot and leg, she confirmed, but was expected to recover. Bill was euphoric at this—then dismayed as she proceeded to explain that only *army* wounded and their nurses were evacuated to Australia before Manila fell. She didn't know what had happened to either the navy patients or the naval medical staff.

By bits and pieces, Bill gradually assembled a fairly reliable composite of what had befallen Barton and where he was most likely being held. It was not intelligence he wanted to share over the phone or in a letter, so in early spring, he secured his first day of leave since war had been declared and booked a train for New Jersey. Helen's and Arthur's calls had grown more frequent and importunate, and he hoped this gesture would calm them. But his good intentions were preempted by an article in the *Red Bank Register*, their hometown paper.

ENSIGN A. B. CROSS THOUGHT PRISONER
WOUNDED AT CAVITE WHICH JAPS HAVE NOW

Ensign A. Barton Cross Jr., son of Mr. and Mrs. A. Barton Cross, is believed to have been captured from a hospital near Cavite Naval Base after the fall of Manila. While there is strict censorship regarding such notices as far as the general public is concerned, it was revealed that during the attack and just before Cavite was abandoned, Ensign Cross was engaged on the dock in duties surrounding the submarine tender of which he was executive supply officer. As the fires raged on the wharves from enemy air action the 22 year [sic] old officer, a former classmate at Harvard of John Roosevelt, was supervising the embarkation of men and supplies when he was struck by a shell splinter.

Attempts are being made to trace Ensign Cross
through the International Red Cross in Geneva Swit-
zerland, but to date all efforts have been unavail-
ing . . . General MacArthur and his Forces still hold
Bataan and Corregidor, the island forts that guard
the entrance to the harbor.

A telephone message from Arthur was on Bill's desk when he arrived at
the White House that morning. After two weeks, with several phone calls and
promises of follow-up in between, a letter from Bill arrived at Lilac Hedges:

The White House
Washington

April 2, 1942

Dear Arthur,

I am sorry about the blow from the _Register_ regarding
Barton. They must have pieced together reports (never
assuredly accurate, by the way) from the Red Cross. I was,
in fact, planning a trip to see you about this when you
[first] called. I regret how matters unfolded.

Yesterday a casualty list came through and on it were
the names of five officers left behind in Manila after
the evacuation to Bataan and Corregidor. Among them were
three in the Medical Corps and one in the Supply Corps.
All of them were known to Admiral McIntyre, the Surgeon
General, who is often here at the White House seeing after
the President. Barton was not listed. Also, Barton's name
was not on the long list of dead that came in today from the

International Red Cross--further confirmation that he is
indeed alive.

I had the occasion to show these lists to the president
and Admiral King and we discussed the possibility of
sending our own doctors over there to tend to the wounded
from Cavite, as well as a great many other related subjects.
I hope to speak with you about this before the end of the
week.

Everyone seems confident that it will only be a matter
of weeks now before we get confirmed information (unlike
that in The Register) that he is alive and in the hands of
the Japanese, if not more.

                              Love,

                              Bill

But Bill's words brought scant comfort:

                              Lilac Hedges
                              Oceanport, New Jersey

                              April 5, 1942

Dear Bill,

Thank you for your apparent efforts, but we continue
to feel terribly depressed by the press accounts we
read daily. Not just about Barton, but the Philippines
generally. Clearly it is becoming another Dunkirk. At
worst the situation may be the complete isolation of the

Philippines and the Japs bomb the hell out of them from every direction.

Why are green men sent to the firing line? What of the wounded? Is this just another instance of Naval stupidity? We pray hourly for Barton and Benny's safety.

Love, Mother

Enclosed in the envelope was an additional note from Arthur:

Dear Bill,

What I cannot understand is that there is no organization big enough to advise the world whether Japanese prisoners are being treated as human beings.

Another puzzlement is that, up to the present, the Navy Prisoner of War Bureau has never issued a statement. On the other hand, the Army bureau is listing personnel weekly. I cannot help but think they are functioning more efficiently.

It does point out to the layman very forcibly that the Army's Colonel Bresee is really on the job. I know of an instance where the Colonel wrote and told a mother how to address letters to her son, in care of the Japanese Red Cross, New York City.

We become incensed with the Navy when we hear these things.

Trusting that this finds both you and your family well,

With Kindest Regards,
Arthur

The White House
Washington

April 9, 1942

My Dear Arthur,

You do the Navy an injustice when you assume the Army
Prisoner of War outfit is functioning more efficiently than
the Navy one. I have been in regular touch with Colonel
Bresee since I very first heard of the attack on Manila, and
he has had a chit on file in his office for months, reminding
him to call me with any news of Barton's whereabouts.

You see, the reports on all branches come through the
International Red Cross in Geneva and funnel through
Colonel Bresee. The Prisoner of War Board is a joint board,
having both Army and Navy officers as members. Captain
Jackson, whom I know quite well, is a Navy member and he
also has a chit to call me the minute any news of Barton
comes in.

What you say about the Army listing personnel weekly is
true, but it just so happens that the Japanese have chosen
to tick off their Army prisoners to Geneva before they get
around to the Navy ones. There is nothing the Navy can do
about this because we don't control the Japanese--yet. Once
more, please be assured that I am leaving no stone unturned
to get the latest intelligence on Barton from any and all
sources.

With Best Regards,
Bill

P.S. Colonel Bresee was very happy to hear that you think so highly of him.

Letters and toll calls continued apace between the White House and Lilac Hedges, but Bill's assurances failed to assuage Helen. She was soon to make matters even more difficult for her middle son. Angry and out of patience, she launched her own official inquiry into Barton's status. Pleas from Helen Cross's prolific pen began pouring into war-wracked Washington: to Red Cross officials, to Bill's former boss at Naval Intelligence (already struggling to locate thousands of missing and captured), and to United States senators, including New Jersey Republican senator William Barbour:

Lilac Hedges
Oceanport, New Jersey

My Dear Senator Barbour,

It never occurred to me that I should ever ask your good offices in a personal way—however the enclosed clipping from the Red Bank Register will explain the grief which has descended on this family.

For three months we were not notified that our son Barton Cross was not with his ship—weekly letters have gone out as though to a ghost. Think also of our awful three months anxiety over him on a ship—a submarine tender loaded with explosives and unprotected— following its progress supposedly from Cavite to Darwin, to the Dutch East Indies—watching for sinkings, bombings. Now we read only "missing" opposite his name after being wounded at Cavite Dec. 10th— where or how he is now, I do not know.

Are our naval officers allowed to disappear like this?

Can you please find out for me if he is a prisoner of the Japanese as well as the following:

1. *How does he live, since no paychecks have been sent out to him since his arrival in the Philippines?*
2. *Will they clothe and feed him properly?*
3. *Could or will he be exchanged as a prisoner of war, so he could go to Corregidor with MacArthur or to the safety of Australia?*

Believe me, I am proud of my son, doing his duty on those blazing docks until struck down and removed to Sternberg Hospital. At 23 years of age, he met Hell unflinchingly. I have another son, an officer on that gallant airplane carrier which was at the Marshall Islands. So I know how to bear anxiety and grief.

I just want to know so that I may sleep again, if Barton is alive, if the Japs will feed him, if America cares about those prisoners at Cavite and Manila or is taking steps to find out about them.

Hopefully, and with appreciation of any reply you may send.

Sincerely,

Helen C. Cross

When his mother's letter to Senator Barbour and others crossed his desk (first routed from Capitol Hill to the Navy Department, then to Bill for reply), Bill was more irritated than embarrassed—but plenty of both. He immediately placed a call to Lilac Hedges, demanding his mother explain her apparent end run around him. Did she really think this would generate better information than he had given her? Did she really think this was appropriate, making inquiry to a United States senator about one missing man with a war spanning the globe going on?

After listening patiently to his rant, Helen explained sweetly ("My dear boy," she began) that she and Senator Barbour were old friends. Why would a little letter to an old friend upset him so?

Bill exhorted his mother to halt her letter-writing campaign, explaining what he would have thought obvious: that such unwanted attention could hurt him professionally, and would certainly not improve her store of information regarding Barton. Bill would have to reply to Senator Barbour, he said through clenched teeth, and with a workday that already spanned sixteen hours, such extracurricular tasks were not appreciated.

> The White House
>
> Washington

My Dear Senator Barbour:

 The Navy's Bureau of Navigation has forwarded me your letter of inquiry for reply. Ensign A. B. Cross is my half-brother, Mrs. Cross being our mother. You may be sure therefore that my interest in his case is more than an official one. I have gone to great lengths to gather any and all information on his case. The unfortunate facts are that Barton was wounded in the bombing attack on Cavite and we've had no further confirmation of his whereabouts. Our fear is that he is now a prisoner of war.

 Mother seems to feel there was some dereliction on the part of the Navy in not having notified her that Barton was missing from his ship; however I believe you will understand that it was, and is, impossible for the Navy to keep in constant radio touch with the Asiatic Fleet, especially regarding individual cases. When on or about the 15th of February I finally received the roster of officers from the boy's ship and found that he was missing, the Navy Department immediately took steps to try and find out what happened to him.

 The Commandant of the 16th Naval District [the

Philippines] conducted an investigation which confirmed that Barton had been wounded at Cavite and was treated in a hospital in Manila. The reasons he probably did not forward this information before he was quizzed by the Navy Department were,

1) That he may have assumed Barton went out on some other ship after the _Otus_ departed, or,
2) He had a war to fight and had not the time yet to take up the case.

Our mother has asked you a great many questions as to how Barton is living, how the Japanese are treating him, possibilities of exchange etc . . . None of these questions have answers at present.

The Prisoner of War Division, working in conjunction with the International Red Cross, is doing everything it can to find out about conditions among our prisoners of war. The Japanese have forwarded them very little information, but all of which I have forwarded to our mother. You may rest assured that I shall make such information as I may be able to gather available to her.

As you know Mrs. Cross has another son in the Navy besides Barton and myself, and I have also written him about this matter since he is on duty in the Pacific and may be able to turn up additional information. I have also written to the Commanding Officer of Barton's ship.

Respectfully Yours,

William C. Mott, Lieut. Cdr.

Weeks passed before Joel Newsom, captain of the USS *Otus*, replied to Bill's inquiry. Finally, in mid-May, Captain Newsom sent his findings after consulting the ship's log of December 10, 1941, to supplement his recall of events that difficult day:

```
                              Submarines
                              United States Asiatic Fleet
                              USS Otus (AS20)


My dear Lieutenant Mott:


    I have purposely delayed replying to your letter of
March 17 until the latest information from Manila was
received. Now that Corregidor has fallen, further delay is
useless. As you say, our departure from Manila on December
10 was somewhat hurried.
```

Newsom proceeded to explain that Admiral Hart had ordered *Otus*—one of the Asiatic Fleet's few critical submarine tenders—to sortie immediately after damaging bombs glanced her starboard side during the Japanese air attack. In the confusion and haste, Newsom couldn't account for why Barton had turned up missing.

```
    Persons who left Manila after we did but before it fell,
stated definitely that Barton was in a Manila hospital with
shrapnel wounds. I cannot confirm whether he reported to
the Submarine Tender Canopus, nor has anyone I can locate
seen him since he was in the hospital. It is known, however,
that the hospital was not bombed. There is a possibility
that upon recovering and finding all naval vessels had
```

evacuated Manila, he escaped to join the guerrillas
in the mountain country, as some did. You are the best
judge of that possibility. I sympathize with you in your
uncertainty . . .

I regret I cannot give you more encouraging news of
your brother. He was a grand shipmate and an excellent
officer. There is no doubt in my mind he is a prisoner
of war. From meager reports received, the Japanese are
treating their officer prisoners of war better than we
might expect from that nation, but reliable information is
scarce, at best.

Next came the news that *Canopus* had been sunk during the siege of
Bataan. After weeks of hoping that Barton had made his way to it, now the
family spent the next several weeks praying that he hadn't, even as they
braced for the ship's manifest and casualty report. When the lists finally arrived in June, Barton was not on either one.

Throughout the spring and summer of 1942, Bill reviewed every scrap
of intelligence from the Philippines—which had narrowed to a trickle since
the termination of all radio traffic at the fall of Corregidor. Even so, while
Barton was still listed as missing, Bill felt sure that Captain Newsom's intelligence was spot on: that Barton was wounded at Cavite, treated at Sternberg, and taken prisoner after Manila fell.

But where was he now? There was a measure of hope in one of Captain
Newsom's references, that perhaps Barton had "escaped to join the [Fili-
pino] guerrillas in the mountain country, as some [Americans] did."

This burgeoning guerrilla resistance movement had been confirmed by
other sources, but Bill was frustrated by the few and erratic details available
on these widely dispersed bands of unsurrendered American and Filipino
military. All that was known so far was that guerrilla groups were organizing
in isolated centers throughout the islands. They were made up of American

officers who had fled to remote hill and jungle communities and banded with armed, resistance-minded Filipinos who knew the terrain. This much was known because some had set up clandestine shortwave radios and were attempting to relay to the world what was happening in the Philippines. These crude broadcasts were first thought to be Japanese feints but had since been authenticated; they were being picked up in Australia as well as at receiving stations as far away as San Francisco. Their repeated requests were for arms, food, and other supplies that would help them resist the Japanese.

The Red Cross, along with the navy and army intelligence operations, built on their meager reserves of information, but limited interaction with the Japanese through Swiss delegations had yielded little more than enemy demands regarding their own prisoners in the Pacific. There were other bits of information coming in that were so disturbing Bill would not share them with Arthur, much less his mother. They were learned via intercepted Japanese communications and other classified documents dispatched to the Map Room. The first, a quote by a Kempeitai official regarding Allied prisoners, had appeared in the *Japan Times*: "They cannot be treated as ordinary prisoners of war. Their defeat is their punishment. To show them mercy is to prolong the war . . . An eye for an eye, a tooth for a tooth. Hesitation is uncalled for and the wrongdoers must be wiped out."

Another dispatch was so disturbing that Bill sought multiple translations to confirm that it had not been an error. In a memo to Captain McCrea, Bill elaborated:

> The following excerpt was taken from a Japanese
> diary captured on New Guinea: "Because of food shortages,
> some companies have been eating human flesh (Australian
> soldiers). The taste is said to be good." (Note: Because of the
> incredible implications of this statement, it was concurred
> in by three individual translations.)

Another entry several days later contained the following crude haiku:

```
When we ran short of rations,
We devoured our own kind to
Stave off Starvation.
```

After writing the memo, Bill put on his cap and walked out of the Map Room in the direction of the Rose Garden. On that early-summer afternoon, a group of military nurses evacuated from the Philippines had been invited to the Executive Mansion. The nurses, bedecked in their crisp whites, were now stationed at Walter Reed Hospital in Washington. When Mrs. Roosevelt heard of their arrival in the nation's capital, she invited them to the White House to officially recognize their good works. Bill was more than happy to escort the nurses to see the First Lady, with whom he had a warm relationship.

After an initial exchange of pleasantries, Bill ventured an inquiry about Barton to the gathered nurses. "Oh yes!" exclaimed one, Mary Lohr. "He's your brother? Oh my, yes, I knew him!"

She explained that she was working at Sternberg Hospital in December when the navy wounded were brought over from Cavite. Barton was wounded in the lower leg and foot, she said; she nursed him from the time he arrived until she was ordered to Corregidor on Christmas Day. He'd told her exactly what happened to him.

Bill was speechless as his new angel of mercy continued her tale.

"He said he heard shrapnel clicking on the road behind him. He'd been running, carrying something, when he got hit. Then he said, 'The good news is, now I'm here with you!' He was always cracking jokes, trying to buck us up," she added.

Bill's questions poured out.

"Yes, he was still there on Christmas, when our group of nurses left for Corregidor. In fact, on Christmas Eve he asked me to send a telegram to his parents, in New Jersey, I think, but from Manila's Army and Navy Club, not the hospital. He didn't want them to know he was in the hospital."

That was the last time she saw him, she said.

Mary couldn't say why only the army wounded were ordered out on the *Mactan*; by then, she was on Corregidor. "There was just no plan for the navy boys, I guess, in all the confusion."

At they talked, the large Red Cross banner was unfurled for the occasion, not far from the circular drive where Filipino stewards polished the running boards and cleaned the windows of President Roosevelt's Packard. Before the ceremonial greeting started, Bill said, "I am so grateful to you for this information, to know that that you saw him alive." And then: "Our mother will be overjoyed to hear these things. This is a feast of news compared to what we've had so far."

11

★ ★ ★

MIDWAY

BOLSTERED BY THE BRILLIANT success of USN Task Force 16 and Colonel Doolittle's Tokyo raid, military intelligence worked furiously to break JN-25, the Japanese naval code. There was no doubt in anyone's mind that the surprise invasion had enraged the enemy and shaken their confidence. A strong Japanese answer to the humiliating home-island strike was expected somewhere, and soon. No foreign power had successfully attacked Japan in more than four hundred years, and its military had assured the civilian government that Japanese skies and surrounding waters were protected and safe. The Japanese, it was soon learned, were formulating a grand reprisal.

Navy cryptanalysts at Pearl Harbor and in Washington scrutinized hundreds of intercepts a day and worked around the clock. The only other Pacific intercept stations—in Guam and the Philippines—had been lost, placing particular pressure on the already shorthanded Station Hypo, Oahu's Naval Intelligence operation.

JN-25 was formidable. It consisted of approximately forty-five thousand five-digit numbers, each representing a word or phrase. For transmission, the five-digit numbers were superenciphered using an additive table. Cracking the code first required intense mathematical analysis to strip off the additive, and then analysis of patterns and sequences to determine the meaning of the five-digit numbers. Under Commander Joe Rochefort, Station Hypo's brilliant, if eccentric, head, the staff made slow but steady progress—thanks to JN-25's rote use of the additive tables.

In May, Hypo cryptanalysts picked through thousands of radio intercepts between enemy ships with intensifying interest. There had been a spike in Japanese naval communications in the Pacific, and each bit of decrypted intelligence from that heightened traffic flow offered tiny clues to the Japanese Navy's whereabouts and intentions. In the White House Map Room, Bill Mott logged the code-cracking progress reports and then presented the eyes-only summaries to the White House inner sanctum and FDR himself.

Bill's own training in codes and ciphers enabled him to follow Station Hypo's progress with knowledge and precision. By the second half of May, Rochefort felt sure that a major enemy strike was in late-stage planning, though the coded traffic had so far revealed little more. Hypo's staff was still deciphering only fractional bits of JN-25 at a time and understood 10 percent to 15 percent of the overall code, at best. Still, a persistent clue from recent intercepts was emerging: the term or location "AF" was mentioned repeatedly.

Meanwhile, *Enterprise* and *Hornet* had been abruptly called back to Pearl Harbor from reconnaissance patrols in the Central Pacific. The cryptic cable from Admiral Halsey to CNO Admiral Ernest King was of far greater weight than the sum of its words:

```
Have Ordered Enterprise and Hornet to Expedite Return.


                          Halsey
```

Bill never feared more for Benny's life. American naval strength against Japan was at an all-time low, and the enemy knew it. Not only was the battleship fleet crippled, the carrier *Lexington* had been sunk in early May at the Battle of the Coral Sea, where an eight-hundred-pound bomb had also ripped apart USS *Yorktown*'s insides. It was unclear whether *Yorktown* could be repaired, and her sister carrier, USS *Saratoga*, was still in dry dock from the broadside torpedo it took at the Gilbert and Marshall Islands.

Official Washington pondered this paltry flattop arithmetic as the clocks ticked down toward a certain enemy assault on beleaguered US naval forces somewhere in the Pacific. Five carriers minus *Lexington* and *Yorktown* equaled three. Three minus *Saratoga* equaled two, leaving only *Enterprise* and her new sister, *Hornet*, which had never engaged in battle. Two carriers to hold the Pacific against an all-out assault by the Imperial Navy?

As the new storm clouds gathered, Station Hypo's wildcatter analysts struck a cryptographic gusher. Acting on a hunch that "AF" was the JN-25 designation for Midway Island, Hypo directed the commanding officer at Midway to send a message in the clear indicating a malfunction at Midway's water distillation plant and that fresh water was needed urgently. Shortly after, Hypo intercepted a Japanese intelligence report indicating that "AF" had a water problem. This breakthrough not only confirmed the identification of "AF" as Midway, but also verified that Hypo had broken JN-25, the General Purpose Code used by the Japanese Navy.

This electrifying revelation also meant that the opportunity for a surprise attack had just reverted from the Japanese to the Americans; they now had a shot at ambushing the enemy's incipient ambush. But even with this powerful advantage of surprise, the engagement still carried long odds for the handicapped US Navy. Intercepts revealed that as many as seventy enemy ships and sixteen submarines were priming to launch against Midway, including at least four, possibly five, aircraft carriers brimming with superior planes and experienced pilots. And the fateful rendezvous was fast approaching, according to Station Hypo; the Japanese assault on "AF" was slated for the third or fourth of June.

Heeding Halsey's curt order, *Enterprise* and *Hornet* churned back to Pearl in late May, and the heavily damaged *Yorktown* hobbled to drydock for repairs. The plan was to refuel and reprovision the first two and to repair *Yorktown*—in four days, not the three months considered minimally necessary. The warships would then sail west and lie in wait northeast of Midway for the approaching Japanese armada.

JAPAN'S DECISION TO ATTACK Midway was based on a grand misperception that would ultimately change the course of the Pacific War. The enemy picket boats that Benny had sighted on April 17—and that *Nashville* torpedoed just before Colonel Doolittle and his men took to the skies—never did get the word to their Japanese superiors that the planes over Tokyo had launched from an aircraft carrier. When queried by the press after the attack, President Roosevelt said with a smile that the B-25s had flown from "Shangri-La"—the mythical city in James Hilton's popular novel *Lost Horizon*. But the Japanese believed they had launched from Midway, the closest American land base to Japan's home islands. As a result, Japanese high command decided to revise its war strategy and attack and occupy Midway to prevent future raids on its home soil.

Admiral Yamamoto had advocated securing Midway, understanding the power of his adversary. He had attended Harvard University and traveled extensively in the United States as a young officer. "I fear we have awakened a sleeping giant," he was rumored to have said after coordinating the successful Pearl Harbor attack. He stood alone among victory disease-ridden commanders in his belief that Japan could succeed against America only if it knocked out its battleship *and* carrier strength early in the war, before the country's mighty shipbuilding industry could mobilize to replace them. This would give resource-starved Japan enough time to seize the oilfields of the Dutch East Indies and Malaya and strengthen its own arsenal before any Allied counterattack.

Only after the humiliating success of Doolittle's surprise Tokyo raid did Yamamoto's superiors yield to his view—and his imperative that the Japanese attack and occupy Midway Atoll, strategically situated 1,300 miles northwest of Honolulu and 2,500 miles east of Japan. Wresting Midway from the Americans, he persuaded, would limit their ability to defend Hawaii, thwart their resistance to Nippon conquests in the entire region, and protect Japan proper. Seizing the objective in an overwhelming surprise attack would further allow the Japanese Navy to annihilate the remainder of the US Pacific Fleet. Under Yamamoto's ambitious Midway annexation plan, the Pacific Ocean would soon become one large Japanese fishpond.

ON THE COOL SPRING evening of May 26, 1942, Bill Mott stood outside the Oval Office with an urgent intelligence update for Admiral Ernest King, chief of naval operations (CNO). King was behind closed doors with President Roosevelt, a relative rarity. Despite King's accurate reputation as generally irascible, Bill respected him for his unalterable—if minority— view that America's interests were best served by allocating more men, money, and materiel to the battle in the Pacific. In a world war in which British and other European interests competed with this priority, the navy's senior flag officer was consistently obdurate on this point.

To his core, King was suspicious of what he saw as British attempts to divert resources from his ability to fight Japan—not just to save their homeland but also to preserve their colonial holdings in the Pacific. The CNO wasn't isolated in this opinion: the Allies' joint South East Asia Command (SEAC) was mordantly nicknamed "Save England's Asian Colonies" by his sympathizers. King was also well known for his rants against MacArthur, using unprintable adjectives to describe his disgust at the general's failures in the Philippines as well as his "absurd" demands on the US Navy. Bill didn't hate that about the CNO, either.

While he waited to speak with Admiral King, Bill chatted with Grace Tully, the president's secretary, all the while nervously fingering the envelope, stamped "Top Secret," in his hand. Grace finally told him she would ring the Map Room as soon as King emerged from the Oval Office; their meeting seemed to be taking longer than expected. Still clutching the envelope, Bill retreated down the cavernous West Wing hallway, now quiet at the relatively late hour of seven o'clock.

The Map Room was tense, hushed, and smoky. Barely audible above the teletype was the murmur of gathering brass conferring over the same eyes-only document that Bill Mott had presented to them a half hour earlier. The communication was from Admiral Chester Nimitz, commander in chief of the Pacific Fleet (CINCPAC). It revealed the shattering news that Admiral Halsey was too sick to engage in the "next operation" and had to be practically forced off the *Enterprise* to be hospitalized at Pearl Harbor, fuming and cursing every step of the way.

To his crew and top Washington brass, the seemingly irreplaceable Halsey was now unable to lead the charge in this next—and most critical— sea battle of the war. The diagnosis was a severe case of dermatitis compounded by exhaustion, for which there was no quick or easy cure. Worse yet, Halsey had apparently decided, with minimal consultation, that a little-known rear admiral by the name of Raymond Spruance was to take his place.

Spruance! The news took Bill by surprise. As if Benny and the crew weren't in enough danger, now subtract the revered, fearless, battle-hardened Halsey and install a cruiser commander—who wasn't even an aviator and who had never commanded an aircraft carrier? Respected? Yes, but untested, and Spruance had never even seen sea-air battle!

War Secretary Stimson said nothing as he reviewed the onionskin paper containing the news. In the uncomfortable silence that followed, Bill walked along the Pacific wall map and inspected the updates. Not one of the men voiced concern about Spruance, as though to do so would have placed a hex. But the discomfiting news hung in the air as palpably as the layer of smoke from Stimson's cigarette.

The facts were these: Admiral Halsey had worked with Raymond Spruance—currently in command of a cruiser division—for more than a decade and had tremendous faith in him. Halsey regarded Spruance as a brilliant tactician with a reputation for making quick, masterful, and precise decisions under pressure. Admiral Nimitz also liked and respected Spruance, but, more importantly, he had immeasurable faith in Halsey's judgment in such matters.

When Admiral King was finally apprised of Spruance's selection to replace Halsey for the Midway operation, he too concurred. He was certainly not about to challenge either Nimitz or Halsey on the eve of battle, from a distance of six thousand miles. Thus the closed society of top brass had spoken by barely speaking. The selection of Rear Admiral Raymond Spruance, cruiser commander, for tactical command of the upcoming Armageddon of the Pacific was not reversible.

ABOARD THE USS *ENTERPRISE*, when the ship and air crews learned of Halsey's illness and the substitution of Spruance, the reaction was seismic. "Spruance! He was against sending Doolittle to Tokyo!" Benny hollered across the wardroom as the men ate their dinner. "I know that for a *fact*."

"He thinks aviators are for the birds, that's what I heard," came a reply. "The pilots are mad as hell!"

These and countless other such conversations reverberated throughout *Enterprise* just hours before the men were to put to sea for certain battle. The crew were stunned and gloomy when they heard about Halsey. Some cursed and fretted, others prayed. With little else to go on in the last six months, they'd placed every ounce of hope, faith, and pride in their feisty and indefatigable admiral. In their heart of hearts, the *Enterprise* crew was in the fight as much for Halsey as they was for their country.

At daybreak on May 28, 1942, *Enterprise, Hornet,* and a rudely patched-up *Yorktown* slipped from their Pearl Harbor berths, followed by an abbreviated band of weary-looking cruisers and oilers. There was a keen sense among all of them that David was trudging to meet Goliath, though the precise details of their mission had not yet been announced.

Early rumors aboard *Enterprise* were that they were on their way to repel an all-out Japanese assault—complete with planned troop landings—on the Hawaiian Islands; it was dramatic, if wildly inaccurate. By early morning May 29, however, the convoy was three hundred miles north of the Hawaiian island of Kauai, a distance at growing odds with rumors of a land attack in the other direction. At 0505 that same morning, just after the ships' sirens wailed general quarters and the men took to their battle stations, a message from Admiral Nimitz was read aloud over the ships' loudspeakers:

"In the cruise just starting, you will have the opportunity to deal the enemy heavy blows. You have done this before, and I have great confidence in your courage, skill, and ability to strike even harder blows. Good hunting and good luck."

Then came Captain Murray's voice:

"We have reason to believe the Japanese may attempt to occupy Midway Island. We are, therefore, moving into such position to counter such an attempt should it develop."

Lastly, the voice of the little-known Admiral Spruance came through:

"An attack on Midway Island is expected. Enemy forces include all combatant types, four or five carriers, plus transport and train vessels. If we remain unknown to the enemy, we should be able to flank attack from a position northeast of Midway. Should our carriers become separated by enemy aircraft, they will attempt to maintain visual contact. The successful conclusion of operations now commencing will be of great value to our country."

Benny leaned back in his seat in the wardroom and let out a long, low whistle. "Jesus, Mary, and Joseph! Four or five carriers and how many escorts? Against what? About two and a half of us?" He turned to face Captain Randall. "I think I'd better go write my mother," Benny said with disdain.

But since *Enterprise* had embarked from Pearl, Admiral Raymond Spruance, a wiry, energetic man whose low-key manner belied a hefty intellect and tremendous self-confidence, had paced several miles on *Enterprise's* flight deck. Senior officers took turns walking alongside him, briefing Spruance and answering questions. The tenor of these conversations was always the same. They were laser-focused, intense, to the point. Almost like a relay race, when one ambulatory meeting concluded, another officer took his place by the admiral's side, Spruance's gait never slowing.

The admiral would question, listen, question, listen, and question some more. He had inherited Halsey's capable, battle-hardened staff, and in these walking meetings, Spruance processed every detail and committed to memory every critical aspect of the upcoming mission. A strategy was developing in his head.

By the last day of May, *Enterprise* and *Hornet* had assumed striking position northeast of Midway—on the flank of the enemy's anticipated thrust. Submarine reports confirmed that the Japanese attack force was approaching from the northwest, as expected. A low cloud cover and poor visibility so far favored the Japanese, because that made it all the harder for the Midway defenders to spot and repel their approaching ships and planes.

For the first three days of June, Benny slept fitfully. His sole comfort those lonely and anxious nights was that he was moving closer to Barton. He would remind his mother of this because he knew it would comfort her—assuming he survived the next two days.

During that same seventy-two hours, the American force maneuvered continuously to avoid detection, then reversed course to arrive at "Point Luck"—code name for the rendezvous point northeast of Midway—on June 4. At 0330 that morning, *Enterprise* reveille sounded, followed by the loud, clangorous general quarters summoning crew to battle stations.

Anticipation coursed through the ship like a high-voltage electrical current. From stem to stern, from flight deck to bridge, in all departments and at all levels, the USS *Enterprise* prepared for action.

Benny made a final gunnery check at each antiaircraft mount. Guns of every caliber and on every level of the ship, port and starboard, were as ready as they would ever be. Planes were also armed and primed for launch. Together with seventeen-year-old Texas sharpshooter Wayne Barnhill (who'd lied about his age to enlist and serve with his older brother), Benny stood in Sky Control, poised for certain action. Wayne was in charge of the sound-operated telephone used to communicate Benny's rapid-fire orders to the gunners throughout the carrier during battle.

Wayne's brother, photographer James Barnhill, nicknamed Barney, set up his action camera on the 0-2 level, halfway down the ship, to capture battle scenes for newsreels to be dispatched to Washington. Though Wayne chose not to speak his mind, he wished his brother would move a little farther back from the rail toward the camouflage draped against the ship's side. When Wayne winced for Barney's safety, Benny understood in a way he could barely express. He slapped Wayne on the back, momentarily holding his shoulder. In a rare act of informality between an enlisted man and officer, he looked him in the eye and said, "Look at it this way, son: he'll have a terrific view!"

Word shot through the ship an hour later that Japanese planes had begun their attack on Midway. The enemy flotilla was two hundred miles northwest of the base and the US convoy the same distance to the northeast. Of the forty-three American planes that launched in the first four hours, only six returned. Forty attacking Zeros had shot the others out of the sky like so many skeet clays. Benny barely took his eyes off the flight deck as the hours ticked away, trying to conceal building unease. The sense of impending disaster pervading Sky Control seemed to confirm the worst-case fears leading up to the Halsey-less mission.

But despite the dearth of returning planes, the American Navy's luck was about to turn. *Enterprise*'s flight leader, Lieutenant Wade McClusky, had inadvertently flown off course to find nothing but vacant seas. Disheartened and low on fuel, he prepared to turn his squadron back toward *Enterprise* when, through a peephole in the clouds, he spied a lone Japanese destroyer heading northeast at flank speed. On a hunch, McClusky ordered his air group to pursue the unsuspecting destroyer instead. Within ten minutes, the hunch paid off. Dead ahead was the entire Japanese striking force, replete with four carriers and a dozen support vessels, including battleships, destroyers, and cruisers.

Benny was so startled to hear McClusky's voice break radio silence over the crackling ship's radio that he spilled his coffee all over Wayne Barnhill. He quickly turned the knob just in time to hear McClusky's staccato delivery of stunning news: not only had they sighted the Japanese carriers, but also their first round of attack planes had just returned from Midway for refueling. Eureka!

Fuel hoses crisscrossed the Japanese carrier decks, and stacks of munitions were piled for reloading in plain view as the *Enterprise* squadron— and, shortly after, *Yorktown*'s fighters—came hurtling through the clouds. From ten thousand feet, McClusky and his thirty-seven bombers bore down on the Japanese anchorage at a seventy-degree angle. In less than thirty minutes, they had handily sunk two of their four carriers and wiped out half their airpower. By sundown, *Yorktown* pilots had torpedoed a third carrier. By the time the planes returned to *Enterprise*, *Kaga*, *Soryu*, and *Akagi* were nosing toward the ocean floor.

The fourth and last Japanese carrier, *Hiryu*, had not been located, but its pilots, seething with revenge, had discovered the American ships' position northeast of Midway and were heading straight for them. Although *Yorktown* and *Enterprise* were steaming less than six miles apart, *Yorktown* was closer to the approaching Japanese fighters. Benny watched enemy dive bombers roar toward *Yorktown* like a swarm of angry bees. Her antiaircraft gunners responded with furious intensity—but their efforts were futile.

With *Enterprise* beyond gun range, Benny and his megaphone were of no use to *Yorktown*. He could only watch helplessly from Sky Control as three bombs and two torpedoes all found their deadly marks. Seconds later, *Yorktown* was belching flames and smoke. Barney Barnhill swept his camera back and forth, back and forth, duty-bound to record the horrific scene. Only a fixed grimace hinted at his internal turmoil while he recorded hundreds of burning sailors jumping into the water. Soon the listing ship's outline blurred into a fireball after which only an urgent water rescue operation was left to film.

The jubilant return of *Enterprise* planes to the flight deck was tempered by the grim spectacle. They were soon followed by *Yorktown*'s fighters—orphaned by the fatal blows to their mother ship. But there was no time for the *Yorktown* pilots to grieve the certain loss of so many shipmates. Within minutes, they refueled and were again airborne, charging at *Hiryu* to exact their own revenge. *Hiryu* soon joined the three other Japanese carriers on the Pacific floor.

FOR BILL MOTT IN the White House Map Room, the suspense—listening moment to moment for the teletype to begin its clicking report of agonizing defeat, failure, and loss—was like waiting for as many pulls on a pistol trigger. The lopsided match between twenty-four American ships and an enemy armada four times that size had him on heart-hammering edge, hour after hour, waiting for Midway's battle status to come across.

Over the course of the three-day engagement, the crowded Map Room was efficient but hushed. Frequently the only sound that could be heard was the semicircular protractor scratching around a table map dotted with two- and three-inch ships. When the dispatch arrived about the loss of *Yorktown*—in advance of any news on the fate of the Japanese carriers—Bill braced for the rash of casualty reports.

When word then came through of the *Enterprise* squadron's brilliant air strikes and the enormity of *enemy* losses—and, best of all, that Japanese firepower was eliminated before it could retaliate against *Enterprise*—Bill threw a celebratory fist in the air and joined in the party-like atmosphere that had fully erupted in the Map Room. Similar celebrations were breaking out throughout the War Department and on Capitol Hill.

Admiral Spruance was forthwith crowned the navy's newest wunderkind. As it turned out, his painstaking preparation, tactical brilliance, and calculated risk of launching all task force planes ahead of schedule to ensure the crucial element of surprise—worked. His strategy not only achieved complete surprise and devastated enemy forces, but also prevented the deadly nighttime counterstrikes at which the Japanese excelled. In a rare moment of cheerful self-deprecation, Admiral King was overheard saying, "I see now that I am only the second-smartest man in the United States Navy!"

The reduction in Japanese Fleet strength wrought by the American Navy at Midway seemed almost too good to be true. Japan had lost four carriers, a heavy cruiser, and well over three hundred aircraft, not to mention its most experienced pilots. The Battle of Midway marked a strategic reversal in the Pacific War; America was now the aggressor, and Japan on the defense.

Admiral Nimitz immediately recalled the remainder of the Midway task force to Pearl Harbor. The mood aboard *Enterprise* was a strange mix of relief, exhilaration, and mourning. They had won and won big, but *Enterprise* had lost numerous pilots and air crews. There had not even been an opportunity to pay last respects on the fantail at a burial at sea service. The airmen had crashed to their Pacific graves without so much as a final salute.

Admiral Spruance came over the loudspeaker and delivered the following message as *Enterprise* steamed to port:

"I wish to express my admiration and commendation to every officer and man of the *Enterprise* and especially to the pilots and gunners for their splendid performance . . . The personnel losses are most regretted, but it is felt that these gallant men contributed materially in striking a decisive blow against the enemy."

The ship's radio buzzed with congratulatory messages. They poured in from President Roosevelt and Allied commands and officials from around the globe. There was also an awkwardly translated and wildly inaccurate report from Radio Tokyo, claiming victory for Japan's navy:

"Japan's forces carried out fierce attacks on Midway Island, inflicting heavy damage on fleet reinforcements in that area, also damaging naval and air installations . . . Japanese sank carrier *Enterprise* and *Hornet* and shot down one hundred twenty enemy aircraft."

Benny allowed a wide grin as he listened to the message. This was the second time the Japanese had reported sinking the *Enterprise*: the first was after the Gilbert and Marshall Islands raid in February. When the translation was read gleefully over the ship's loudspeakers, crew on every level stamped their feet approvingly. It was getting to be a good omen. Admiral Halsey's sobriquet for his beloved flagship, the Galloping Ghost of the Oahu Coast, had been well earned.

On the afternoon of June 13, 1942, every soldier and sailor in Pearl Harbor lined the docks to welcome *Enterprise* home. Deafening cheers and waving flags greeted the task force as it approached. The beginning of a forty-eight-hour congratulatory liberty found Benny and hundreds of other boisterous *Enterprise* celebrants crowding the bar at the Royal Hawaiian Hotel. None of them paid for their own drinks that night.

Over the ukuleles, laughing, and back slapping, one comment made the rounds countless times: "That Spruance! Brilliant, by God, *brilliant!*"

12

★ ★ ★

UNDER SIEGE: JN-25

WHILE SLIGHTLY HUNG OVER the morning after *Enterprise*'s victorious return to Pearl from Midway, Benny penned a reply to two letters from Bill that awaited him:

June 14, 1942

Dear Bill,

    I haven't had much time to write, as you might imagine, but many thanks for your welcome words of encouragement. Your letters always give me something to look forward to. I would very much like to talk with you right now--I'm sure we could find many things of mutual interest to discuss without the veil of censorship.

    We've been lucky so far--the line has been held once

again. But there is such a thing as riding a good horse to
death. I am bone tired. The situation remains grave however
and there will be no respite, as you know.

To be honest, the thing that keeps me going are thoughts
of Bart. After four years at sea they say I could stay and
work ashore for a month or so, recognizing that one does
need some rest to be of any use. But I feel the worse because
when he came through here, he knew conditions were bad,
and I told him not to worry too much, as we would be out
there, ready and waiting if anything broke. I want to make
good on that assurance before it's too late.

As for how badly you want to go to sea, Bill, I want to
say again I think you can do more and serve better where
you are. I know how you feel about Bart, but I believe if I
could see you and have a talk with you I could convince you
of that . . .

Well Bill, that's all for now except I have some good
ideas I wish I could talk over with you so you could pass
them on to the right people.

> Do your best always,
> Love,
> Benny

BILL READ AND REREAD Benny's somewhat disjointed response
to his letters. He was relieved to finally get direct word from his brother,
and for the moment dismissed the usual admonition about his desire to
go to sea. Right now he was focused on a different phrase Benny had used:
"veil of censorship." Bill had just learned that an unbelievable tear in that

veil had occurred, quashing his jubilant mood over the victory at Midway. The breach could potentially endanger Benny and his crew as much as any incipient Japanese assault.

The Midway task force had just prevailed because of a combination of intelligence work, skill, and luck in breaking the Japanese naval code. Even better, the Japanese were unaware that their code had been cracked; they continued to use JN-25 after Midway to encrypt naval messages. But the work of one Stanley Johnston—World War I veteran, champion sculler, and heady Australian war correspondent for the *Chicago Tribune*—had potentially reversed Station Hypo's crucial code breaking gains.

Johnston had distinguished himself while on assignment covering the Coral Sea Battle back in early May. When the *Lexington* received her fatal bomb blow during that engagement, Johnston, in the heat of battle, heroically rescued burning sailors from "Lady Lex's" doomed hold. He was one of the last to leave the ship. Then, while the crew members thrashed desperately in the oily water, Johnston, a strong swimmer, was further credited with saving a number of lives by helping them to land into lifeboats.

Both *Lexington*'s skipper and his executive officer, M. T. "Mort" Seligman, were so impressed by Johnston's actions that they recommended him for a navy heroism citation. In fact, their experience of surviving the harrowing *Lexington* disaster forged a bond between Johnston and Seligman, who shared a cabin from the Coral Sea back to the States aboard the navy transport *Barnett*. During that voyage, a secret dispatch containing the decoded Japanese order of battle for the upcoming Midway engagement was selectively distributed.

As *Lexington*'s XO, Seligman received a copy of the classified dispatch, its blue lines standing out from the other papers on his desk. Versions vary on what happened next. One is that Johnston, being a good reporter and sleuth, observed the document and took note of its contents. Another holds that Seligman shared the very interesting top secret document with

Johnston, whom he now considered a close friend and confidant. Either way, Seligman would soon be in very hot water.

On return to the States, Johnston caught the first flight to Chicago, his priority to finish and file his story on the Coral Sea drama in which several men, including Mort Seligman and himself, were cast as heroes. But Johnston was also roughing out another story on his L.C. Smith & Corona Standard—bearing the electrifying draft lede that the US Navy had broken the Japanese naval code.

On June 7, while the Midway battle was still in progress, the *Chicago Tribune* presses cranked out hundreds of thousands of copies of the day's broadsheet, with Johnston's article appearing on page A1, above the fold. The headline: "Navy Had Word of Jap Plan to Strike at Sea." The story also appeared in other newspapers that subscribed to the *Tribune*'s newswire, including conservative Cissy Patterson's *Washington Times-Herald*.

The opening lines of the article, which carried a Washington dateline, soon had jaws dropping all over the capital:

```
Washington, DC, June 7--
The strength of the Japanese forces which the Ameri-
can Navy is battling somewhere west of Midway Island
in what is believed to be the war's greatest naval
battle, was well-known in American naval circles, re-
liable sources in Naval Intelligence disclosed here
tonight.
```

The story named the four carriers of the Japanese striking force and listed the Japanese order of battle. It further noted that all American outposts in the Pacific had been given the advance warning. The Washington dateline on the story was designed to conceal that Johnston in Chicago was the source of the breach, implying instead that the leak was from Naval Intelligence in Washington.

As news of the catastrophic leak settled in, military and political lead-ers began vying for first blood. An enraged Roosevelt threatened to send marines to Chicago to shut down Tribune Tower, home of the loathed newspaper, which he viewed as a thinly disguised organ of the Republican Party. Roosevelt already famously despised its publisher, Colonel Robert McCormick, a conservative and vocal anti–New Dealer—and old nemesis of the president's, going all the way back to their boarding school days at Groton School.

The navy went straight to work to rout the leaker. Astoundingly, the article had managed to clear censorship channels, with the critical nature of the contents somehow eluding the readers at the US Office of War Informa-tion (OWI).

The Japanese had only to read the *Chicago Tribune* to find that their codes had been compromised! Admiral King was said to be in "a white fury" that months of exhausting, round-the-clock effort to break JN-25—a singu-lar feat on which the tide of the Pacific War had just turned—could soon be for naught. For days, Bill shuttled endlessly between the White House and the Navy Department as the navy and administration attempted to under-stand how this crucial secret had been compromised—not to mention how such a story could have slipped through the censors' fingers.

The investigation quickly confirmed that Commander Morton T. Seligman, the *Lexington*'s XO, had shared a cabin with correspondent John-ston, "in which the reporter observed the classified documents, including a JN-25-C decryption containing the Japanese order of battle at Midway." Whether Seligman intentionally shared the information or Johnston ob-tained it by sleuth, the result was the same. Seligman's naval career was ef-fectively over. Still, more bloodletting was sought.

This was one of many instances in which Bill was grateful that none of his White House associates were aware of his Republican background. Burning with partisan rage toward McCormick, Roosevelt and other prominent Democrats demanded a grand jury investigation; party loyalists on both sides lined up to watch the goring. Roosevelt was not interested in Stanley Johnston's resignation or censure of the hapless Seligman. He wanted Colonel McCormick's scalp.

Miraculously, however, in the first week following the initial news leak and its subsequent coverage, the Japanese barely tweaked JN-25. Navy cryptanalysts began to wonder: Was it possible that no Japanese sympathizers or spies had read the article or its reprint in any American newspaper? Code breakers scrutinized new intercepts with bated breath, expecting at any moment for them to become indecipherable. But only small, manageable changes to JN-25 were detected. This wasn't necessarily unusual—minor code modifications happened all the time. But was Johnston's article the reason? Only the Japanese knew the answer to that.

BILL FOLDED BENNY'S LETTER and put it back in his briefcase. He was now trying to absorb the latest development in the crisis: a White House visit earlier that day by his old friend "Saffo." US Navy Captain Larry Safford was the brilliant, low-key head of OP-20-G, the code breaking division within the Office of Naval Intelligence. Saffo had come to Bill with an idea and a request. He hoped Bill might impart his thoughts to higher-ups and tame the hysteria.

The last thing Captain Safford wanted was a long-drawn-out grand jury investigation, trial, and more publicity than had already been generated by the original article. He fretted this would *ensure* the Japanese would learn that their naval code had been compromised, if that hadn't happened already. "Bill," Saffo had said, "we think that with no more publicity on this thing, we can crack the changes the Japs have made to their code since Midway. I'm telling you, they make changes all the time. But if this thing doesn't go away, we are going to have a much, much bigger problem. You've got to stop this lawsuit."

Bill looked at Safford, mouth agape. "Who, *me?*" was all he could muster. "Come on, Saffo, I can't do that." The old Roosevelt-McCormick political rivalry had overshadowed all reason. "You don't know how much these two people hate each other."

Safford shook his head. "Well, Bill," he said somberly, "if this story gets any bigger, if that grand jury gets going, we'll never be able to break the Japanese naval codes again. *Never.*"

Before Bill left the White House late that evening, he put the finishing touches on a memo to Captain McCrea explaining Safford's grave concerns and recommendations. He had promised Saffo he would give it a try, using his best legal and personal powers of persuasion—and not only because it was the right thing to do for the United States Navy and the war in the Pacific. Almost certainly, Benny stood to gain or lose in the outcome.

Several weeks later, JN-25 was still being used by the Japanese, with only minor changes. Admiral King wasted no time barring Commander Seligman forever from promotion and made sure the only vessel he would see thereafter was an "LSD": a large steel desk. Stanley Johnston's award for bravery at the Battle of the Coral Sea was disallowed by the White House. But, inexplicably, the grand jury investigation of the *Chicago Tribune* was abruptly dropped. No concrete reason was ever given to the press by William Mitchell, the special prosecutor in the case.

13

★ ★ ★

TO DAVAO: *EN AVANT!*

CONDITIONS AT CABANATUAN IMPROVED from dire to grim over Barton's first three months there, from a loss of 1,300 men in June and July 1942 to fewer than 300 in August. This was primarily due to prisoner-generated solutions to waste management disposal and control of malaria-carrying mosquitoes. Though mistreatment by their guards had not abated, these and other morale-building improvements helped the prisoners beat back despair.

The men were heartened as well by persistent rumors of American gains in the Pacific. Despite strict Japanese rules against dispensing war information to prisoners, news accounts managed to trickle in—primarily via Filipinos working at or near the camp.

But when a draft of 400 Cabanatuan prisoners was abruptly shipped to Japan as laborers for the Nippon war effort, the remaining POWs had fresh cause for apprehension. They loathed Cabanatuan in every respect, but shipment to Japan was by far their biggest fear. The prisoners assumed little chance of survival on enemy home soil. So when word leaked of Japanese plans to ship a second, much larger detail out of Cabanatuan, tensions spiked.

Lieutenant Colonel Mori ended their speculation by announcing that a thousand "able-bodied" prisoners would be selected for relocation to a prison farm on Mindanao, the southernmost Philippine island. The "able-bodied" designation disqualified a wide swath of prisoners suffering from various diseases, including dysentery, pellagra, and diphtheria.

The news sparked an outbreak of optimism—despite nagging suspicions that this could be a Japanese trick to get them to depart peacefully and then route them to Japan. But once a knowledgeable senior American officer confirmed—after conferring with the Japanese—that this was not the case, men rushed to volunteer in a rare display of enthusiasm. A move from Cabanatuan but not to Japan was regarded as improving their chances of survival.

The new place, named Davao Penal Colony, became a beacon of hope. It brought the imagined prospect of better food and improved living conditions, plus the psychological benefit of its southern location: nearly a thousand miles closer to Allied-held Australia. Cabanatuan prisoners of all stripes eagerly signed up for the Davao draft; in the end, hundreds were crushed to learn they'd been turned down.

JUST BEFORE SUNRISE ON October 25, 1942, the first of two groups selected for Mindanao was awakened, fed a small breakfast of tea and rice, and ordered out on foot. Barton and Charles and the rest of the first five hundred prisoners marched the several kilometers back to Cabanatuan City in the now-familiar four-abreast formation. With many barefooted and their bodies wrecked and undernourished, the hours-long march proved the most difficult one so far. But they pressed on, eager to appear fit for the journey lest they be removed from the draft of "able-bodied" prisoners. All along the way, local Filipinos flashed their signature V signs and tossed fruit and other victuals to the grateful prisoners.

The next leg of the long southbound journey to Mindanao meant reboarding the dreaded narrow-gauge boxcars that would carry them back to Manila. Barton checked his incipient panic when he saw that the cars had been cooled by hours of overnight rain. Better still, the guards agreed to leave the cars' sliding doors ajar so the men might get fresh air. Whether this was a rare show of goodwill or a reflection of the guards' disdain for handling suffocated corpses upon arrival in Manila mattered little to the prisoners.

The prospect of distancing themselves from the much-loathed Cabanatuan had the prisoners actually smiling as the train jerked to life and began rumbling toward Manila. From there, they would board a ship to Mindanao. They chatted quietly, calmly among themselves, swapping yarns and talking, as always, of family.

A locomotive's rhythmic movement had always had a somnolent effect on Barton, and he eventually dozed off as he so often had on the late train home from the city. Did he hear the stationmaster's insistent calls in his slumber? *"Red Bank! Perth Amboy! Hoboken! Long Branch!"* And was that Mother? Out the window on the platform? Scanning faces in the passing windows? But the train in all his dreams would pass right through those familiar stations without so much as a pause.

The long, low screech that brought the prison train to a halt awoke Barton with a start. His attention was redirected to the sound of Filipinos gathering on the station platform of a small barrio. Suddenly rice balls, bananas, and bits of fried chicken were being tossed toward the boxcar openings. Only a few reached their car, but Barton let out a signature barrel laugh after fielding a chicken leg and a fat, sweetened rice ball. When the train resumed, he divided his spoils into impossibly small portions and distributed them to those who had failed to score.

At the next station, the group of local well-wishers was even larger and better prepared. More food was handed to the prisoners through the boxcar openings, but the larger gift was a chorus of young boys at the far edge of the platform humming a melody. They dared not sing the words for fear of enraging the guards, but the familiar tune "God Bless America" could be heard loud and clear throughout the train compartments. The strengthening effect this had on the prisoners was at least equal to the proffered foodstuffs. "Victory, Joe!" one young boy called out as the train pulled away. Two of his small, dirty fingers were fixed in a defiant V.

Hours later, the men arrived at Manila—hot, tired, and thirsty. Without respite, they formed up and marched back to the familiar intersection of Azcarraga and Quezon. Just before they passed through Bilibid's gates, one of the men, "Ship" Daniels, collapsed. He had been placed on the Davao roster by a well-intentioned superior hoping that Mindanao's climate might improve his failing health. Fellow prisoners looked on helplessly as repeated beatings by the guards failed to revive him. Ship was finally picked up and carried into Bilibid. He died later that night.

The returned Cabanatuan prisoners were kept in cramped quarters at the northern end of the Bilibid compound, sequestered from the other inmates. Despite the discomfort, they prayed for only one thing that night: that tomorrow's voyage wouldn't prove a ruse for shipping them to Japan.

The next morning, Barton and Charles stayed close as the prisoners assembled into groups of one hundred and began yet another march past throngs of careworn Manilans. Women wept openly at the sight of the diminished, half-clad American soldiers and sailors. But defiant V flashes were also spied and murmurs of "*Mabuhay*," or "Long life," were heard all along their route to the waterfront.

This would be Barton's third such post-capture stroll, again past the Manila Hotel, the high commissioner's residence, the Manila Polo Club, and his onetime home, the Manila Army and Navy Club. Despite the many months away, it still stung to see a large Japanese flag flying atop its flagpole.

Its gardens were weedy and unkempt, but the club had so far been spared the destruction that surrounded it; bomb rubble, boarded-up shops, and piles of debris now defiled the once-pristine Dewey Boulevard.

The terminus of their march was Pier 7, another familiar landmark. The loading of so many prisoners onto the awaiting ship, an old coal-burning vessel named *Erie Maru* (which the Japanese had requisitioned from the Americans before the war), took several hours in the hot sun. Enthusiasm diminished as the men were packed tightly into nightmarishly dark holds thick with coal dust. The sleeping bays were three feet high, five feet wide, and ten feet deep, and twelve prisoners were crammed into each one. Worse, they were met in the holds by a tenacious new enemy: millions of tiny, crawling body lice, well established in the deep coal dust. Soon virtually every man's skin crawled with them.

A competitive game developed: prisoners tallied and compared the number of lice on their bodies. When Charles's grousing did not improve with the game, Barton urged him to count his blessings instead—for their ever-widening distance from Cabanatuan.

On October 27, 1942, the *Erie Maru* cast its lines and moved out of Manila Bay. They were all attentive to the ship's course, nervous that a turn north would confirm their worst fears. But when *Erie Maru* heeled to port and turned south into the South China Sea, there was collective relief: here was irrefutable confirmation that they were not going to Japan.

The ship proceeded to follow a nine-hundred-kilometer zigzag, hugging the Philippine shoreline as closely as its captain dared, demonstrating an early Japanese fear that American submarines might be lurking off the coast. The prisoners were confined belowdeck at night but were allowed topside during daylight hours. After the second day of the journey, Barton, Charles, and a fortunate group of other naval officers somehow negotiated to remain topside for the balance of the voyage. Free of the desperate confines of the past ten months, they luxuriated in the healthy dose of sea air. Even Charles remarked positively on this development.

Better yet, the food aboard ship was a feast compared with anything since their capture, despite the rueful observation that several of the chow containers bore a "US Navy Base Cavite" stamp. But three meals a day, variously of cabbage soup with any combination of pork, spinach, meat, milk, dried fish, corned beef, and squash, had most of the men feeling much improved almost immediately—particularly in the absence of harsh camp labor to dissipate their new energy stores. Such allowances alone made their *Erie Maru* overseers seem more humane than those at Cabanatuan. Could this be a harbinger of better treatment ahead?

More heartening still was the explanation for their prolonged layover at an anchorage on the island of Panay. A Filipino stevedore at the Iloilo City docks tipped off the prisoners: a fierce sea battle between the Japanese and Allied navies raged near the Solomon Islands. As a result, the *Erie Maru* was ordered to remain at Panay until further notice. "Japanese Navy *losing!*" the stevedore exuded in a triumphant whisper. This was a shot of adrenaline for Barton, who thrilled at the prospect that Benny was there in the Solomons—thousands of miles closer to the Philippines than he could have imagined—directing fire from *Enterprise*.

When the *Erie Maru* finally departed Panay and steered east through the Surigao Strait and into the open Pacific, Japanese crew and guards warily donned life jackets. Fear of American submarine strikes loomed even larger as word had circulated of hit-and-run strikes on Japanese shipping in the area. Not one of the Japanese transports that had been struck—whether carrying goods, munitions, or people—had seen its presumed American attacker. That the *Erie Maru* bore no markings as a prisoner-of-war transport made her fair game.

During the wait at Panay, Barton had become acquainted with a number of the older naval officers in the Davao draft. One, Commander Melvin McCoy, had been two years ahead of Benny at Annapolis, a connection the two men enjoyed exploring for days on end. But when McCoy's talk turned to the possibility of the naval officers taking over the ship, Barton declined comment. Reprisals for a failed mutiny attempt would be severe—likely re-sulting in the torture and death of many innocent friends, if not all of them.

Strengthened by the improved rations, McCoy and others had whis-pered the possibility of charging the ship's crew and commandeering the *Erie Maru* to Australia. Philippine constabulary troops were also aboard and, although under Japanese control, they were presumed to be sympa-thetic with the prisoners' plight. Barton was relieved when the would-be conspirators concluded the odds were too great to risk so many lives, and the matter was dropped.

Despite obvious uneasiness among the crew, the *Erie Maru* sailed un-molested all the way to Davao Gulf at Mindanao. On November 7, eleven days after departing Manila, her lumbering engines finally downshifted and the ship dropped anchor by a simple wooden pier. The place was called Bar-rio Lasang, a tiny logging anchorage northeast of Davao Harbor.

After the lines were secured, an American voice boomed from the rusted loudspeaker: "Now hear this. Now hear this . . . We are to disembark [at Barrio Lasang] and march to Davao Penal Colony, a distance of twenty-seven kilometers (sixteen miles). Food will be distributed at the end of the gangplank. When you leave the ship, form a column at the far end of the pier. That is all."

After a meal of rice and *camotes*, however, the prisoners were ordered to sit in the midday sun for several hours without explanation. The men had come to call this familiar exercise the "sun treatment," which they believed the Japanese guards deliberately employed to weaken them so they would be easier to control.

They were finally rousted to their feet in the peak-afternoon heat, as-sembled into columns, and directed up a narrow jungle road that cut through dense vegetation. The prisoners marched deep into the night, and by the wee hours, the road had tapered to a steep, deeply rutted trail. Visibil-ity was practically nil, despite bright flecks of moonlight filtering through the rainforest canopy.

Several fell out from sheer exhaustion as the going grew more difficult. But unlike earlier marches where they might have been slapped, bayoneted or shot for the same transgression, collapsing Davao-bound prisoners were loaded onto a truck trailing the columns and driven the rest of the way. Approximately halfway to the camp, Charles was loaded onto the truck. By then, Barton's world had narrowed to the dirt path directly in front of him, and he managed to make the entire trek to the promised land on foot. It ended at 0400, after nine grueling hours.

Barton was among the first to stumble into what initially seemed like a jungle clearing, but once his eyes adjusted to the dim, a tidy compound of barracks and other outbuildings spread out before him. In the predawn glow at least, Davao Penal Colony appeared as hoped for: a significant improvement over Cabanatuan. The prisoners were herded into a large warehouse-like building. After the order "Fall out. This is the end of the line," an exhausted Barton Cross curled up on the floor alongside a thousand other hopeful arrivals and surrendered to a deep and welcome sleep.

DAVAO PENAL COLONY, OR DAPECOL as it was called, was a maximum security prison established by the Philippine government for habitual and incorrigible prisoners. Its location—still marked "Unexplored" on a 1940 map—was in the middle of a rain forest barely north of the equator. But to the prisoners from Cabanatuan, it seemed the answer to so many prayers. It had acres of rice fields, and crops of coffee, papaya, and mung beans. It also boasted pig and chicken farms, a lumber mill, carpentry shop, hospital, and chapel. Though rough and unpainted, the tin-roofed barracks were water tight, alone a substantial improvement over Cabanatuan. The prisoners felt the promise of survival.

After inspecting the new arrivals, however, DAPECOL's camp commander, Major Kazuo Maeda, complained angrily to the assembled group that they resembled walking corpses. He had been told, he said, that he was being sent the strongest of the POWs for his mission of running the farm to supply food to Japanese soldiers in the Philippines.

Nonetheless he proceeded to deliver the following speech, with his *l*s replaced mostly with *r*s—the prisoners' scant and only source of humor for the day: "You have had soft, easy life since your capture. All that will be different here. You will learn about hard labor. Every prisoner will work unless he is in hospital. Punishment for malingering will be severe."

14

★ ★ ★

AND THEN THERE WAS ONE: USS *ENTERPRISE* VERSUS JAPAN

IN MID-OCTOBER 1942, THE USS *Enterprise* was again poised to move out of Pearl Harbor's narrow channel, bound for the South Pacific. The ship had been in drydock for two months, undergoing repairs from three bomb hits she'd received in August at the Eastern Solomons battle. One hit alone had killed thirty-eight men in the gun gallery on the carrier's aft starboard side.

Benny worked with navy dentists for hours following to help identify his dead gunners. The boys' clothes were vaporized by the initial blast, and identification was made harder yet by the furious gunpowder-fueled fire that ensued. Like uncovered remains at ancient Pompeii, a number were frozen in the stances they'd held on impact: one still seated, leaning into his sights, training his gun on an incoming plane; another handing over a powder keg, the hands of both giver and receiver still outstretched; pointers and trainers were hunched over in their seats as though resting. Benny had the further unhappy task of writing to the families of the fallen men. His heart heaved with each note, knowing how his own mother might receive such news.

Stories of the fierce clash in the Solomons had been fully reported by the time mutilated *Enterprise* limped back into Pearl Harbor for repairs. Waiting for Benny was a hastily composed and badly typed letter from Bill:

```
Dear Benny,


     The suspense I have gone through since hearing from

you last has been terrific. If you do get this letter which

Praise God you will, call me collect at the White House at

your earliest opportunity, sometime between the hours of

eight and twelve in the morning or five to seven at night. I

have told the White House operators that you might call, so

they will be expecting it. The times given above are Eastern

War Time which is the same as Zone Plus Four.



                         Devotedly,

                         Bill
```

Benny placed the call immediately. As he waited for the White House operator to put him through to the Map Room, he tore open his one other piece of mail: a legal notice indicating that his wife Jeannette had requested that his life insurance policy eliminate Helen Cross as a joint beneficiary and name her as sole beneficiary. The explanation given was that she would need all the proceeds to support herself and their daughter, given the high probability that something would happen to her husband. Benny was crushed.

He set aside the rude shock when Bill's voice broke in on the line.

"Jesus, you had me worried this time!" Bill said, trying to sound jocular, but his voice was thick with emotion.

"Yup—well, this one was a nail-biter, I don't mind telling you," came Benny's reply, also tinged with forced cheerfulness. "Thanks for your note. I just got it. Matter of fact, we just got in."

The two brothers spoke at length of their shared relief that Benny had survived another terrifying ordeal, the details of which Bill already knew well. *Enterprise* had pulled through again, if barely, this time listing and afire, spewing black smoke and loaded with charred bodies. Benny had lost many friends, and he admitted to Bill he was badly shaken. "Worst one yet, this one—for me, anyway." Benny let out a disconsolate chuckle before sharing the contents of his other letter. "Nice homecoming present, eh? Guess she was hoping I was one of our casualties."

Bill assured Benny he would assume the task of responding to Jeannette's shabby request and that "two-bit lawyer" she had engaged even as her husband had steamed toward battle. When they hung up, Bill heaved a deep sigh and scrolled a piece of White House letterhead into his typewriter. In an instant, he went from enormous relief to a controlled state of rage. Still, rigorous legal training had taught him to hew to the facts. He was pleased to report, he began, both as Commander E. B. Mott's brother and now his legal representative, that Benny had survived the recent engagements in the Pacific, rendering Jeannette's concern over his life insurance policy premature.

In any case, the policy was indeed being revised, Bill continued coolly—by giving Helen Cross, the existing joint beneficiary, special new powers. Her role would be to see that any amounts that might at some future point be due Jeannette would instead be placed into trust for young Jeanne Marie. Bill could be contacted at the White House if the lawyer misunderstood any of the foregoing. Only on the last line did Bill yield to temptation, concluding the missive with the following remark: "I cannot understand for the life of me why any woman would want to torture and make miserable the life of anyone who is already giving so much for his country, but I guess this war has shown there are a lot of things about human nature that are inexplicable."

As Bill saw to Benny's painful marital matters, Benny returned to urgent ship business. While *Enterprise* was under repair, he'd managed the critical installation of powerful and more precise 40-millimeter quad-mounted guns, plus new mounts to the bow of the ship on the forecastle. Forty-six new 20-millimeter guns were installed as well. In all, the carrier now had much more powerful and protective antiaircraft batteries than in the Eastern Solomons, and Benny was confident they would do valiant service in upcoming battle.

With customary good rapport, the Gunnery and Air Departments worked together to train the ship's gunners—both green and veteran—on the new equipment. Benny and *Enterprise*'s air officer, Commander John Crommelin, met on the flight deck each morning for target practice with the new guns. The two officers worked closely together on the complex carrier minuet that combined air combat with sea fighting. Thousands of lives and survival of the ship itself depended heavily on the quality of their cooperative efforts.

During these exercises, Crommelin would order a group of planes to fly over the ship so that the gunners could practice training their gun sights onto enemy aircraft. Benny would then give commands over the flight deck bullhorn to commence and cease fire. They would conduct these exercises for hours at a time.

Whenever the men called for a break, Benny, with the quick, flat wit of a train conductor, would issue the following over the bullhorn: "Boys," he said, then sighed and paused for effect, "I'd like you to think about something on your little break. There are two kinds of people in gunnery. The quick and the dead."

That usually made the point that the long, hot practices were crucial. In battle, the time a gunner had to train his artillery on a dive bomber and then fire on it was between five and eight seconds. In that minuscule flash of time, the attacking plane would have to be downed or the aim of the pilot spoiled if the ship was to be spared. Only practice improved those odds.

★   ★   ★

ON OCTOBER 16, 1942, *Enterprise* departed Pearl Harbor for certain battle. After six days at sea, she merged with the USS *Hornet's* convoy and several new crew members zipped over to *Enterprise* via high line, a conveyance cable suspended between support and troop vessels and warships. Benny and Commander Crommelin interrupted their morning rehearsals while the new recruits came aboard. Both men commented on the questionable wisdom of adding inexperienced crew members so soon before battle.

Their musings turned from concern to salty invective when a smiling young ensign swayed and dangled on the high line between the troopship and *Enterprise*, and then dropped to the deck with golf clubs slung over his shoulder and carrying a tennis racquet.

Other newly boarded men would distinguish themselves in a different way. One was a naval aviator named Robert Emmett Riera, a 1935 Annapolis graduate who had also worked in gunnery before attending flight school in Pensacola, Florida. Riera was joining *Enterprise* from his first Pacific piloting assignment with Scouting Squadron Sixteen. Benny naturally liked the fact that Riera knew gunnery and was also an Academy man—particularly with so many novice pilots joining the fight. This was the type of naval aviator that rose quickly in rank in officer-starved 1942, assuming he continued to make good decisions.

The brutal work ahead for the *Enterprise* crew was the continuation of what they had begun in August in their harrowing foray to the Solomon Islands. Their mission then was to assist in the landing of the First Marine Division on a little-known island called Guadalcanal. It had been a deadly two months since. The protracted air, land, and sea battle to control that remote but strategically invaluable jungle outpost was showing no sign of letting up.

It all began in July with a tip from hidden Australian coastwatchers that the Japanese were building an airfield on Guadalcanal. Admiral King reacted immediately. Not only did Guadalcanal mark the outer perimeter of mainland Japan's defense, but King instantly understood that an enemy airfield there would also give long-range Japanese bombers a launch pad for decimating US-Australia shipping and supply lanes. With Roosevelt's direct support, King ordered an immediate naval counteroffensive.

When Admiral Nimitz asked for Seventh Fleet ships to assist with the campaign, General MacArthur registered his fury with Washington. Alleging that the "navy cabal" was attempting to relegate him to a subordinate role in the Pacific, he claimed Nimitz had violated the divided command structure by not going *through* him to request access to the US Navy's Australia-based ships. And, he declared, any US Navy offensive to seize Guadalcanal was a further "breach," as Guadalcanal was part of the Solomon Islands chain, the dividing line between his command purview (Southwest Pacific) and Admiral Nimitz's (Central Pacific).

In a radiogram to both the War Department and the White House Map Room, MacArthur alleged:

"IT IS QUITE EVIDENT . . . THAT NAVY CONTEMPLATES ASSUMING GENERAL COMMAND CONTROL OF ALL OPERATIONS IN THE PACIFIC THEATER, THE ROLE OF THE ARMY BEING SUBSIDIARY AND CONSISTING LARGELY OF PLACING ITS FORCES AT THE DISPOSAL OR UNDER THE COMMAND OF NAVY OR MARINE OFFICERS."

The incoming rant raised plenty of eyebrows in the Map Room, but at the Navy Department, the veins in Admiral King's neck reportedly bulged at the news. Imagine his having to request permission from General MacArthur for access to the navy's own ships! MacArthur's petulant missive thus effectively reignited the Washington turf battle over which service would take overall command of the Pacific theater of war. As the command scuffle was thrashed out in Washington, the Japanese made handsome progress toward completing their airfield on Guadalcanal. Many senior navy officers were implacably hostile toward MacArthur forever after.

THE ISSUE OF OVERALL command in the Pacific had been simmering between the army and the navy since war was declared seven months earlier. To CNO Admiral King, the matter was simple: the battlefield in question was a multimillion-square-mile expanse of open ocean—emphatically and logically suited to naval command. Army Chief of Staff General George Marshall, however, argued in favor of awarding command of the Pacific to General MacArthur—himself a onetime army chief of staff and already on duty in the Philippines. Marshall was not about to let MacArthur become subordinate to naval command.

Admiral King, just as adamantly, refused to allow the precious remaining ships of the Pacific Fleet to be placed under Army General MacArthur. This was not only because King disliked and mistrusted MacArthur—whom he considered a megalomaniac—but also because MacArthur's knowledge of basic naval operations was critically deficient. King's own solution for overall Pacific command was, to him, the obvious choice: the commander in chief of the Pacific Fleet (CINCPAC): namely, Admiral Chester Nimitz, who was also at the ready in Pacific-bounded Hawaii.

Unable to reach consensus on either the army's or the navy's proposal, the Joint Chiefs of Staff (JCS) elected to *split* Pacific command between MacArthur—by then in Australia—and Nimitz. The command area dividing line was drawn along the Solomon Islands chain. MacArthur was named commander in chief of the Southwest Pacific Area (SWPA) and charged with subduing the Japanese at Port Moresby, New Guinea, and then driving his forces north from Australia to the Philippine archipelago.

Admiral Nimitz was named commander in chief of the Pacific Ocean Areas (POA) and charged with advancing easterly across the Central Pacific—clearing enemy resistance in the Marshall Islands and the Marianas—and ultimately converging with MacArthur's forces in the waters off the Philippines. The combined Allied force would then retake the Philippines, beginning logically with Mindanao, its southernmost island, and then make its final move against mainland Japan.

Under the Joint Chiefs' agreement, if either service happened to be operating within the other's command area, they would become subordinate to that area's theater commander, even if interservice radio channels were poor or nonexistent—a risk at any time, but particularly during war. The JCS's imperfect resolution solved the immediate spat but seemed destined to produce fractured communications, a disunity of effort, and enormous loss of life. Moreover, it had only temporarily solved the Pacific command scuffle.

MacArthur's petulant objections delayed the urgent Guadalcanal counteroffensive for weeks while a revision to the command geography was hammered out between General Marshall and Admiral King. The resulting amendment nudged the dividing line westward, placing the lower Solomons—including Guadalcanal and nearby Tulagi—under Admiral Nimitz's command. The agreement also allowed General MacArthur to lead future Allied moves against Rabaul, New Guinea, as well as New Britain, located northwest of Guadalcanal.

Finally, in early August, carriers *Enterprise*, *Wasp*, and *Saratoga*—and a cobbling together of nearly every available support naval vessel in the Pacific, including Seventh Fleet ships from "MacArthur's Navy"—had pressed toward Guadalcanal at flank speed. They were carrying a landing force of 19,000 marines. The mission was named Operation Watchtower, but a nickname quickly circulated among Washington military planners: "Operation Shoestring."

The stakes were high for both sides. The Allies could not allow a completed enemy airfield on Guadalcanal, especially since the Japanese could use it to attack all remaining Allied bases in the South Pacific—as well as Australia and New Zealand—with land-based bombers. The Allies also wanted Guadalcanal, the "unsinkable aircraft carrier," as a launching point for their own land-based bombers. Neither side could afford to lose it to the other.

The First Marine Division was landed on Guadalcanal and Tulagi, but nearly everything else about the operation's launch went badly. In this very first amphibious landing of the Pacific War, the newly named amphibian force commander, Admiral Richmond "Kelly" Turner, was forced to withdraw his ships prematurely "in view of heavy impending air attacks." The aircraft carriers—commanded by Admiral Frank Jack Fletcher—had withdrawn first, denying Turner's supply vessels crucial air cover. Turner was forced, therefore, to order withdrawal of *all* remaining ships, which had not yet unloaded armaments, rations, and medical supplies—and a thousand-man reserve force. In one of the proudest chapters of Marine Corps history however, the food-and-supply-strapped Corps on Guadalcanal still managed to seize the airfield, which they promptly rechristened Henderson Field in honor of a fellow marine killed at Midway.

Loath to lose the strategic benefits of the Guadalcanal airstrip, the Japanese staged a series of counteroffensives to repel the US Marines and retake the island. For the next two months, both sides poured blood and treasure into their dueling claim for that malarial speck of jungle in the Central Pacific. On October 22, the Japanese, supported by a forty-warship naval force, launched a massive ground offensive, with the additional objective of striking a decisive blow against approaching US naval forces, especially her aircraft carriers. For four days and nights, outnumbered, underfed, and exhausted, the marines continuously beat back the strengthened attack force at the airfield perimeter. Incredibly, on October 26, when *Enterprise, Hornet*, and their escorts arrived to assist with the counteroffensive, the marines still held Henderson Field.

THAT MORNING, *ENTERPRISE* STOOD west of Guadalcanal, just north of the Santa Cruz Islands. At first light, Admiral Halsey's order came through from his island headquarters at Nouméa, New Caledonia, 5,700 miles southwest of their location. The radiogram required no signature to identify its sender: "Attack. Repeat, Attack."

At 0630 Benny was in Sky Control, squinting eastward through his field glasses. Tense and expectant, he had just learned that one of *Enterprise*'s PBY scouting planes had been spotted by the Japanese. Suspecting their position, the enemy naval force had turned north to confront the American convoy. All was ready for certain battle; now only the dreadful wait.

"Guad-al-*canal.*" Benny had sounded it out the first time he'd located it on a map—the largest of the Solomon Islands on the northeastern approach to Australia. He'd never heard of it, but nor had a single US Navy admiral until July when the vigilant coastwatchers first reported the landing of laborers and heavy construction equipment there. Since then, loss of life and limb had mounted nonstop—by the troops battling ashore, by the sailors at sea, and by scores of carrier pilots all seeking to both attack enemy positions and defend hard-won ground.

The sun had barely cleared the horizon when *Enterprise* got its next scouting report—another disappointing one. A sizeable Japanese air squadron had launched and found *Hornet*. Benny focused his field glasses astern. *Hornet* was at least ten miles away, but he had a clear view of the evolving battle.

Through fiftyfold magnified lenses, Benny could plainly see one after another of *Hornet*'s planes getting shot down—then, worse, a bright orange geyser of flames erupting from the ship itself. He'd witnessed a similar sight just ahead of *Yorktown*'s incineration at Midway. By the size of this explosion and the profusion of smoke, he knew *Hornet* was also doomed. Within seconds, Benny was notified that *Hornet*'s crew had been ordered to abandon ship and her remaining planes redirected to *Enterprise*'s flight deck.

Meanwhile, both *Hornet* and *Enterprise* fighters had scored hits of their own on two of the advancing Japanese carriers. But the carriers had still managed to launch their Zeros and were steaming toward *Enterprise* like wounded, raging bulls. In a flash, Benny calculated the shrinking distance between the ship and the incoming planes and relayed firing instructions to his AA gunners with the urgent, rapid articulation of an auctioneer.

Bullets ricocheted off Sky Control's metal overhang, and for the first time since the war's outbreak, Benny understood the sudden mortal grip of fear. Only adrenaline and the repetitive rigors of years-long training kept him from seizing up.

He was not one to forget the timeworn aviator creed that flyers were a ship's first line of defense; her antiaircraft guns, a close second. Seaborne radar had risen in value and accuracy since Pearl Harbor, but at the moment, it offered little defense against the sky itself. *Enterprise* radar units had detected the Zeros closing in, but low clouds limited pilot visibility to less than five feet. As a result, neither the *Enterprise* pilots aloft nor the ship's AA gunners could get an early fix on the Japanese planes.

Suddenly a second wave of planes, this time Aichi Val bombers, dropped from the clouds, and Benny, following their course through his binoculars, alerted his portside gunners to the planes' position. The gunners whipped their weapons to a seventy-five-degree angle and, in a split second, unleashed a torrent of hot lead on the Val bombers bearing down on the ship.

From his summit post, Benny had a commanding view of the unfolding battle. Perspiration drenched his khaki uniform as he stood in the open aft section just forward of the stack. He gripped his bullhorn with one hand and the railing with the other as the ship zigzagged violently to spoil the multiple attackers' aim.

Jack Rountree and Roger McCabe, Benny's spotter and phone talker, were with him, both battle hardened from *Enterprise*'s August clashes in the Eastern Solomons. When either sighted a plane, Benny hollered the bearing and elevation over his bullhorn, and Rountree repeated it over the ship's sound-operated telephone. Later he couldn't remember whether the plane or the new 20-millimeter portside gun had fired first during this wave of attacks, but he remembered his amazement at the tremendous burst of fire from the new equipment.

Twenty-millimeter tracers soared over the stack, thirty feet aft of Sky Control. The leading aircraft crumbled in flames and dropped to the sea. A simultaneous whoop went up in Sky Control and the portside gun gallery.

Japanese Val bombers dove in a shallower pattern than their American counterparts, generally about a fifty-degree dive. They bore down expertly on *Enterprise*, one after another after another. As each plane closed in, antiaircraft batteries opened up, and a barrage of tracer shells riddled the planes. Benny, Rountree, and McCabe watched in a combination of horror and admiration as exploding shells hit their marks over and over, and enemy planes became so many flaming shards slamming into the sea.

Every time Benny barked out the bearings, he reminded his gunners to *lead* the plane, which they did with repeated success thanks to those countless hours of mind-numbing rehearsals. If the plane kept steady in its dive, the pilot would likely be killed and the bomb not released. But even if the pilot tried to "jink" out of the cone of fire from the ship, time-tested theory had shown that the bomb would still miss the ship because the tracers would follow and heckle the plane. Benny had always contended that the main function of antiaircraft fire was to throw off the pilot's aim; planes shot down were a bonus.

Line after line of fifteen-plane air groups continued to drop below the cloud cover and hurtle toward *Enterprise*. After each wave, there was just enough time to reload the burning-hot AA guns before the next phalanx came at them in a glinting, buzzing fury. Gone was Benny's fear now; it had been replaced by pure competitive instinct—and anger as hot as a spent tracer shell. *Goddamn it, this one's for those boys I lost in the Eastern Solomons.*

Benny's bullhorn was wet from the spit of his orders, but his voice came through strong and clear. The gunners processed his staccato directions almost simultaneously and threw plane after enemy plane off target. Victory was beginning to feel possible—even imminent. At this point, Benny greeted Associated Press correspondent Eugene Burns, who'd made his way up to Sky Control for a better view of the action. Jubilant, Benny clapped Burns so hard on the back that Burns winced in pain. "Ha, you think that's bad," Benny said in a moment of dark humor. "Stick around!" But the jovial moment was short-lived.

Rountree tapped Benny on the shoulder and pointed at the first airplane in yet another wave of bombers. At eight thousand feet, it punched through the bruise-colored cloud ceiling and, with steely accuracy, bore down at 120 degrees toward *Enterprise*'s starboard beam. In a split second, Benny shouted coordinates into the bullhorn. The ship jerked radically to throw off the pilot, but this time it also threw off the gunners' aim. Their tracers only glanced the attacker, and the pilot managed to release his deadly load. Seconds later, the bomb tore through the flight deck and exploded just off the stern; an earsplitting explosion of fuel tanks followed.

The rest of the planes in that wave were either shot down or they missed badly, except for one near miss that violently rocked the ship—even as repair and rescue crews raced to the initial explosion site. While they triaged among the wounded and dead and trained fire hoses on the burning flight deck, another squadron of fifteen Japanese dive bombers lowered toward *Enterprise*. This time the five-inch-gun batteries found their targets, again and again. The first shell hit an incoming plane in the engine. The bomber disintegrated eerily before Benny's eyes and then dropped silently from the sky in a series of spare parts. Thirteen more were either shot down or their aim was thrown off. But *Enterprise* was not to be spared. The last plane in the attack wave came screaming in, astern of the ship, its machine guns strafing and winking at Sky Control as it dove.

Bullets clicked and bounced off the overhang like a hailstorm. Benny ducked but managed to keep his sights on the plane and continued shouting instructions. But he knew as soon as its bomb was released from the bay that it would hit the ship. He gripped the railing and braced for impact.

Enterprise rocked and shook with repeated explosions as the bomb penetrated deep into her infrastructure.

The report came up that the bomb had exploded in the ammunition-handling room, instantly killing its entire gunnery and damage-control group. The forward aircraft elevator was on fire, too, and more than thirty officers' rooms below were destroyed.

In the brief lull that followed, Benny spotted movement in the water a few hundred yards out. Two Japanese pilots were clinging to what appeared to be an aircraft wheel and tire. Thinking they should be taken as prisoners for interrogation, Benny made the announcement over the loudspeaker. He was horrified in the next instant when all the automatic weapons on the starboard side opened up on the clinging pilots. He shouted, "Cease fire at once!" but not soon enough to save them. Burning grief and rage over lost comrades and a desire for revenge had overwhelmed the gunners, who had fired almost in unison.

Seconds later came another shock. Rountree hollered to Benny and pointed astern of the ship: *another* fifteen torpedo planes were charging at full throttle and low over the water, this time bearing down on both sides of the bow, intent on ensnaring *Enterprise* whichever way she zigzagged. The bow gunners went right to work on them, as did gunners from *Enterprise*'s screening vessels, just as the attackers opened their payloads for a devastating double-sided strike.

But at once from amidships, port, and starboard, every gunner started firing at the incoming planes. Despite the raw terror of what they'd just been through, their aim remained intact. The most remarkable strike was made by a forward port gunner. He had fixed his sights on the nose of the plane but due to a slight deflection, he hit the tail instead. The plane flipped backward into the sea as if lassoed by an ace cowboy's rope. More than half this group of planes was neutralized, but the last two managed to release their payloads, sending two more torpedoes plunging deep into the ship. Fire and rescue crews raced toward multiple sites of concussive explosions and horrific carnage.

As suddenly as it began, after sixty planes in four waves of continuous attacks, in what became known as the Battle of the Santa Cruz Islands, was over. It had lasted one hour and fifteen minutes, the longest sustained aerial attack ever on an American ship. Smoke from the fires and the reek of cordite from untold thousands of rounds of expended ammunition hung like a pall over bloodied *Enterprise*. But at least the Japanese had failed in their mission of the day; the air and seas around Guadalcanal remained under Allied control, and *Enterprise* remained afloat.

Other ships were not so lucky. Just over the horizon, fires continued to rage aboard the doomed *Hornet*. The pocked and burning deck from which Colonel Doolittle had valiantly launched his Tokyo-bound squadron of B-25s was slanting toward a certain descent to the ocean floor, three miles down. She'd been in service a year and six days, and would be at the bottom of the Pacific by the next morning.

Drained and weak from exhaustion, Benny slumped against the railing to catch his breath as wounded *Enterprise* retreated to the Allied base at Nouméa for urgent repairs. His chest tightened at the prospect of the impending sea burials, the gunners he would need to replace, the grieving mothers he would need to write.

But here again, *he* had survived. For what? His resilience now ripped away, he felt a deep and unshakeable loneliness. But then came the answer: for his daughter, Jeanne Marie, of course. It was her future he was working to protect out here, no matter what her mother did to hurt him.

WHEN FINALLY RELIEVED FROM Sky Control, Benny felt his way along dim, watery passageways to the forward handling room, in ruins from the first bomb hit. He waded on, navigating in the knee-high water by patting his hand along the passageway wall. With the aid of a flashlight, he located where his quarters had once been. Ajar from the blast, the warm

metal door creaked open. He took one tentative step inside to test the footing, and then ventured another. His old surroundings were barely recognizable; the room was a smoky tumult of wet, scorched debris.

The impact of the blast, the leakage, and the heat from the nearby fires
had each wrought damage. Benny poked around the compartment as long
as he dared, recovering only a dented box containing the remains of his
white dress hat and his Naval Academy sword, still warm from the heat of
the blast and bent in a semicircle.

It would never again be extracted from its sheath, but somehow that
didn't bother him. He fingered the scabbard's ornamental filigree, and
then tucked the ruined weapon under his arm and continued down the
dim passageway. His next stop would be the battle dressing stations and
his next task identification of his dead gunners. He paused on the hangar
deck in front of a large, defiant sign erected by crew members, still wet with
industrial-grade paint.

"Enterprise vs. Japan" was rendered in large, uneven letters. The reality
stunned: at the conclusion of the Battle of Santa Cruz, the USS *Enterprise*
was now the only operational American aircraft carrier in the hostile waters of the Pacific. One by one, every other prewar flattop had either been
lost in battle or forced to withdraw for lengthy repairs. *Lexington* had gone
down in May at the Coral Sea battle. *Yorktown* was lost at Midway less than
a month later. On the last day of August in the Eastern Solomons, *Saratoga*
had taken a second devastating torpedo hit and retired to drydock at Pearl
Harbor. *Wasp*, en route to Guadalcanal two weeks later, was fatally struck by
three torpedoes. And now *Hornet's* pyre burned over the horizon.

Over the course of 1942, *Enterprise* had been struck a total of six times
by Japanese bombs or torpedoes and had suffered hundreds of casualties.
The painted sign reflected both the grimness of the situation and the grit
of a determined crew: this sole surviving American aircraft carrier in the
seventy-million-square-mile Pacific war front was in no mood for backing
down.

15

★ ★ ★

THE OTHER WAR: ARMY-NAVY FOOTBALL

ON NOVEMBER 1, 1942, a mangled USS *Enterprise* staggered into Nouméa, New Caledonia, for repairs. Compared with other war-darkened Allied outposts in the Pacific, Admiral Halsey's Nouméa headquarters was ablaze with lights, as hordes of Seabees—the navy's skilled construction and engineering battalions—worked around the clock. With so few ships and *Enterprise* now the only functional carrier, the urgency of nighttime repair work outweighed security concerns.

The Santa Cruz attacks on *Enterprise* were the fiercest ever launched against a single vessel in the war, and the damage was extensive. The forward section of the hangar deck—from the number one aircraft elevator clear to the quarterdeck—was a grotesque collage of charred and twisted metal. The powerful blasts had also recast the hangar deck into a bizarre configuration of mountains and valleys. Every inch of it had to be cut, flattened, and rewelded.

The number one elevator shaft was so badly damaged that it was beyond repair entirely. The only positive note was that it was stuck in the upright position at the flight deck level, and so wouldn't hinder launching of aircraft. The officers' living quarters had to be pumped dry, repaired, and resealed to be usable. In the meantime, makeshift sleeping quarters were created by stringing up curtains in open areas to provide a modicum of privacy.

Seabees from the repair ship *Vestal* boarded *Enterprise* at her docking. The foreman estimated it would take three weeks to repair the damage, but Admiral Halsey made it clear that was three weeks he didn't have—they would have to get it done in ten days. For those living aboard the carrier, there was no respite from the spark and sputter of the welders' arcs.

Benny called Bill shortly after the ship arrived.

"I'm not sure if it's worse for you there," Bill said, "or me here, waiting for word—over and over again—whether you made it through! Jesus!" Bill had read the Santa Cruz dispatches about the damage *Enterprise* had sustained, and the casualty estimates. But there had been no casualty list, only word that losses to gunnery had been particularly high. He was electrified when the call came through and grateful beyond words that his brother had survived yet again.

"Listen, Bill," comforted Benny, "in the things that count, we're getting the upper hand. If they want to trade some more, well, let 'em. I think they'll find the exchange even less in their favor going forward."

"Anybody taking furloughs while they fix her up?" Bill asked. The abrupt topic shift reflected his concern about discussing too much war information over the phone lines. Nouméa was a free French island and friendly port, but it was known to have its Axis sympathizers. From half a world away, he couldn't be sure that Benny was safe from determined eavesdroppers. But the subject change was not unwelcome.

He could hear the wistfulness in Benny's voice. "My God, wouldn't I love that! I'd hoped to get out of the trenches for the holidays, but it's not looking that way now. You'll have to have a few good eggnogs for me, I guess."

"You do know the big game is on, don't you?" said Bill. "It'll be different this year, of course, but wish we could go together like the old days."

"Are you actually *going*?" Benny asked in a raised voice tinged with envy. "Are you going to the army-navy game?" he repeated, now hollering into the phone. Last Benny had heard, Congress was pushing for the game's cancellation. "Well, I'll be there in spirit, you can count on that—wish I could lend you my topside megaphone!"

The rest of the conversation centered on the game's executive level rescue, relocation, and various other war-related adjustments—and, lastly the odds, a ritual the brothers had held dear for years. The distance between them closed with time-honored bets on score spreads and game stars before they reluctantly said their good-byes.

With the tireless vigilance of a surgical team bent over a life-support patient, the Seabees labored day and night so *Enterprise* could return to the urgent contest for Guadalcanal. Tipped off by coastwatchers and confirmed by scout planes, Halsey knew the Japanese were returning with an armada to strengthen their garrison and regain control of Henderson Field.

Enterprise had scarcely arrived at Nouméa before being ordered out again, taking the hard-working Seabees and their thrumming pneumatic drills with her. *Enterprise* hastened out of Nouméa on November 11 and made straight for the treacherous waters off Guadalcanal. From November 13 to 15, the solitary carrier and her escorts resumed their offense—an increasingly dangerous mission as fewer and fewer screening vessels were available to provide cover. At least eighteen American warships had already gone down off Guadalcanal, giving Savo Sound at the island's southern end its nickname "Ironbottom Sound." Japanese ship losses were even more numerous.

Finally, on November 15, Halsey received word that the Japanese Fleet was retreating to the north. Given the rapid attrition of its ships, planes, and pilots, it appeared—at least for the time being—that the enemy had quit the scrum for Guadalcanal and Henderson Field.

There was a collective sigh of relief among a mourning *Enterprise* crew. Several more screening vessels had gone down protecting her this time and taken scores of good friends with them, compounding the crew's battle distress. Every officer, pilot, and sailor aboard needed a respite from months of near-constant battle.

Admiral Halsey ordered the ship and a grateful crew back to Nouméa. *Enterprise* had survived multiple attacks over the past two months, and the Seabees needed to complete urgent repairs from the devastating Santa Cruz strikes. This time the ship would be there for weeks of sorely needed overhaul—and rest for her crew.

IN MID-NOVEMBER THE MAP Room teletype barely rested as it spit out obituary after obituary of sunken American ships in Savo Sound. On edge, Bill watched and waited. When confirmation came through on November 15 that the enemy was in retreat and Guadalcanal was secured, cheers went up. With this, Bill's relentless anxiety over Benny's safety got a temporary reprieve. He also had a cautious sense that better intelligence about Barton might be coming through soon. For the first time since the fall of Bataan and Corregidor, intercepted messages from unsurrendered individuals in the Philippines were providing concrete intelligence. Station KFS, a powerful commercial San Francisco station that also furnished relay services for the military, was now forwarding them to Washington with some regularity.

The senders were scattered Filipino guerrillas using contraband radios. Several had managed shortwave contact with MacArthur's headquarters in Australia as well. The messages were clear: "We are resisting the Japanese. Can you hear us? Can you help us?"

Equally intriguing was the startling news about one naval reserve officer, Lieutenant Charles "Chick" Parsons, who cloaked his American naval identity after Manila fell by assuming the guise of his onetime role as Pana-manian consul. After persuading the Japanese of his diplomatic status, he secured passage out of Manila.

When he showed up unannounced at Naval Intelligence in Washing-ton, Parsons caused quite a stir. Not only had he eluded capture, he had secreted out with him high-value intelligence on everything from the state of the burgeoning guerrilla movement to the treatment, status, and location of Allied prisoners of war. Parsons's escape, attendant story, and detailed documentation of activity behind enemy lines had jaws dropping all over Washington.

Lieutenant Parsons confirmed that the intercepts picked up in Austra-lia and by station KFS were not Japanese feints; they were from guerrilla bands cropping up all across the islands. But he had more. From the shad-ows of occupied Manila, he had taken dozens of pages of detailed notes on the occupiers' cruel crackdown. Before he and his family gained passage out of Manila on a Red Cross ship, he had fully chronicled meticulous details on the new puppet government, food supplies, enemy troop strength, tor-turous interrogations by Japan's ruthless Kempeitai, guerrilla espionage po-tential, and the condition and movement of prisoners of war. He presented a fifty-one-page document complete with underground contact names and places and other crucial intelligence. Navy officials were stunned.

Built like a boxer, Parsons was five feet seven inches and tanned to a deep umber. He could easily pose as Filipino on one mission and a Pana-manian on the next. The Tennessee native spoke English without a drawl, Spanish like a native, and numerous Tagalog dialects without a trace of an accent. And from his years of running a Manila stevedoring business and marriage into a well-respected Filipino family, he knew the islands cold.

During his Washington debriefings, Parsons volunteered to return to the Philippine war zone. His potential for high-value intelligence gather-ing and bolstering the developing resistance movement were considerable. Parsons ticked off a list of what he could accomplish: evaluate guerrilla assets such as leadership, armaments, and personnel; set up intelligence networks; and establish additional coast-watcher stations, which would be positioned on key islands so as to track enemy shipping and monitor war prisoners' movements. He could also smuggle in personnel and supplies and generally advise Filipino citizens on best methods for resisting their occupiers. Parsons wasn't offering to undertake the high-risk mission for just the navy's or even the Allies' sake—he had powerful personal motives as well. He had left behind an extended family, a thriving business, and his entire life savings.

But since the lieutenant was navy and the Philippines war zone was now under General MacArthur's control, returning Parsons to Manila under US Navy auspices could be complicated. As it turned out, however, MacArthur's attitude toward Parsons would be different, despite his usual antipathy toward anything concerning the "damn navy." Some interservice bartering—instead of bickering, for a change—would be in order.

The navy proposed to MacArthur that Chick Parsons go to Brisbane under the tutelage of Captain Arthur "Mac" McCollum USN, the Seventh Fleet's intelligence officer. The officials bristled at the Seventh Fleet's new nickname, "MacArthur's Navy," due to its anchorage within SWPA, but with respect to Parsons, it served their purposes perfectly.

It was no secret that MacArthur craved control over the widening Pacific War, particularly with respect to the Philippines—the command he had lost under humiliating circumstances. Getting the general's headquarters to forward their guerrilla-derived intelligence to anyone in Washington had been nearly as difficult as getting the guerrilla transmissions past the Japanese.

This was because the Office of Strategic Services (OSS), the powerful, Washington-based secret intelligence agency, was operating in every Allied theater of war except SWPA. MacArthur had firmly and repeatedly declined OSS assistance; instead, he elected to use the services of Australia's Allied Intelligence Bureau (AIB), which was now under his full control.

Underlying this choice was that MacArthur did not want any of his GHQ (General Headquarters) functions brought under the War Department's or any other Washington-based agency's purview. OSS director William "Wild Bill" Donovan expressed concerns about the depth and quality of AIB, yet his offers to send experienced field agents to MacArthur were all in vain.

But Parsons was different. He wasn't a Washington insider or even a navy insider. A longtime expat, Parsons had married a Filipino woman, started a family, and had managed and grown a thriving Manila business for more than a decade.

In fact, Parsons's naval career began only when he was awakened on December 8, 1941, and told that his entire Luzon Stevedoring Company—personnel, equipment, and ships—had been taken over by the US Navy. Admiral Hart swore him in the same day. Freshly minted lieutenant Charles Parsons, USNR, was as unsullied a naval officer as a navy-hating army general would ever find. MacArthur, it turned out, was interested.

In late November 1942 the navy's proposal to send Parsons to Brisbane under the tutelage of Captain McCollum and the Seventh Fleet received an affirmative response from MacArthur. "Send Parsons," wrote the general himself, with uncharacteristic brevity.

ENCOURAGED BY NOVEMBER'S DEVELOPMENTS, Bill took a rare Saturday off for a beloved cause: the army-navy football game. Though the Cabinet and Congress had both debated cancelling the time-honored match to conserve rubber and gasoline for the war, Bill's navy-football-loving boss FDR ended the debate by personally ordering that the game be played.

Annapolis coach John "Billick" Whelchel and assistant coach Edgar "Rip" Miller generously credited Bill Mott with nudging the decision, but he insisted their gratitude was undeserved. While Bill had weighed in enthusiastically during the official bickering, the leader of the free world had already made up his mind. The army-navy gridiron face-off was key to morale at both academies, Roosevelt declared, and good for the country, too. Game on.

The game was relocated from Philadelphia's traditionally neutral ground to Thompson Stadium at Annapolis, and wartime travel restrictions would limit attendance to mostly local spectators. How Bill Mott got around the ten-mile radius restriction may never be known, but exceptions were in fact made. He might have happily volunteered to chauffeur one or more Washington-based sweethearts of fourth-year middies—all of whom were allowed to attend.

Since West Point's Corps of Cadets, Army's traditional cheering section, was not allowed to make the trip, another novel accommodation was made. The Academy's third- and fourth-year midshipmen were ordered to sit behind the Army bench and cheer for the visiting team. The 1942 match grew more unique by the hour.

Newsmen in attendance wrote enthusiastically about Army's Navy-populated cheering section. Midshipmen braying the Corps cheer was living proof of interservice comity, they reported. Even the touchdown-starved Army players expressed their gratitude to the cheerleaders, despite their 14–0 loss in a match they had been heavily favored to win. The 1942 game would be Navy's fourth consecutive victory over West Point.

Game attendance may have been a tenth the size of the usual hundred thousand Philadelphia sellout, but President Roosevelt had correctly gauged the broad national interest in the match. An unprecedented forty million Americans tuned in to the live radio broadcast. The defiant, patriotic fervor at Thompson Stadium compensated for the reduced spectator size. From the emotional opening remarks to the extra staccato in the last stanza of the Annapolis school song, "Navy Blue and Gold," fans wept, cheered, and sang themselves hoarse on their country's behalf.

Bill always belted out his alma mater anthem with gusto, and always off key. It was impossible not to recall doing the same with Benny and Barton at his side in 1937, the last time all three Jersey brothers attended the match. Today, Bill surely sang it for them instead of with them.

Rip Miller wrote Bill after the game, thanking him for his "splendid work in keeping the navy football team before 'the big head coach.' I don't know where we could do any better for our cause here than what you have made possible for us."

Bill continued to refuse credit, but he was so pleased by the overall turn of events that he started advancing the idea of sending the game reels to Admiral Halsey's men in the Pacific. As it happened, the garrulous Admiral William "Windy" Calhoun, commander of the Service Force of the Pacific Fleet, was in town to meet with officials from the White House, State Department, and War Department in the days following the game. Bill was assigned as his escort.

During their banter to and from the meetings, Bill mentioned that he had seen the army-navy game films and casually suggested sending them out to the Pacific. Calhoun's eyes widened. "Terrific idea, Commander! Great for morale!" He clapped Bill on the shoulder and asked for copies of the reels to take back to Pearl Harbor with him. Bill savored the prospect of telling Benny he'd had a hand in dispatching the films to the war front, particularly given Navy's shutout victory.

16

★　★　★

HAPPY DAYS AT THE
PENAL COLONY

WHEN THE PRISONERS AWOKE to their new home at Davao Penal Colony in November 1942, there was universal agreement: the move had been an open-and-shut case of divine intervention. Housing and sanitation were a dramatic improvement over Cabanatuan, and the rations, while still spare, were double the size. They knew the purpose of the latter was to strengthen them for heavy farm labor—logging, sawmill operation, field and railroad work—but the quantity and quality of the food was measurably better than at any previous Japanese accommodation. With the addition of vegetables purloined on farmwork details, Barton, Charles, and the other ensigns began to regain weight and strength.

Still, Davao was a prison camp. Scurvy was rampant, and the men despaired at the sight of wild citrus rotting beyond their reach or being devoured by bands of plump parrots. And there were trillions of disease-carrying mosquitoes that bred in the swamps of the surrounding rain forest.

Dark, whining clouds of them feasted on the prisoners as they toiled in the fields, and cases of malaria skyrocketed.

On the other hand, prisoner details were lightly guarded, a marked shift from the oppressive oversight at Cabanatuan. Major Maeda believed that heavy guarding at Davao was unnecessary because it was surrounded by impenetrable, alligator-ridden jungle, not to mention by roving bands of Moros, Mindanao's reclusive but fierce Muslim tribe, widely feared for their head-hunting practices. Another surprising bright spot at DAPECOL was its corps of Filipino convicts. When Barton's draft arrived, 80 percent of the camp's existing inmates were convicted murderers serving life sentences. These men understood all aspects of the farm operations better than the guards or camp administrators, and they were ordered to train the Caba-natuan newcomers.

The cutthroats, who dubbed the new arrivals "gentlemen prisoners," promptly got to work instructing them on the primitive sugar and sawmill operations and the dangerous business of bringing down massive mahog-any trees and processing the lumber. They also taught them how to harness caribou and Brahman steer and guide them to the fields. The convicts were friendly, helpful, and seemingly pro-American. The POWs were uniformly sorry when these kindly mentors were rotated out of DAPECOL for lack of space.

BARTON, CHARLES, AND ANOTHER Cabanatuan colleague, Ken Wheeler, made several new friends at Davao—mostly young naval ensigns like themselves. They spent nearly all their time together as their Davao overseers also quartered prisoners by service and rank and usually applied the same groupings to work details.

Together these friends shared the smallest of pleasures: a contraband banana, a fistful of coffee beans, a captured lizard—executed, cooked, and cut up—or a tin of canned fish extracted at a dear price from the camp's black market. Even seeds from a withering tobacco plant discovered on a work detail were a source of shared entertainment. They planted the seeds underneath their barracks, and the yield of bitter green leaves was "cured" on short poles. The greatly anticipated first smoke from the pathetic harvest became a deep and happy memory.

Decision-making also became unusually communal. When the prisoners learned that they would be allowed to write one postcard (of no more than fifty words), they debated at length who they would write (parents? wife/girlfriend?) and shared many a joke about the disfavor they would earn from those not selected. But despite generous advice, Barton stuck with his first choice. Even as a prisoner of war on the other side of the world, he had no appetite for the imagined rebuke; he knew he must write his mother.

"Am hoping the time draws near when we may see each other again," he wrote, somewhat stiffly. "Think of you all constantly, and also of William's many accomplishments in the culinary department."

On some level, Barton knew this bit of humor would telegraph that, despite his unfortunate circumstances, he was intact mentally. He was prohibited from disclosing where he was, what had happened to him, and very nearly anything else of a personal nature. Beneath the section of the card marked "Health," he underlined "fair" (versus "good" or "under treatment").

This was likely due to the recurring infection of his shrapnel wound, thanks to its daily exposure to mud and muck on the rice detail. He and Ken Wheeler had also contracted vicious cases of malaria. It made them shaky and weak, but the malady was so commonplace it was not sufficient to excuse them from the fieldwork. Every hand was needed during peak rice planting season.

Each rectangular paddy measured thirty-five by forty yards. A rope with knots spaced at six-inch intervals was laid across the short end of each tract, and a planting team of twenty-eight prisoners was then distributed along the rope. Standing midhip in mud with the rope in front of them, each prisoner took six seeds from his satchel and plunged them deep into the mud, bare-handed. They then stepped back a precise eight inches and repeated the process. So when the opportunity to switch to the carpentry detail "to build a new prisoner barracks" arose, Ken and Barton—despite some uneasiness that they would instead be assigned to rumored local Japanese airfield construction—were among the first to volunteer.

To qualify, they were marched to the DAPECOL carpentry shop and quizzed on the identity and use of such tools as saws, hammers, and planes. A chorus of wisecracks followed Barton's proud performance on the carpentry exam. "Who knew I had this aptitude?" he joked. He and Ken bonded all the more on their new detail. The work was hard, but it was on dry ground, in the shade, and infinitely more interesting than planting rice. And they did indeed build a new barrack, as well as a new prisoner galley— the men took great satisfaction in the finished products. Their next work detail was even better.

An interpreter came into their barracks one evening and asked for "four navy men" to run a boat. After a hurried conference, Ken, Barton, and two more senior officers stepped forward. The four happy sailors were taken via hand-cranked cart over the prison's narrow-gauge railroad to a place called Anebogan, on the Tuganay River. The very smell of the water excited them, and they eagerly scanned the dock area for their new vessel. When Ken spied the dangerously listing diesel tug, he quietly scaled back his dream of engineering a possible escape. The rusted, leaky hauler would not be capable of making an open-sea trip.

Still, working on a boat was infinitely better duty than toiling in the rice fields or in a wood shop. The men were first charged with repairing the tug, and then towing supply barges from Davao City upriver to the prison camp and small Japanese outposts along the way. They got right to work. Because the boat had B. P. stamped on the bow—for Bureau of Prisons— they cheerfully nicknamed their new command "Bo Peep."

After days of patching, caulking, and engine tinkering—and prodigious use of the kind of language that gives "sailor mouth" its name—they coaxed a belch of black smoke from the tug's engine and it sputtered to life. They then nosed *Bo Peep* into the Tuganay River under the careful scrutiny of four guards—one per man. The sailors divided their shipborne duties quite professionally and were pleased to find they had largely retained vital seafaring skills—including how to bail bilges, which they did frequently, even after plugging a number of newly discovered leaks with flattened tin cans.

The break from tedious prison routine was a true pleasure, and it felt good to be on the water again. The river breeze offered reprieve from DAPECOL's mosquito swarms, and the guards had brought along more and better food than they'd received inside the camp. There was also unexpected entertainment along the way: the jungle-lined shores were a *National Geographic*–worthy movie reel of iguanas, frolicking monkeys, and baboons by the hundreds. A veritable orchestra of animal and bird sounds filled the air—as surely a salve for the prisoner soul as the water itself.

When *Bo Beep* approached the mouth of the river and egress to open sea, the guards became especially attentive to their charges. There were ample disincentives for escape: heavily armed guards, a vessel that was hardly seaworthy, and head-hunting aboriginal tribes in the jungle. But if *Bo Peep*'s crew had known what lay ahead for them, might they have attempted escape anyway?

IN DECEMBER 1942, DAPECOL was full of anticipation. To the prisoners' universal surprise and pleasure, they were notified that they would be allowed to hold a Christmas service. Every man who was able took part. The preparation was earnest and intense, and the result was a rare and emotional evening that brought together the prisoners, local Filipinos, and even the camp's Japanese overseers.

The service was scheduled for seven o'clock on Christmas Eve and was held in the camp mess hall-turned-chapel. A light rain fell that afternoon, but it did little to dampen local spirits. The room filled to capacity quickly—and while the prisoners were carefully sequestered from the local Filipinos, smiles and eye contact between them reflected a tacit solidarity.

Lieutenant Yuki, a Christian camp official, served as interpreter and master of ceremonies. Barton's a cappella group was the first to perform, and the crowd hushed as the forty-strong choir assembled. Barton stood proudly in the front row, not only because of his size but also because of his role as lead tenor. It was a fleeting moment of pure joy, doing what he loved and did well before a very special group of friends.

He and the two other ensemble leaders then issued a synchronized hum in middle C. The chorus followed in unison, during which the hall went completely silent. Only the evening sounds of the rain forest could be heard in that brief lull before the group burst into "O Holy Night."

By the last stanza, Barton and the rest of the singers had tears in their eyes, and most in the audience were openly weeping. But then the pace picked up, and laughter replaced tears as the chorus broke into Hoagy Carmichael's popular tune "Stardust." The crowd chimed right in, alternately clapping and humming along. The refrain was bittersweet:

> Sometimes I wonder why I spend
> The lonely nights
> Dreaming of a song
> The melody haunts my reverie
> And I am once again with you.
> When our love was new and each kiss an inspiration
> But that was long ago, and now my consolation
> Is in the stardust of a song.

On cue several members of the chorus then paired off and gave brief but hilarious demonstrations of the jitterbug, rumba, and tap dance as the singing continued. The crowd clapped with delight. The hours of rehearsal were evident as bass, tenor, and alto sections harmonized perfectly. At the closing note, the crowd jumped to its feet, wild with whistles and applause.

The choristers joined hands and took a deep bow. This wasn't the *Radio City Christmas Spectacular* in which Barton had once fantasized taking part. But if one measure of success in life is a moment of contentment derived from deep fellowship and hard work, the evening's performance easily surpassed that dream.

A group of local Filipinos took the stage next. They performed a series of traditional island dances and sang native folk songs. The prisoners whooped and hollered in approval. Then, to the surprise of all present, an ensemble of Japanese soldiers rose and crooned a series of classic Oriental tunes followed by an elaborate sword dance demonstration. Next up was another group of Americans who performed Indian sun dances of the Iroquois, Sioux, Navajo, and Pueblo Indians—thanks to generous prisoner representation from Texas and Oklahoma.

Cigarettes and small gifts were passed around at the end of the revue, and the hall was alive with conversation, laughter, and general goodwill. While the stage was converted to an altar for the service that would follow, the Americans and Filipinos mingled, speaking in English, an unusual opportunity that was not interrupted by Major Maeda. For the duration of the evening, in fact, the differences between foe and friend were put aside.

After the break, the audience returned to their seats for the Christmas service. A manger and crude but recognizable nativity scene—created by children in Davao City—now adorned the brightly lit stage. A small group of Catholic and Protestant chaplains officiated together. They opened the service by thanking Major Maeda for allowing the important Christmas observation, and also Lieutenant Yuki for serving as translator and master of ceremonies.

A simple but deeply moving homily followed readings from the New Testament and a few liturgical prayers.

"Tonight we celebrate the birth of Jesus in a place far from home, far from your loved ones, mothers, fathers, brothers, sisters, wives, and children. We celebrate tonight in an entirely different way from your various traditions. Whether you are from the North, South, East, or West, you miss such familiar scenes—for me it is snow and the sound of bells . . . But let me lead you for a moment away from those cares and toward a place called Bethlehem. There a child was born this very night that we may forget our earthly sufferings."

Communion, the last rite of the service, was taken simply and silently by nearly all attendees, no matter their denomination. The majority of prisoners had experienced some form of spiritual awakening during their incarceration, and the Christmas service carried unusual significance as a result. Many tried unsuccessfully not to cry. Barton surely understood this—his own unbidden religious renewal had sustained him, from Christ School on, in ways he could not have imagined at the time.

As the prisoners filed out of the building and moved toward their barracks, guards were already posted with fixed bayonets; camp life had quickly returned to normal. Barton and a gaggle of choristers sang rounds of "Oh Christmas Tree" while they walked, as if in mock challenge to the alien surrounds of mahogany and palm trees.

Their upbeat chorus likely drowned out a quiet exchange between two marine lieutenants, also heading toward the barracks. Trailing the others, they talked intently and in low voices all the way. The gist from one of them, a Texan, was that this was going to be the last damn Christmas he planned to spend as a prisoner of war—a resolution that would have a far-reaching impact on his fellow residents at Davao Penal Colony.

PART

TWO

17

★ ★ ★

WINTER'S GRIEF

CHRISTMAS OF 1942 AT Lilac Hedges came and went, slowly and painfully. Helen confided to her diary: "A different Christmas this year. A tiny tree, subdued decorations, no Barton. We all tried to be cheery as he'd like to think us."

Even Bill's letter confirming that Barton's name remained absent from the most recent casualty lists was only enough, she wrote, "to keep dinner from sticking in our throats on Christmas Day."

The dining room at Lilac Hedges had long since become its own well-appointed Map Room. The mahogany table was covered with Pacific maps, maps of the world, and maps of the Philippines, all variously marked up. International Red Cross reports and Bataan Relief Organization newsletters littered the floor, and several colored pencils, a ruler, and a magnifying glass could reliably be found on one or another of the dining chairs. Locations in the South Pacific were circled or had notations or question marks beside them, and pads of paper with daily notes were permanent fixtures alongside the sterling tea service, long in disuse.

After Christmas dinner, Helen wasted no time reverting the dining table—which had been cleared for the first time in a year—to Map Room status. It had become all important for her to walk into the room at any hour, pore over her maps, or look down at the red circle around the Philippines and "visit."

On the day after Christmas, she was off to participate in another such ritual, this one at the local chapter of the American Red Cross. Here mothers, wives, daughters, and sisters donned aprons and gloves and lined up at a conveyer belt to pack boxes for prisoners of war in the Pacific. Before turning off her bedside lamp that night, long after Arthur had nodded off, Helen picked up her diary and pen.

Packed boxes for prisoners all afternoon at the Red Cross. Seven thousand of them rolled by me on the conveyor belt and who knows? One may be going to Barton! I found myself caressing the contents before packing them in, as though sending my love and prayers along with the food stuffs. God be with him!

IN WASHINGTON, TOO, CHRISTMAS of 1942 was barely a footnote as war operations ground on. The new year, 1943, dawned icy, cold, and gray, but the frigid weather didn't delay the January opening of the massive new War Department headquarters in Arlington, Virginia. Dubbed "the Pentagon" for its five-sided shape, the building was ready for occupation after only sixteen months of construction—right on schedule. In addition to their other duties, Bill Mott and his Map Room staff now had to retool a number of procedures to adapt to the daunting relocation of the army and the navy, soon to be across the river instead of a short walk down Constitution Avenue.

In early January, they were also busy coordinating the president's imminent and very secret meeting with Prime Minister Churchill in Casablanca, Morocco. Preparations included the assembly of dozens of briefing binders as well as the execution of an elaborate series of ruses to preserve the secrecy of the meeting location. They also needed to fabricate a foolproof story on FDR's whereabouts during his White House absence.

At midnight on January 9, Bill allowed a sigh of relief as President Roosevelt, Harry Hopkins, Captain McCrea, Admiral McIntyre (as FDR's physician), and the rest of the covert entourage finally departed the Executive Mansion for the first leg of the seventeen-thousand-mile journey to Morocco. Bill was exhausted, and looked forward to a respite from the frantic activity of the past several days.

But on the evening of January 12, the Map Room telephone shattered the relative calm of the previous seventy-two hours. Bill answered it on the first ring, his custom, and stiffened when he heard the voice on the other end of the line. The caller was Lieutenant Commander Randall Jacobs, head of the Navy Casualty Section. Bill braced for what surely was news of one of his brothers. Why else the unusual late-night call?

He was uncharacteristically quiet for nearly the entire call. "Good God," he said finally. Then, "Yes, I see, yes, all right . . . Of course . . . Right away," and replaced the heavy black receiver.

A flurry of press calls followed on the same subject; they were on deadline and pushing for details. The horrific story took Bill some minutes to absorb, and his own anxieties on behalf of his family suddenly paled in comparison. He simply couldn't imagine his own mother absorbing such news.

Bill handled each media inquiry deftly, with promise after promise of a return call. But first things first. He sat down at the typewriter to compose a memorandum for Captain McCrea and the president for immediate dispatch to Casablanca:

The White House

Washington

January 12, 1943

Memorandum for: the President and Captain McCrea

Lieutenant Commander Jacobs from the Casualty Section of
the Bureau of Naval Personnel has just called to say he is
preparing a letter for the President's signature regarding
the death of five brothers, the Sullivan boys, in the
sinking of the light cruiser Juneau off Guadalcanal.

These boys were the sons of Mr. and Mrs. Thomas F.
Sullivan, 98 Adams Street, Waterloo, Iowa. They enlisted
in January 1942 contingent on the Navy's promise that they
could serve together. Every effort was made to dissuade
them from this course both at the time of their enlistment
and after they joined the Fleet. However these efforts were
of no avail and they all went down with their ship. Only
one of these boys was married. His wife is Mrs. Albert Leo
Sullivan, 2228 Hawthorn Street, Waterloo, Iowa.

The parents were notified today by the Lieutenant
Commander [Truman Jones] in charge of the Navy Recruiting
Station at Des Moines, Iowa. The press is anxious for a
story on this, but the Department is reluctant to give
any details, such as the name of the ship, because of the
significant publicity on these five brothers when they
first enlisted together. The thinking is that a letter from
the President would make good copy and they are anxious to
get one signed as soon as possible.

I have told them nothing, of course, about the

President's whereabouts, but will forward their proposed
letter to you by the next pouch.

You may recall that President Lincoln once had to write
the same kind of letter and did such a good job of it that
all students of composition have been using the same as a
model ever since.

                                        Very Respectfully,
                                        W. C. Mott

The Sullivan brothers' ship, USS *Juneau*, had been one of *Enterprise*'s
protective screening vessels in the deadly seas around Guadalcanal. Bill
couldn't help but feel this one a little deeper in the gut. He sat back to review the memorandum, but his mind was still on the conversation with
Commander Jacobs.

Jacobs told Bill that when Lieutenant Commander Jones and two other
officers approached the Sullivans' front door in Waterloo, Iowa, the boys'
father, Thomas Sullivan, greeted them.

"I have some news for you about your boys, sir," Jones had said.

"Which one?" asked Thomas.

"I'm sorry, sir," Jones replied. "All five."

18

★ ★ ★

ESCAPE: CRIME AND PUNISHMENT

BY PRISON CAMP STANDARDS, the Christmas festivities had been a high-water mark, but the best day at DAPECOL came a few weeks later, in January 1943. The men were already buoyed by news relayed by a friendly Filipino working near the camp: the American Navy had held in the long struggle for Guadalcanal, meaning Australia was safe and that the sea-lanes between it and the United States were protected. The good news was confirmed by broadcasts over a contraband shortwave radio occasionally tinkered to life by one fearless inmate.

Moods swung higher still when word circulated that the International Red Cross had shipped gift boxes to the DAPECOL prisoners via the *Gripsholm*, a Swedish goodwill vessel. The boxes had arrived at Davao City! It was their first official acknowledgment that the Allied world knew where they were, knew they were in need, and that they cared. The effect on prisoner morale was profound.

On January 12, 1943, Barton, Ken Wheeler, and *Bo Peep* commander

Alan McCracken made their way to Anebogan with two Filipinos and three Japanese guards. Full of anticipation, they boarded *Bo Peep* and set a down-river course to *Gripsholm*'s anchorage.

Bo Peep's ad hoc crew were the first Americans to see the huge stacks of lovingly packed boxes, each stamped with the reassuring and familiar Red Cross insignia. It took hours to transfer the precious cargo from *Gripsholm* to the waiting barge, but it was more thrill than labor.

The smiling *Bo Peep* crew navigated the tug upriver, blowing smoke rings from the Lucky Strikes their guards had filched out of a box and mag-nanimously shared. They were in a fine mood that afternoon, and not only because of the Red Cross boxes; *Gripsholm* had also off-loaded several sack-fuls of mail—the first word from home since their capture.

Assembly of the Red Cross boxes had been a true Allied effort. They were filled by volunteers in Canada, South Africa, Britain, and the United States. Inside each box was a variety of precious goods: evaporated milk, hardtack and cheese, vitamin pills, soap, shoe polish, a container of cocoa, cans of corned beef and pilchards, chocolate bars, sugar, orange concen-trate, instant coffee, dried soups, pudding and tea (British), and Roy and Lucky Strike cigarettes (American). The boxes were uniform in size, and each weighed eleven pounds. The prisoners all got a good laugh out of the shoe polish; few of them still had shoes. Their primary foot protection at this point consisted of crude wooden slats called "go-aheads," which they strapped to their feet. But the very sight and smell of familiar American goods made their eyes well up.

Agony replaced delicious anticipation as neither the boxes nor the mail was distributed on arrival at DAPECOL. A Japanese Special Service Unit intercepted the treasure-laden trucks as they rumbled through the camp gates. The unit's purpose was to "inspect" the shipment and "censor" the mail. The men on the truck detail, including Charles Armour, were ordered back to the barracks empty-handed. Charles quickly reverted to his grumpy self, theorizing that "the goddamn Nips" were sore about the war news and jealous over the contents of the boxes.

Several anxious days later, two boxes were finally distributed to each prisoner. Though they had been rifled through and some original contents were missing, the men were thrilled nonetheless. Impromptu trading posts popped up in every barrack as the men swapped for favorite items. Medicines, sugar, and many of the coveted cigarettes had been lifted by the Japanese, but the remaining Red Cross box contents nourished body and soul and undoubtedly saved lives.

It took days longer for the Japanese to "sort" the equally priceless mail. The men knew it had arrived, and the wait seemed interminable. Finally, one by one, names on the envelopes were read aloud and the mail distributed. Several of Barton's barrack mates received two and three pieces of mail in that shipment; they wept as they read and reread the reassuring missives from mothers, fathers, wives, and girlfriends. Barton agonized over who his mail might be from. Had the lovely Eve—that distant erotic memory from his visit to Pearl Harbor—cared enough to inquire how to write him? He hoped they wouldn't *all* be from his family, though he could hardly wait for word from them. Rosemary? Bill? Benny?

But Barton received no mail in the January 1943 shipment of ten thousand letters to Davao, nor any in the next shipment two months later. By that time, some of his colleagues' letters numbered a half dozen or more. Did everyone think he was dead? he wondered. Had they simply given up? He tried to make light of it and joke about it, as he had with so many other adversities he'd endured over time. But this hurt Barton more than all the privations and insults in his long, dark months of incarceration, and it was obvious to his close friends.

Charles made every effort to convince him that it was the goddamn Nips' fault. Those letters were out there for him—*somewhere*—his friends insisted, and they went to great lengths to take Barton's mind off his pain just as he had done for them so many times. But whatever the cause, the inexplicable silence from home caused a sharp prick of sadness in Barton, and a tinge of resentment, too. The next precious card the guards allowed him to write went not to his mother or father but to a Chapel Hill classmate, whose postal address, remarkably, he still remembered. Let his parents hear of him from that, he thought.

ON THE EVENING OF April 3, 1943, Major Maeda arranged for movie night at Davao. That night's feature was a Japanese propaganda film on the bombing of Pearl Harbor. Over the past few months, Maeda had grown anxious that the prisoners might become troublesome if they learned the details of steady American gains against the Japanese at sea. He was also nervous about the strengthening guerrilla presence in the jungles around the penal colony. Lightning-quick hit-and-run raids on local roads had resulted in the gruesome slaughter of a number of Japanese soldiers.

Some guerrillas had been apprehended and punished brutally, but many more had notched deadly blows against the occupiers. Maeda knew that the local guerrilla movement—with both American and Filipino elements—had grown in strength and size and that they were in contact with distant Allied commands. Weeks earlier, Japanese planes had dropped pamphlets over Mindanao, warning of mortal consequences for collusion with the guerrillas.

Central to Maeda's concern was that Mindanao was the closest Philippine island to Australia—an obvious first step in any Allied move to retake the Philippines. In view of the looming threat, anything the major could do to dampen prisoner morale—reduce rations, impose longer and harder work details, or feature a movie on the decimation of Pearl Harbor—was a worthy countermeasure.

The men sat quietly through the pummeling of the USS *Arizona*, understanding well the wisdom of not provoking their captors with sneers or catcalls. Still, as they watched the guards struggle with changing the reels on the projector, Barton couldn't resist whispering a mock dare to Charles (now widely known as "Ensign Goddamn"): "Okay, who wants to ask if we can watch the bombing of Tokyo next?"

Despite Major Maeda's concerted efforts to the contrary, camp morale *had* improved. Enough war news had leaked through to boost prisoner confidence that chances for their eventual rescue were improving, if they could just keep themselves alive. The evening's film feature had a particularly galvanizing effect on one small contingent in the audience. These men were poised for a long-planned escape—scheduled for the very next day.

THE MORNING OF APRIL 4, 1943, began as most Sundays did at Davao: stifling, dreary, and overcast. Reveille pierced the air, but since it was Sunday, only a few voluntary work details were scheduled to go out. Sometimes prisoners signed up for these out of boredom; others went hoping to score an extra piece of fruit or a few husks of rice. Beneath their mosquito nets, Barton and Charles took little notice as two of their barrack mates roused for Sunday detail. They likely gave no thought as to whether either might be a member of his shooting squad.

Ten Americans—eight officers and two enlisted men from all three services—lined up at the camp gate, initially in separate groups. They were heading out on routine details: a few to build a rain shelter; others to feed and water the animals used to haul a bull cart that carried tools and supplies around the colony. In plain view of sentries toting machine guns, the men walked calmly out the gate and down the road as though it were just another workday.

Once out of sight of the sentries, they left the road and crept noiselessly through tall cogon grass toward a prearranged rendezvous point; there they recovered hidden supplies and met their guides, two Filipino convicts who had left the prison camp on a separate work detail. The DAPECOL system of rotating guards to work details rather than assigning all-day overseers to each group was critical to the plan's success. The expanded escape party then proceeded into the rain forest, unobserved, and began their dash to freedom.

The escape had been planned for months, each element precisely thought out. The jungle-wise and more savvy Filipino convicts were recruited to guide them through thick and dangerous forest and swampland. Supplies needed to survive outside of camp were gradually stockpiled at a secret location over a period of several weeks. The choice of a Sunday, in hopes they wouldn't be missed until they did not return at the end of the day, would give them a full day's lead over certain pursuers.

In fact, it was not until evening *tenko* that the numbers failed to add up. "*Ichi, ni, san, shi . . .*" At first, the Japanese thought they had miscounted and ordered the some two thousand prisoners to stand for a second, hours-long count. When it, too, came up short, but by a different number, Major Maeda flew into a rage and ordered a third, fourth, and fifth tally, each with varying results but all still short of the previous evening's count. It was after midnight by the time the ten missing men were identified. Mr. Shusuke Wada, the perpetually angry hunchback interpreter, reminded the prisoners of the shooting squad rule with a sneer. "For every man who escape, nine die!"

Search parties were immediately dispatched with orders to shoot on sight. Fearing a mass prison break coordinated with a guerrilla attack on the compound, Maeda also placed guards in each barrack and set up a perimeter defense around the camp. The men from barracks five through eight, where the ten escapees had variously lived, were particularly fearful of the ten-for-one death-sentence trigger. Which would it be? Shot? Bayoneted? Beheaded?

Every occupant of those four barracks was taken to Japanese headquarters for questioning. While the men waited their turn, arguments over prisoner escapes were renewed. Some spat curses, while others reminded the group that they were duty-bound by military doctrine to attempt escape if captured. "Even if we're held by fucking barbarians who ignore the Geneva Convention?" came a bitter response. "To hell with your goddamn doctrine. It's no good to me dead."

From that day forward, nothing was the same at Davao Penal Colony.

Guards who had been friendly were reassigned. Those who remained were mistrustful, hostile, and quicker to punish with slaps, kicks, or rifle butt strikes. Rations were cut drastically. Religious services were again forbidden; any prisoner gathering had the potential for collusion.

On April 11, as the frantic search for the escapees lengthened into a second week, residents of barracks five through eight were marched to a maximum security pen at the north end of the compound. The grim enclosure was surrounded by guard towers and three concentric rings of barbed wire fencing. Inside the cramped prison within a prison, Barton spent the next day—his twenty-fifth birthday—fighting claustrophobia and a creeping fear of inevitable execution.

Between interrogations, the sequestered men were kept in wire-screened, double-decked cages resembling rabbit hutches, alive with bedbugs. Nesting rats scurried beneath them. Their rations were cut to rice only, twice daily, brought in by oxcart. They were forbidden to speak to one another and ordered to "meditate" on their wrongdoing.

Instead, they contemplated their dimming prospects for survival. What would the final punishment be? All signs pointed to a mass execution. They wrote wills and last messages and buried them in tin cans during latrine breaks—the only times, other than for interrogation, that they were let out of the cages.

The incarceration lasted for a month. In mid-May, they were marched outside the guardhouse and ordered to line up. Trembling, they obeyed and braced for the worst.

19

★ ★ ★

FAREWELL TO THE
WHITE HOUSE

SPRING AND SUMMER OF 1943 found Bill Mott busier than ever, increasingly besieged by both personal and professional concerns. His wife, Romie, had been restricted to bed rest due to complications with her second pregnancy. At the same time, Map Room personnel were providing critical support to Trident. This third strategic conference of Allied leaders was taking place in Washington, with meetings at both the White House and the Federal Reserve Building. Prime Minister Churchill was again in residence at the White House, and he and his entourage had Bill and the Map Room watch officers hopping day and night, with demands both official and unofficial.

In this same time frame, Bill was also waiting for a response to his request for release from White House duty so that he could go to sea and join the fight. Impatient, he could no longer bear standing by while the enemy held his brother, particularly in light of recent intelligence regarding Japanese treatment of POWs in the Philippines. The new information shocked the senses, even in a wartime context.

The first dispatch came from Luzon in February 1943. MacArthur had radioed the information to Washington:

> A guerrilla leader on Luzon confirms reports from Filipino escapees that at Camp O'Donnell . . . deaths of American and Filipino prisoners by execution or disease, numbered 23,000 by November 1; Executions daily for such causes as disrespectful or insubordinate attitude or inability to work, deaths by disease resulting from dysentery, malaria, influenza, beriberi, pneumonia in order of importance; no medicine and two Red Cross trucks with medicine doctors and nurses from Manila refused entrance; meals consist of cold rice twice daily, sometimes with rotten camotes; no sanitation; for every prisoner that escapes, the Japs shoot five [sic] hostages; attempts by loyal Filipinos to smuggle in food, medicine punished by rough treatment and shooting; also prisoners had no blankets and only their original shoes and clothing.

Bill chafed at the "No Action" recommendation on the circulated radiogram. He knew the reason, of course. This was very bad, but not a priority to resource-strapped war leaders.

Then another, more significant dispatch came through concerning a different prison camp, this one on the island of Mindanao. The highly classified memorandum reported that a group of American officers, including at least one naval officer, had escaped from the very same camp where Bill felt sure Barton was being held prisoner. His heart had jumped at the news.

The men had escaped in early April and were now safe in the hands of Mindanao guerrillas. Thanks to Chick Parsons, arrangements to get them to Australia by navy submarine were in process. Bill was acutely disappointed to learn that Barton was not among the escapees, but apparently these men had quite a story to tell—one that would make all previous reports pale in comparison. Horrific details were trickling in via the Filipino guerrilla unit protecting the men. He would know more once the escapees arrived in Washington.

Bill was hopeful that they would bring concrete news about Barton, but another thought also nagged him—one that always crossed his mind with good news from the Pacific, as with the recent downing of Admiral Yamamoto's plane over Bougainville, the largest of the Solomon Islands. He had a recurrent, consuming anxiety that any Allied gain—whether the elimination of a revered Japanese admiral, a victorious sea battle, or a large-scale escape from an Allied prison camp—could trigger enemy retribution against the war prisoners under their control.

Around this time, the White House had new senior naval aide: Admiral Wilson Brown—the same Wilson Brown who'd been Naval Academy superintendent the year that Barton was forced to withdraw from Annapolis. Captain McCrea had departed to command the USS *Iowa*, the first of the new "fast battleships" churning out of American shipyards. Bidding farewell to his important mentor and friend was difficult for Bill. But Captain McCrea had also been driven to take part in the fight—on the war front instead of from inside the secure marble confines of the White House.

This was Admiral Brown's fourth stint as White House naval aide; the previous three had been under Presidents Calvin Coolidge and Herbert Hoover, and an earlier iteration (in the 1930s) under FDR. Despite their sizeable age difference, Bill and Admiral Brown found a quick and easy rapport. They had strong common ground in their mutual devotion to Annapolis (including its gloried football lore).

They swapped stories throughout the days and evenings as their work allowed. Brown savored one story in particular—likely with a twinkle in his eye—during an afternoon lull in the Map Room. Apparently Helen Cross's 1938 letter dressing down the Naval Academy for its "unpedagogic methods" had left quite an impression on then superintendent Brown. Bill shook his head and held up his hands in mock surrender, as though in belated apology on the family's behalf.

But Admiral Brown recalled Barton's situation sympathetically. Even when Academy rules didn't make sense, his job was to enforce them, he offered, in half apology. This was the first that Brown had heard of Barton's post-Annapolis reentry into the navy (he thought the boy had pursued a singing career) and of his wounding and capture in the Philippines. From that point forward, he asked frequently about both Barton and Benny, touching Bill more than he ever let on.

When the timing seemed right, Bill summoned the courage to ask Admiral Brown to endorse his waiver request regarding his nearsightedness. Doing so, he explained, would greatly improve his chances to get to the Pacific front. Though Bill's eyesight was now correctable with something called contact lenses, only a formal waiver would clear him for sea duty.

Brown worried that finding a qualified replacement to run the Map Room could be as big an obstacle as the waiver request, but Bill pointed out that the able and well-liked Lieutenant George Elsey—whom Bill had hired back at ONI and subsequently brought over to the White House— could assume his responsibilities seamlessly. Not only was Elsey familiar with Map Room operations, the president liked and trusted him. Bill had learned to spot discretion and talent, he assured the admiral, and Elsey possessed both. Brown agreed.

After conferring with the president, Wilson Brown penned an enthusiastic endorsement of Bill's formal request to the chief of naval personnel.

Two days later, three bells sounded outside the Map Room door, the all-important signal that the president was on his way. Bill and the duty officers readied themselves quickly for the day's briefing and question-and-answer session that always followed. When the door opened, Mott took the wheelchair handles over from the president's valet (who was not allowed in the room) and carefully steered Roosevelt into position for the briefing.

Before it started, Roosevelt turned to Bill, now beside him, affixing his blue eyes on Bill's own. "William," he said, "Admiral Brown spoke to me of your request to leave us and go to sea. You must know, I was reluctant. Eleanor was most disappointed to hear it, too. We don't want you to go."

Bill was a combination of stunned, pleased, and embarrassed, wondering all the time that Roosevelt was speaking how to respond appropriately. When the moment came, his answer poured out.

"Thank you, Mr. President. I am deeply honored, but you know how when you first come into this room and look on the maps for your sons' ships—even that of your Hyde Park butler? Well, sir, every day I look at the postings of the *Enterprise* and then the Philippines where my little brother is a prisoner of the Japanese. I feel compelled to go, to fight."

The president nodded somberly, already having turned his gaze to the Pacific wall map, scanning for the USS *Wasp* on which his son John was serving. "Yes, son, I do, I do understand," he said. By then, his mind seemed half a world away from the conversation.

Optimistic, Bill wrote Benny of the development:

```
You know I have been trying for some time to get some
kind of sea duty, but my every way has been blocked because
of my eyes . . . Admiral Brown recommended me to the course
at the Naval War College at Newport, which coupled with the
President's approval, will mean, I hope, that orders will
come through soon . . . Please don't blow me a blast about
leaving my nice soft job in the White House, because it
means a lot to me to become one of the fighting brothers . . .
    I visited both Rockaway and Oceanport last week
and found things in pretty good shape. Mother of course
grieves over Barton, and as could be expected, is slightly
irrational on the subject. She can't understand why we
don't turn all our effort into the Pacific in order to
avenge the heroes of Bataan. Emotionally, I agree with her,
```

but realize the Combined Chiefs of Staff are the people
to make that decision. Incidentally, we have had a very
interesting guest at the White House in the last few weeks,
as you probably have heard.

When Prime Minister Churchill arrived for the Trident Conference, he rejected the Queens' Bedroom, named for the many royal White House guests it had hosted in the past. Instead, he took over the more comfortable Rose Bedroom, also on the second floor, just as he had during his June 1942 stay. Churchill also brought along his legendary traveling map room. But when its director, the tall, handsome, and very proper Captain Richard Pike Pim, saw how sophisticated the White House Map Room had become, he proposed to Bill that the British contingent move in with them. Maintaining separate maps would be inefficient and superfluous, Pim insisted.

So Pim and Churchill made full use of the Map Room—morning, noon, night, and very late night. Bill built on the convivial rapport established during the PM's previous visits. In addition to inaugurating an afternoon tea ritual, the Map Room watch officers supplemented their regular daily map postings with incoming war cables from the Admiralty and London's War Office.

Churchill made himself very much at home, often appearing at the Map Room door in the wee hours. He was always in his Royal Air Force jumpsuit, usually barefoot, and never without a lighted cigar. One such evening during Trident, the Map Room sentry admitted the prime minister, this time carrying both a cigar and a snifter of brandy. "Good evening, my boy," the PM said to a startled Bill Mott as the door closed behind him, and he began to pace its perimeter thoughtfully. "How's Hitler?" he growled, pausing at the European map, then, drawing himself up, "the *bah*-stard."

On occasion, Bill delivered dispatches and briefing materials to the Rose Bedroom. On such visits he was often asked to pull up a footstool and read the material aloud or provide an impromptu summary of the world naval situation while the ample, pink-fleshed Churchill listened pensively from the bathtub. The naked prime minister, ringed in cigar smoke, always responded with insightful and impeccably phrased questions.

On Wednesday morning, May 19, 1943, Bill escorted Churchill to another recently converted White House coat room, this one into a movie theater. They took their seats to watch the latest war newsreels and the film to be premiered at the upcoming White House dinner honoring the prime minister. The documentary *The Battle of Britain* was the latest in Frank Capra's popular series Why We Fight. Halfway through the feature, however, the president's butler, Alonzo Fields, stepped into the darkened, smoky theater and tapped Bill on the shoulder. Given his charge, Bill might have been annoyed by the interruption had Fields not said immediately, "Congratulations, sir. It's a girl."

The prime minister's eyes grew wide, and an impish smile spread across his face. The onscreen fighting for country momentarily lost its audience. "Goodness, William," said the PM, "you are too modest! Congratulations indeed!"

That afternoon, a generous bouquet of pink roses and a charming note of congratulations arrived for Romie Mott and hours-old Janie (Jeannette Baker) Mott, causing quite a stir in the Garfield Hospital maternity ward. The card was signed in elegant script, "Winston S. Churchill."

BILL HAD SEEN LITTLE of his wife during the final days of her pregnancy, thanks to late hours in the Map Room and Trident's long, contentious Combined Chiefs of Staff meetings. Unlike the easy Anglo-American Map Room camaraderie, these sessions laid bare the mutual suspicions between the respective Allied countries' senior representatives and their aides.

Admiral King's reflexive exhortations about the dearth of resources going to the Pacific always flustered the London brass, sparking fresh concern of a possible US defection from the Europe First policy. Nor did the

American delegation hide its uneasiness that Britain might drop out of the Pacific War once Britain was made secure by Germany's defeat. Battle lines on maps were drawn and redrawn as the meetings themselves seemed to teeter on the brink of hostilities.

But just as Romie endured a long and difficult labor to productive end, the quarrelsome Trident Conference ultimately bore a fruitful resolution: Allied forces would launch a cross-Channel invasion of Europe in May 1944. A stepped-up campaign against the Japanese was also approved, as was accelerating the development of a devastating new weapon that harnessed atomic energy, possibly for use against Japan to speed her surrender. Though details were few, Bill found the last two decisions personally encouraging.

NOT LONG AFTER THE conclusion of Trident, a thick envelope addressed to Lieutenant Commander William C. Mott was delivered to the Map Room along with the morning's locked pouches full of classified documents from the War Department. When Bill first spied the manila envelope, stamped "BUPERS" (Bureau of Personnel), his heart jumped. He was sure the envelope contained orders that would either change his life completely by allowing him to go to sea or indefinitely tether him to his present course. He slipped the sealed envelope into his briefcase. He would open it at home, where he could react in relative privacy.

Meanwhile, Romie and a seven-pound, twelve-ounce, pink-blanketed Jeannette, forever after called Janie, had finally been released from Garfield Hospital and returned to 7 Newlands Street. Friends and neighbors streamed through, bearing good wishes and all manner of pink gifts and posies. Romie had been unwell for the last month of her pregnancy, and the fact that both mother and child were in good health and home was cause for neighborhood celebration.

Bill was not so unwise as to open the BUPERS envelope on arrival home that evening, though he ached to know its contents. The first order

of business was to greet his weary wife and new baby girl, who was alread.
demonstrating strong vocal cords, and reassure a slightly bewildered three-
year-old Adam.

When the family finally retired for the evening, Bill engaged in a quiet
ritual, rarely enjoyed of late. He walked into the kitchen and turned on the
tap, letting the water run while he opened the glass-paned cabinet and retrieved his favorite cut-crystal tumbler and bottle of Old Grand-Dad. He
poured until the glass was a third full and then held his finger under the tap
stream, staring out the kitchen window as he waited for it to cool.

Stirring the drink with his finger, Bill walked back into the living room
toward the stuffed briefcase slumping against his easy chair. He paused to
savor the charm and tranquility of his surroundings with a new perspective—
of one who might be taking leave of its comforts—and confines—for an
indeterminate period. How many men, he wondered, would lunge for his
position, the excitement, the prestige, the proximity to power and safety
from harm—and count themselves lucky? Here was a beautiful wife and
family, a lovely home, a terrific job. Was it right to want to go?

But reading daily about Benny and *Enterprise*'s brilliant and daring exploits and worrying hourly over Barton had worn him down, leaving him
feeling more and more a useless bystander in the world's titanic struggle
against determined enemies. He had to do this.

Bill sank deep into the armchair and placed his bourbon and water
on the polished mahogany side table. The first letter was from his mother,
which had also arrived that day.

Billy dear,

*A censored letter I wrote as secretary of my Club came back to me
after months yesterday. Perhaps this is why mail is so slow now; I do
hope you get this note in better time! We are all thrilled about baby
Jeannette and that Romie is improving . . .*

*You now have one more good reason to stop this talk of going to
sea—it seems to me that you are doing very useful work where you
are—God knows we need badly some men with brains in Intelligence
work! When I think of Benny and Barton and such stupidity at the
top—whee! But these Pacific island attacks have been glorious haven't
they? I suspect Benny was right there . . .*

*It would be such a comfort to hear directly from Barton; I know
something unusual prevents it . . . I am proud of them both out in the
thick of it, and of you too, trying to carry on at home. I hope you won't
go to sea unless really needed. I do need one son left and you have more
to lose than either Benny or Barton, the truth be told. One has hardly
lived at all and the other has had enough mental suffering so that
action might well help him right now.*

*Maybe you can slip up here for a rest very soon—we will make it
a real rest for your nerves, away from Washington entirely. We think
often and fondly of you, Bill. You are dear to me, my son.*

Mother

Bill's first reaction to her letter was a wince at the praise for Benny—
"out in the thick of it"—and her pride in "those glorious island attacks."
These things stood out as though she had written nothing else, uppermost
were they already in his mind.

He folded her letter and put it back in the powder-blue envelope with
"Lilac Hedges" embossed on the back and collected himself. The BUPERS
envelope rested on his lap. With his recent bid for orders that would take
him to sea, he had played his last best card. If a recommendation from Admiral Brown—who had cleared it with the president—had not done the
trick, there was no higher appeal short of Almighty God. Should the contents of this envelope prevent it, he could be sure that was the final answer.

Certainly the sleeping inhabitants of this house would prefer that outcome. But again, he told himself, in that endless quarrel between head and heart, what good was he to his family if he didn't join the fight and do what he was trained to do? Or stand aside with a lifetime of halfhearted explanations ahead—that it was his *eyes* that prevented him from fighting, not a shortage of courage or ability?

Bill finally tore open the envelope and pulled out a sheaf of papers, flipping through the pages, scanning the contents from the first to last. He then reread the cover memorandum:

```
From: The Chief of Naval Personnel
To: Lieutenant Commander William C. Mott
Office of the Naval Aide to the President,
The White House


Subject: Change of duty.


When directed by Admiral Brown, you will regard yourself
detached from duty at the White House, Washington, DC, and
from such other duty as may have been assigned you; you
will proceed to Newport, Rhode Island and report to the
President, Naval War College, for duty under instruction.

     You will be assigned government quarters in one of the
officers' dormitories of the Naval Training Station. These
quarters are not adequate for your dependents.
```

He might well have imagined a divine light shining down on him in the dimly lit living room. After tucking his new orders back in the envelope, Bill allowed a measure of relief. This would be difficult news to break to his family, but his prayer had surely been answered. With luck, he would finish his training at the Naval War College in Newport and be in the Pacific by year's end.

★   ★   ★

A MONTH OF HASTY preparations followed, interrupted in late May
by a whirlwind trip to Pearl Harbor with a planeload of navy luminaries
for a very special ceremony. If Bill needed any additional visuals to seal his
resolve, his happy reunion with Benny on the occasion of *Enterprise's* receipt of the Presidential Unit Citation—the first ever awarded an aircraft
carrier—certainly did.

Bill had stood in the oval office as FDR signed the executive order.
He'd barely been able to contain himself when the president—knowing,
of course, that Benny was *Enterprise's* gunnery officer—then suggested Bill
attend the ceremony.

A battle-scarred USS *Enterprise* had returned to Pearl Harbor to receive the award and also, after nine hard months at sea, to undergo a major
structural overhaul. Benny was grateful for the chance to catch his breath
and savor Bill's surprise visit. Here was a long-deferred reunion in which
a pent-up checklist of items that could only be shared in person—the war,
Lilac Hedges, Barton, their complicated parentage, their own marriages and
children, Bill's decision to go to sea, and Benny's weariness of it—would be
covered in an adrenaline-charged conversation in Sky Control preceding
the citation ceremony.

Bill was particularly excited to relate the recent intelligence that a
group of men had escaped from Davao Penal Colony on the island of
Mindanao. He was sure, he said, that this was where Barton was being
held. Benny was incredulous. "Are you saying Barton was one of them?
Oh my God!"

"Sadly, no," Bill replied. Barton wasn't among the escapees, but this was
still an encouraging development, he insisted, even as his brother's disappointment registered. It was the first and only contact with any captured
American since the fall of Bataan and Corregidor. The navy was going to
send a submarine to rescue the escapees, who were under the protection of

Mindanao guerrillas. He would know more after they were safe in Brisbane and could be debriefed.

He repeated that the escape was good news. "One," he said, holding up his index finger: "The men got out alive. Two"—he raised a second finger— "word is, there's a navy commander in the group; an Academy graduate. If they were at the same camp, and I'm fairly certain they were, he had to know Barton and will have news of him. Three, these men will have other dope on the prisoners in the Philippines—plenty of it."

Knowing this last could be a mix of bad and good news, Bill elected not to speculate. "Meanwhile," he said, shoring himself up with some emotion, "you're safe! Amazing what you've been through, what you've accomplished. Honest to God. You have been getting closer to Barton in your own right."

He was referring to *Enterprise*'s relentless westward foray against one after another enemy-held islands in the Pacific. Every battle, it seemed, had brought *Enterprise* a thousand miles closer to Manila. "Between the two of us," Bill said, "we'll get through to him."

Benny sighed. "Well, I sure as hell hope you're right, Bill. To tell you the truth, I wouldn't mind some new orders myself, but then it's hard to think about much else. Even though we're lickin' 'em, they're still holding Bart in a pen somewhere. That keeps me going on the worst days."

With that, band music sounded, and their precious time together was up. Top brass had begun to assemble on *Enterprise*'s flight deck, and Bill would have to return to Washington shortly after the award ceremony. Taking his place behind a phalanx of captains and admirals, he watched with patriotic and familial pride as Benny and the crew, in dress whites, stood at attention.

The flags on *Enterprise*'s yardarm snapped in the stiff Pearl Harbor breeze as Admiral Nimitz, CINCPAC, stepped forward to read the Presidential Unit Citation. Poignantly, he stopped just aft of the patched-over impact point of the bomb that had wiped out Repair Crew II at Santa

Cruz, and a few feet forward of the new starboard quarterdecking where Benny's thirty-eight gunners were incinerated by the bomb blast in the Eastern Solomons.

Admiral Nimitz cleared his throat, leaned into the microphone, and began his address to the white-clad assembly. The text before him was a large ceremonial document signed by President Roosevelt:

For consistently outstanding performance and distinguished achievement during repeated action against enemy Japanese forces in the Pacific War area, December 7, 1941, to November 15, 1942. Participating in nearly every major carrier engagement in the first year of the war, the Enterprise and her air group, exclusive of far-flung destruction of hostile shore installations throughout the battle area, did sink or damage on her own a total of thirty-five Japanese vessels and shoot down a total of a hundred eighty-five Japanese aircraft. Her aggressive spirit and superb combat efficiency are fitting tribute to the officers and men who so gallantly established her as an ahead bulwark in the defense of the American nation.

The admiral then listed action after heroic action, all which the ship's crew recalled well, if painfully.

Enterprise's current captain, Samuel Ginder, followed Admiral Nimitz. His every booming syllable echoed off the ships moored along a restored Battleship Row and drew cheers from hundreds of sailors manning those rails. Captain Ginder smiled and turned to acknowledge the rising crescendo of admiration and gratitude before continuing. "Your record has never been even remotely approached by any ship of this or any other navy."

Captain Ginder then proceeded to read a telegram from Admiral

Halsey, now commander of all South Pacific naval forces, but once and for-ever *Enterprise*'s symbolic leader and champion:

"It is with deep pride and gratification that I learn of the Presidential Unit Citation for *Enterprise*. This eminently deserved award expresses the appreciation of a grateful people for your outstanding accomplishments in this war.

"Keep fighting, ever mindful of the glorious traditions you have estab-lished. My heart is always with you."

At this the crew could not help, to the last man, grinning so hard it hurt.

Bill was left nearly wordless by the serial superlatives his brother's ship had earned. For eighteen months, USS *Enterprise* had been to him a thimble-sized marker that he had moved, always carefully, thoughtfully, around a map inside a window-blackened room six thousand miles away. The force of finally being aboard her with Benny, at such a charged and his-toric moment, was overwhelming.

After exchanging words of encouragement and a crisp salute—though they both would have preferred a hug—Bill said his last good-byes to Benny and boarded the waiting military aircraft.

The Washington-bound plane lumbered off Ford Island's runway into graying eastern skies. Pearl Harbor and a storied Oahu sunset retreated into the distance through a porthole-sized window. This day's experience made all the clearer the chasm between the insulated world of the White House Map Room and life aboard a ship at war. He would come to appreciate all the differences soon enough. What was that niggling feeling this realization gave rise to—was it fear?

ON HIS LAST DAY at the White House, Bill made the rounds, bidding farewell to the close-knit staff who had become a surrogate family to him. There was a perceptible sense among all of them that they might never see Bill again. The somber White House staff was still grieving over the recent loss of Daniel Callahan, another well-liked Roosevelt naval aide who had been drawn to the front. He was killed in the action off Guadalcanal.

Eleanor Roosevelt's farewell was especially unnerving, though Bill didn't let on. She clasped his shoulders with her hands and looked directly into his eyes, as though trying to memorize his features in case he didn't return. She had taken to him during his tenure there, always asking about his family and producing the occasional plaything for his young son. Her affection had been returned in kind by a young man who'd experienced too little maternal warmth and attention.

Bill's last stop was the Oval Office. Grace Tully pressed his hand in her own, said good-bye, and then opened the president's door. Roosevelt was sitting in his wheelchair beside his desk instead of behind it, his Scottish terrier Fala lounging at his feet. "Good afternoon, Mr. President," Bill said. "I've come to say good-bye and to thank you for your many kindnesses."

"Well, William," the president said, and then paused and leaned forward. "You know you really should stay here." The comment seemed more a gesture of affection rather than reproof, and Bill took it that way.

"Well, sir, the Japs have my brother in a prison camp, as you know. I really feel I must go."

Their eyes met, and the president nodded.

After a few minutes of small talk, Bill finally said, "Well, Mr. President, I hate to leave, but you may be sure I'll be back for the peace conference." Roosevelt's ice-blue, half-hooded eyes again met Bill's gaze. Then he looked away. The dark circles beneath them had deepened in recent months, and he had clearly lost weight. And though it was June, he still had a wool cape draped over his shoulders.

"Well, son," the president said, "I'm not sure there will ever be one."

20

★ ★ ★

A TALE OF ATROCITIES

THE FIRST THREE OF the escaped Davao prisoners to be rotated out of Mindanao by submarine were William Dyess (army air corps), Melvin McCoy (navy), and Steven Mellnik (army). When they arrived in Perth, Australia, two could barely walk, and the third emerged through the sub hatch on a stretcher. Within hours, all three received a stern summons from MacArthur's Brisbane headquarters: proceed to GHQ for debriefing as soon as physically able. They were also ordered, in no uncertain terms, to otherwise keep their mouths shut:

```
    Do Not, Repeat, Do Not, Discuss Experiences with Anyone.
Imperative You Arrive in Brisbane Soon as Possible. Have
Notified Your Family of Safe Arrival.


                        MacArthur
```

The ex-prisoners got a warm reception in Brisbane, however—especially Steve Mellnik, who had served on General MacArthur's prewar staff in Manila. They were particularly surprised when the general pinned Distinguished Service Awards on their very new uniforms. While accepted graciously, all three men commented to the assembled brass that the real heroes—both dead and alive—were those they had left behind.

After the awards, the gathered officers and their note takers listened, mostly in silence, alternately horrified and entranced as the escapees told the tale of their capture, the grisly methods used to exterminate thousands of prisoners of war, and the particulars of their escape. Except for their repeated expressions of gratitude and respect for the Mindanao guerrillas who had rescued and delivered them, the details were relentlessly grim. The AIB's Colonel Allison Ind paused the proceedings every twenty minutes or so, as much for the weakened officers as for the weeping stenographers.

Dyess, Mellnik, and McCoy chronicled the marches that killed tens of thousands, the beatings and bayonetings, the burying of men alive, the starvation and gruesome torture—all carried out with bland and unemotional Japanese efficiency. This was the very first report to the outside world of the Bataan Death March and the savage abuses of daily prison camp life that followed. The men spoke haltingly at first, and then with more energy and animation, likely motivated by reawakened outrage.

There was particular interest in their method of escape, which had been months in the planning. Key to their success, they explained, was the Japanese practice of sending out unchaperoned details on Sundays; they stressed that DAPECOL was lightly guarded compared with Bilibid, O'Donnell, and Cabanatuan—the prison camps on Luzon.

The lax oversight gave the incipient escapees the opportunity to preassemble food and essential equipment, including a compass, precious canned goods from their Red Cross packages, a sextant, quinine tablets, and maps of Mindanao and sea routes to Australia. They gradually removed the vital supplies from the camp on a bull cart used for hauling and hid them near the jungle perimeter until Sunday, April 4.

The Brisbane audience was also intrigued by the critical assistance provided by two longtime Filipino convicts, both in for murder. In fact, among the escapees' first requests was that MacArthur arrange for President-in-exile Manuel Quezon to formally pardon these criminals. This had been the bargain the American prisoners had gladly struck with the convicts early in the planning.

The two men, Benigno de la Cruz and Victorio Jumarong, had risked their lives—or worse, recapture and torture by the Japanese—to aid the Americans in a life-threatening, weeks-long ordeal, during which the escapees had hiked, half starved, across more than sixty miles of dark jungle, treacherous swamps, and rugged mountain ranges—nearly always within whispering distance of enraged Japanese search parties. Only with the convicts' help had the men miraculously made good on the escape.

Even with the convicts' knowledge of the jungle, they encountered difficulty from the start. After initially losing their way, they had unwittingly doubled back toward the prison camp, potentially squandering their all-important head start. With Japanese troops in hot pursuit, they narrowly avoided recapture.

Weakened by days on the run, wading chest deep through snake- and alligator-infested swamps, their rations running short, and the Japanese close on their heels, the escape party was finally picked up by Mindanao guerrillas, who promptly led them to safety. The guerrillas fed and clothed them, and treated their malaria, skin ulcers, and other raging ailments. Guerrilla-protected villagers even threw fiestas to celebrate the Americans' newfound freedom. These events, in further display of Filipino loyalty to the American cause, featured platters of food, flowing *tuba*, an alcoholic beverage coaxed from jungle vines, and music and dancing.

There had been one significant exception to the escapees' positive guerrilla experience, however: "Colonel" Wendell Fertig, an unsurren-

dered American mining engineer who had muscled his way to leadership of the various Mindanao guerrilla bands. Fertig had treated them
with suspicion and arrogance and initially resisted their request that he
radio authorities in Australia and notify them of their escape. Only when
McCoy, Mellnik, and Dyess confronted Fertig and displayed a gun they
had acquired did he relent and allow the encrypted message to be sent to
GHQ receiving stations in Brisbane.

After this part of the story was told, General Charles A. Willoughby,
MacArthur's intelligence chief, launched into an explanation. "Colonel Fertig was with the Corps of Engineers working to construct airfields on Mindanao when hostilities broke out," Willoughby began. "He fled to the hills
and later came down, gradually assuming control of local guerrilla units,
which were struggling to oversee food distribution to the local villages and
generally maintain civil control. Fertig then established radio contact with
us here in Brisbane, and when those units understood he was in contact
with us and had accorded him rank, they gradually allowed him to organize
and oversee all the guerrilla bands on Mindanao. We understand his drawbacks, but he's done a decent job distributing supplies and providing intelligence. He's set up a number of radio 'stations' on the island—including the
one from which your dispatch was relayed—as well as formalized a coast-
watcher network that monitors enemy shipping.

"His personality has grated on more than just you; I'm not sure the
guerrilla leaders on the island fully trust Fertig. After all, he assumed control over indigenous units that they had organized. But they ceded control
because of his power to distribute supplies, not his leadership ability. The
local leaders probably pay him lip service in proportion to what Fertig can
furnish them.

"That said, it's our impression he didn't quite know what to do with you
initially—I believe he meant no harm. Fertig desperately needs skilled men
to help him, and he probably saw you as potential recruits! We are aware

that he is egotistical and difficult, but he has been helpful to us in many ways, including resolving power skirmishes between the guerrilla bands. They are no good to us if they are fighting with each other. That is why we granted him the temporary senior rank of colonel—so he can assert Allied authority. We need Fertig to organize those bands into a cohesive military operation on Mindanao for when we *return*."

General Willoughby emphasized the final word, echoing MacArthur's famous pledge.

WILLOUGHBY WAS PLEASED TO have the opportunity to demonstrate his command of Mindanao's state of affairs before such an attentive audience. He was senior in rank and experience to Courtney Whitney, who had recently arrived in Brisbane and become his chief rival for MacArthur's attention. Willoughby had been in charge of Philippine affairs until MacArthur appointed Whitney to head GHQ's new and semiautonomous Philippine Regional Section (PRS). PRS now oversaw all Philippine operations for MacArthur, including guerrilla operations. To Willoughby's further chagrin, Whitney was now also the GHQ liaison to the navy's Seventh Fleet—and thus in control of Chick Parsons's covert submarine supply operation as well.

The clever Courtney Whitney had risen in stature at GHQ thanks to a steady stream of glowing, ingratiating praise of General MacArthur. It is said that a fool flatters himself but a wise man flatters the fool, and from the moment of his arrival at GHQ, Whitney had proven himself a master among masters at manipulating his new boss. It began with comments he had made on MacArthur's draft press statement to be broadcast on the anniversary of the fall of Bataan.

"This is superb," Whitney wrote to MacArthur. "It has the classical quality of imperishable statements. I predict that someday it will be carved in stone on monuments in the Philippines. I predict a tremendous emotional effect. American history is shot through with the power of such words and slogans. Like 'Remember the Alamo'... it has the dignity of distinguished literature."

Whitney's stature at GHQ soared following this early and memorable exchange, and his meteoric rise was vexing in the extreme to General Willoughby—especially because he'd lost command of Philippine affairs. Now it was the ambitious Whitney who controlled the guerrilla leader Wendell Fertig and who was charged with bringing MacArthur's iconic "I Shall Return" pledge to fruition. Whitney would control the vain Fertig with similar tactics—by implying that his own place in history would be secured by following Whitney's lead.

Willoughby was furious that the potential of Mindanao's twenty-two-thousand-strong guerrilla movement was now being undermined by Whitney's politically motivated tolerance of Fertig's limited leadership skills and poor people skills. Even Fertig's principal aides, American captains Ernest McLish and Clyde Childress, regarded him as paranoid and consumed with personal ambition. They did not like or trust him.

Willoughby had continued to push for trained military personnel and intelligence officers to be sent to Mindanao to take over operations from the one-time mining engineer, but Courtney Whitney had blocked him at every turn, preferring his tight control over the vain, inexperienced Fertig. Whitney liked the arrangement just as it was.

STEVE MELLNIK LISTENED AND nodded quietly during Willoughby's explanation, while also watching the body language—including that of the inscrutable Whitney—of all present. The experience brought back precapture memories of all the petty rivalries that had animated MacArthur's Manila headquarters before the war. It was one of the very few things, he realized, that he had not missed during captivity.

The conversation moved quickly beyond the escapees' interactions with Wendell Fertig. The men continued in their high praise of the other

Mindanao guerrilla leaders, whose operations they'd had plenty of time to observe in the nearly two-months hiatus between their escape and submarine rendezvous with Chick Parsons. One leader stood out: Captain Claro Lauretta, head of the Davao region guerrillas and the first with whom the escapees had come in contact. Lauretta's operational ingenuity and sophisticated level of organization, particularly given his primitive surrounds, had especially impressed them.

The GHQ audience showed intensified interest. They were hungry for well-sourced details on how the guerrilla units functioned, their living conditions in the jungle, their morale, their ability to gather enemy intelligence, and the extent and nature of their interactions with the Japanese. The escapees filled in the many blanks with hard facts.

Numbering several thousand, the Mindanao guerrillas were tough and smart. They knew the terrain like the backs of their hands, enjoyed widespread Filipino loyalty and support, and dealt ruthlessly with the Japanese, who increasingly feared and avoided them. The Japanese garrison on Mindanao persistently underestimated their strength and cunning. Not only had the guerrillas inflicted hundreds of Japanese casualties, but their very presence tied down thousands of other Japanese troops who could have otherwise been deployed elsewhere. Whenever the Japanese tried to attack them, the guerrillas melted expertly into the jungles and mountains, taking their food, supplies, and radios with them.

When the stenographers' work was finally done, MacArthur sent the word-for-word transcript to the White House by special air dispatch, on orders of President Roosevelt.

After the debriefing, General Willoughby said, "I'm convinced the guerrillas will play a major role during the liberation. Their potential for intelligence and sabotage is enormous. We need someone familiar with their operations to help us develop that potential." Looking at Steve Mellnik, whom he remembered well from prewar Manila, Willoughby then announced to the group, "Steve will need to take off for several weeks' debriefing in Washington, but when he's through, I'd like him to return and join our staff." Only after General MacArthur nodded in agreement did Courtney Whitney concur quietly.

Mellnik could not have been more pleased. Though he didn't say it at the time, he was already envisioning another role for the Mindanao guerrillas, one in which he might now play a critical part: as facilitators of a mass rescue of the two thousand remaining prisoners at the Davao Penal Colony.

21

★ ★ ★

AUGUST 1943: ALLIED WAR SUMMIT, QUEBEC, CANADA

WHEN IT WAS DECIDED that a fourth major Allied war summit was to be held in August 1943, Washington's stifling summer heat was rejected in favor of Winston Churchill's suggestion that they meet in cooler climes: Her Majesty's Quebec, Canada. That he might have the honor of hosting the president at the British Empire's largest North American fortress, the Citadel—proudly overlooking the site where the British defeated the French in 1760 to claim the spoils of all of Canada—was reason alone for the prime minister to favor the location.

But in addition to the historic Citadel and Canada's infinitely superior summer weather, Quebec also boasted a large, comfortable, and secure château-hotel where the Allied leaders' sizable military and civilian staffs could hold their "pick-and-shovel" sessions, the detailed meetings that converted the war leaders' big decisions into workable plans. So on August 1, 1943, some three thousand reservations at the famed Le Château Frontenac, the magnificent Gothic Revival edifice perched high above the rushing

Saint Lawrence River, were abruptly cancelled. Preparations for the war conference began immediately. Secrecy shrouded the arrangements, and rumors regarding the unexplained cancellations abounded. The two most remarkable were that Pope Pius XII was leaving war-torn Italy to set up temporary Vatican headquarters there, and that the storied hotel was to be converted to a military hospital.

In two weeks' time—with the addition of several miles of barbed wire, portable antiaircraft batteries, and armed sentries—the site's conversion to a first-rate world war summit location was complete. Hundreds of American, British, and Canadian officials began descending on Frontenac: from senior staffs, to secret service agents, to military intelligence officers, to Signal Corps communications specialists. President Roosevelt and Prime Minister Churchill took up official residence within the Citadel's elegant residential quarters, an ideal environment for informal and confidential discussions, as well as for high-level meetings.

The priority at Quadrant was to refine the timing and strategy for Operation Overlord, the seminal cross-Channel Allied landing in France that would launch the all-out assault on "the Axis in Europe." Still to be addressed were the sticky details of "combined" commands over American and British land, air, and sea forces, as well as other turf-related Overlord logistics.

Also vying for attention at Quadrant was the simmering intra-Allied battle over strategic next steps in the Pacific. Whenever the discussion turned to that topic, the British delegation appeared more focused on approaches favoring its lost imperial colonies—Hong Kong and Singapore in particular—than on prioritizing men and ships for an attack on Japan's home islands.

From Day One at Quadrant, the Anglophobic Admiral King pressed relentlessly for more aggressive action against Japan—and sooner rather than later—with George Marshall voicing his strongest support yet for King's position. Building on his Casablanca and Trident fulminations, King turned up the heat at Quebec, all but alleging that Britain lacked serious commitment to defeating the Japanese once Europe was liberated from the Nazis. The meeting room quieted at the accusation.

British representatives grew red with irritation whenever Admiral King opened his mouth. King was brilliant, but even on his best days, his personality was like a blowtorch. It wasn't that he was singling out the British for especially harsh treatment—he treated just about everyone that way. General Dwight Eisenhower, in charge of the US Army's European operations, once confided to his diary: "One thing that might help win this war is to get someone to shoot King. He's the antithesis of cooperation, a deliberately rude person . . . [and] a mental bully."

But popularity seemed utterly unimportant to Ernest King. In fact, by all accounts, he held dear his tough, lionlike defense of the United States Navy. When he was tapped to replace Admiral Harold Stark as CNO in the post–Pearl Harbor shake-up, he said famously, "You see, when things get tough, they call in the sons of bitches."

To Admiral King, the Pacific War—in which America and her navy had the greatest stake of all the Allies—had always come first. He pressed inexorably for the American Navy's needs and priorities, no matter the venue. At Quebec, he reminded the august assembly of the US Navy's string of Pacific victories, earned despite a paucity of men, ships, and materiel—a paucity not only compared with enemy assets but also compared with those being allocated to the European front.

King's clear implication was that the navy's heavy casualties in the early battles were greater than they *should* have been and a direct result of misplaced priorities of higher-ups. This was particularly true of sailors of the surface fleet, among whom the Guadalcanal toll alone was more than 5,000 young lives—a stratospheric number even when compared with the much-publicized losses by the US Army and Marine Corps during the protracted struggle ashore. That casualty estimate stood at 1,592.

In fact, Pacific naval commands had been appallingly underfed in the past two years compared with commands in Europe, arguably because of the time it took to convert US industrial capacity to a dedicated output of war goods. But here it was August 1943, King argued, and *still* only 15 percent of the supplies pouring out of converted American plants and factories were designated for the Pacific War. Moreover, the number of troops deployed to battle the Nazis was double that sent to the Pacific, which occupied a larger and more complicated theater of war.

In what one British representative deemed "very undiplomatic language," Admiral King demanded an agreement at Quadrant that more ships and personnel be sent to the Pacific front. King had already assigned the shrewd and equally irascible Admiral Kelly Turner as commander of Pacific amphibious forces. Recalling that Guadalcanal had been nicknamed Operation Shoestring, what Turner needed now, King exhorted, were the men, ships, and equipment to win the decisive next rounds of amphibious assaults as they closed in on Japan's home islands. With proper resources, Admiral Turner would get the job done.

At Quadrant, King's and Marshall's exhortations for stepped-up aggression against Japan seemed to have a greater urgency than at previous summits. The reason was that both men—as well as President Roosevelt—had very recently read the sworn statements of the escaped Davao prisoners. In addition to being outraged, they wanted an accelerated action plan agreed to by Allied war leaders at Quebec ahead of the inevitable release of these atrocity reports to the American public.

ON THE NEXT-TO-LAST DAY of the conference, as a final punctuation to their position throughout the week, King and Marshall won President Roosevelt's approval to have one of the escaped POWs' sworn statements read aloud to the combined military chiefs.

And so on August 23, with Major William Dyess's affidavit in hand, General Marshall rose from his seat in Le Château Frontenac's elegant Salon Rose Room, a circular space with rose-colored walls and floor-to-ceiling windows affording sweeping views of the Saint Lawrence River. Just outside the meeting room, lunch was waiting to be served. Perspiring pitchers of ice water and lemonade were perched next to a grand silver service of steaming coffee and tea. Beside the beverage table was a brimming buffet of fresh fruits, salads, breads, and platters of chicken, beef, and Canada's fine smoked salmon.

General Marshall began:

At daylight, 10 April, 1942, we started marching on the National Road off Bataan . . . This march is referred to by American prisoners of war as the Death March of Bataan. Had the Americans or Filipinos known the fate in store for them, though beaten, hungry, and tired from months of hardships, never would they have surrendered to our dishonorable foe . . . It was a terrifically hot day as we marched along the road without food, cover, or water.

We frequently passed men lying on the side of the road. Many had been run over by Japanese trucks and flattened. The next day, still with no food or water, we were marched twenty-one hours continuously. Men started falling out frequently, but the guards did not allow us to aid them. We could hear gunshots behind us. The Japanese had clean-up squads marching behind us, killing those who had fallen out . . .

At three a.m. we were placed in a barbed-wire bullpen that might have ordinarily housed two hundred men. In this pen were at least two thousand men. Human filth and maggots were everywhere . . . Three Filipinos and three Americans were buried alive, and one of the guards went so far as to make one of our own American sergeants hit one of the men in the head with a shovel when he tried to get out of the grave. Many of the men went crazy, and several of the delirious were dragged out and shot.

The secretary of the army cleared his throat as he read the statement, so replete with gruesome bayonetings, beheadings, and descriptions of mass starvation, brutality, and disease that some of the meeting attendees seemed to be fighting nausea. Still, General Marshall read the document in its entirety, pausing periodically so that the full impact of the narrative could be absorbed by even the most ardent Pacific Second advocates in the room. During his closing statement, however, seemed to draw the greatest attention:

> "In my opinion, it is not only advisable, but absolutely nec-
> essary, that all civilized people of the world know the condi-
> tions of the Japanese prison camps and the atrocities against
> American prisoners of war."

When the meeting broke, the sumptuous buffet lunch outside Salon Rose was hardly touched. Admiral Ernest King had suddenly become the least of the meeting attendees' concerns.

At the conclusion of the weeklong Quadrant, a weary President Roosevelt was wheeled into his temporary office next to the Citadel residence's drawing room, a bright, windowed space with river views on three sides. Roosevelt settled in for a day of reading and responding to accumulated correspondence that had been dispatched from Washington.

The president's secretary, Grace Tully, had developed a fine sense over the years of what was urgent, what could wait, and what could be responded to adequately by someone else. With four thousand letters a day pouring into the White House since the beginning of the war, Tully culled to a fraction the mail that actually reached the president. In further efficiency, she always attached a brief note summarizing each piece of correspondence. Letters of a personal nature were decorated with a red tag.

So marked was a letter atop that morning's tidy pile, written on powder-blue stationery. In a long, sweeping hand, the linen envelope carried a return address of Lilac Hedges, Oceanport, New Jersey. In the cover note attached to the letter, Tully had written:

     Letter from Mrs. A. Barton Cross. Her son was an officer
in the White House (Lt. Com. Mott), has another son, Chief
Gunnery Officer on aircraft carrier, a daughter--an
officer in the WAVES, and third son is a Japanese prisoner.
Is grieved over her youngest son in the Philippines. Was
John's [Roosevelt] classmate at Harvard. Asks the President
if these prisoners are forgotten as he never mentions them
in his [speeches] etc. . . . Since Mrs. Roosevelt is away and
this is addressed to both the President and Mrs. Roosevelt
and is from Commander Mott's mother, perhaps you would care
to answer.

Roosevelt read Grace's note and the letter itself, which he was told
Eleanor had already seen and urged be sent on to him. No doubt the president paused before penning his reply. The escapee depositions sent him
by MacArthur had stunned him. Their sworn statements stressed the dire
circumstances these men had escaped, but perhaps the most haunting as-
sertion was William Dyess's: "If any American could sit down and conjure
the most diabolical of nightmares, he might come close to . . . the tortures
and horrors that these men are going through." Roosevelt was surely also
mindful of the personal note he received from MacArthur just prior to his
departure for Quebec:

[O]ur quiescent policy with respect to the Philippines . . . is
in no small degree responsible for the unfolding of a drama
the stark tragedy of which has no counterpart in American
history. Our prisoners of war are being subjected to slow and
deliberate extermination through disease, starvation and
summary execution. So have many thousands already perished,
and few, if any, will survive unless we arouse ourselves into
a more dynamic military aid policy.

Roosevelt recalled the many conversations he'd had with his former naval aide, William Mott, and his ill-concealed anxiety about his brother Barton, one of those very prisoners in the Philippines. The president had always extended words of sympathy and encouragement to Mott; at the time, it was all he could do.

But now, God help him, with the burden of this new and terrible information on the treatment of these men, here was a letter from Mott's mother! What could he possibly say to comfort her, given what he now knew? Helen Cross's maternal tenacity was not so different from that of Roosevelt's own late mother, Sara—legendary for her fierce protectiveness and involvement in all matters relating to Franklin.

When the president was deep in thought ahead of dictation, he would pause and tap his fingers on the arms of his wheelchair. His secretary knew that dictation would usually begin when he stretched out his arms and placed his hands flat on the top of his desk. He would then push back his chair a bit, grab hold of a trouser leg at the knee, swing the leg over the other knee, and fold his hands. This was the familiar series of gestures he repeated before dictating the following:

                              The Citadel
                              Quebec

                              August 24, 1943.

My dear Mrs. Cross,

     Mrs. Roosevelt and I have read your letter of August
10th and we want to assure you that the subject of American
prisoner of war, their treatment and the distress and
anxiety of their relatives, is among our many grave

concerns. Having in mind the character of our enemies, it
seems improbable that repeated declarations of that anxiety
or concern would help the prisoners or improve their
condition.

The most effective step at this time appears to be
through the good offices of the Red Cross with the help of
the benevolent neutrals.

Every effort is being strained to end the war at the
earliest possible date and one of the most urgent reasons
for that haste is the desire to release our prisoners. I
know that your sons understand how anxiously all our
country look forward to their day of release.

At the White House we miss your son, William, and I am
sure you must feel equal satisfaction for the fine work of
your other sons and your daughter in the Service.

> With all good wishes,
> Sincerely yours,
> Franklin D. Roosevelt

When the freshly typed letter was handed back to him, he read it
through. He then slowly unscrewed the cap of his fountain pen. First, he
scrawled an *s* after "prisoner" in the opening paragraph, correcting it to
reflect the grim plural that it was. Plural in the tens of thousands, he knew
too well. Then, pressing hard on his fountain pen nib, he scratched his signature.

He had answered a mother's lament as best he could. Never far from
his mind were his own four children, also in uniform and in harm's way. In
that, the parental anguish of Helen Cross and Franklin Roosevelt were one
and the same.

Soon thereafter, the president received an effusive response:

> Lilac Hedges
> Oceanport, New Jersey
>
> September 9, 1943
>
> To the President and Mrs. Roosevelt,
>
> Dear Friends,
>
> How can I consider you other than friends when you were good enough to give me time out of your busy lives? Time to say a few words to assuage a mother's real and protracted anxiety! Your letter must have brought good luck, for the next day a postcard arrived from Barton, from Military Prison Camp Number Two in the Philippines. It bore his dear signature in a firm hand and the information checked that things are not too bad.
>
> Thank you also for your kind words about William. I am proud also of his brother, Commander E. Bertram Mott of the "workhorse of the Pacific"... and our Ensign Rosemary Cross of the Brooklyn Navy Yard.
>
> God bless you in your wise and single hearted direction of our land!
>
> Sincerely Yours,
> Helen Cross

In time, however, the tone and content of Helen's correspondence with President Roosevelt would change dramatically.

22

★　★　★

REVENGE ON THE INNOCENT
AND A COVERT PLAN

AFTER CROUCHING FOR THIRTY days in feces-strewn wire hutches and in constant dread of summary execution, the fellow tenants of the four escape-party-occupied barracks were let out of their cages and ordered to line up outside their isolated compound. A weakened Barton Cross and a subdued Charles Armour fell in with their fellow prisoners. It appeared their deaths were near, in keeping with the Japanese ten-for-one shooting squad rule on prisoner escape.

In his immaculate uniform and shiny boots, Major Maeda twitched his riding crop as he paced up and down the nervous, hollow-eyed assembly. His demeanor betrayed a mix of contempt and disgust—but also something else: Was it resignation? Maeda began his address to the prisoners. When the interpreter translated the remarks into broken English, the men could barely maintain their fixed expressions.

They had been "bad boys," the interpreter delivered, for having allowed their barrack mates to escape, and they were ungrateful to the benevolent

Japanese for having spared their lives. Their punishment, therefore, would be severe: the prisoners would lose all the monies they had "earned" during their imprisonment, which, Maeda asserted, had been deposited on their behalf in Japanese postal savings accounts.

The comedy of the punishment was lost on none of its recipients. That they might have ever received such funds—and this was the first they'd heard of their existence—was not a prospect they could even contemplate. A dead man can't spend a penny, and all they could think when the interpreter finished was that, incredibly, they were not going to be executed.

Resisting the urge to throw his head back and laugh out loud had to be difficult for Barton. But as sure as he stood unsteadily on his filthy bare feet listening to Maeda's dispensation from the harshest rule of prison life, he believed the worst was over. If they could survive this, he would say later, they could survive anything.

Still, when the sequestered prisoners were returned to the main camp, they found a changed attitude among their captors, even among the previously friendly guards. Lieutenant Yuki, once compassionate and understanding, barely spoke to the ensigns after their return, indicating only that he felt betrayed for his previous kindnesses.

Reduced rations were now the new norm, and random beatings increased. Not surprisingly, unguarded work details were also a thing of the past—which drastically reduced the prisoners' ability to supplement paltry rations with food skimmed during farmwork. Some had lived this long only by snatching from these sources to supplement their starvation diet. To those men, this was the worst consequence of the escape.

Barton was among a small faction of prisoners who did not begrudge the escapees: to survive in the jungle and reach safety (if indeed they had; nobody knew) seemed a feat larger than life itself. Perhaps they felt this way because the navy man, McCoy, and the marine, Austin Conner Shoffner, had been respected as men of conscience. Surely these men would get word back to their families, let them know they were alive, tell them where they were; surely they would do at least that on behalf of the prisoners left behind.

This prospect was especially keen to Barton. Here it was summer 1943, and he still had not received a single piece of mail from his family. Nor did he know whether they had received the cards he had written them. He agonized over the possible reasons. For all Barton knew, his family had given him up for dead. *Maybe those escaped men will get word about us to the outside world*, Barton hoped. *That would make it all worth it.*

Such had been his ruminations during those long nights in the rabbit hutch. Some good might very well come of this.

But the majority of prisoners were bitter about the escape and ensuing crackdown. They could barely speak the escapees' names without modifying epithets. In their minds, those ten men had willfully inflicted mass punishment on nearly two thousand innocents. To the majority of prisoners at Davao, this was unforgivable.

IN SEPTEMBER 1943, AFTER lengthy hospitalization in Brisbane, Steve Mellnik and the other escapees flew thirty-six hours across nine time zones to Washington, DC. Their debriefings at the Pentagon, the State Department, and other relevant agencies went on for weeks. Throughout the process, he was reminded repeatedly that his experiences were a military secret. Like his fellow escapees, Mellnik was under strict orders not to divulge, even to his family, any detail of what he had been through. It was a new and cruel form of incarceration for all of them, especially because these men believed their escape would be justified—and their guilt assuaged—*only* by exposing what the Japanese were doing to Allied prisoners.

Mellnik took particular offense at disdainful bureaucrats who intimated he had lost sight of the greater war because of his singular concern for the prisoners he had left behind. Others, however, listened respectfully. Once Mellnik realized the degree to which a calm and professional demeanor improved his credibility, he conducted himself with special care.

The combined stress of the debriefings and forced repression landed Mell-nik back at Walter Reed Hospital for recuperation from a vicious recurrence of malaria. But the respite gave him an opportunity to refine his plan.

The idea had first come to him during the escapees' Brisbane debriefing. Mellnik's detailed description of the strengths of Mindanao's guerrillas was met with intense interest by MacArthur and his colleagues. What he had de-scribed wasn't an underground resistance with a few shortwave radios but a broad, deep, and sophisticated military network that included an island-wide supply, defense, and communications system. The guerrillas also commanded the deep respect and loyalty of virtually every island resident—thanks to their reliable enforcement of law and order and their ruthless treatment of the hated Japanese occupiers.

The original and core purpose of the guerrilla organizations—on Min-danao, in particular—had been to restore civil order when local authority crumbled at the war's outbreak. This function expanded rapidly to include harassment of enemy garrisons across the island. Word of their brutal and highly efficient ambushes spread fast, and the Japanese increasingly feared them.

How did they accomplish these feats with so few resources? At Bris-bane's GHQ and later at the Pentagon, Mellnik quoted the words of one guerrilla leader over and over: "What we don't have, we make, what we can't make, we steal, what we can't steal, we do without and still get the job done."

Brass curtain rods were melted down to make bullets, gunpowder was extracted from firecrackers, and the jungle was so laced with trip wires, sharpened bamboo spikes, and other death traps that the Japa-nese were afraid to stray from the main roads. And they stayed well away from the guerrilla strongholds dotting the island. The guerrillas had some natural advantages as well. They knew Mindanao's treacherous ter-rain intimately and navigated easily through even its most inhospitable areas. They had adapted and formalized military protocols to jungle life and abided by them. The American escapees—all professionally trained military officers—had been suitably impressed by the guerrillas' twenty-four-hour combat readiness.

Just as he had at Brisbane, Mellnik methodically spread the Mindanao guerrilla gospel throughout the warrens of the Pentagon, detailing the operation's leadership, breadth, size, and sheer gutsiness. He fascinated every interviewer with the guerrillas' methods and astonishing effectiveness.

Mellnik always began by differentiating Mindanao from Luzon, which was heavily garrisoned and controlled by the Japanese. The guerrillas controlled 95 percent of Mindanao, with enemy activity limited to patrols on major highways. In fact, Japanese soldiers were terrified of the jungle—home to both the guerrillas and the legendary head-hunting Moro tribes. "The possibility that the Japanese will send a strong force to Mindanao to neutralize this resistance does . . . not . . . exist." Mellnik would repeat the last three words slowly and succinctly.

Perhaps Mellnik's most important Washington meeting was with Lieutenant Harold Rosenquist, an officer with MIS-X, an unpublicized section of the army's G-2 (Military Intelligence) branch. MIS-X was an ultrasecret POW communication, support, and supply program operating with vaunted success in the European theater. Mellnik was stunned to learn that such an organization existed. So clandestine was MIS-X, code-named "1142" for the box number at which it received top secret correspondence, that relatively few within the military establishment had even heard of it.

Rosenquist was entranced by Mellnik's story and responded with a description of what MIS-X did to assist men trapped behind German lines. Its primary purpose there, he explained, was to rescue downed airmen as well as maintain communications with those inside German POW camps. Monopoly game boards and checkerboards loaded with real currency and forged documents were smuggled into camps throughout Germany. Chess pieces, shaving brushes, and other hollow items were packed with compasses, tools, and money. Decks of playing cards, when stripped of their backs and laid out, became full-color silk maps of Europe. Cribbage boards were actually radios, and rubber shoe heels were carved with the word "Visa" and other official stamps that could be inked and imprinted on forged papers.

Mellnik could barely contain himself.

"Why aren't you operating on Mindanao?" he asked, incredulous.

"Many reasons," replied Rosenquist. "First off, we're not bombing the Philippines—yet—so there's no urgent escape-and-evasion training required. Second, we had no information about conditions on the islands; your group was the first to bring back any solid data. Third and last, we had no way of getting to you! Darwin, Australia, our closest base, is twelve hundred miles from Davao."

Mellnik then outlined the very new Seventh Fleet submarine operation that was ferrying supplies to the guerrillas from Australia. Rosenquist responded with the confident tone of a man accustomed to overcoming the difficult and dangerous: "Well, then," he said, "we could reach the Mindanao prisoners by that means."

An elated Mellnik agreed. And, he ventured, there was one particular guerrilla unit on the island, headed by a Lieutenant Colonel Claro Lauretta, that already had the manpower to storm DAPECOL and rescue the prisoners. "All Lauretta needs," Mellnik said, "are supplies and guidance. I know that springing two thousand prisoners sounds like a major undertaking, but if you could see how well they function in that jungle area, you'd agree with me. I have it in mind to persuade GHQ to do something along those lines."

"I'll volunteer for that rescue operation," said Rosenquist. "I've had training in escape-and-evasion techniques. I'd like to put it to practical use."

"Well, if you do go in," Mellnik said, "it will have to be under MacArthur and GHQ's auspices; no one can operate for long without guerrilla support, and the guerrillas look to General MacArthur."

"I wouldn't have it any other way."

While jubilant at this turn of events, Mellnik felt it only fair to disclose the difficulties of the jungle—its intrinsic dangers to health and life, and the near certainty that a mistake or moment of carelessness would mean certain death.

"I'll chance it," said Rosenquist. "You people took worse risks when you made your break. I'll have GHQ and the guerrillas at my side."

Shortly afterward, Mellnik was contacted by General Richard K. Sutherland, MacArthur's Brisbane-based chief of staff, who was then in Washington at a war planning conference. With Pacific strategy beginning to crystallize, MacArthur had tapped Sutherland to negotiate his priorities with the War Department. In fact, Sutherland traveled between Brisbane and Washington extensively for this purpose. When he heard that Mellnik was in town, he requested a meeting with his old colleague from prewar Manila days.

"Sorry I couldn't welcome you in Brisbane, Steve," Sutherland said when they got together. "But I read your entire report with great interest—it has caused comment at the highest level of government! Tell me, what are your plans for the future?"

Mellnik said that General Willoughby had requested he return to Brisbane to work on guerrilla matters at GHQ. Sutherland nodded approvingly. "Excellent. It's about time we beefed up that new Philippine Guerrilla Section."

Remembering the contentiousness between Willoughby and Whitney on this point, Mellnik carefully pivoted the conversation back to rescuing the POWs at the Davao Penal Colony. He again described to an attentive General Sutherland the island's tough and well-organized guerrilla assets, with specific praise for Colonel Lauretta's unit that had controlled the Davao region so effectively since the fall of the Philippine government. Mellnik then repeated, nearly word for word, what Lauretta had told him one night regarding a possible POW rescue:

" 'Steve,' he said, 'we've been operating effectively against the Japs without support for sixteen months. We are an agricultural island, so we have plenty of food, and some of the best-known physicians and trained nurses in the Philippines are operating clinics in the hills for guerrillas and civilians alike.

" 'My headquarters are about seven miles from the penal colony. The heavily jungled area in between is under absolute guerrilla control. So we could easily raid the colony, which has garrisoned, at most, two hundred and fifty Japanese soldiers—mostly low-ranking guards. But we cannot do it without more ammunition.

" 'It's a matter of simple arithmetic,' Lauretta said. 'So you see, I have four times the manpower of the Japs at the penal colony, and control the entire area between the prison camp and my headquarters, but I have only one hundred and fifty rifles. If I had a thousand rifles, we could overrun the colony and move the POWs to the mountains, where we have the resources to protect and feed them. The Japs simply don't have the troop numbers or knowledge of the terrain to challenge that.' "

A rapt Sutherland did not interrupt, and Mellnik continued full steam ahead: "Lauretta said they could take rifle and supply delivery from a surfaced navy submarine after sunset. It's already been done many times and works beautifully," he said. "His men wait in nearby *bancas*"—a canoe-shaped boat indigenous to the Philippines—"exchange recognition signals, load the supplies onto the *bancas*, and get them ashore. The sub is exposed only briefly, and the guerrillas have hours of darkness to move the supplies to safety."

Mellnik emphasized the guerrillas' unique dominion over Mindanao, as opposed to other islands in the Philippines. To curtail guerrilla control on Mindanao, the Japanese would have to send ten times as many men as they now had. He then told Sutherland about his meeting with Lieutenant Harold Rosenquist and MIS-X—about which, to Mellnik's surprise, even Sutherland knew little.

He explained MIS-X's capability for supporting behind-the-lines resistance. Not only could they arm and train the guerrillas in the art of rescue, escape, and evasion, he said, but also they could help map out multiple prisoner escape routes. Mellnik then related Rosenquist's offer to lead this very mission. "General," he concluded, "I think we have the ingredients for a successful jailbreak."

Sutherland had heard more than enough to be convinced. Mellnik's knowledge was detailed, and the information well presented, eliminating any concern that the former POW was pursuing the rescue plan out of guilt or outsized rage at his former captors. He had made a strong and persuasive case.

"It's a wonderful idea," Sutherland said, "and Harold Rosenquist sounds like the right man for the job. But don't underestimate the difficulties. It's a long way to Mindanao, transportation is limited, and our buildup is just beginning. But with those cargo subs the navy is lending us, we can send a hundred tons of cargo over at a time—and carry out a hundred passengers."

Steve Mellnik nearly skipped out of General Sutherland's Pentagon office. If General MacArthur's chief of staff—one of the most powerful men in the US Army—had viewed his rescue plan as wishful, impractical, or of secondary importance, he most certainly would have said so. Instead, Sutherland *approved* it.

The cargo subs that Sutherland mentioned referred to GHQ's recent agreement with the US Navy to commit a pair of Seventh Fleet submarines to supply the Philippine guerrillas. As agreed previously, the navy counterpart in the clandestine supply and intelligence operation would be naval reserve officer Commander Chick Parsons.

The army-navy negotiations over the subs had been delicate. Parsons's boss, Captain Arthur McCollum, and McCollum's boss, Seventh Fleet Commander Admiral Arthur S. Carpender (a vocal MacArthur detractor), had wanted a few things in exchange for lending from their precious submarine supply, particularly for fateful missions into enemy-controlled waters. Could MacArthur deliver coast-watcher reports of the navy's hit-and-run strikes against Japanese shipping in Philippine waters? The navy was sure that it was having measurable success with these raids, but its subs did not stick around to see if the ships it hit actually sank. They could get credit for these "kills" only with confirmed reports from coastwatchers in the Philippines—who reported directly to MacArthur.

When Whitney agreed to forward the coast-watcher reports to the navy, a deal on loaning its submarines was struck. That final detail also resolved Mellnik's one remaining logistical question regarding the Davao prisoner rescue. The freed men could be rotated out of Mindanao in these very submarines. With this, he immediately began devising a detailed rescue plan to present for General Sutherland's approval.

23

★ ★ ★

SECRETS INSIDE THE
OXYGEN TENT

DECEMBER 1943: EVEN IN his miserable, pneumococcal state, Bill entertained a feverish reverie inside an oxygen tent at the Naval War College infirmary. *A prisoner rescue mission? Is it too good to be true?* The dreamy vision came and went as if regulated by his wildly fluctuating body temperature. How hot he was, how cold now! The monotonous *whirrrr-tap-tap* of the oxygen pump, the beads of moisture on the plastic windows, the dampness of the sheets, the din inside the rubber enclosure—all combined to challenge his tether to reality as the monstrous double pneumonia fought to take over his lungs.

At a series of Pentagon briefings during Bill's brief Thanksgiving trip home—hardly a respite from the long hours of coursework and drills at the War College—he was stunned to learn from the Seventh Fleet's intelligence officer, Mac McCollum, that a plan to rescue the prisoners at Davao Penal Colony on Mindanao was in the works. Ever since March 1943, when Helen and Arthur were notified of the change in Barton's status from missing in action to prisoner of war, Bill had sought to triangulate his precise location by every possible means. When Barton's first, electrifying postcard subsequently arrived at Lilac Hedges from "Military Prison Camp Number Two," he confirmed this meant Davao Penal Colony on Mindanao.

Captain McCollum had also been elated to learn of the plan, for both personal and professional reasons. He too had a family member—his favorite first cousin, Shivers McCollum—being held at Davao. Bill's first question was inevitable: "After they're rescued from the prison camp, how the hell are they getting them out of the Philippines?"

"By navy submarine," came the answer, as though from the breath of an angel.

McCollum explained the arrangement that he and Admiral Carpender had negotiated with MacArthur's staff regarding GHQ delivery of coastwatcher confirmations of enemy ships sunk by US Navy submarines lurking in Philippine waters. With this proof, the navy would finally get due credit for its serial successes eliminating Japanese vessels. And besides, the two submarines McCollum had offered, *Narwhal* and *Nautilus*, weren't useful for combat: their torpedo capacity was limited, and their driving time slow. But with significant interior capacity, they were ideal for ferrying guerrilla supplies in—and men out.

McCollum had nothing but praise for the subs' covert trial missions under Commander Chick Parsons. Bill remembered Chick from his astonishing arrival in Washington from occupied Manila the previous fall. He was now back in Australia working to supply the Filipino guerrillas. It was Parsons who had arranged sub passage out of Mindanao for the ten escaped prisoners from Barton's camp.

McCollum explained the now-standard operating procedure: After unloading supplies, Americans who had been trapped behind enemy lines since the fall of the Philippines were boarded onto the empty subs. First evacuated were those of political or military significance, followed by American civilians, and, finally, other asylum seekers. As many as possible, as quickly as possible—that was the imperative. Parsons had been given significant leeway to save as many American lives as he could. McCollum had said they wanted to save these prisoners. "Not just Shivers—all of them."

The news had seemed incredible to Bill at the time, and now, in his oxygen-tent delirium, even more so. He liked—no, cherished—the fact that the navy would play a role in the covert operation. And what luck that the rescue was to be of prisoners from Barton's camp! Of course, he could tell their mother nothing of this, not until Barton was out safely. Bill so looked forward to that moment.

When would it take place? Not sure, replied McCollum, but the mastermind of the operation, Lieutenant Harold Rosenquist from MIS-X, meant business—that much was clear. Rosenquist would depart for Australia in January, but he was already hard at work on the rescue plan, McCollum explained.

There were risks, of course. The escapees' sworn statements cast plenty of doubt on any prisoner's ability to survive his ordeal much longer. Could Rosenquist get to Davao in time? Get them out without a bloodbath? Every worry spiked a coughing fit and expulsion of phlegm into the sputum cup.

Bill had paid close attention to any mention of MacArthur's GHQ during the Washington briefings he'd attended over Thanksgiving. For each section in Brisbane—G-1 (Personnel), G-2 (Intelligence), and so on—there was a corresponding oversight unit at the War Department. Useful information on developments in Brisbane could be extracted from these Washington counterparts.

Clouding matters right now was the fact that Courtney Whitney—no longer General Willoughby, who, Bill understood, had greater sympathy for the prisoners of war—had total control over Chick Parsons and his submarine supply missions. Rosenquist couldn't execute a rescue operation without access to those subs. It was no secret that "Colonel" Whitney was more MacArthur loyalist than military professional, one of a select circle of GHQ insiders that had fled Corregidor with the general—as well as partaken of enormous last-minute payments by the Philippine government to exiting US Army leadership before the doomed command was abandoned. Wealthy civilian Whitney had also been MacArthur's prewar Manila attorney, and the general placed considerable trust in him.

Of all the general's aides, Whitney seemed the most focused on ensuring the success of MacArthur's all-consuming objective: returning to the Philippines in a reputation-restoring blaze of glory, forever removing the humiliating blot of defeat.

Given Whitney's narrow objective and bewildering power at GHQ, it was unclear how MacArthur's overriding objective of retaking the Philippines squared with Washington-based Rosenquist's orders to rescue these prisoners—from the very island where the general planned to make his initial landing. Maybe it wouldn't matter. After all, Sutherland, MacArthur's chief of staff, had already approved the mission, hadn't he?

Still, there was cause for worry, especially given GHQ's obsession with interference from Washington. Normally Bill didn't concern himself with the army's petty rivalries or gnarled bureaucracy; there was plenty in the navy to keep him busy. But the question begged an answer: How would Brisbane's complicated office politics affect the rescue plan?

He remembered MacArthur's early and emphatic refusal of OSS intelligence support from Washington; it would be inefficient, the general had said. But everyone knew the real reason: MacArthur wanted complete control of intelligence gathering and distribution within his command area, *especially* with respect to the Philippines.

THE SEVERE BOUT OF pneumonia had Bill alternately gasping for air and coughing up blood-stained phlegm, prompting his transfer to Newport Naval Hospital. Even Eleanor Roosevelt's anxious phone calls to the night nurses ("Yes, this is Mrs. Roosevelt calling again. Can you tell me, please, how is Billy Mott?") did little to buoy his spirits or condition. He'd been lying there for three days, teetering on the edge of delirium as his fever climbed and plummeted, climbed and plummeted.

Bill could see the nurse through the tent's rubber-seamed windows, periodically checking the oxygen-ration meter, the pumping apparatus, and the tent's temperature readings. What a hell of a time to get sick. For now, all he could do was dream of this rescue plan's success and a Pacific reunion for Bill, Benny, and Barton.

24

★ ★ ★

HERO OF BATAAN VERSUS
THE WAR DEPARTMENT

IN THE FALL AND winter of 1943, the Davao escapees, especially
Major William Dyess, continued to chafe under the government's gag order
forbidding them from divulging any details of their imprisonment and escape. Dyess had become so outraged that he requested a meeting with General "Hap" Arnold, chief of the army air forces, to appeal for his help. While
sympathetic, Arnold told Major Dyess there was nothing he could do. The
Joint Chiefs of Staff had not changed their official position: the matter remained classified at the highest level of national security. Arnold could arrange a flight command in Europe for Dyess, but he was powerless to help
the hero of Bataan get his story aired.

But the war censors were worried about Dyess, and for good reason. Possessed of the Silver Star, Legion of Merit, and Distinguished
Service Cross with an Oak Leaf Cluster, Major William Edwin Dyess
was already well known to the American public. The tough Texan's
daring exploits against the Japanese had been splashed across every

newspaper's front page throughout the slow, agonizing fall of the Philippines.

Stories abounded about his daring seaborne raid against Japanese amphibious landings. He had personally led twenty of his men and wiped out an entire enemy battalion. Then, with one of the few remaining airplanes on the Bataan Peninsula, Dyess took to the skies, alone and incredibly outnumbered. Yet he succeeded in destroying an enemy supply dump and sinking a twelve-ton Japanese transport, a pair of hundred-ton motor launches, and several loaded barges in Subic Bay. In the same daring run, he also seriously damaged another six-thousand-ton Japanese vessel. One article dubbed him the "Red Baron of the Philippines."

Pressure to grant his story's release swelled like an untapped fire hose, due largely to Dyess's own efforts. Ever since his escape, he had used his name recognition for one high purpose: to reveal what was really happening to the tens of thousands of prisoners left behind in the Philippines. He was certain that the resulting outcry would become a force in itself—one powerful enough to elevate, once and for all, the subordinate status of the war with Japan.

Dyess was just as sure that the resulting publicity would shame the Japanese into improving treatment of their prisoners. He was astounded that official Washington was preventing him from going public—and even more astounded by the given reasons. The War Department was holding firm that publicizing the story would *further* endanger those still in captivity, as well as jeopardize the mission of the *Gripsholm*, the neutral Swedish merchant ship delivering the desperately needed Red Cross boxes to POWs throughout the enemy-controlled Pacific. Again, Dyess disagreed vehemently. The prisoners would fare better, he countered, because the Japanese hate nothing more than being shamed publicly.

While the War Department may have named these concerns, its true motive for muzzling the escapees was common knowledge in closed military circles: that releasing the story now would derail the Allied grand strategy of prioritizing the European war—just as plans for the seminal cross-Channel invasion were entering their final, climactic stages. The policy of defeating Germany first, and then Japan, had been born out of a consensus that the former was the more powerful and destabilizing opponent; final implementation of that strategy could not be jeopardized. General Marshall had cautioned repeatedly since Quebec that when the Japanese atrocities did come to light, the home front would be as outraged as it had been following the attack on Pearl Harbor. Their eyes would turn toward avenging the enemy in the Pacific, and the hand of war strategy would be forced to follow.

From the start, however, the War Department's attempts to silence the escapees—especially Dyess—had been flustered and ineffectual. First, it sent the feisty pilot to "recuperate" at the Greenbrier resort in West Virginia, which had been converted temporarily to an army hospital (named Ashford General) for recuperating soldiers returned from the front. Dyess was placed in the hospital's top-security wing. But the news media knew how to get to the Greenbrier, and whisking away the freshly escaped war hero only intensified their interest in breaking what was surely a headline-grabbing tale. Newspapermen from all over the country swarmed the coffee shops in nearby White Sulphur Springs, waiting for their chance.

Throughout the final months of 1943, conservative maverick Colonel McCormick—owner of the *Chicago Tribune* and long a thorn in Roosevelt's side—was adding First Amendment muscle to his quest for government clearance to publish Dyess's account. The War Department finally allowed veteran *Tribune* reporter Charles Leavelle to take down Dyess's story at the Greenbrier, but Leavelle was not given permission to publish it. Now his fourteen-part series was ready to go, but the War Department still declined to permit its release, repeating its national security concerns.

When the *Gripsholm* returned unmolested from the Pacific after completing its dispatch of Red Cross packages to Allied prisoners of war, the newspaper renewed its petition for release of the Dyess story. With the ship's humanitarian mission no longer at risk, the *Tribune* argued, it was the paper's constitutional right to report this important story.

Leaks were springing too, despite the blanket gag order, worrying the censors all the more. Horror stories from others repatriated from the Philippines had reached the Bataan Relief Organization chapters that had been created by POW families across the country and were hinted at in their newsletters. Now these groups were joining ranks with the *Tribune*'s growing band of advocates to ratchet up pressure on the government to allow release of the story.

Even Great Britain, which had plenty to lose by a radical change in American sentiment, now favored the story's publication. Why? The British had several times more prisoners in Japanese hands than the Americans did—caught when the former colonies Java, Singapore, and Malaya fell early in the war.

In a December 1943 memorandum to the Joint Chiefs of Staff, President Roosevelt himself revealed an increasing inclination to release the story. He requested a recommendation from the JCS as to when, not whether, the White House should permit its release. Then a tragic but galvanizing event occurred just before Christmas.

By this time, a fully recovered William Dyess—promoted again, to lieutenant colonel—was in California flying practice drills in preparation for his return to combat. On December 22 his P-38 Lightning caught fire while on a training mission over the heavily populated city of Burbank. In heroic Dyess fashion, he remained aloft in his burning aircraft—despite ample opportunities to bail out safely—in order to guide the crippled aircraft to a vacant lot on Myers Street. His action saved the lives of countless civilians on the ground.

His plane crashed, however, killing William Dyess on impact. The tragic event was the fatal blow to Washington's resolve to contain the POW story. Dyess's grieving—and media savvy—father, Judge Richard T. Dyess, as well as Colonel McCormick, was now threatening to have a member of Congress read the entire story into the *Congressional Record*.

After a final flurry of tense meetings and consultations in Washington, a compromise was reached: an official joint army-navy statement would first be made public regarding the sworn statements of the escapees. Following its release at midnight, January 28, 1944, Charles Leavelle's fourteen-part series would be published.

25

★ ★ ★

BAD TIDINGS

ON JANUARY 16, 1944, in New York City, Helen Cross made the following diary entry:

> *Rosemary came to see us tonight, a respite from her work for the*
> *Commandant at the Brooklyn Navy Yard. Her news was so disquieting*
> *that Arthur and I lay awake all night practically. The navy has struck*
> *us foul blows—I wish none of mine had put on their uniform.*

Helen was tense for the rest of Rosemary's visit, barely able to contain her anxiety. She and Arthur had hoped to distract themselves from their ceaseless worries by spending January in New York City—to escape the isolating snows at Lilac Hedges, visit friends, attend the theater. But with Benny back in the Pacific and Bill soon to be, and with no word from Barton since September—and little, at that—the unconfirmed rumors had Helen on edge.

The next few days passed slowly, cruelly. Her diary entries from January 17 to 21 recorded forced distractions, including her attendance at the Broadway performance of *The Duke in Darkness*, and Olympic gold medalist Sonja Henie's figure skating show at Madison Square Garden. She also went to Red Cross headquarters to again partake in packing boxes destined for Allied prisoners of the Japanese, hoping that she might overhear something there to refute for a day, an hour, Rosemary's troubling report.

ON JANUARY 25, 1944, Bill's train rolled into Grand Central's bustling track yard. Still recovering from his bout of pneumonia at the War College, he buttoned his long overcoat before shouldering into New York's damp, snowy streets. Bill was thinner from his hospitalization, and he still had a deep, raspy cough, but he wanted to say good-bye to Helen and Arthur before leaving for the war zone. He had another mission in coming to see them, too, and not a happy one.

Despite the icy wind tunneling up the avenues, he walked the several blocks to the Henry Hudson Hotel on West Fifty-Seventh Street. It would give him a little more time to decide exactly what he wanted to say, and how. Feeling compelled to prepare them, Bill had decided to come tell them in person about the coming publication of Dyess's account before the story broke in the newspapers. He wished he could share the counterbalancing good news, but of course that was out of the question. The risk of Helen Cross not keeping that secret was greater than the risks inherent in the rescue operation itself.

It was just past five o'clock in the evening, but blacked-out New York was winter-dark, chill, and comfortless. Still, the hotel was not difficult to spot: the boxy high-rise loomed over the aging brownstones on West Fifty-Seventh like a Nebraska grain elevator. Entering through its revolving door, Bill made for the lift. The lobby's music and conversation faded as the car creaked up the shaft, stopping several times before finally reaching the fifteenth floor, giving Bill a few more minutes to rehearse.

When the elevator operator called out "Fifteen!" and cranked open the lift's brass accordion door, Bill headed toward room 1547 in a state of half anticipation, half dread. When he reached their room, he put an end to his internal deliberations, took a deep breath, and gave three quick raps on the door.

His heart jumped when his mother answered, smiling up at him. She was quickly joined by Arthur, who took Bill's damp woolen coat from him but kept the other hand, for an overlong moment, on his stepson's shoulder. "Bourbon?" he offered, gesturing proudly to the makeshift bar he had set up in their small accomodation. Bill gladly accepted the drink offer.

As Arthur prepared the beverages, Bill couldn't help but notice how tired and careworn both he and his mother looked. What else did he sense? Something told him that their seeing him uniformed and ready to depart— even his new commander's bars—triggered more anxiety than pride.

They sat with their cocktails, uncomfortably close in the tiny quarters. Bill showed them recent photographs of Adam and baby Janie ("almost eight months old!") and exhausted every other possible family topic until Bill knew the time had come. He took two long draughts of his bourbon and water, more than half the glass, in preparation for the conversation's next phase.

"There are some other things I thought you should know," he started. At this, they sat still, listening expectantly.

"The Joint Chiefs of Staff," he said, choosing his words carefully, "met earlier this week and decided to recommend the release of a story about the Japanese and their"—he paused, thinking—"*treatment* of the prisoners of war in the Philippines." Helen leaned forward and clasped her hands, appearing to believe something good was coming. Here was Rosemary's rumor, debunked! Arthur sat back and crossed his legs, reserving judgment. They seemed to barely breathe.

"You remember," Bill resumed, "there was an escape from a prison camp on Mindanao in the Philippines last spring? Barton's camp?" They nodded silently, but their expressions registered *That had been good news, hadn't it?*

"Well, when those men got out, they gave sworn statements on every aspect of their . . ."—he paused again—"experiences. But the War Department would not allow them to divulge any of the details—not even to their own families—for fear the Japanese might retaliate against the prisoners still being held. Among other reasons, they did not want the revelations to get leaked and possibly interrupt delivery of those Red Cross boxes." On this last point, he gestured to his mother, knowing how much effort she had devoted to the packing project.

Helen and Arthur nodded again, but with visibly waning enthusiasm at the word "retaliate." Still, this was perfectly acceptable so far; they knew Barton was among the hopeful recipients of the boxes. Packing them had brought Helen almost as much satisfaction, she'd mused, as they likely would bring the prisoners themselves. Here had been something she could *do* to manage her pain.

"But now," Bill continued, "the Joint Chiefs think—and the president thinks—that it's time for the American people to know about these atrocities."

"Atrocities?" Arthur repeated in his proper British accent. He shifted in his chair. "What do you mean, atrocities?"

Bill fingered the rim of his glass before responding. He hadn't intended to put himself in this corner. "Well, actually, before I get into all *that*, I have some good news. Some very good news. Just this week past, I spoke with one of those escaped prisoners, the navy man. He knew Barton, and saw him in April, just before they got out."

"Was it as far back as April?" Arthur asked. "You do mean April of 1943, I assume?"

"Well, yes, but it took some time to get them back to the States," Bill said, trying not to sound defensive. "This fellow said that when they left,

Bart was alive and in pretty good shape, considering. In fact, he said that Barton had done real credit to himself under difficult circumstances. Other prisoners look up to him, he told me—the ensigns especially. I thought you would like to know that." Bill remembered his own flush of pride when he'd heard this about his brother.

Helen leaned back in her chair and let a moan escape her lips. Arthur, in an effort to check another of his wife's teary descents, jumped in. "Well, that *is* good news, Bill; let us pray it is still the case *now*." Bill nodded. That round had ended in a draw.

Helen and Arthur could tell by Bill's demeanor that something hard was coming. They had grown accustomed, over time, to Bill's method of breaking the sparing news he had gathered about Barton. First came the good news and reasons why they should be encouraged, updates from well-placed sources—after which came the less good news, often couched in maddeningly optimistic language.

Tonight was different, they detected; they were about to hear something from which even Bill couldn't protect them. Helen braced for affirmation of Rosemary's rumor (of tortured prisoners), which had plagued her since hearing it. Bill took another long draught of his drink, nearly empty now. He then started talking again, a little faster.

"So, anyway, back to the other. I thought you ought to know ahead of time that the story these prisoners had to tell about their experience in the Philippines is going to be published—in all the papers—sometime in the next week, I expect. And it's, well, I wanted you to be prepared that some of it is quite graphic."

He paused again and then said, "Frankly, you might be better off not even reading it." For several seconds—the seeming length of an eternity—the three of them said nothing. Bill broke the silence.

"Remember, the best information so far is that Barton has come through. And the thinking now is that when this story is made public, the

Japanese will be shamed into treating the remaining prisoners . . . better. They know they are losing right now. General MacArthur himself is preparing a stern warning to the Japanese that's going to be released with the government's statement.

"I just thought you should be prepared—for the media sensation around it all, too," he finished, wishing he had not used the word "sensation."

What registered on their faces when Bill stopped talking was that if Bill was willing to say to them words and phrases such as "atrocities" and "really bad," given his propensity to soft-pedal the negative to them, this must be *really* bad.

"Billy, dear, you must tell us, what exactly is this story going to say?" Helen entreated, almost in a whisper.

Worn down by the conflicting desire to both shield and inform them, Bill proceeded with mixed emotions to reveal the nature and content of the escapees' sworn statements, all of which he'd read several times. While omitting the most chilling details, he went as far as he did because he knew they *would* read the story—and would have lost their trust in him had he kept it from them.

What Bill did keep hidden was that he too was angry—very angry. He was in a pent-up, self-blaming, roiling rage for being the very person who had unwittingly put Barton, despite his best intentions, in harm's way. It had eaten at him day and night for weeks, months, and now years. Only getting on a ship and getting to the front—and eventually to the Philippines itself—would relieve the building pressure in his chest.

When he finished talking, Bill looked down at his hands and rubbed his Academy ring, a habit when he was nervous. "They will pay with their lives, Mother," he blurted out, feeling the color in his cheeks rise. "Their army hasn't just been lying to the International Red Cross; they've been lying to their own people. This story will—"

He stopped abruptly. His mother had buried her face in her hands and begun to sob. Arthur, who had sat pale and stoic throughout Bill's difficult revelations, moved only when Helen broke down—raising his right hand, trembling, as a signal to Bill to pause.

Her hair fell forward, thrown out of place by her shuddering. Bill saw streaks of gray that he had never noticed before and suddenly realized how Barton's removal from her life had utterly transformed their mother. It was as though a vital organ had been ripped from her core, and she could not get on without it.

Bill saw full force that no matter how hard he or Benny or even Rosemary tried to make her proud, to fight the good fight, this pain was deep and untouchable. There was no earthly remedy for it. He had never felt so helpless.

Bill said no more about the impending news story after that, except to again suggest tenderly that she avoid reading it. All he could muster was to repeat, "The Japanese will pay for what they've done, Mother; you can be sure of that." At this, Helen shored herself up and narrowed her eyes contemptuously.

"By the time *they* get around to it, it will be too late for Barton, I fear," she said angrily, her old imperiousness making a brief reappearance. "*They*," Bill knew, meant all the people he worked for, right to the top.

The visit did not last much longer. He embraced his mother and shook Arthur's hand after putting on his overcoat and reclaiming his cap from the end table. "I am doing the best I can, please know that at least," he said, his voice thick but the words forceful and clear. They nodded.

"Be careful, Billy dear," Helen said, regaining her composure. "I do need at least one son left to carry on." Bill was both touched and taken aback, just as he had always been by her brief spasms of warmth. This was the best he could hope for, he understood now.

THREE DAYS LATER, A Friday, Helen remained in her New York hotel room for the entire day with the dreaded copy of the *New York Times*. Her eyes welled with tears each time she reread the opening line of the front-page story. "A pent-up story of atrocities perpetrated by the Japanese army on the captured heroes of Bataan and Corregidor was released by the United States government today in sickening detail."

Contrary to Bill's advice, she pored obsessively over the article, alternately sobbing and lying down. Arthur was stricken, too, but by early afternoon, he implored his wife to get dressed and go for a walk with him. Getting some fresh air would help them both, he urged. But Helen declined, remaining in her bedclothes the entire day.

The story went on for pages, the details beyond the opening paragraphs so much worse than her worst expectations that Helen had to pause every few lines to absorb the shock. Before switching off the light and ending the day's misery, she opened her diary and unscrewed her fountain pen, hand shaking slightly:

> The Japanese atrocity stories are out. Oh God! They cannot be true!
> A million bayonets pierce my heart—my dear one, my lad of peace and kindliness—where are you? How fare you, beloved one? I die for you in your pain. No food, no solace in this life until Barton comes! If only I could bear each insult, torture, pain for him. I will not even call on the name of God again.

And the next day, written diagonally across the page, was only: "Sick, sick, in body and mind."

By the end of January, the story had been told and retold in thousands of newspapers and magazines across the country and around the world. It punched the public with predicted emotional force and the response was universally vengeful. At the Brooklyn Navy Yard's ceremonial christening of the USS *Missouri* the day after the story's release, a somber Vice President Harry S. Truman stated, "May this great ship be an avenger to the barbarians who wantonly slaughtered the heroes of Bataan."

Whether Helen saw the coverage of the *Missouri* ceremony in the New

York newspapers is unknown. There were no further entries in her diary until February 6, 1944. On that day, she wrote:

For Arthur, I cannot go on this way. I must keep living in the slipping hope that my boy may come back. And Rosemary came by today too and said, coldly but logically, I suppose, "Either Bart returns or he doesn't. There is nothing you can do to alter that fate. But you can prevent it from killing all of us, Mother."

I must, I will face it.

26

★ ★ ★

POLITICS IN BRISBANE

HAROLD ROSENQUIST ARRIVED IN Brisbane in early December, and he and Steve Mellnik went right to work fleshing out the logistical details of the rescue proposal. Under General Willoughby's guidance, they crafted a staff study that covered every aspect of the mission. For comparison purposes, Mellnik also prepared a memorandum on the potential for escape from the Cabanatuan prison camp and the significantly greater logistical challenges it presented. Luzon was far more heavily garrisoned than Mindanao, and Cabanatuan significantly more so than Davao.

In a race against time, they focused primarily on the details of a Davao rescue, which had the greatest potential for success. Mellnik laid out the proposed timetable based on his own escape and knowledge of the island. First, he explained that Rosenquist's submarine would need to rendezvous with local guerrilla units in the waters off the Davao Gulf on the east coast of Mindanao. Once ashore, he would then have to make his way to Major Lauretta, whose Davao guerrilla unit would be central to the plan's implementation.

Under Lauretta's guidance, Rosenquist would then initiate contact with select Davao prisoners. Letters from Mellnik, written on GHQ stationery, would be passed to trusted prisoners inside the camp. This aspect of the operation was not as daunting as it might seem, Mellnik assured Rosenquist, as many locals came and went from the penal colony daily, and prisoner work details moved in and out of the compound frequently.

Once these clandestine contacts were established, the next priority would be to smuggle in vitamins, medicines, and badly needed quinine tablets to bring rampant malaria under control. The prisoners would have to regain as much strength as possible ahead of a mass evacuation.

Rosenquist assured Mellnik that this would be the least of his problems: his MIS-X expertise was camouflaging and smuggling such items past hostile parties. Compared with what his team of experts had concealed and smuggled into German prison camps—money, maps, radios, compasses, even weapons—vitamins, medicine, and quinine tablets would be a cakewalk.

The men spent countless hours refining the elements of the rescue itself, including the logistics of the predawn raid and the distribution of prisoners to multiple safe havens within the Mindanao hill and jungle communities and other outposts under guerrilla control. Sophisticated escape-and-evasion maps, complete with topographical data, were prepared, in addition to "Plan B" maps detailing alternative escape routes to the sea.

Ultimately, the men would be rotated off Mindanao by submarine. *Nautilus* and *Narwhal,* and additional navy submarines as they became available, would provide the conveyance. In the cover memo of the detailed Staff Study submitted for General Sutherland's approval, Mellnik wrote:

"Recommend that Lieutenant Rosenquist, MIS-X, be authorized to proceed immediately to Mindanao and that Colonel Fertig be directed to make arrangements for his trip to Major Claro Lauretta's headquarters. Its proximity to the POW camp . . . makes it the logical point of contact from which active assistance to the POWs can be initiated. It is further recommended that Lieutenant Rosenquist work directly under the auspices of G-2."

General Willoughby signed off on the Staff Study on December 11, 1943, and immediately forwarded it to General Sutherland for final approval. Mellnik and Rosenquist were jubilant when the plan came back in January with General Sutherland's consent, after which he departed Brisbane for Washington for an indeterminate length of time to promote General MacArthur's control of the entire Pacific theater. Rosenquist prepared to depart on the very next Mindanao-bound submarine scheduled for February 16, 1944.

But from the moment Courtney Whitney got Rosenquist's dispatch request and learned the details of the rescue plan, he raised loud and continuous objections. Thus was launched the GHQ battle royal over control of the Philippine theater. The rescue plan—placed under G-2 auspices—had been specifically designed to bypass Whitney and his new Philippine Regional Section, with the exception of his control over its use of the submarines. Rosenquist would need to be transported to Mindanao by submarine, and the freed prisoners evacuated in them.

Whitney objected that the rescue operation would endanger the Mindanao guerrillas' primary goal: the eventual facilitation of MacArthur's return—the principal reason, he argued, that PRS had been supplying the guerrillas in the first place. He further objected that the plan rendered Colonel Wendell Fertig—GHQ's anointed Mindanao guerrilla leader—subordinate to Rosenquist's orders, and by extension, General Willoughby's. Whitney adamantly opposed Rosenquist's "unwarranted" authority over Fertig.

Lacking veto authority, Whitney's tactic was to delay the operation, at which he proved very effective. Each new delay was cleverly disguised as a "concern." As the lives of Davao's prison population hung in the balance, dueling memoranda between PRS's Whitney and G-2's Willoughby locked Australia's army headquarters into inaction. With General Sutherland on a possibly months-long mission to Washington, he was unavailable to break the tie. General Richard Marshall, acting chief of staff during Sutherland's absence, declined to mediate. "I'm staying out of this . . . brawl," he said flatly. "Take the problem up with Sutherland when he returns."

And so, on February 16, 1944, Courtney Whitney's cargo list for the Mindanao-bound USS *Narwhal* emphatically excluded one Lieutenant Harold Rosenquist.

27

★ ★ ★

"PROCEED TO KWAJALEIN"

IT HAD BEEN A long time coming. Bill slung his duffel over his shoulder and stepped onto the gangway of the USS *Rocky Mount*, the Fifth Fleet's amphibious flagship. Anchored in the central lagoon at Kwajalein, in the heart of the Marshall Islands, "the Rock" had just completed a victorious sweep of the southern half of the Kwajalein chain, the world's largest coral atoll. The operation had been supported by two naval task forces—one, the new, hard-hitting "Fast Carrier Force" (TF 58), and the other led by the battle-hardened *Enterprise* and her screening vessels.

Bill was to report to Admiral Richmond Kelly Turner, Allied commander of the Fifth Fleet's new Joint Expeditionary Force—responsible for the seizing of designated Japanese-held islands across the Central Pacific, and for all naval, air, and landed troops in each operation. Bill's new position was flag secretary to Admiral Turner. He was also designated the fleet's legal officer. Turner desperately needed a new flag secretary; many had already been chewed up and spit out by the famously abrasive admiral.

As head of the Navy Department's War Plans Division in the crisis-ridden years of 1940 to 1942, Turner recalled young Lieutenant Mott as one of the few people there that he hadn't fought with and also that Bill had been quite helpful to him on occasion. In his note requesting Bill's services, Turner wrote:

Between 1940 and 1942, I was the Director of War Plans in the Office of the Chief of Naval Operations. During this period, Lt. Commander Mott was on duty in the Office of Naval Intelligence and very frequently came under my close observation. I observed his great energy and attentiveness to duty during long hours and well in excess of prescribed hours, including most Sundays. I would welcome his attachment to my personal staff.

In the exponentially expanded US Navy of 1944, résumés for top staff positions requiring both amphibious and code-and-communications backgrounds were "as scarce as glassy seas in the Bay of Biscay," one admiral mused; those selected would require a strong work ethic and hard, on-the-job training. Bill Mott amply satisfied both requirements, and with the rare quality of never having previously crossed hairs with Admiral Turner, his orders to *Rocky Mount* were drawn up.

He was needed immediately. With completion of the Allied occupation of Kwajalein—relatively lightly defended but valuable for its large and deep natural harbor and sturdy, coral-surfaced airfield—Turner's forces had begun planning their next series of amphibious assaults: Eniwetok, followed by Truk and then Saipan, the most prized of the inner protectorates of the Japanese islands. A continuation of the amphibians' thrust across the mid-Pacific, this next phase was designed to pierce the enemy's perimeter-island defensive arc that protected mainland Japan itself.

★   ★   ★

HIS NEW HOME, FLAGSHIP USS *Rocky Mount*, was unlike any ship Bill had ever boarded. Its superstructure was dominated by a geometric tangle of radar and radio gear. Above the bridge was another curious gnarl of transmitters of various shapes, sizes, and heights, all positioned next to a phalanx of receivers. In most other respects, *Rocky Mount* resembled little more than an old supply transport—a purposeful disguise. Experience had shown that enemy bombers went after this sort of ship last.

Rocky Mount was not only the Amphibious Force Command headquarters; it was home to its Combat Information Center (CIC), the fleet's electronic nerve hub, and served as the floating residence for top brass from every service taking part in each island offensive. The Rock was to Pacific amphibious campaigns what the Map Room was to the world war: the decision-making epicenter for all commands. In sight of all action at all times, it was the lead vessel in every action. The monumental challenge of coordinating combined amphibious operations, among the most demanding of military missions, was soon to become Bill's life—heart, soul, body, and mind.

For the three months prior to Bill's arrival at Kwajalein, Admiral Turner and the amphibians had been busy seizing Makin and Tarawa Islands and gaining a toehold in the Gilberts and Marshalls. But personnel losses from those operations had numbered in the several thousands due to stiff enemy resistance, inadequate resources, and flaws in their advance reconnaissance—as well as in planning and execution. This was especially the case with Tarawa.

The objective had been narrow: seize Tarawa's strategic mid-Pacific airfield. But the losses were staggering and caused a storm of stateside protest. Was that seven-hundred-yard-wide scrap of mid-Pacific coral and sand, smaller than New York's Central Park, really worth the lives of a thousand marines, and twice that wounded? MacArthur wasted no time pouncing:

he placed square and very public blame on the navy for Tarawa's "tragic and unnecessary massacre of American lives."

Kelly Turner was not taking time off to celebrate his recent promotion to vice admiral; the next objective was imminent, and lessons from Tarawa needed to be understood and applied. First of all, four million pounds of explosives dropped on the island ahead of the landings had not made a dent in enemy positions. Unmolested, 4,600 Japanese ambushed the landing marines. Another ugly surprise had been the dual effect of Tarawa's jagged coral reefs and a lower-than-hoped-for tide—a deadly combination of landing conditions that exposed wave after wave of marines to murderous artillery fire as they struggled toward shore through wide stretches of razor-sharp coral.

Admiral Turner wasted no time applying these hard-won lessons to future planning. Naval and air pre-bombardment was revised following grim proof of its ineffectiveness at Tarawa. Henceforward, pre-invasion firepower would focus on destroying specific enemy capabilities, not neutralization. More amphibious landing vehicles (amtracs) with better armor were also ordered, as well as side armor for the marines. And underwater demolition teams were created to search out and clear all natural and artificial beach obstacles ahead of future landings.

And so it was that one of Bill's first reading assignments was to memorize his new boss's post-Tarawa memorandum, "Recommendations for Changes and Improvements in Tactics, Techniques, Existing Instructions and Material," as well as that of Turner's senior amphibious subordinate: Rear Admiral Harry Hill's sobering "Lessons from Tarawa."

According to Bill's position description, he was to "supervise and direct production plans and execution of major amphibious operations." This meant coordinating among a myriad of constituents the logistics and battle plans that make up an expeditionary force invasion: naval support groups; underwater demolition teams; meteorologists; beachhead organization (beachmasters); the amphibious corps; marine personnel; medical personnel; and the strategists who determined the timing and disposition of the multiple landing forces and whether they were variously supplied with rations, water, ammunition, tourniquets, and morphine in advance of battle. And, of course, there would have to be major contingency plans to all the above—for according to naval doctrine, "No battle plan survives contact with the enemy."

Bill read his orders with the appropriate humility of one whose longest prior ship duty was his post-plebe midshipman cruise more than a decade earlier. He was terrified and thrilled in unequal parts by the enormity of the challenge. But the home front had done its part. Turner's Joint Expeditionary Force encompassed 634 ships and more than 300,000 navy, marine, and army personnel. With the country's industrial might ramped up to full war footing, the sailors' joke now was that they could walk for miles across Pacific anchorages without getting wet: the ocean was paved with steel.

BEFORE SETTLING INTO HIS duties aboard *Rocky Mount*, Bill requested permission to board the *Enterprise*, lying astride recently annexed Kwajalein. Time was short: *Enterprise* was preparing to depart for its next enemy raid of Truk. Benny had been cautiously optimistic that he and Bill would intersect at Kwajalein, but he had avoided setting his heart on it, given the potential for snafus in the navy generally and in the middle of a war zone specifically.

So when Bill came through the heavy door of *Enterprise*'s Sky Control, Benny let out a howl of delight. One proud introduction followed another, Benny making great hay out of Bill's new job as "Terrible Turner's" latest flag secretary.

The brothers' reunion was brief but upbeat—until the end, when Bill shared the difficult details of his January visit in New York. He didn't need to brief Benny on the Japanese atrocity story; it had reached the farthest Pacific outposts in no time, smacking Allied forces like a rogue wave. With each printed word, every man on the front lines seethed for revenge.

Bill told Benny of his exchange with one of the Davao escapees while he was recuperating at Walter Reed in Washington. And that "positive developments" had him hoping for a three-brother reunion. When it was time for Benny to share his own news, he wished he had told Bill sooner. But perhaps it was obvious. The toll of alternating days, months, and years of high alert, worry, and fatigue had gathered in darkening ditches beneath Benny's normally bright eyes.

"Bill, I've been on this ship for four years, and I'm proud of the work we've done, what we've accomplished. But I'm exhausted. My marriage is in shambles, and I've only seen Jeanne Marie once in eighteen months. I have put in for a transfer to Washington. I can really help those desk captains there in Ordnance—they need an experienced hand from the field. So I guess that means it's up to you now to see the rest of the way through to Barton."

Bill took in Benny's every word without interrupting. He was a combination of sad and relieved at Benny's news, but not surprised. Remembering his own anxiety during engagement after engagement, wondering if Benny was dead or alive—if it had left *him* emotionally whipsawed, he could only imagine its effect on Benny. Bill knew he would find out soon enough.

They stood together for a few more minutes, having no idea when—or if—they would see each other again. No more was said about Barton, but they did agree that Benny's reassignment was a wise move for their mother's sake, not to mention his own.

Benny fought welling emotion as he watched Bill make his way toward the idling launch that would take him back to *Rocky Mount*. With forced cheerfulness, he called out to his brother, "Just remember, Bill, hell, be *careful*. It can get dicey out here!"

PART
THREE

28

★ ★ ★

THE BEST-LAID PLANS

IN APRIL 1944, GENERAL Sutherland finally returned to Brisbane. He left behind the bitter scrum in Washington over whose military strategy would dominate the balance of the Pacific War—only to step into the GHQ turf war that had been simmering in his absence. The widening scope of Courtney Whitney's PRS and its control over the submarine missions had become the sorest of points to G-2 generally and to General Willoughby specifically.

As PRS activities had expanded—adding more coastwatchers, clandestine radio receivers, and Filipino agent nets, plus stepped-up supply and support of the guerrillas—so had Whitney's free agency and access to MacArthur. Severely irritated by his rival's increasing stature and erosion of his own authority over Philippine affairs, Willoughby greeted General Sutherland with a formal recommendation for a GHQ reorganization regarding the handling of Philippine affairs. They should be split among staff sections, Willoughby argued, and, as head of G-2 for SWPA, the majority of Philippine activity should be returned to his purview. Willoughby also asked Sutherland to immediately re-approve the Rosenquist prisoner rescue mission, which had been inexcusably thwarted by Whitney during his long absence.

For the previous twelve weeks, Willoughby, Mellnik, and Rosenquist had all tried to placate Whitney with revision after revision of the rescue plan so that Rosenquist could depart for Mindanao. After Whitney scuttled his February departure, Rosenquist made a brief diary entry: "Ready to go on mission, but Whitney's influence too strong." He had begun to fear privately that they were running out of time.

Tensions were exacerbated further by the media sensation over the Davao escapee story. Whitney and Willoughby had quarreled endlessly over whether the story's publication had likely worsened (Whitney) or improved (Willoughby) the Japanese captors' treatment of Allied prisoners. Inevitably, the argument expanded to include their respective opinions on whether or not this had a bearing on Rosenquist's incipient mission.

When General Sutherland returned to GHQ, Whitney fired off a memo justifying his actions:

```
My objection to [the plan] lay in the:


(a)  Status given Lieutenant Rosenquist rendering him
     subject only to the direction of G-2, GHQ [Willoughby];
(b)  Rosenquist's unrestricted right to call upon the local
     commander [Fertig] for such personnel, supplies,
     communication and transport facilities and other
     assistance as may be necessary to accomplish his
     mission;
(c)  Establishment of an intelligence system within the POW
     camp by written directive from this Headquarters to
     certain officer prisoners and;
(d)  Plan for mass evacuation or escape of prisoners.
```

... I believe that we should but ask these prisoners
to continue to show the fortitude that alone will make it
possible to survive the difficult and trying ordeal which
yet lies ahead.

C. W.

Sutherland was unmoved by Whitney's arguments, and General Sutherland had the final say—always with MacArthur's presumptive authority. He was MacArthur's top confidant at the time and widely regarded as his full and equal partner. In fact, it was an open secret that General MacArthur was positioning Sutherland for the highest office in the army, one that he himself had held: army chief of staff. As popular as "Court" Whitney was with General MacArthur, Sutherland's power trumped any amount of shameless flattery Whitney could pour on.

RICHARD KERENS SUTHERLAND HAD been unwavering in his endorsement of the Davao prisoner rescue mission from the start—despite the risks it might pose for MacArthur's planned Mindanao landing, for the Mindanao guerrillas, or for the prisoners themselves. To Sutherland, its potential rewards outweighed all imagined downsides.

But to say that General Sutherland had a complicated relationship with the whole idea of POWs would be a serious understatement. For eighteen months, he had been conducting an intense and surprisingly public affair with one Elaine Bessemer Clarke, the Australian wife of a British captain whom the Japanese had taken prisoner at the fall of Singapore.

The married Sutherland had met Clarke and her infant son in Melbourne, Australia, in March 1942, shortly after he, MacArthur, and other senior MacArthur staff had fled the Philippines. According to sources present, Sutherland and Clarke were attracted to each other from the moment they met. The new couple quickly became the subject of endless staff gossip.

When MacArthur's headquarters moved offices from Melbourne to Brisbane, eyebrows rose further as Clarke, her toddler son, the nanny, and their cocker spaniel packed up and made the six-hundred-mile journey with them. And they rose all the more when Sutherland pulled strings and appointed the Australian Clarke a captain in the American Women's Army Corps (WAC), making her the first non-American woman to join those proud ranks. Captain Clarke became the receptionist at GHQ's new Brisbane headquarters at the AMP Building on Queen Street.

The couple's bold intimacy became increasingly apparent over time, with Sutherland playing father to Clarke's young son. All the while, the uncomfortable subject of her POW husband reportedly weighed heavily on them both. It is unknowable whether Sutherland and Clarke's intense relationship propelled his support of the Davao prisoner rescue plan. Was he allaying his guilt by supporting the rescue of an unrelated group of war prisoners? What if the plan had been to rescue the British prisoners in Singapore?

Sutherland's relationship with Clarke would eventually put him in an untenable position with MacArthur, but at the time, Sutherland still had his mentor's full support. So in April 1944, when Sutherland overruled all objections and reasserted his earlier approvals of the rescue mission, even Court Whitney had to accept it. Lieutenant Rosenquist would depart for Mindanao on the next available submarine.

Whitney conceded defeat reluctantly; this was the *third* time Sutherland had ruled in favor of the Rosenquist plan. Yet even as he agreed to arrange Rosenquist's submarine conveyance to Mindanao, Whitney continued deploying delay tactics. In his capacity as head of PRS, he had the final say on *when* submarines could be dispatched to the Philippines. On the April night of Sutherland's latest ruling, Rosenquist confided to his diary, "Okay again by General Sutherland, but again, delays."

Rosenquist did not board the USS *Narwhal* until May 10, 1944, but with cautious optimism, he wrote his boss at MIS-X's secret headquarters in Virginia. Both men understood each and every carefully veiled reference in the letter, including its high praise for Steve Mellnik:

Lt. Colonel John H. Starr

P.O. Box 1142

Alexandria, Virginia

May 10, 1944

Dear Colonel Starr:

    At last! After much fussing around, I can write you that my mission is now set and I'm going shortly. The good news came quite unexpectedly after many trying months of nursing the project.

    Eventually and without question . . . everything hoped for should materialize. You can be certain, Colonel . . . my designation is fixed and reachable . . .

    Knowing the responsibility of this job, perhaps more than people realize, makes enthusiasm secondary to firm patience. I realize the big opportunity to save lives and the joy my presence will bring people who have untiringly waited for word of encouragement.

    I pray God I can completely execute the job you have assigned me, through the untiring efforts of one who for so many months has pushed this assignment . . . in the face of many obstacles. For him, and you know of whom I speak, I have the highest admiration and respect. Knowing he will be on the job here is of great consolation to me . . . and I

know that reports will get through to you as he finds them
possible.

My best regards to all at PO Box 1142. I sincerely hope I
can do the job with credit to our Section.

H. A. R.

Rosenquist was delayed another five days at the Darwin rendezvous
point without explanation. On May 15, 1944, he confided to his diary:
"At last . . . after eleven months, on our way." He estimated that the voyage
would take ten days, putting him in Davao by early June.

But on May 27 and 28, a dismayed Rosenquist was still aboard *Narwhal*. He wrote, "We are way off course . . . no contact . . . disappointed . . .
navigation lousy . . ." Then again, on May 30: "Marking time . . ." On the
thirty-first of May, he reported: "Sight of land through periscope."

That faint outline of land, however, was the *southwest* coast of Mindanao, hundreds of kilometers (hundreds of miles) from Rosenquist's
explicitly planned debarkation point near Davao, on the island's *southeast*
coast. But Rosenquist had no alternative. He and the other *Narwhal* passengers, weather observers carrying a supply of weapons, pistols, daggers,
emergency rations, and numerous thermometers, were told they must debark and make the best of it.

The disoriented party paddled ashore in a rubber boat and, fortunately,
was intercepted by local guerrillas instead of the Japanese. Colonel Robert
Bowler, the senior-most guerrilla in that part of Mindanao, questioned the
group, but Rosenquist declined to disclose his mission. When Bowler told
him that Wendell Fertig insisted on seeing him personally before he could
proceed, Rosenquist reluctantly agreed. Fertig's Tenth Military District
headquarters in the Agusan Valley, however, was even farther from Colonel
Lauretta and the Davao Penal Colony than the submarine's erroneous landing point, causing Rosenquist still more costly delays.

The guerrilla-guided journey, however, confirmed everything Mellnik had told him about Mindanao's skilled and fleet-footed guerrilla population. Rosenquist's journey across miles of jungle, enemy-infested mountains, and treacherous inland waterways was made possible only by his seamless conveyance from one guerrilla unit to the next. They fed, housed, and protected him every step of the way, and even arranged for a dentist and barber en route. Rosenquist was impressed.

The orders he carried from GHQ explicitly sanctioned his mission and ordered the guerrillas to fulfill it. They also made clear that Rosenquist reported directly to General MacArthur's command, not Wendell Fertig's:

> "Captain Harold Rosenquist, O-278037, has been placed
> on temporary duty . . . for the purpose of acting as advisor
> in the planning of assistance to prisoners of war in your
> military area. Such matters will be conducted in accordance
> with the policies of [General MacArthur] as communicated
> to you from time to time."

In addition, he carried letters from Steve Mellnik to specific trusted individuals inside Davao Penal Colony, men who could be relied on to facilitate the escape from the inside. One letter, dated February 10, 1944, was written after the broad publication of the atrocity stories. It was addressed to Lieutenant Colonel Memory "Doc" Cain:

> General Headquarters,
> Southwest Pacific
>
> Dear Doc,
>
>   It's been almost a year since we talked about things
> at Barracks Number 8. I pray you are still there to read
> this . . . The country has just heard the news. Congress

and the people have sent up a cry that's echoing around
the world. Things are afoot to do things. I won't give
any "target dates." This letter, written from General
MacArthur's headquarters, is sufficient proof of what is
happening. He is taking a great and active interest--I
should know.

Much has to be done, Doc. I'm depending on you to do it. The
source of this message was sent by me to you. Trust him. He is
H. A. R. He will get in touch with you. You've got to consider
yourself C.O. of the camp with this. Mobilize all of [his]
activities. Exercise extreme security precautions . . . Take
your time, be awfully careful, and remember all of this is
being done to speed up the DAY. I cannot reiterate too strongly
that the success of our plans depends on 100% secrecy.

                         Steve Mellnik

En route to Wendell Fertig's headquarters, Rosenquist encoded a preliminary report for relay to Brisbane once he reached Fertig's radio station.
Despite the serial setbacks and detours, the indefatigable Rosenquist remained optimistic:

Guards and outposts covering trails, roads, and rivers
everywhere; one rifle, fifteen rounds of ammunition per two
men of front line units, who are familiar with respective
sectors. Plan formulated for roadblocks, bridge construction,
trail coverage, and delaying enemy action . . . Troop and
civilian morale high. Our trip untold value.

BUT WENDELL FERTIG—WEARING locally crafted silver stars of
a brigadier general on his collar despite his actual US Army Reserve rank

of lieutenant colonel—was of another mind when Colonel Bowler radioed him that an unannounced submarine had surfaced off the coast of southwestern Mindanao and unloaded five surprise guests: four enlisted weather observers, and one highly ranked intelligence officer on an undisclosed mission "of great importance."

Fertig said to his aide de camp, Commander Wheeler (no relation to Ken), who had delivered the dispatch, "You send a message back to Bowler. Tell him to disarm those weather people and turn their stuff over to people who can use it . . . Make clear," he added sarcastically, "we won't interfere with their basic mission of wetting their fingers to detect which way the wind is blowing."

Fertig was just getting warmed up. "And tell Bowler," he continued, "to make sure these people understand that all persons reporting to Mindanao *must* come under my direct command, and that all activities will be directed by *me*. And Bowler is to tell this Rosenquist that as far as we're concerned, he is a visiting staff officer without authority. Until I find out what his mission is and *I* approve it, he is not to issue orders to any of our men. I need to find out from Headquarters what the hell is going on."

Then Fertig gave Wheeler a second order. "Send a message to GHQ asking them what the hell is going on with Rosenquist. Tell them all activities on the island of Mindanao *must* be controlled by me." Then he muttered, "Thickheads." A bewildered Wheeler left to carry out the orders.

Fertig sat back, absorbing what he had just learned. Weathermen were one thing; hopefully their presence presaged an increase in US air reconnaissance, which hopefully presaged an imminent landing by MacArthur on Mindanao, a moment he had been savoring for some time. But a high-ranked intelligence officer on a secret mission? That was something else entirely.

Fertig's disposition did not improve when Wheeler returned with a response from Brisbane. "Headquarters," he reported, "says we are to furnish Rosenquist with any aid and assistance he may require."

Fertig spun around, eyes wide. "What is his mission?"

"They won't say," Wheeler said, "just that it's of the 'greatest importance' and that all we have to do is follow orders."

Fertig then spat, "I haven't stayed alive here for over two years by allowing a crowd of dreamers fifteen hundred miles away to tell me what I have to do. And, by God, I'm not going to start now. I'm not going to have them sending special missions in here that could get my tail in a crack without my knowing what's happening until it's too late. Therefore, you will tell Bowler to send this Rosenquist to me, and *I'll* decide whether we'll help him or not."

Since late May, Fertig had been hearing the distinctive drone of US Navy carrier aircraft strafing in the distance. He had interpreted this as further corroboration that MacArthur planned to make his first strike at Mindanao—*his* military district—meaning, hopefully, his place in history would soon be secured. After that first landing, or so he had heard, Allied troops would slog their way north to Leyte, and then Luzon—and its prize, Manila. Both Fertig and the Japanese were expecting this scenario to unfold in the coming weeks.

So when Rosenquist finally arrived at Wendell Fertig's headquarters, the colonel's guard was up. Whatever this stranger was up to, Fertig was determined that it not derail his grand plan at the last minute.

Rosenquist shook Fertig's hand enthusiastically. "It won't be long now," he told the guerrilla leader at their introduction. "I don't know when it's going to be, but it's an open secret it's going to be soon."

He then complimented Fertig on his work of the past two years, adding that GHQ thought that he'd "done one hell of a fine job."

"My instructions are to give you any assistance I can," replied Fertig, in a tone of one unaffected by compliments. "Whether I do depends on whether I decide your mission is practical. I want to make that clear."

Rosenquist replied that it was. He had great confidence in his mission, he said, and the potential for its success had been confirmed by everything he had seen in his smooth guerrilla passage across the island.

Fertig listened without expression, and then replied flatly, "If I decide not to help you, you will remain in this area as a staff officer without command authority, subject to a letter of instruction that will be furnished to you."

Rosenquist was taken aback. Ever since the first mention of this proposed mission, back in Washington the previous summer, he had maintained a singular focus on freeing some two thousand systematically beaten, tortured, and starved Americans. After surviving General Whitney's serial delays, he thought the only remaining obstacle was the enemy.

"I don't mean to be abrupt," Fertig continued. "I just want you to understand that I will be the judge of any operations within my area. Now, just what do you intend to do?"

It was a shocking moment for Rosenquist. Armed with orders from General MacArthur's chief of staff, as well as other weighty documentation from Brisbane's SWPA Headquarters, Rosenquist had imagined that all he needed to do was direct Fertig to put men under his command, no questions asked. To surrender any classified information to Fertig violated everything this intelligence officer—trained and experienced in top secret missions—held dear.

But Rosenquist realized there was no way out: Fertig would have to know if he was to proceed. Moreover, precious time was slipping away. "We intend to free the American prisoners from Davao Penal Colony before they can be moved," he said.

"I have no information that they're about to be moved," replied Fertig, genuinely startled by Rosenquist's confident pronouncement. "When are they going, and *where* are they going?"

Rosenquist answered the question with a question. "Do you think it's impossible to get them out of there?"

"Certainly not," Fertig said. "The prison camp is not heavily guarded. Twelve of my men have already escaped from it. They were working on a road gang under one Japanese guard. One day they rushed the guard, beat him with shovels, and walked away."

Relieved, Rosenquist felt his old enthusiasm return. "How many men do you think I'll need?" he said eagerly.

"Tell me this," Fertig said. "Is headquarters going to supply a hospital ship to pick up the prisoners as soon as they're freed?" The look on Rosenquist's face supplied the answer.

"I know what's going on in that camp," Fertig said. "Some of those men are friends of mine. But can you imagine anything more stupid than releasing two thousand weak and sick men on an overburdened local economy? You'll attempt no such rescue. Headquarters can call my refusal to cooperate with you any damn thing it likes."

Rosenquist was stunned. Fertig's response constituted willful disobedience of a direct order from high command—surely the man knew its potential consequences. Fertig had no trouble reading the disbelief on his face. "You go to Davao and see for yourself," the colonel said, ending the conversation. "But you are to make *no* attempt to get those men out of there."

29

★ ★ ★

INITIATION AT SAIPAN

IN MARCH 1944, WASHINGTON military planners decided the next amphibious operation would be to seize the primary islands of the Mariana atoll. The trifecta conquest of Saipan, Tinian, and the former American base at Guam would be the Allies' bold first strike at Japan's inner defense perimeter. Preparation for a fanatical resistance began immediately.

Operation Forager had two overarching goals: to sever the enemy's north-south supply and communications route, and to secure mid-Pacific bases for the Superfortress of the air, the B-29 bomber. From the Marianas, B-29s could easily reach Japan's home islands and begin fire bombing, a tactic designed to shake the country's resolve and hasten surrender.

The decision to strike the Marianas next was made despite unrelenting pressure from Douglas MacArthur to do something entirely different with the naval forces in the Pacific. He wanted those forces to report to him as soon as possible to support his advance on the Philippines—and sooner rather than later. MacArthur had proposed seizing Rabaul, New Guinea, and then basing the Fifth Fleet there. From that vantage point, the navy could assist him in retaking the Philippines. In a dispatch to General Marshall in Washington, MacArthur wrote:

"I propose that with the completion of the operations in the Marshalls [Kwajalein, et al.], the maximum force from all sources in the Pacific be concentrated [to assist] my drive up to Mindanao."

But the vote taken by the Combined Allied Chiefs of Staff at Cairo, Egypt (Sextant conference) the previous December, concurred with the US Joint Chiefs' recommendation: that whenever there was a conflict over resources, the US Navy's crucial thrust across the Central Pacific would take priority over MacArthur's objectives. Undeterred, MacArthur continued to lobby for a strategy shift in his favor. This was the reason he had dispatched General Sutherland to Pearl Harbor in January 1944: to negotiate this revision with Admiral Nimitz. When that effort failed, Sutherland pushed on to Washington to make the case.

Admiral King had one word for the proposal to divert the bulk of the Pacific Fleet to MacArthur's command—*absurd*. King's negative opinion of MacArthur had been formed early in the war by Admiral Hart's highly charged eyewitness account of the general's role in the disastrous fall of the Philippines. But King's mistrust of MacArthur wasn't the only reason for his opposition. He was convinced that the Central Pacific thrust—which included seizure of the Marianas and additional islands to their west—was the key to dominion over Japan because of their B-29 base potential. Not surprisingly, King had the full backing of Army Air Forces Chief General Hap Arnold.

Furious that the "navy cabal" had won again, MacArthur reacted bitterly to what he viewed as a barely concealed plot to prevent him from taking overall command of the Pacific War. "The navy fails to understand the strategy in the Pacific," MacArthur scolded. But the Joint Chiefs held firm. MacArthur's Mindanao landings would be allowed to proceed only after the Central Pacific forward areas were secured.

★   ★   ★

THANKS TO A COMBINATION of factors, the war in the Pacific was finally getting its share of resources. Admiral King's relentless push for a stepped-up Pacific offensive was key, but so also was home front outrage over the widely publicized accounts of Japanese atrocities against American prisoners. All that was needed now were the right men to lead the effort.

Admirals Nimitz and King had easily agreed that Raymond Spruance, now a vice admiral, should be placed in overall command of the Central Pacific sweep. King, Nimitz, and Spruance had also been unanimous in their choice of Kelly Turner as the Central Pacific's amphibious assault commander. He was bold and brilliant, if exceedingly profane—even by US Navy standards. But in their view, Turner alone had the unique combination of talents and skills to seize the target assets and lead the navy's vast armada of ships and troops all the way to Japan's doorstep.

The amphibians had their work cut out for them. Operation Forager would be their biggest operation so far, by orders of magnitude. Saipan was sacred ground to the Japanese, and a full-blooded samurai defense was expected. Nor was it a tiny islet bluff measurable in yardage. Saipan's seventy-two-acre terrain was a hellish montage of coral-aproned beaches, high plateaus, rolling hills, jagged ridges, blind ravines, sheer cliffs, and an extinct volcano—plus a new logistical nightmare for amphibian planners: a vast network of caves.

Saipan's human defenses were also formidable. In addition to a Bushido-stout army, it was home port to Pearl Harbor villain Admiral Chuichi Nagumo and his fleet. It was also home to tens of thousands of Japanese civilians. The stakes were sky-high for both sides, just as they had been at Guadalcanal, but in that action, the navy had snuck into Japan's side yard. At Saipan, they would be breaking into their house. Forager would be an assault of unprecedented scale, and Bill Mott wasted no time immersing himself in the planning.

If he was going to keep this job, he needed to learn quickly, perform optimally, and make Admiral Turner happy. Many of his predecessors had succeeded at the first two but failed at the third. But Bill was optimistic. Hard work had always propelled him toward his goals, and this would be no exception. In this case, he had two aspirations. One was career advancement—stellar performance in this job would ensure his dream of transferring from the naval reserves to the regular navy. The other was to advance toward the Philippines and Barton. Some days he wasn't sure which was the greater motivator.

The planning process itself was byzantine. Fine-tuned sequencing of every land, sea, and air offensive was essential, and a daunting mobile logistics force had to be assembled. Avoiding the sorts of horrific and costly errors that had unfolded at Tarawa was always uppermost in his mind.

He rose well before dawn each morning to analyze documents, maps, memos, manifests, intelligence estimates, and massive to-do lists—and then create his own. He marshaled every scintilla of his accumulated knowledge of complex communications and radio transmission codes and distribution networks among and between the services, in order to build a largely unprecedented mastery of multiservice amphibious assault operations. It was the toughest task he'd ever undertaken, and his new boss was a living, fire-breathing homing device for the slightest human error. President Roosevelt himself had been easier to please.

Battle plans were drafted and redrafted with continuous input from a vast orchestra of individuals from all the services, from Generals Marshall and Arnold to Admirals King and Nimitz. Updated intelligence was layered in daily, requiring more drafting and redrafting. Operation Forager planning was then put to the test, repeatedly, with rigorous landing rehearsals at Maui. After each multiday rehearsal, plans were revised and more rehearsals were conducted.

At Turner's behest, Bill marshaled the preparation of inventories, indexes, and execution orders. The logistics of long-distance provisioning alone seemed infinite. With Saipan 3,500 miles from Pearl Harbor, the closest full supply depot, 120 days' worth of everything was needed for more than three hundred ships' companies. All combatant and auxiliary ships required capacity stores of ammunition, fuel, lubricants, fresh provisions, dry goods, clothing, and medical supplies. An additional 60-day supply was required for the landing forces—some one hundred thousand men in all.

Compounding these dizzying logistics were the complications of fueling hundreds of vessels at sea, with each class of vessel having different protocols. There were also the details of aircraft replacement, repair facilities, salvage operations, and coordination of the four hospital ships to move wounded from the beaches to the ships—with the added consideration that all the above would likely take place in the heat of air and sea battle and in the vicinity of torpedo-bristling enemy submarines.

Coordinating the multiple services' contributions to this quadrille of an assault plan—designed to put eight thousand men ashore every twenty minutes—was another herculean undertaking, alone requiring thousands of man-hours. And, of course, there had to be contingency plans for each one of these carefully laid plans, because battles rarely go according to plan. As samurai warrior Sun Tsu had observed centuries earlier, "Many calculations lead to victory and few calculations to defeat."

Successful amphibious operations also required reliable intelligence estimates of the number and types of enemy forces and the location of fixed artillery and other equipment, as well as anything else that might improve assessment of enemy potential. After collecting such intelligence, the estimates then needed to be scrutinized, questioned, and revised over and over and *over* again. Admiral Turner—in a style that overwhelmed and terrorized nearly everyone around him—demanded it all at his fingertips, funneled to and from him through his fledgling aide and flag secretary.

In addition to these duties, Bill was also the ship's legal and personnel officer, in which capacity he was responsible for issues ranging from promotion and decoration recommendations, to dereliction of duty, drunkenness, and assault. He was also the ship's media censor: he had to read and approve all copy written by the dozens of war correspondents aboard before it could be transmitted from *Rocky Mount's* communications center. Despite the other demands on his time, Bill attached no small importance to this task. He had witnessed firsthand how one errant news report had the potential to derail the war effort.

Lastly, he was to see that a discreet group of Navajo Indians aboard— whose assignment was the synchronous transmission of radio messages between the flagship and landed parties in their little-known Native American tongue—coordinated properly with their multiple constituents in the amphibious force's complex communications chain. The Navajo code system was valued for its unique ability to transmit real-time battle-status updates to and among units onshore and to and from the fleet without time-consuming enciphering and deciphering.

All this planning was for a landing nearly the size and complexity of the impending Normandy invasion (deferred from May to June, 1944, due to weather)—but which had to be assembled in a fraction of the time. It was the busiest Bill Mott had been in his life. Admiral Turner arose each morning at 0430, and by 0700, the admiral's orderly would have made several trips to Bill's quarters with instructions relating to the full range of matters listed above. So many notes from Turner's personalized notepad would arrive before breakfast each day that Bill came to refer to them as "snowflakes." Like his own boss, Admiral Spruance, Turner famously believed in delegating authority. Bill felt the full brunt of this management style early on.

The only way to become an accepted member of Kelly Turner's rarified inner circle was to be able to interpret and respond to his orders intelligently and on the double, as well as to have the physical capacity to remain alert and quick on the uptake at all hours. One also had to accept the occasional "spit in the eye," by way of the admiral's famously foul mouth, bad temper, and general dearth of charm. His transport commanders were said to fear Kelly Turner more than they did the Japanese.

But Bill got on well with his new boss. In fact, a bond formed between the two men, just as had been the case with virtually all of Bill's previous mentors and bosses—sequential father figures so lacking in his early childhood. After Bill's relatively mild trial by fire at Eniwetok (at the end of the Marshall Islands campaign), Admiral Turner made clear he was impressed with his new charge. For one thing, Bill never seemed to fall behind on the formidable list of tasks assigned him. For another, the irascible Turner observed, Bill was "unfailingly courteous." Even the admiral understood this challenge.

FOLLOWING ONE LAST DRESS rehearsal in late May 1944, Admiral Turner approved the plan for Operation Forager. The volume dwarfed all previous Pacific assault directives. Including the 163-page executive order issued by CINCPAC Admiral Spruance, Turner's master plan ran 800 pages; it had been assembled and tested to the teeth in an impressive three months. Saipan would be invaded on June 15, followed quickly by Guam on June 19, and Tinian last.

Between May 29 and June 6, 1944, the various contingents of the huge invasion fleet sortied from multiple ports for convergence off Saipan. As the world's eyes fastened on events unfolding on the beaches of northwest France, the largest naval convoy ever assembled in the Pacific set sail in 550 ships, auxiliary vessels, and landing crafts; 128,000 troops with 75,000 tons of supplies were in tow. Fanned out ahead of them were dozens of armed, prowling submarines, primed for the kill.

On the long voyage to Saipan, Bill began to feel ill. Initially, he wrote it off as seasickness, but in time, he knew it was something more serious. He wondered if departing for the Pacific the previous January before fully recovering from double pneumonia was the cause. But these were different symptoms. He could barely keep down food, and coffee, critical sustenance for months of long days and short nights, burned into his stomach and intestines like battery acid. Bill returned to his cabin each night doubled over in pain.

When the ship's doctor, Captain Gillette, suggested he take to Sick Bay, Bill declined. After years of scheming and countless setbacks, he was finally at sea on the eve of battle; surely he could make it through Operation Forager. Instead, he requested a hefty supply of magnesium hydroxide for its antacid properties, and aspirin. The latter, it turned out, would only make matters worse.

One night, during a break in the earsplitting pre-invasion shore bombardment of Saipan, Bill mixed a rounded spoonful of magnesium hydroxide in a metal cup of water and swallowed it with two gulps and a wince; this usually kept the symptoms at bay for a few hours. He then left his cabin for the deck. At the forecastle rail, he beheld a sight as spectacular as the one that spread out before him on the sea. The star Sirius—the brightest in the night sky and crucial to nautical navigation—was the centerpiece of a celestial light show of shooting stars and crystal-clear constellations. These jewels of the night backlit a dark and quiet Saipan.

The vast waters surrounding *Rocky Mount* were studded, too: hundreds of ships reached beyond the horizon in every direction. The prodigious fruits of America's war industries were arrayed before him like a feast. In fact, the exponentially expanded United States Navy of mid-1944 was about to surpass the size of all the navies in history combined.

Bill allowed a measure of relief to mingle with his physical discomfort. So far he had delivered fully on each task required of him. He'd grown confident in this daunting new role. Despite the initial—and steep—nautical learning curve, his sea legs now stood firm. Battle would be quite another thing; he would find that out soon enough. This moment, he knew, was a rare snatch of tranquility.

Enterprise was visible in the middle distance. With Benny now in Washington, Bill was grateful that perpetual worry over his safety, if not his happiness, was behind him. He also indulged in a deep sense of optimism about reaching Barton. He had measured in centimeters the shrinking distance on the map more than once over the past few weeks. In Washington, he had been some 14,000 miles away; now Mindanao lay less than 1,500 miles to the west.

Unable to sleep after retiring to his quarters, Bill switched on the tiny light over his bunk. He had always enjoyed penning spontaneous verse when the muse called, and tonight its bid would not be ignored. He turned over a spare map and scratched the following lines across the back:

At Sea, off the Marianas
June, 1944

Peace at War
Through many a year I've failed to dream
And soothe my heart and soul with fancy,
Too long a slave to life's routine
And none of nature's necromancy.

But now by Ares' paradox
My mind is free; no longer chained,
And damned up worry burst its locks
To loose those cares which long have reigned.

How easy here it is to dwell
On beauties dead and long forgot,
On stars and birds and ocean swells
And other charms that God hath wrought.

My ship for me a castle fair
And all around the sea, a moat
The drawbridge up; no stranger dare
Invade my world with boresome rote.

Time was the clouds could never be
Much more than shadows passing by;
But now they are the world to me,
And here, my other self, is why:

Confess, in all these years, to you
A cloud has been a cloud, naught more;
No towering castle in the blue –
Or tufted rug on heaven's floor.

The sea, alas, has seemed but water
And salt, at that, your dull mind said,
Because poor fool, you never sought her
And only stared while beauty bled.

Now the truth burns through at last
And you, the light from dark can sift
Away the worry of the past
And in mind's cup pure beauty lift.

Drink in the ocean's white nip'd breasts
Pay court to her in all her moods
Come skip from cloud to flowing crests
And fill your mind with fancy's foods.

See how the west wind comes a' prancing
And slices wavelets at their crest,
To spin and swirl them off a' dancing
Like Spanish Capes to castanets.

Thrill with the east wind's vicious strafe
Which cleaves the billows through and through;

A pure white counterpane to make—
The spread for Neptune's bed of blue.

And mark the ocean's face when still,
An image of the clouds and sky,
No song do breaking waves then spill,
A breathless beauty to the eye.

Save when the south wind's zephyrs trace,
The mirrored surface with design,
As water striders in a race
Or school fish airing in a line.

Seek out these beauties for, each day
The guns and falling death ignore
But if they speak, as soon they may,
Remember peace can come with war.

Naval bombardment of Saipan resumed the following morning: loud, lurid, and violent. Overhead, US planes circled and strafed. At 0400 tens of thousands of marines were served a princely breakfast of steak and eggs. For an unknown number of them, it would be their last meal. Chaplains were on hand to hear confessions and offer last-minute prayers.

At 0542 Admiral Turner's voice bellowed through the ship's loudspeakers: "Land the landing forces!" As rehearsed, the first marine-laden amtracs kicked up their wakes and churned toward the beaches of Saipan.

Rocky Mount's flag staff watched from the ship's rail as the battle, its blueprint so long in the making, unfolded before them. The plan had called for the simultaneous landing of two marine divisions on a beachfront spanning six thousand yards. Eight thousand marines were to go ashore in the initial wave; another twelve thousand would follow shortly thereafter.

But from the first hour forward, Operation Forager did not go according to plan.

The initial sign of trouble was a crescendo of murderous artillery fire when the leading line of amtracs reached the outer lip of Saipan's coral reef. Death rained down as their ramps splashed into the surf and marines hurtled out, only to slog toward the beach through heavier than predicted surf and larger than anticipated hummocks of coral.

Almost immediately, a chorus of desperate wails competed with the deafening artillery barrages. "Corpsman! Corpsman, Corpsman!" rose up from men cut down all along the shoreline. The less fortunate floated voicelessly in the seaweed, lapping to and fro in the reddening tide.

Three days of brutal cannonade ahead of the landings—165,000 large shells and another 2,400 sixteen-inch shells—had done little to dislodge well-concealed Japanese blockhouses and gun emplacements. The fleet's new, fast battleships had been trained for sea battle, not routing out hidden land targets. And they had fired their volleys from ten thousand yards offshore to protect the ships from return fire, too far for any real measure of accuracy. These errors would be grimly noted for future campaigns, as those at Tarawa had been.

Navajo radiomen positioned onshore sent their first chilling message back to anxious receivers in *Rocky Mount*'s communications center: "They're being killed all around us." There would be two thousand American casualties in the first hundred hours of the battle for Saipan, and it would get worse. Transports overflowing with the wounded rushed men from the beaches to the hospital ships throughout the day. Every sailor and officer who could donate blood did so.

Then came another staggering piece of news.

When Bill returned to the flagship's communications center after giving blood, it was buzzing with excitement. A cryptic piece of radio traffic originating from a coastwatcher in the Philippines had been picked up by

San Francisco's KFS Radio and beamed to the fleet. If the stunning report could be verified, the largest amphibious campaign of the Pacific War— now under way and not going particularly well—was about to become its largest sea battle as well.

ON THE MORNING OF June 15, 1944, twenty-three-year-old coast-watcher Gerald Chapman picked his way barefoot up a craggy path to his lookout post: a sea cliff overlooking the San Bernardino Strait on the southern tip of Luzon. Lieutenant Chapman had previously covered the strait from the island of Samar as part of the expanding coastwatcher network in the Philippines. On Luzon, Chapman had a much better view of both the strait and surrounding waters, but heavy Japanese presence made his current operation much more difficult and dangerous. Here he had to keep well hidden and limit his airtime to avoid enemy triangulation of his position. Detection would result in his instant execution.

On that morning, Chapman sat down and prepared for another hot, solitary day. But no sooner was he in position than he scrambled back to his feet. Undernourished and weak from malaria and tropical ulcers, he didn't trust the initial report of his naked eye. Chapman grabbed his binoculars and adjusted the focus, blinked, and adjusted it again.

Training the magnified field on the top of the waterway, he was sure now. Ships! No, an entire fleet! My God, such a fleet as he had never seen in his life! First, the outline of slim gray destroyers, and then the broader beams of cruisers, and then a phalanx of flat, boxy aircraft carriers hove into view. Soon there was no need for binoculars; he could see Japanese sailors all along the rails of an endless parade of vessels; they were looking out at both sides of the Strait, laughing and talking among themselves. Chapman ducked down as shadows of aircraft, their engines grinding, swept over his cliff outpost and fanned out eastward ahead of the flotilla, toward the Pacific Ocean.

When the last ship had passed, Chapman raced back to his low-slung, brush-covered radio shack. He cranked up his set with its meager 4-watt output and tapped out the message to Wendell Fertig's Mindanao station, call letters KUS, praying that his rusty instrument would not fail him now. Optimally, his urgent message would move from Fertig along the flash line engirdling the Philippines and then beam south to Australia and east across the Pacific, alerting likely Allied recipients of the surprise armada's approach:

```
Going east northeast . . . Jap Naval Fleet consisting of
two small patrol boats, eleven destroyers, ten cruisers, three
battleships, and nine aircraft carriers, last ship passed two
four degrees nine min lat one from west.
```

The Japanese immediately blasted Chapman's already weak transmission with intense jamming signals. But Chapman persisted, sending out the same message over and over again.

Bob Stahl, another coastwatcher posted on Samar, picked up Chapman's repeated relay attempts. He noticed that the enemy's jamming was unusually intense and that Chapman was struggling to get his message through. Stahl also knew how vulnerable Chapman's lookout post was and that he was supposed to limit his airtime—and that Chapman was fully aware of the swift and gruesome fate that befell apprehended coastwatchers. Yet he doggedly repeated his relay attempts.

The intensity of the jamming, Chapman's audacious persistence, and gut instinct told Stahl that this transmission must be of special significance. Without knowing its contents, he copied the entire message code and sent it out himself from his sturdier 12-watt radio. For hours, he received no response, even as Chapman boldly continued to relay.

Finally, Stahl received a response from KFS in San Francisco, directing him to move to a higher frequency. He complied, and resent Chapman's message, still unaware of its contents.

After what seemed an interminable wait, a coded response from KFS chirped through Stahl's headset:

```
Message received.
```

Then, later:

```
Well done.
```

Stahl's relay had also been picked up by navy submarine USS *Flying Fish*, lying off the Philippines. Her skipper corroborated what Chapman had observed:

```
Large enemy fleet headed east from San Bernardino Strait
at 20 knots.
```

What Chapman reported was the gathering strength of the entire Imperial Fleet en route to prevent the US Navy's seizure of Saipan. Its plan was to attack the Fifth Fleet—standing off Saipan in support of the marine landings—by a sneak attack from the rear. It was the same surprise strategy that had been deployed by Admiral Spruance at Midway—only applied in reverse. If the Japanese flotilla could take the Americans by surprise and strike a swift and decisive blow, it could save the hallowed Saipan.

AS THE BATTLE RAGED ashore, Admiral Spruance convened his commanders in the *Indianapolis* wardroom following receipt of Chapman's relay. "Well, gentlemen, the Japanese are coming after us," he said calmly, and then delivered another of his thoroughly risk-assessed decisions. Despite pressure to dispatch the bulk of his force as far west as necessary to obliterate the Japanese Fleet—a thrilling temptation with realistic potential—Admiral Spruance had concluded that his primary mission was to protect the vulnerable landings at all costs and to capture Saipan. He was also mindful of the Japanese penchant for diversionary lures, as well as the painful lessons from the first landings at Guadalcanal when the navy pulled back its ships prematurely—with nearly disastrous results for the marines ashore.

So, in this instance, Spruance decided to both protect the Saipan beachhead *and* sortie to meet the Japanese Fleet. He ordered Admiral Marc Mitscher and his powerful Task Force 58—comprised of fifteen new Essex and Independence-class aircraft carriers (with a total of 956 planes), as well as fast battleships, cruisers, and destroyers, all of which could sail at an impressive thirty knots—to ply northwest to meet the approaching armada. But also, guided by his primary mission of guarding the beachhead, he ordered a disappointed Mitscher to restrict his foray to a two-hundred-mile radius of Saipan. This was so the carriers could return quickly in case of a Japanese end run on the vulnerable island. Spruance further ordered a small but sturdy staple of escorts and carriers to remain in the immediate waters to provide continued bombardment and air cover to the beachhead— reassuring a visibly relieved Turner. "I'm going to join up with Mitscher and TF 58, but I'm also going to keep the Japs off your neck," Spruance told him.

For the next thirty-six hours, Mitscher's task force and the Japanese Fleet raced toward each other across the reaches of the Philippine Sea— the section of the Pacific Ocean between the Marianas and the Philippines. Finally, the location of the enemy fleet was confirmed: two hundred miles west of Saipan and on the move. Admiral Jisaburo Ozawa, in command of the Imperial Fleet—large, but inferior in airpower to the Fifth Fleet—had mistakenly assumed he could advance so close because he would be supported by five hundred land-based planes on nearby Japanese-held Guam. Unbeknownst to Ozawa, however, those planes had been dispatched elsewhere.

On the morning of the June 19, Mitscher launched his planes to greet Ozawa's first wave of 545 aircraft, to deadly effect. Three hundred and sixty-six were shot down by American planes. Another nineteen were downed by antiaircraft fire. The sinking of three Japanese carriers, the Shokaku, the *Taiho*, and the *Hitaka*, as well as a destroyer and a fleet tanker, soon followed, along with the downing of hundreds more enemy aircraft. An *additional* three carriers, a battleship, three cruisers, and three fleet tankers were also maimed. So lopsided was the aerial battle that a pilot from the new USS *Lexington*, a Texan, said it reminded him of a good old turkey shoot at home. The Battle of the Philippine Sea was thereafter nicknamed the Great Marianas Turkey Shoot.

Admiral Spruance's measured strategy not only broke enemy hopes of saving Saipan and destroying the Fifth Fleet, but it diminished forever their remaining carrier strength: they were floating airfields without aircraft. The engagement would rank into the twenty-first century as the biggest aerial battle in American history.

GERALD CHAPMAN'S RELAYS MEANT abrupt alterations to Forager's timetables, which meant that Bill Mott would not see his bunk for nearly seventy-two hours. With fleet adjustments and battle plans in rapid flux, he loped from cabin to deck to transport to wardroom and back to *Rocky Mount*'s CIC to relay real-time updates to Admiral Nimitz at Pearl Harbor, Admiral King at the Navy Department, and his former staff in the White House Map Room—waiting anxiously, he well knew, for battle news.

Meanwhile, mounting marine casualties quickly overwhelmed the fleet's hospital ships, and scores were diverted to *Rocky Mount* for treatment. Stretcher after stretcher was handed up the gangway as Bill raced by. Many had limbs blown off. Others had bloodied bandages covering gruesome trunk wounds. Still others wore stained strips of cloth over their skulls or empty eye sockets. The ship's surgeons, dentists, and medical corpsmen worked around the clock, in both sick bays and wardrooms. The latter had been hastily converted to emergency dressing stations outfitted with plasma, morphine, whole blood, dressings, instruments, splints, litters, and an ample supply of body bags.

The first of several Japanese prisoners was brought aboard as well—for medical treatment and questioning. Though he had known to expect it, Bill was taken aback by his first encounter—face to face and in the flesh—with an enemy who had so inflamed his passions over the previous thirty months. He had been more prepared for a defiant, insolent soldier than this frightened, bloodied teenager before him. The prisoner glanced nervously between Bill and the interpreter as he answered the basic questions: name, rank, division. The boy was hardly the embodiment of evil Bill had conjured so fully in his mind.

By sunset on June 19, the battle outlook on Saipan had improved. The ships composing Spruance's ad hoc shore defense were doing their job and the marines had established a beachhead and were advancing inland. The US Army's Twenty-Seventh Infantry Division, which had been standing in reserve, had also joined the fight. Saipan's all-important airfield passed into American hands the next day, and the Fourth Marine Division reached the sea on the opposite side, bisecting the island. Given these positive developments, Admiral Turner handed over complete control of the landed forces to USMC general Holland "Howlin' Mad" Smith. And with the return of Mitscher's task force following the "Turkey Shoot," the tempo of the invasion was stepped up.

But two days later, a new kind of trouble started simmering—between the marines and the Twenty-Seventh Infantry Division. Here Bill found himself in familiar territory: in a bitter war of words between the army and the navy. He might just as well have been walking the halls of the Pentagon.

On June 22, USMC's Holland Smith had positioned the Twenty-Seventh Infantry Division between the Second and Fourth Marine Divisions in preparation for a broad sweep across the island. The two marine divisions advanced on schedule, but the army division did not. By nightfall on the twenty-third, instead of a straight line of advancing troops, the line had taken on an ominously concave U shape. On June 24, the army infantry division was still bogged down, threatening momentum and dangerously exposing marine flanks on both sides.

A jowly bulldog of a man, Howlin' Mad Smith stormed aboard *Rocky Mount* clutching his battle maps. He'd had enough. In an invective-laced conversation with Turner, the marine general lived up to his nickname, conveying in no uncertain terms his opinion of the Twenty-Seventh and its relatively young commanding officer, Army General Ralph Smith (no relation). Holland Smith had drafted a letter for Turner's signature removing Ralph Smith from his Saipan command. But Admiral Turner—while never noted for his tenderness toward the opposite service—wasn't going to relieve an army general at the height of battle without some flank of his own. Good reasons notwithstanding, there would be hell to pay between the services.

So Admiral Turner, Holland Smith, and a handful of hastily summoned aides, including Bill Mott, took *Rocky Mount*'s launch over to *Indianapolis* to confer with Admiral Spruance. Could Spruance fix this problem with Ralph Smith and the Twenty-Seventh Army Division? Spruance listened to his Forager commanders present their complaint and then asked what, precisely, they recommended he do. Both men advised that Ralph Smith be replaced by the more seasoned army general, Sanderford Jarman, who had already been designated to take over the Twenty-Seventh once Saipan was declared secure.

Spruance rightly paused before answering. Yes, there would be hell to pay: the open firing of an army general by a navy admiral on the joint recommendation of another navy admiral and a Marine Corps general? But lacking better alternatives—and with the faltering army line becoming dire—Spruance concurred. He issued the following order to Holland Smith:

```
You are authorized and directed to relieve Major General
Ralph Smith from command of the Twenty-Seventh Division,
US Army, and place Major General Jarman in command of this
division. This action is taken in order that the offensive on
Saipan may proceed in accordance with the plans and orders
of the Commander, Northern Troops and Landing Force.
```

When General Jarman stepped in, the line advance dilemma resolved quickly, but a furious reaction by army brass ensued. The long-simmering interservice rivalry in the Pacific—rooted in the struggle for theater primacy between Admiral Nimitz and General MacArthur—roared into public view. Bill admonished war correspondents aboard that this was a strictly military matter and not fodder for newspaper reports. He then shuttled endlessly between *Rocky Mount* and *Indianapolis* as part of an attempt to contain the firestorm.

But it was too late, thanks to reporters in Pearl Harbor who had somehow sniffed out the story. The controversy was lustily played out by the largest newspaper chain in the country. Strong coverage of the "navy scandal" story gave its owner, conservative William Randolph Hearst, an ideal opportunity to advance his political agenda in support of MacArthur. Hearst editorials spewed blame at the marines for excessive loss of life in the Pacific and called for General MacArthur, whose leadership resulted "in little loss of life, in most cases," to be named supreme commander of the Pacific.

MacArthur's abject failure and subsequent personnel losses in the Philippines, and the fact that he hadn't had much enemy contact since, factored little in the press accounts. Scandalous headlines dominated: Holland Smith was the butcher he had been declared to be after Tarawa, and he fired gallant Ralph Smith for refusing to send his men into certain slaughter. The precipitating facts and factors in the Smith vs. Smith contretemps faded into the background. Another press account competed unsuccessfully for attention: that Ralph Smith was not sufficiently battle tested and/or lacked the requisite training and discipline necessary to advance men under fire.

On July 9, Admiral Turner declared the island of Saipan securely in Allied hands. The final carnage was staggering: the Americans suffered 16,000 casualties (dead, wounded, and missing). Japanese losses were worse: at least 24,000 dead and 3,612 missing. Enemy casualties climbed sharply toward the end when defenders launched a series of final banzai charges, and Japanese-born civilians by the thousands rushed to the island's steep cliffs and jumped to their deaths. When the battle outcome was certain, Admiral Nagumo, General Saito, and their senior commanders all committed ritual suicide rather than surrender. The loss of Saipan also prompted the once-powerful prime minister, Hideki Tojo, to resign his cabinet—all proof of how catastrophic the sacred island's loss was to the Japanese.

Turner and the amphibians went on to prevail at Tinian and Guam as well, and on August 9, the Marianas conquest was complete. But Operation Forager had taken its own toll on Bill Mott. Over the two-month campaign, he had progressed steadily from unwell to seriously ill. On August 10, the day after Guam was secured, he collapsed on the bridge.

When Bill regained consciousness, he was on a stretcher alongside numerous battle casualties awaiting airlift to Pearl Harbor's Aiea Heights Naval Hospital. Humiliated that he hadn't kept the pace he demanded of himself and further embarrassed to be evacuated alongside gruesomely wounded marines who'd given nearly their all, Bill sank into despondency. Not only did it likely mean back to a desk job, but it also meant he had failed in his quest to reach Barton—a possibility he had never even considered until now.

It was in this morose frame of mind that Bill, waiting for trans-Pacific air transport, looked up to see Admiral Turner standing over him, holding an Armed Services paperback edition of *The Razor's Edge*. He'd been looking all over for him, the admiral said cheerfully. He thought Bill might like to read W. Somerset Maugham's brand-new novel while recovering. Even at this zenith of self-loathing, Bill thanked and then apologized to Turner, who he was sure was about to become his ex-boss.

But Turner seemed to miss none of the turmoil that was clawing holes in Bill's stomach. "You've done a fine job, Commander," said the admiral, a man not given to flattery. "If you can get yourself well by the time the ship returns to Pearl, consider your job as my flag secretary and legal officer a permanent assignment."

30

★ ★ ★

DECAMPMENT

AS EARLY AS MAY 1944, changes in guard behavior and camp routine at Davao augured another mass prisoner move. Agitated by yet another successful escape, camp administrators had been further spooked by rumors that local guerrillas, whom they believed to be greater in size and strength than their own tiny garrison, were planning to storm the camp and free the remaining prisoners.

Nearly all productive work details had stopped. Rice paddies and vegetable gardens were not replanted, and tools and equipment were being crated and shipped out. In addition, all prisoners were given dysentery tests, presaging the dreaded possibility of shipment to Japan.

The most recent escape had taken place in March. An eleven-man work detail, armed with heavy shovels, had left the camp to reinforce fences around a cucumber field near the jungle perimeter. Following a work break, one of them clubbed the head guard to death. Another prisoner struck the second guard, but not hard enough to kill him. The group then fled into the rain forest. Six of the escapees survived the jungle trek, met up with the guerrillas, and joined their forces.

Not long afterward, guards overseeing another work detail discovered a cache of vitamins, chocolates wrapped in papers with "I Shall Return" stamped on them, and a copy of *Free Philippines*, the Filipino resistance publication printed by the US Army, all compliments of Courtney Whitney's PRS advancement efforts. Reprisals, including further food curtailment, fell once again on the innocent.

But the point of having nothing left to withhold was fast approaching; the Japanese needed a new strategy to prevent escape. Each day some action by camp administrators or a comment by the despised hunchback interpreter, Shusuke Wada, increased prisoner suspicion that they were going to be moved. The men had long feared being sent to Japan, but now even more so; thanks to contraband radio reports, they knew that the war had turned decisively in their favor and that liberation of the Philippines was approaching.

In late April, 750 prisoners had been trucked off-site with orders to finish constructing two nearby airfields. The sudden urgency to accelerate completion of the airstrips—one near Barrio Lasang and the other near Davao City—was yet another sign the Japanese feared that the Allies were closing in. Communications were severed between the airfield detail and the prisoners that remained at DAPECOL—another precaution taken by the increasingly uneasy prison administration.

Speculation finally came to an end on June 5, 1944, when a fleet of empty flatbed trucks rolled in and parked across from the camp compound. The prisoners were told at *tenko* that evening to prepare for an early-morning departure; they were leaving Mindanao for good. Each was handed an ominous-looking thirty-six-inch strip of white cloth and told to bring it with him the following morning, along with any remaining personal belongings.

At first, the men were oddly nostalgic, remembering their initial elation upon arriving at Davao nineteen months earlier. Then an almost festive

mood swept the camp. Charles and Barton, their surnames near the beginning of the alphabet, would be in the first echelon to move out. They wasted
no time organizing activities for their final night, of which the guards were
surprisingly tolerant. After a moment of hesitation at the thought of his precious spaniels Jasper and Sable back home, Barton joined Charles and Ken
Wheeler in the sacrifice of the protein component of the last supper, the
camp's stray dogs and Susie the cat and her offspring. Barton's motive was
pure: to live long enough to see Sable and Jasper again at Lilac Hedges, at
which time he would somehow make it up to them.

The ensigns stripped all remaining edibles from individual gardens and
the prison kitchen—mostly cassavas and squash—rounding out the final
Davao repast. Against the din of screaming scarlet macaws and raucous parrot
chatter, the men talked and even laughed as the unfortunate animals sizzled on
spits and the potpourri of residual victuals simmered in a pot over a campfire.

In an unexpected act of clemency, the Japanese distributed several bags
of mail that evening that they had inexplicably been holding back. It was on
this occasion that Barton Cross received his first letter from home, from his
mother, dated a full year earlier—June 1943. He was overjoyed. Written in
her familiar, sweeping hand, it included family news, greetings from neighbors, and photos of her, Arthur, and Rosemary. Bill's and Benny's activities
were not mentioned, perhaps because of their military positions and combat activities.

Barton was euphoric, and the photos made numerous rounds during
the festivities. While the prisoners indulged themselves under the stars that
night, they speculated endlessly on their destination, about which camp administrators had been tight lipped. The men suspected and hoped for Manila, but, as ever, they worried about being shipped to Japan.

The next morning, the first group was ordered to assemble at 0400.
Barton and Charles rousted themselves from their hard bunks and took
one last look around. At each juncture of their now two-and-a-half-year
imprisonment, hope had vied with apprehension as to how their next set

of living conditions would compare with the last. But with the amulet of a letter from home tucked into a tiny satchel, Barton radiated optimism that things were on the upswing.

ON THE MORNING OF June 6, 1944, as the epic cross-Channel invasion of Western Europe—D-day—unfolded continents away, 1,239 war prisoners were marched to the awaiting trucks outside the Davao Penal Colony. Those who still had shoes were ordered to remove them and tie them around their necks. Any prisoner who failed to follow orders exactly received a rifle butt reminder. The guards' generous demeanor of the previous evening had vaporized; they were visibly nervous and determined to prevent another escape.

The twenty-two truck beds were loaded to overcapacity. Thirty men were jammed into each, tight against one another, then ordered to remain standing even though the slatted sides were barely eighteen inches high. A guard with a long rope then boarded each truck bed. Beginning in the right forward corner, he tied the rope around the waist of the first prisoner, and successively tied him to the man on his right and left, or to the person in front of him if he was at the end of the row. This continued until all thirty men on each truck bed were tethered together with a single piece of rope.

As the truck engines growled to life, the men were ordered to blindfold themselves with the strips of white cloth they'd been issued the previous evening. With these tasks complete, two armed guards boarded each truck, and the convoy rumbled out of Davao in the semidarkness.

It was a difficult trip. The men lurched and reeled; they couldn't brace for stops, acceleration, turns, or cavities in the rutted road that they couldn't see. Slowing jammed them forward, accelerating swung them backward, and turns pitched them outward. More than once, an entire truckload nearly toppled over the low railing.

When the tethers and blindfolds were finally removed, the prisoners found themselves at the Lasang dock, not far from where the *Erie Maru* had first off-loaded them in October 1942. Once on the docks, the men were ordered to sit in the hot sun for hours while the trucks left to collect the rest of the prisoners. Anchored out in the harbor was a single ship: a rusted freighter with *Yashu Maru* painted on its side.

With signature adjectives, Charles Armour noted that the ship did not carry any markings indicating that it would be carrying prisoners of war. They all knew Allied submarines lurked in nearby waters. How would the submariners know to let them pass? "Maybe they should just paint a big bull's-eye on her," Charles remarked, but in a tone less defiant than in the past.

When the second group of prisoners arrived, those that were removed from Davao in April to work on the airfield were not among them. When questioned, Mr. Wada declined to disclose their whereabouts. Speculation on the fate of these many friends rippled through the group as they waited.

In the peak afternoon heat, the prisoners were ferried out by launch to *Yashu Maru*, and the dreaded boarding began. Barton and Charles were among the first to descend the ladder into the dark, steaming hold; alphabetical loading made their very surnames a curse. The first group was jammed so tightly into the hull's canted rear that they couldn't sit, much less lie down. The men girded themselves for a miserable trip. No reminder was necessary that their voyage to Mindanao had taken eleven days.

Ominously, the Japanese guards began removing all life jackets from the hold's storage area. But just when it seemed things were going from bad to worse, they distributed Red Cross parcels to every prisoner—for which any prisoner would have happily traded a life jacket if given the option. Such was the unpredictability of their captors. Spirits gradually declined again as *Yashu Maru* languished in the harbor for an impossible six days. Some prisoners became so agitated after crouching so long in the airless hold, they had to be tied up like dogs.

Finally, on June 12, the engine sputtered to life. A cheer went up as the movement generated a subtle flow of air belowdecks. *Yashu Maru* departed its prolonged anchorage in a small convoy, and the captain steered a careful northward course. Fearful of attacks from above and below, he hugged the coast so closely it seemed at times the ship might run aground.

Once under way, the men were allowed to rotate to the deck for rations and to relieve themselves. To ease the crowding below, a few lucky ones, including Barton and Ken Wheeler, were allowed to sleep on the deck, a tremendous reprieve. However, that privilege ended after only a few days when two prisoners, army officers John McGee and Don Wills, jumped over the rail into the ocean. This time the hatch was bolted shut.

Defiant and hopeful that McGee and Wills had made good on their escapes—despite the thirty-foot drop to the water and the hail of gunfire that followed their overboard leaps—the locked-down prisoners began to sing. Hoarse, repeated strains of "God Bless America" drifted up through the floorboards. A visibly irritated Mr. Wada finally opened the hatch and glared down at them. "You crazy Americans," he spat, and slammed it shut again.

Misery below mounted as the convoy plied glacially north for three more days. Then suddenly the prisoners lurched as the ship turned abruptly, accelerated, and headed toward land. It seemed they were making an unscheduled stop at the island of Cebu, south of the San Bernardino Strait. The date was June 15.

To the prisoners' relief, the hatch opened, and they were ordered to exit the ship. The guards yelled, *"Speedo! Speedo!"* as the 1,237 men struggled up the ladder. Squinting out into Cebu Harbor, they were taken aback by an enormous formation of Japanese warships.

The bewildered prisoners were herded ashore and marched to an old American bastion, Fort San Pedro. The building, which still bore the sign "USAFFE Headquarters," had been heavily bombed, but its shell was intact. The interior was a heap of stones, dirt, and coal ash.

The men were held here, without explanation, for five days. Eventually a local Filipino tipped them off as to the cause of their detour: the

Americans had landed at Saipan, and the Japanese Fleet that they had seen in the harbor was now battling the US Navy in the Philippine Sea. The thrill of hearing that their countrymen were so close shot through the group like an electric current. The outcome of the engagement was not yet known, but to the prisoners, the Allies were hard by and on the offensive, nourishing their hopes of imminent liberation.

On June 21 the prisoners were rousted off the fort's floor and marched back to the docks. Smudged black from the coal ash, they drew sympathetic stares from Filipinos all along the route. At the dock, their guards were testy and brusque, leading to upbeat prisoner speculation on the winner of the naval clash. But the grins soon vanished.

Crammed belowdeck on an even smaller ship, they braced for another stretch of misery. The prisoners murmured prayers and clung to their sanity for five more days inside a hold normally used for coal storage. A collective sigh went up at the clank and grind of an anchor chain followed by a splash. They were back in Manila Harbor.

The psychological relief this brought was short-lived as the desperate men remained in the hold for another four days in the scorching June heat. They fretted and cursed. Why had they not disembarked? Was this just a stopover en route to Japan? The uncertainty was as maddening as the dim and increasingly fouled quarters.

On the afternoon of June 26, three weeks since departing Davao, an unfamiliar guard finally opened the hatch and called down, "All men go now!" The body of a prisoner who had died of heat exhaustion was lifted out first, followed by a long queue of litters. The hold's rear echelon, including Barton and Charles—badly depleted but able to walk—were the last to emerge.

In stark contrast to his appearance and present circumstances—and the emotional state of many of the others—Barton's morale was "sky-high." The news at Cebu surely meant that the US Navy was on the way! Armored in optimism, he gulped the harbor air and lined up for the march back to

Bilibid Prison. Given the range of lesser alternatives, all the prisoners were encouraged by this development. Here was a place they could walk around, breathe fresh air, and even lie down—if on a cement floor. And also reunite with old friends.

The Davao returnees were greeted warmly by several familiar faces, including some of the original navy doctors and medics from Canacao Naval Hospital. These were the men who had cared for Barton and so many other wounded during and after the attack on Cavite. But the doctors were shocked by what they saw.

After examining their group, Surgeon Thomas Hayes confided to his journal, "1,234 prisoners arrived from Davao after 21 days in route . . . A horrible, miserable lot, many officers, both Army and Navy, among them. A wild eyed, dirty mob, many changed almost beyond recognition."

The resident prisoners at Bilibid must have made similar observations; they showed extraordinary sympathy toward the returnees, despite their own privations. Miraculously, they produced a tub of ice water to welcome them. *Ice* water? From where in all of war-torn Manila was there ice to be found, the Davao group marveled—much less at Bilibid Prison? Many described feeling the most grateful they had felt in their entire lives at that sole gesture.

But the reprieve was brief. After four days at Bilibid, some of the Davao draft received bad news; others worse. Nine hundred were to go back to Cabanatuan. The rest would be shipped to Japan.

31

★ ★ ★

SEPTEMBER 1944,
LILAC HEDGES

ON EVERY SEPTEMBER FIRST in memory, Helen Cross had launched her autumn garden preparations as if prompted by the same lunar pull that stirs birds to journey south. Just as winged migrants detect a scent in the wind, a shift in the stars, or the changed direction of a late-summer breeze, something tugged at Helen's soul when the calendar page turned to September. The first day of that month always marked the start of a weeks-long autumn gardening ritual.

The summer of 1944 had been unusually hot and dry in New Jersey, killing some of her plants outright, despite Helen's vain attempts to keep them hydrated. To her diary, she complained:

Pretty hot, diary mine! Rainless for over a month. I have visions of a nice stand of hay where lawns used to be! Jupiter Pluvius must be on some Olympian holiday. The flowers and bushes droop for his

attention—the expected thunderstorms seem to pass right out to sea—
poor garden!

Barton's twelve-year-old spaniel, Sable, trailed behind her during this autumn's garden rounds at a noticeably slower clip. Helen lamented:

I think this may have been his last summer—he is very feeble, yet he
follows me slowly and faithfully all over the yard. He's now blind and
deaf to all but my whistle. Queer, but he seemed to fail fast once Barton
went away. I remember him sharp as a trigger years ago, cute as a fox,
and fast on his little feet. He is Barton's dog, and I hope he lives for his
homecoming.

As usual, Helen began her fall inspection at the outer-perimeter beds and worked her way in toward the house. She would set out each morning in the early-autumn cool, wearing sensible shoes and her favorite apron, with its wide band of pockets, home to a notepad, trowels, and other gardening implements. Her auburn hair was tucked under a broad straw hat the color of sunflower petals.

She noted first that the plants in the unshaded southwest corner of the property were parched and wilted; they must be dug up and replanted. ("It will look nice, I think, for Barton to see," she wrote that evening.) Moving on, she decided to plant a new bed of yellow tulips and relocate the red ones to the side lawn.

She would then address the routine tasks: dig up and divide her daylilies, which had come back crowded that summer, barely able to breathe. Her rosebushes needed cutting back, too, after which she must lay down a protective winter blanket of good straw. The next job would be an all-day project: fertilizing her dozens of precious lilacs from the lovingly tended compost pile behind the shed. But first, some fall adornment to cheer her as she worked:

Geraniums came for the beds—a blaze of scarlet glory!

As skeins of southbound geese passed over Lilac Hedges in military-like V formations, Helen worked her trowel with the same focus and passion that she did her pen. And for nearly nine months out of the year, the glorious gardens at Lilac Hedges repaid her with pendulous blooms of every description—one of her few remaining sources of pleasure.

But on the fifteenth day of that September, Helen's hopes, plans, and gardens were fouled—like so many other events of late—by circumstances beyond her control. What would go down in history as the Great Atlantic Hurricane of 1944 slammed into coastal New Jersey.

Sixty-foot trees toppled like sticks, pulling down wires and telephone poles with them. Whipping winds dashed a 250-ton freighter onto the shore like a toy boat. Atlantic City's iconic boardwalk and Steel Pier were laid to waste, and hundreds of homes were reduced to rubble. Lilac Hedges—and Helen's gardens—were not spared:

> *Last night the house shook, windows rattled, and trees bent before the onslaught . . . And oh! Never can I forget the sight which met our eyes this morning. Trees crashed through the garage, all smaller trees bent to 45 degrees, the lilacs—as though beaten nearly to death by some sinister force.*
>
> *Sick at heart as we survey the damage, try to straighten small trees and tie up plants. Every one of the Jap lilac trees on our western border is devastated, huge centre haunches broken off at the base . . .*
>
> *The horror at the shore is terrific—everywhere trees through rooftops—wild demonic destruction—worst storm in 75 years and it must come now?*
>
> *God in heaven, isn't war's anguish enough?*

For the next two weeks, Helen cleaned up from nature's vicious attack. She stumbled through fallen boughs and heaps of brush as she worked, wringing her hands over the destruction. The wreckage that surrounded them, she mused to Arthur, matched the wreckage in her heart.

SOME RELIEF ARRIVED WHEN Benny, now stationed in Washington, arrived by train. It was only his second visit to Lilac Hedges since his orders to the Pentagon. There had been little respite from his work as the harried new chief of Ship Characteristics and Fleet Requirements—or from vexing negotiations with his estranged wife.

Over a rare home-cooked meal with Helen and Arthur—prepared lovingly by William and Nelly in his honor—Benny covered many topics, including Bill's recovery. He was much better and had finally been released from Aiea Heights Naval Hospital at Pearl Harbor, Benny reported. He hoped to be back in the fight soon. But Helen's focus never wavered. To her diary that evening, she confided:

> Benny had news of Bill, healing from ulcers of the stomach. But he [Bill] had apparently done nothing to get news of Barton. I had asked him to call on the Provost Marshall.

Benny's visit to New Jersey was actually official business. He was scheduled to honor the workers at a converted sewing-machine factory in Elizabethtown for their extraordinary productivity. He had hoped a respite at Lilac Hedges would restore his flagging spirits, but the arrival of bad news the following morning foiled that plan.

> A letter came today from a Bataan Relief correspondent confirming the Japs' report to International Red Cross of the sinking by an American submarine of an American prison ship. It was said to be carrying hundreds of American prisoners of war, and was off the coast of Mindanao . . .

The sick continuous ache, the shaking fear the Japs will kill their
prisoners as help approaches, and now—this! It is the final horror.
Dear God, dear God, grant that this not be true! After three years, must
American lads be sunk by their own country? I stumble around in a fog,
talking to Barton's picture and crying until I am weak. I got out all his
baby pictures, his Christ School pictures, my son—my dear lad! Come
soon!

Benny did everything he could to calm his mother. Too little was known for her to draw the worst conclusion, he reasoned. He pointed out the unreliable and often strident nature of the Bataan Relief Organizations' reports—particularly since, in this case, the enemy was its source of information. But privately, he too was troubled, making it harder to muster reassuring arguments in which he didn't fully believe.

The Pacific Fleet—including *Enterprise*—was closing in on the Philippines, and its carrier planes and submarines routinely fanned out ahead of the fleet to soften enemy resistance—in this case to prepare for MacArthur's imminent landings. The cruising formation of the now-gigantic fleet was forty miles long and nine miles wide. With a fleet that size, communications in the heat of battle were challenging under a single, unified command; under an unrehearsed command divided between the army and the navy, such tragic incidents would not surprise Benny.

Tacking away from the topic, Benny tried a different approach. Why didn't she come with him to Elizabethtown? It would be an interesting excursion with the added benefit of taking her mind off the news. Helen was reluctant, but Benny prevailed on her to fix her hair, put on some nice clothes, and go hear him speak on behalf of the navy she was coming to despise.

At Elizabethtown, wearing a black dress with little adornment, Helen took her seat among the thousands of war-industry workers. Benny's mission was to present a special award to the plant's workforce for its phenomenal output: a coveted fourth star on its hard-earned army-navy E flag. The E on the pennant stood for Excellence. As a way of acknowledging the importance of home front workers to the war effort, the E flag was awarded to individual plants rather than to parent companies for exceptional yield and product quality; additional merit stars could be earned, as was the case on this occasion. The hard-earned E flags flew over war materiel facilities all over the country, and lapel pins reflecting the honor were worn proudly by every plant employee.

Benny received an introduction that would have made any mother proud. "Please welcome USS *Enterprise* gunnery and antiaircraft officer, Commander E. Bertram Mott—New Jersey's own!" Benny was hailed at length for his role on the storied *Enterprise* in the formidably difficult early months of the war, where he had "seen action at Pearl Harbor, Tokyo, Midway, Guadalcanal, and other points in the Southwest Pacific, fighting against overwhelming odds."

There was full, respectful applause as Benny approached the lectern and held up his hand to acknowledge the accolades. When he cleared his throat and looked out at the sea of faces, the room quieted in anticipation. Despite her darkened mood, Helen allowed a sense of pride in her firstborn son as Benny began to speak:

"Because of your faithful efforts toward victory, the Armed Forces today are *again* conferring upon you the highest civilian honor on the production front. The depth-charge pistols and booster extenders you make here are playing a dramatic part in our antisubmarine warfare in the Pacific.

"We normally think of depth charges as only being carried by destroyers and escort vessels, but not any longer—this critical antisubmarine ordnance is on *all* aircraft carriers. I know that our flyers on the *Enterprise* spotted many Jap submarines from the air, and we successfully depth-charged them more than once—thanks to you!" Benny smiled and gestured to the crowd with both hands.

Young Bill and Benny play in
a New Jersey alleyway while
staying with relatives during
Helen and Arthur's nuptials in
England. A network of aunts and
grandparents took loving care of
the young brothers, despite the
apparent paucity of playthings,
Bill's safety-pinned coat, and
their general dishevelment.

Bill, in acolyte robes,
poses for a photo in 1925
with young Barton and
Rosemary on the side lawn
of Lilac Hedges. Helen and
Arthur indulged Barton
and Rosemary, who had a
less disciplined upbringing
than Bill and Benny.

Left: Arthur and teenage Barton on the Atlantic City boardwalk. Helen and Arthur enjoyed dressing Barton and Rosemary in fine clothes and taking them on indulgent family outings. *Right:* Bill and Benny in Annapolis, 1929, before the brigade of midshipmen marched from Bancroft Hall to the football stadium, a tradition that continues to precede every navy home game. Bill and FDR shared a passion for navy football, which they discussed often. When Congress threatened to cancel the 1942 game to conserve rubber and fuel for the war, the Roosevelt White House would not hear of it.

St. Joseph's Chapel, Christ School for Boys, Arden, North Carolina. Daily homilies here helped shape adolescent Barton's character. These lessons would later guide him as a prisoner of war. An alumni war memorial stands near the entrance of the chapel.

Bill and Benny pose with Barton after his graduation from Christ School in June of 1934. The older brothers took an active interest in Barton's academic performance, as they wanted him to follow them to the US Naval Academy.

Barton poses at Lilac Hedges with proud Helen and Arthur following his graduation from US Naval Supply Corps School at Harvard University and US Navy induction ceremony. Barton would be wounded and taken prisoner barely three months after this photo was taken. *September 1941.*

Barton at Allenhurst, the Jersey Shore locale where he learned to swim in the Atlantic surf. His strong skills and confidence in the water are credited with his assistance to several prisoners struggling in the water at Subic Bay after their prison ship was bombed.

Barton raises a glass in toast at a bar in New York City prior to his departure for the Philippines. He was always at the center of social activities, at both after-work parties in New York City and as a prisoner of war. *November 1941.*

Nurses walk the grounds of the lovely and spacious Sternberg Hospital before the war. Barton, Charles, and a number of other navy patients were ferried across Manila Bay to Sternberg after Cavite Naval Base was bombed on December 10, 1941, but when Manila fell, General MacArthur only ordered that the facility's army patients be moved to safety.

Bill and Romie on their wedding day. Benny (right of groom) was Bill's best man and only attendant, the custom of the day. Rosemary Cross, standing to the left of the bride, was one of Romie's attendants. The marriage suffered from Bill's long hours at the White House after war was declared and subsequent orders to the Pacific. *Chevy Chase, Maryland, September 10, 1938.*

12

A naval intelligence officer re-plots battle lines in an exhibit in Churchill's subterranean map room, the heart of his secret complex hidden beneath Westminster between Parliament and #10 Downing Street. Churchill's map room served as the model for the White House Map Room, which was established in the White House basement in 1942 by Bill Mott. That map room was also a closely guarded, twenty-four-hour center, run by rotating shifts of carefully selected watch officers, fielding incoming cables from intelligence sources, war officials, and Allied leaders.

13

A rendering of the White House Map Room, where Bill spent sixteen months keeping Allied leaders informed and protecting the war's secrets. The furniture was moved to the room's center so Roosevelt could observe the updated war activity from his wheelchair. Bill Mott is seated at a teletype table to the far right of Roosevelt. This rendering was created in 1994 based on former watch officer George Elsey's recollections, as told to artist William Gemmell, head of White House Calligraphy and Graphics. The illustration hangs in the Map Room today.

This three monkeys cartoon was taped to the back of the Map Room door, which was guarded around the clock. The penciled edits were added by Secretary of War Stimson. Bill Mott used the cartoon as a visual aid to train new watch officers on the need for absolute secrecy concerning the room's activities.

Photo of FDR, a gift to Bill Mott at his departure from the White House. The inscription reads: *For Bill Mott from his friend, Franklin Roosevelt*. Bill Mott often described his close relationship with the president and FDR's and Eleanor's frequent inquiries about his brothers, Benny and Barton.

Benny Mott on the platform outside Sky Control, USS *Enterprise*, 1942.

Benny's genial nature, valuable understanding of carrier battle maneuvers, and the vantage point of his Sky Control post attracted the company of war correspondents. *Enterprise* narrowly escaped the Pearl Harbor sneak attack and was one of the few carriers available to conduct early 1942 hit-and-run raids on Japanese-held islands. Here he is sharing a sandwich with Keith Wheeler, *Chicago Sun-Times*, and Joe Custer, UPI, while they wait to hear the results of one of the raids.

Benny in civilian clothes visiting with his toddler daughter Jeanne Marie (Mara, later) before the war. Jeanne Marie was always uppermost in Benny's mind during *Enterprise* battles; he fought to protect her future liberties and to keep her safe from a scurrilous enemy.

Benny Mott (left) and two unidentified officers try to relax aboard *Enterprise* at the end of the Marcus Island raid, March 4, 1942.

Bilibid Prison was such a desolate, crumbling facility that the Filipinos had closed it before the war. The Japanese reopened Bilibid to serve as a way station for processing prisoners of war being shipped to Japan. Barton, Charles, and their ensign fraternity were held at Bilibid a number of times during their imprisonment and passed through its forbidding gates one last time on December 13, 1944, to board the *Oryoko Maru*, the last ship out of Manila Bay before it was sealed off to enemy shipping.

"I KNOW OF NOTHING OUT HERE THAT HAS DONE MORE GOOD."
Lieutenant Rosenquist

When MIS-X operative Harold Rosenquist was finally allowed to board USS *Narwhal* to initiate his belated rescue of the prisoners at Davao Penal Colony, he carried with him several copies of the *Life* magazine article about the electrifying stateside effect of the atrocity stories told by the ten Davao escapees. The story spread rapidly through Mindanao's "jungle telegraph." It was their first confirmation that the home front understood their struggles and successes, and passionately supported them.

Admiral Chester Nimitz signs the Japanese surrender agreement on USS *Missouri*, September 2, 1945. The inscription reads: *To Captain William C. Mott, with best wishes, warm regards, and great appreciation of your contribution to the war effort, which made possible the above scene. C.W. Nimitz, Fleet Admiral, USN.*

First group of jubilant ex-POW's pose for navy photographers as they depart the Pacific for their home countries. Helen Cross scrutinized this photo when it appeared in the *New York Times* in early September 1945.

After three years of reading about her brilliant exploits in the Pacific, crowds gather as victorious *Enterprise* returns stateside after the war. More than a quarter million visitors toured the Big E during Navy Day festivities in New York City the week of her return.

Shusuke Wada listens to charges against him at the Japanese War Crimes Tribunal in Tokyo. The despised interpreter's life sentence for inhumane treatment of war prisoners was commuted after the end of Allied occupation of Japan. His boss, Davao Commandant Lieutenant Toshino, was convicted and executed for ordering the killing of war prisoners in his charge.

Conference delegate Bill Mott at the 1947 International Red Cross Convention in Stockholm. Here he helped draft the Geneva Convention's new Article III, which put in place the strongest ever protections for prisoners of war. The measures were adopted by the Swiss Federal Council in 1949. To date, 196 countries, including Japan, are signatories.

The author's parents before a White House dinner in the early 1950s.

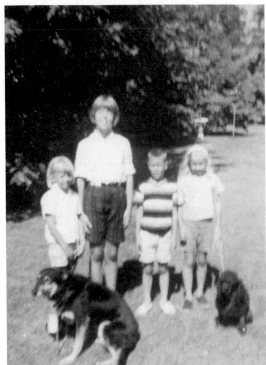

Three Mott siblings (author far left) with cousin Barton Cross-Tierney and a new generation of Lilac Hedges dogs on the property's south lawn. The photo was taken during a visit that ended abruptly after an emotional adult argument on the porch.

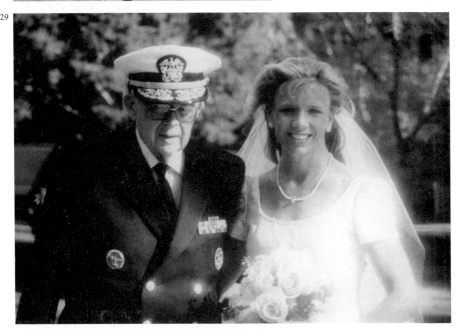

Author-bride with her father in the Bishop's Garden of Washington National Cathedral before her marriage to John Freeman in 1996. Bill Mott passed away on All Saints' Day in 1997 at the age of eighty-six.

At this, the thousand-strong audience clapped and cheered. Already fierce patriots, enthusiasm for their work had reached and remained at a new high after the Dyess story detailing the Japanese atrocities toward American prisoners broke. They were as fired up now as they had been in the immediate aftermath of Pearl Harbor. Benny then took them back to those first days of the war, recalling the desperate position of the country following the Pearl Harbor attack:

"The expansion of our military and naval establishments to their present formidable proportions would have been impossible without the complete mobilization of our war industries to provide these vital tools. If we have emerged from the shadows of unpreparedness and initial defeat, the credit belongs in enormous part to the skill, labor, and cooperation of the production front. The credit belongs to you."

He paused again, smiling at the wild, self-congratulatory applause and more than a few whistles.

"At the time," he continued, "the job of the US Fleet—or what was left of it—was to hold the line. We faced battle every time we left port. We knew we were overmatched, yet did not dare lose a single action. We were at sea constantly, under great nervous strain. Without a doubt, every single officer and crew member realized his enormous personal responsibility—to the nation."

The applause was building in enthusiasm, if that was even possible. Benny responded with a controlled nod, despite a surge of emotion welling up inside. It had been exactly as he'd said just now, hadn't it? That was the very feeling, every hour of every day aboard the *Enterprise*—no exaggeration.

He would never forget KGMB's Webley Edwards's somber farewell to him at Pearl Harbor in the early-morning hours of December 9, 1941. They had been standing amid the ruins in the predawn darkness, their faces lit only by the burning USS *Arizona*.

"It's up to you carrier boys now," Edwards had said, slapping Benny on the back. "You're all we've got left." Prescient words.

Benny was home now, which had been his fondest wish. But all he could think of right now, right here in the middle of giving this speech, was that ship. *His* ship. He yearned for her explicit rules and creeds and clarity of purpose. It was a hard life, but orderly, honorable, and worthy. He ached for the simplicity of a sailor's order of priorities, drilled into him from plebe year forward: Ship. Shipmate. Self.

In fact, the very hardships from which Benny had sought relief, from the inconsequential to the significant—hard bunks; earsplitting shelling; lack of privacy; a constantly vibrating deck; navy chow; the uncertain sequence of anticipation, fear, relief, and euphoria; and the monotonous, ticking meter of the sea when the bombs weren't dropping—were what he missed now. All those things, as well as the ready companionship of thousands of shipmates struggling under identical pressures. He was so lonely now, and so alone. Benny had to work to suppress the sudden, indescribable longing to be back aboard his beloved *Enterprise*.

After clearing his throat, he returned to the task at hand. "Planes from the *Enterprise* reached Pearl Harbor at the height of the sneak attack on December seventh. The task force to which *Enterprise* was assigned reached the blasted harbor the following day to see the saddest sight any of us had ever seen: battleships, cruisers, installations, blasted beyond recognition."

He paused an overlong moment at the memory of it. The audience grew quiet. Hundreds of heads nodded somberly; many began to cry. Virtually everyone in the audience had someone dear off fighting the war, and a considerable number had already lost loved ones.

"For the next year, the *Enterprise* was in one action after another—Gilbert and Marshall Islands, then Wake and Marcus Islands, in quick succession. Then came our raid on Tokyo in which *Enterprise* joined *Hornet* and her task force—"

He couldn't finish the next sentence. The audience had snapped out of its momentary mourning as though a switch had been flipped. Every last person was out of his or her seat, cheering and stamping their feet. Benny smiled and nodded, smiled and nodded.

"We fought against overwhelming odds, endured great hardship, living for the day when our great new fleet would be ready. That fleet—thanks to millions of American men and women in shipyards, mines, and factories such as yours—is near completion. If we have come out of the shadows of initial defeat, again, the credit belongs to the skills and labor and cooperation of the production front. And because of that, at long last, the initiative is ours. We have the ball, and we are going places."

Helen smiled and lifted her leaden hands from her lap to join in the next ovation. With time and a measure of luck, perhaps these fiery, patriotic words would again have meaning for her, she hoped, half listening as Benny wound down with highlights from the battles of Midway, Guadalcanal, and Santa Cruz.

"And now," Benny said after the room quieted, "here is your flag. Fly it proudly above your plant until the Stars and Stripes wave in triumph over the ruins of Berlin and the ashes of Tokyo."

AFTER SEEING BENNY OFF on the train back to Washington, Helen returned directly home and sat down at her desk with a full draft of ink in her fountain pen and a clean sheet of powder-blue Lilac Hedges stationery. Benny had done a fine job, but it seems her mind had been elsewhere during most of his speech. She had a letter to write, and by the time she got home, she knew what it had to say.

October 5, 1944

Dear Mr. President,

Word has come to me of the sinking of Japanese transports loaded with American prisoners off the coast of Mindanao on September 7.
I do not yet know if my youngest son Barton was among them—like those doomed men, he too was imprisoned at Davao Penal Colony.

However the horror and stupidity remain the same. To endure nearly three years of Japanese treatment—then to be sunk like a rat in a trap by one of your own American submarines!

Why sink transports in the first place? Why sink transports going north in any event? What about the colossal stupidity of the Joint Chiefs of Staff, not to foresee such movement of those abandoned American men and forbid the shelling of any northbound transport in waters off Mindanao?

If your son, a classmate of Barton's, had been imprisoned on Mindanao, you would have seen to it, wouldn't you, that such stupidity of the Joint Chiefs were corrected by orders from you?

Mr. President, you will probably never see these lines from any other agonized mother. To think, Americans, trapped in a hold being sunk by an American submarine!

Yours very sadly,
Helen C. Cross

The next day, she unburdened to her diary:

No sleep, no food. Rosemary called from New York—it seems Arthur has known it for two weeks and carried the awful news alone. Whether Barton was on that ship or not, the horror of it sickens me. But I must keep up, somehow. Arthur and I try to keep on, but we are so lonely for our lad.

32

★ ★ ★

HOPES DASHED

BY EARLY JUNE, TENSION at GHQ in Brisbane had risen to a fever pitch. Had Harold Rosenquist made contact with the prisoners at Davao without arousing Japanese suspicion? Were the friends Steve Mellnik had left behind, Doc Cain and Johnny King, still alive and able to help? Without word from Rosenquist, the agonizing days passed slowly. Mellnik made repeated visits to the GHQ's radio receiving room to check for incoming messages. For weeks, nothing.

Finally, the news arrived via Signal Corps radiogram in mid-June. Signed by Rosenquist, it said, "Walked around Penal Colony. Found no, repeat, no POWs . . . Convicts say they were evacuated ten days ago, probably to Manila."

Momentarily unsteady, Steve Mellnik lowered himself into his chair and reread the cryptic message, maddening in its dearth of detail. He then covered his face and sobbed.

★ ★ ★

SUBSEQUENT MISSIVES FROM ROSENQUIST contained better news: all was not lost, it turned out. There were still several hundred Dapecol prisoners on Mindanao. Two separate work details had been detained to complete airfields on the island, including one called Lincayan. Rosenquist was racing the clock, he intimated, to rescue those remaining prisoners. With American planes flying frequent reconnaissance missions overhead, the nervous Japanese were expected to ship them out, and soon.

This time Wendell Fertig did not interfere with Rosenquist's rescue planning, likely due to guilt over the fate of the more than 1,200 prisoners removed after his first meeting with Rosenquist. With the aid of Claro Lauretta's guerrillas and Jim McClure and Jim Haburne, two escapees from a Dapecol fence detail, the scheme began to crystallize. "We are working to locate the garrison where [the prisoners] are quartered, the guard strength, and the [potential for] their release," Rosenquist radioed Mellnik.

With mounting resentment toward Courtney Whitney, whom Rosenquist privately blamed for his failure to reach the other prisoners in time, Rosenquist asked escapees McClure and Haburne to pen statements on the potential success of a Dapecol rescue had Rosenquist been allowed to depart Australia earlier, as planned originally.

Haburne wrote:

```
"After staying in this particular prison camp for nineteen
months, going to and from Davao City on work details, see-
ing the communication system of the Japanese, the number of
guards in the prison, how they were armed, and after stay-
ing with various units in Davao Province for months after
I escaped, I am sure that those prisoners of war could have
been saved if Major Rosenquist had gotten to Davao Province
before he did."
```

McClure was more specific:

Major Harold Rosenquist told me he was here to release the
prisoners at Davao Penal Colony . . . and should have arrived on the east coast of Mindanao by a submarine [no
later than] May 28, 1944, but that the submarine commander
was off course and decided to proceed to the west coast . . .
I gave all the information I could to Major Rosenquist
about the conditions . . . when I left the prison camp--
number of guards, how they were armed, location of Japanese outposts, communications from the Colony to Davao City
and . . . the best possible way to attack the Colony . . . I
believe that [had] Lieutenant Rosenquist arrived in Davao
Province not later than May 1944, all of the American prisoners of war could have been released . . . [T]he job could
have been completed with minimal loss of troops.

Rosenquist refocused his efforts to rescue the men laboring at Lincayan
Airfield. First, he dispatched a letter via Filipino courier to smuggle into the
prisoner barracks at the airfield. It was addressed to Colonel Rufus H. Rogers, a trusted friend of Colonel John McGee, one of the two *Yashu Maru*
passengers who had jumped over the rail and survived. McGee had made it
back to Mindanao and joined the guerrillas, and he felt certain that Rogers
was alive and on the Lincayan detail.

August 11, 1944

TO: Lt. Col Rogers USA

Prisoner of War.

    This message is written with a prayer to God that it may
be safely delivered to you, that you and all the remaining

POWs at Lincayan may know that you have not been forgotten
all these months, that you can be encouraged that freedom
from the Japs is near. It has taken some time and the
hurtling of some obstacles to get here . . . but whatever
may happen, it is the result of the untiring effort of Col.
Steve Mellnik to bring you a message, and perhaps help to
the boys who were at the Penal Colony.

You will be glad to hear that the entire story of
the atrocities of the Japs on the "Death" March, their
treatment of Americans at Cabanatuan and Davao Penal
Colony were given by Mellnik and McCoy to Life Magazine
which published the whole story . . . in the February 7,
1944 issue. I have a battered copy, shown to hundreds of
Filipinos who have befriended our party as well as many
Americans now fighting with the guerrilla units here.
Remember Lt. Jim McClure? He is now with me, escaped with
Wohlfield, Watson, Campbell, and Haburne. We heard that
the others were recaptured and killed. Is that so? And were
there any reprisals?

Col. John McGee escaped from the boat taking the 1,220
[sic] to Manila, jumping off at Zamboanga, now safe at
"A" corps Hq . . . McGee gave me your name as a reliable
contact . . . so here's hoping fervently that you get this
message, and that you believe it!

Accomplishing that first step, we have to rely on you
for some facts to effect your release and that of others.

1.   What hours of the day do you work, where, under what
     guards?
2.   Help us to help you by giving us all the information
     possible. We have at least 100 men with arms, ammo and

grenades. The risk should not be too great for the
protection of you and your comrades.

Most any day now, maybe before you receive this message,
Lincayan Airfield will be bombed. SWPA and General
MacArthur know you are there and have been informed of
your barrack location. The advantage of the bombing and
resulting confusion may offer you the best opportunity for
escape. If that comes true, make for the guerrilla units
north of you; they are not far. I am writing this letter
within 25 kms of the Airfield.

The war progress is given on the back of this letter.
Is it any wonder you can be encouraged . . . It has been
so long but read the news and judge for yourself. May God
grant the delivery of this message and your reply safely
here.

                        HAR

It is not known whether Rosenquist's missive reached Colonel Rogers,
the senior officer of the Lincayan detail, before US Navy planes swooped
down and began dropping bombs on the airfield in mid-August. The prisoners cheered as the bombs blasted large craters into the runway they had
just built, rendering it unusable. Their incensed guards slapped and kicked
the men nearly insensate before marching them back to the barracks, which
were, in fact, untouched during the raid.

From that point forward, the prisoners were put on reduced rations
and confined to the heavily guarded barracks. Then, on September 3, they
were marched barefoot to the local dock, where they joined the hundred-
man prisoner detail that had been rebuilding the airfield east of Davao City.
Together the 750 men crammed into the hold of the *Erie Maru*, the same

unmarked Japanese freighter that had taken them from Manila to Davao in October 1942. The ship departed immediately in a Manila-bound convoy; it would make one Mindanao stop en route—at Moro Bay in Zamboanga Province.

When the news of the sudden departure of the final DAPECOL draft reached him at Claro Lauretta's guerrilla headquarters, Rosenquist was devastated. "Guess I won't get the chance to do what I really came here for," he wrote mournfully. Ex-prisoners McClure, Haburne, and the guerrillas of Lauretta's regiment were equally distraught. They had been so close.

THE MINUTE THE LOCAL coastwatcher saw American prisoners being loaded onto *Erie Maru*, he sent a radio dispatch to Mindanao's guerrilla headquarters. With American carrier planes and submarines now patrolling Mindanao waters in force, *Erie Maru*—lacking explicit markings as carrying prisoners of war—had little chance of making it past the patrols.

When guerrilla headquarters received the dispatch, it promptly radioed MacArthur's headquarters in Brisbane, which in turn notified the navy. Thus alerted, the submarine patrol allowed *Erie Maru* to pass. When her convoy stopped overnight at Zamboanga, another coastwatcher, Don LeCouvre, sent another dispatch through the same channels, and *Erie Maru* was again allowed safe passage when it departed the following morning.

But late on the night LeCouvre sent the first dispatch, the prisoners were removed from *Erie Maru* and loaded onto another ship, *Shinyo Maru*. LeCouvre promptly tapped out a second message, marking it Priority. The prisoners had been moved, it said, and were now aboard a different transport named *Shinyo Maru*, also unmarked. He directed that patrols be advised and allow it to proceed unmolested.

LeCouvre's urgent bulletin was forwarded to Brisbane, as required by the Divided Command structure, with directions to transmit it immediately to navy submarines patrolling off Zamboanga. But this time, LeCouvre's flickering message languished at an empty switchboard at MacArthur's Brisbane headquarters (GHQ). By the time the message was transmitted from there to the navy, *Shinyo Maru* had already departed Zamboanga.

JOHN MORRETT WAS ONE of the lucky survivors of the torpedo attack by the USS *Paddle*. He remembered two massive blasts inside the hull of the *Shinyo Maru* where they were quartered. The first pulverized men all around him, and the second brought large ceiling beams crashing down on them. Prisoners were covered in blood and piled in mangled positions all over one another—arms, legs, and bodies broken.

Miraculously spared, Morrett climbed the ladder to find the deck strewn with dead Japanese soldiers. But others had grabbed their weapons and were firing through blast holes and hatch openings at the trapped prisoners below and at any that had escaped into the water.

Denver Rose was beyond relieved when he was plucked with several others from the sea by a circling Japanese patrol boat. But his reaction was short-lived. "They tied our hands behind our backs . . . [and] started to machine gun us, but then changed their minds . . . One by one they took us to the aft end of the ship and shot us with a rifle . . . I was the fourth man up." But Denver Rose escaped back into the water after severing his rope manacle with a wire cable.

Japanese executions of prisoners trying to escape the doomed *Shinyo Maru* were not just acts of Bushido-sanctioned rage. They were following explicit orders. An August 1944 War Ministry order, issued to all prison camp commanders, directed that all remaining POWs be killed. It also proposed methods for their final disposition. The order read, in part:

```
Whether they are destroyed individually or in groups, or
however it is done, with mass bombing, poisonous smoke, poi-
sons, drowning, decapitation, or what, dispose of them as the
situation dictates. In any case, it is the aim not to allow
```

```
the escape of a single one, to annihilate them all, and not
to leave any traces.
```

On September 12 a chilling radio dispatch from a coast-watcher station in northern Zamboanga lit the airwaves. Local guerrillas had picked up eighty-three survivors of a torpedoed ship, it said. They had floated with the tide to the shoreline and were being cared for by Filipino civilians in a local barrio. The rest of the prisoners aboard *Shinyo Maru* were presumed dead.

Colonel John McGee, now working with a guerrilla unit near Zamboanga, received a subsequent dispatch: the eighty-three survivors needed immediate medical attention and were being taken to Sindangan City. Before departing to assist his onetime fellow prisoners, McGee radioed GHQ in Brisbane. Could these injured men gain submarine passage to Australia?

In Australia, Courtney Whitney reviewed the dispatches concerning the *Shinyo Maru* sinking and its relatively few survivors. With casual detachment, he penciled a note on the radiogram regarding a submarine rescue of the surviving prisoners. "This is a headache," he wrote in his elegant script, "but can be worked out."

As Shakespeare penned in *Richard II*, "Such is the breath of kings."

33

★ ★ ★

SETBACKS

MEDICAL AIR EVACUATION FROM the mid-Pacific to Pearl Harbor was by far the fastest option, but it had its downsides. The shriek of the Douglas C-54 Skymaster transport's engines as it climbed ten thousand feet from Guam's reclaimed Northwest Field surely caused Bill Mott's head to ache as much as his ailing gut. The flat chill of the prone aluminum berths, hinged to the metal curve of the plane's interior, felt less like a bed than being splayed on New Jersey's frigid Mill Pond after an ice skating spill, minus the laughs. But Bill was in decent spirits.

The reason was none other than "Terrible" Turner himself. The boss had a hard, gruff exterior, Bill mused, but inside, the irascible admiral was as soft as a grape. With everything the commander of the Pacific Amphibious Forces had been through during Operation Forager—and with everything he still had to do—Kelly Turner had personally arranged for this junior officer's transportation and (relative) comfort, as a father might a son. Better yet, his parting words had been for Bill to get well and to return as his permanent aide and flag secretary!

He *would* get better, Bill thought—he would *will* it. His grandmother Lauretta had marveled over his determined boyhood recovery from a grievous bout of typhoid fever. Perhaps he imagined her voice above the engines' high whine, remembered her soft hands, with their gentle scent of Hinds hand cream, caressing his burning forehead. Thoughts of his kindly grandmother, who had cared for that small, sick boy when it seemed nobody else had the time or inclination, were always a source of strength.

Inside the plane, disfigurement and pain were everywhere. By their first hop at Kwajalein, two marines—barely visible under a tangle of tubes draining pus and administering morphine—had died. The flight nurse, in baggy GI shirt and pants, took their pulses one last time to be sure before recording the names and serial numbers and pulling the sheets over their ashen faces. Such scenes of misery and mercy characterized the entire flight from the Marianas.

Under the circumstances, Bill could not yet bring himself to engage in Turner's parting literary gift: Somerset Maugham's popular tale of a young man's search for meaning in a postwar world. He drifted in and out of fitful sleep through the time zones. When awake, he cradled Turner's pronouncement that his orders would be made permanent, but he worried about not being found fit to resume duty—yet another hurdle in his quest to reach Barton.

It was nearly dusk when the pilot lowered his blighted cargo through the mist onto the concrete strip at Hickam Field. After a final insult of precautionary vermin delousing, Bill and the handful of other "walking wounded" made their way into a waiting hospital bus. Stretcher cases would follow separately.

The patients gazed out the bus window at the passing sights: the dimming harbor, reconstructed hangars, and an acres-wide stretch of white crosses marking the graves of those killed on December 7, 1941. A baritone grind of gears and a sudden shift into low signaled the final approach to Pearl Harbor's base hospital. The reticent driver steered his last load of infirmities of the day up the steep macadam drive.

Made of fireproof steel and concrete, Aiea Heights Naval Hospital was a brand-new, four-floor beacon of modern architecture. Surrounding the main hospital was a veritable village of temporary structures—mostly trailers and corrugated iron Quonset huts—that had been erected hastily to meet the hospital's rapidly expanding patient load. The new structures were painted dark green to blend into the towering backdrop of primeval-looking Norfolk and Keiki pines. Rising sharply behind the evergreens was the darkening Pali Lookout, its peak shrouded in cloud. Aiea Heights seemed a world unto itself.

Bill grasped an outstretched hand at the foot of the bus steps. Nurses armed with clipboards and the sort of kindly warmth unknown aboard any navy ship greeted the walking wounded. *Maybe this won't be so bad after all.*

In January 1944, the year-old hospital had rostered only 1,709 patients—1,358 of them still recovering from wounds received at Tarawa the previous November. But patient intake at Aiea had exploded by midsummer when the last group of Operation Forager casualties arrived. In June and July an additional 6,256 casualties from Saipan were logged, followed by 1,848 from Tinian and Guam. When Bill Mott arrived at Aiea in August, he had 7,667 fellow patients—in a facility built to accommodate an imponderable 5,000 casualties at any one time.

Bill was placed under the joint care of Aiea's chief of medicine, Captain Manley Capron, and the deputy chief, Commander Edward Delbridge. The next few weeks were a blur of waking, sleeping, poking, prodding, and invasive gastrointestinal procedures. His days at Aiea blended one into the next, punctuated only by rotating call nurses and Somerset Maugham's needling reminder that this phase of his life would in time yield to some unknown other.

A bright spot was the weekly call from ever-loyal Benny, who happened to be well schooled in the byzantine process of reaching a patient in the back warrens of Aiea's mini-bureaucracy—a mission as challenging, they would joke, as getting past the enemy alive. What fine medicine to laugh with Benny again! And whether or not Benny expressed his relief in those calls, he had feared as much for Bill's life at Saipan as Bill had ever worried over him on the *Enterprise*.

They talked at length about their unwitting role reversal: Benny now getting his fill of hard-nosed, self-important admirals, generals, and bureaucrats, and Bill now all too familiar with cramped quarters, K rations, carnage, and ever-present death. But the switched roles gave them all the more in common. After each restorative conversation, Benny always dutifully promised to communicate Bill's improving health status to the rest of the family.

JUST BEYOND AIEA'S STEELY confines, the long-simmering Pacific command rivalry had resurfaced once again. In late July 1944, President Roosevelt himself finally entered the army-navy fray over the direction and overall command of the Pacific War. FDR had been frustrated by months of conflicting advice from his top advisors on how to resolve it. As commander in chief of the army and the navy, he decided to sidestep all the bias and go hear from his Pacific commanders himself. The seminal meeting took place a stone's throw from Aiea Heights Naval Hospital, which the president visited afterward.

More than two and a half years into the war, command of the Pacific War zone was still divided in half. General MacArthur was still the supreme allied commander of the Southwest Pacific Area (SWPA), and Admiral Nimitz, commander in chief, Pacific Ocean Areas (POA), in charge of the rest of the Pacific theater. Conflicts had burned between the two commands since the start of the war—over strategy, objectives, delegation of ships, and jealously guarded latitudes and longitudes. Each fracas had been handled on a case-by-case basis by the Joint Chiefs of Staff, with neither Admiral Nimitz nor General MacArthur ever having to answer to the other.

The two commanders had progressed across their respective Pacific battlegrounds, however, and were both now on the doorstep of enemy home territory. The time for the separate command axes to converge had come. Critical decisions were now at hand, including where and when that convergence should occur, and which commander would lead the combined final thrust against mainland Japan.

The core conflicts had not changed. By pay grade measurement, MacArthur was the more senior in rank of the two flag officers and would not report to someone junior to him, but the Pacific was a naval theater by its very nature, and placing an army officer in overall command of an ocean battlefield was still just as unacceptable to the navy.

Not inconsequential to the unique Pearl Harbor summit was that 1944 was an election year, and Roosevelt had just accepted the Democratic Party nomination for a fourth presidential term. At the same time, MacArthur was enjoying broad media speculation as a possible Republican presidential contender. Summoning MacArthur to Hawaii—over his strenuous objections to "leaving his command," especially for the Nimitz stronghold of Oahu—served the additional purpose of cementing FDR's credentials as MacArthur's boss.

MacArthur agreed to attend the conference only when directly ordered by General Marshall. He still managed to convey his displeasure by rolling up late to Admiral Nimitz's dockside ceremony greeting FDR's ship—in a flag-wielding, open-air touring car, flanked by a deafening escort of motorcycles and wearing a bomber jacket with his corncob pipe between his teeth. Reporters crowded around him nonetheless, their cameras flashing, as MacArthur knew they would.

Despite that inauspicious beginning, the July 27 summit proceeded amicably in a luxurious villa at the Pearl Harbor Officers Club. Inside a map-hung room with balconies offering sweeping views of Waikiki, the parties discussed the various topics and even agreed on some of them. There was consensus that Japan could not continue to aggressively wage war without continuing to draw food, oil, and raw materials from its southern supply sources in the Dutch East Indies and Malaysia. How best to accomplish the crucial goal of cutting Japan's access to those supplies was disputed vigorously.

In a plan known in senior navy circles as "Admiral King's baby," Admiral Nimitz proposed bypassing the Philippines entirely—inspiring clenched jaws in the MacArthur delegation—and seizing the more proximate Formosa (present-day Taiwan). Nimitz argued that, with Formosa in Allied hands, a fail-safe blockade could be imposed that would decisively sever Japan from its supply sources. Simple geography. Nimitz also favored Formosa over the Philippines as the logical forward base for subsequent attacks on mainland Japan. It was closer to China, from which Allied bombers could easily reach Japan's home islands, and was ideally suited as a rendezvous point from which to invade mainland Japan—if and when that time came.

By seizing Formosa, Nimitz added tactfully, the Allies could end the war more quickly and with significantly fewer *Filipino* casualties—certainly fewer than would occur during a complex and lengthy invasion of the seven-thousand-island atoll of the Philippines. Chafed by his exclusion from the meeting, Admiral King had vigorously urged Nimitz to make another point in his absence: that war progress should not be slowed, nor excessive blood shed, for the purpose of servicing MacArthur's sentimentality or restoring his reputation. The more genteel Admiral Nimitz declined to make that point.

General MacArthur countered with commanding eloquence for the retaking of the Philippines. He presented strongly and without notes, fully aware that his reputation and military legacy depended on it. He reminded the group that the Philippines was an American commonwealth, and the United States had a constitutional responsibility to liberate her people. Taking the Philippines first would also enable the Allies to sever Japan from its supply sources. He reiterated his "personal guarantee"—previously circulated in Hawaii and Washington by General Sutherland—that the

Philippines campaign could be accomplished in thirty days to six weeks, with "inconsequential" losses.

"The eyes of all Asia will be watching," he then admonished Roosevelt, warning that America's postwar image in that part of the world would be tarnished forever if the Philippines were bypassed. Nor did he miss the opportunity to salt the old wound of "America's failure" to send ships and reinforcements to beleaguered Bataan and Corregidor in their hour of need, abandoning not only an alleged promise to do so, but also loyal Filipinos and tens of thousands of Americans as well.

Any plan to bypass the Philippines, MacArthur declared, was "utterly unsound." With signature theatrics and sweeping hand gestures, he stood before the map and patiently explained his long-planned amphibian invasion—beginning at Mindanao and thrusting northward up the island chain to Leyte, and then Luzon. He emphasized the flow of intelligence from Filipino guerrillas since the enemy occupation, maintained at great risk to those involved. It was unconscionable, he concluded, that the United States even *consider* not honoring MacArthur's much-publicized promise to return.

"Give me an aspirin," ordered the president after enduring three hours of General MacArthur's oratory. "In fact, give me another aspirin to take in the morning. In all my life, nobody has ever talked to me the way MacArthur did."

Roosevelt would need that second aspirin. On the following day, MacArthur took advantage of a private moment with the president to press one last point. "I daresay [if the Philippines were bypassed], the American people would be so aroused that they would register the most complete resentment against you at the polls this fall." To Candidate Roosevelt, this was heard as a threat—exactly as MacArthur had intended it.

WHAT THE SUMMIT PARTICIPANTS did not yet know was that the US Submarine Service had already imposed a virtual supply blockade of Japan. From recently won bases at Saipan and Guam, bands of roving submarine "wolf packs," as they were known, were sending one merchant vessel after another—carrying hundreds of tons of oil, iron ore, coal, bauxite, rubber, aluminum, arms, ammunition, aircraft, and enemy troops—to the ocean floor. By the end of Operation Forager, few enemy merchant vessels entering or departing Japanese-controlled ports were spared by Allied submarines. In fact, what they had already accomplished would come to be known as the most effective undersea war in the history of human conflict.

The submarine force had grown in size, agility, and effectiveness since December 7, 1941, when the United States ordered unrestricted submarine warfare—that is, submarine attacks on merchant vessels without warning—voiding its international treaty to the contrary. Under the gutsy guidance of Vice Admiral Charles Lockwood—"Uncle Charlie" to his devoted men—these wolf packs swaggered along the Pacific's undersea lanes like vigilante posses: mission driven, armed to the teeth, and bristling for kills.

They went by such names as Ben's Busters, Ed's Eradicators, Clyde's Cannibals, and Whittaker's Wolves, and the enormity of destruction they conferred on the enemy vied with that of Allied surface fleets many times their size. Just like their warships and aircraft, Japanese merchant ships transporting military personnel and cargo (including food) had to be destroyed in order to prevent them from aiding Japan's war effort or inflicting future harm.

The submariners possessed another deadly weapon: code breakers. By 1944, their cryptanalysts were reading Japanese transmissions with relative ease, providing the undersea combatants with exact sailing dates and times and course, speed, and composition of formations and convoys—though much less precise data on their cargo. This made it possible to triangulate convoy positions, allowing the wolf packs to lie in wait and then fire torpedoes deep into the unsuspecting ships' hulls. The nimble subs would then dive hundreds of feet to evade depth charges dropped by the enemy ships. Barton Cross would have swelled with pride at the war performance of the submarines that had once been under his care. But he might also have been justifiably nervous, given the dramatic rise in 1944 of Allied prisoners traveling between enemy ports in unmarked Japanese merchant ships.

WHILE NO FINAL AGREEMENT was reached at the Pearl Harbor conference, it was clear that MacArthur's emotional arguments and political intimations made their mark on Roosevelt. MacArthur's enduring—if self-propagated—status as American Hero, his broad conservative newspaper following, and his "strongest nonconcurrence" for any plan that omitted the Philippines would ultimately force the hand of a campaign-minded president.

The final decision was handed down six weeks later, on September 8, 1944: the next military objective in the Pacific would be the Philippines. MacArthur would land at Mindanao in October and progress to Leyte Island by December 20, 1944. In the meantime, the Joint Chiefs directed Admiral Nimitz to prepare for the subsequent invasions of Iwo Jima and Okinawa. An invasion of Formosa was tabled, much to Admiral King's disappointment.

But just four days after these decisions were handed down, Admiral Halsey—whose aggressive Third Fleet had been clearing Japanese shipping in the southern Philippines—reported minimal enemy resistance around Mindanao. In fact, said Halsey, "there was no shipping left to sink."

He followed with a bold three-part suggestion to Admiral Nimitz: that (1) Mindanao be bypassed entirely, (2) the invasion of the Philippines instead begin at Leyte, and (3) the Leyte invasion date be set for October 20.

Nimitz and the Joint Chiefs agreed, believing that Halsey's proposal could shorten the Pacific War. The Philippines invasion plan was thus revised accordingly. But there was a crucial omission in this grand revisiting of Pacific strategy in the summer and autumn of 1944. Both President Roosevelt and his Joint Chiefs had dodged their last, best chance to put the Pacific theater under a single, unified command. Interservice rivalries and political considerations had teamed to prevent that logical course of action—even as the mammoth forces of the US Army and Navy were about to converge.

In the upcoming Philippine invasion, therefore, the navy's Seventh Fleet, with its home port in Australia and under MacArthur's purview, would continue to report to Brisbane GHQ. Admiral Halsey's Third Fleet would operate under navy command. These two fleets, consisting of many hundreds of ships of every description, were about to converge in enemy-infested waters without so much as a common radio frequency.

This flawed command structure was in stark contrast to the one in place throughout the island-by-island sweep across the Central Pacific. In that sequence of campaigns, Admiral Spruance oversaw all aspects of each invasion, from shore bombardment, to air cover, to fire support, to troop landings, to operations ashore. A unified command structure had made crucial split-second decision-making possible—especially at the Battle of Saipan.

At Saipan, Admiral Spruance directed Kelly Turner to land tens of thousands of troops under heavy enemy resistance while Navajo code talkers communicated minute-by-minute enemy positions to marines ashore and to ships offshore. Spruance simultaneously ordered his fast carrier task force to sortie from Saipan and attack the Japanese Fleet in the Philippine Sea and another contingent of ships to remain and protect the Saipan landings. The continuous and coordinated flow of intelligence and communications to and among these disparate units and attack forces—under rapidly shifting battle conditions—saved lives and ultimately determined the battle's positive outcome. Conversely, army and navy forces merging off the Philippines would answer to two separate maestros—each with vastly different training and each free to indulge his respective interpretation of risk and success. This arrangement would prove particularly detrimental to urgent communications in the heat of battle.

Thanks to MacArthur's insistence on complete control of communications within his command area, the Seventh and Third Fleets would not be permitted to communicate directly with each other. Astoundingly, they instead had to relay their messages through an intermediary army radio station. The messages would be rebroadcast to the intended recipients only after army receipt and evaluation. It was a prescription for mortal trouble, as already evidenced by the preventable sinking of the *Shinyo Maru*. It could take hours for a dispatch to get from one fleet to the other, and they could easily arrive out of sequence—or too late.

WHILE DELIBERATIONS OVER FUTURE Pacific strategy coursed their way to this imperfect solution, Bill Mott's condition improved. By early September, he was declared healed and itching to get back to Admiral Turner and the Iwo Jima and Okinawa invasion planning. Negotiating his way out of Aiea Heights, however, was proving difficult.

Orders for his release had stalled somewhere in the bureaucracy, with few explanations forthcoming. Finally, Bill discovered the problem, and it was serious: diligent Dr. Delbridge had recommended, due to the severity of Bill's initial diagnosis—bleeding, potentially perforated stomach ulcers, with possibility of relapse—that he not return to sea duty. Bill was stunned and furious in equal parts. To come this far and then be sidelined not by his eyes but his *stomach*?

From his hospital cot, Bill began working the navy's front and back channels, a skill long in the honing. And he wasn't above charming Aiea's nursing staff to his cause. But his real weapon was feisty Admiral Turner, who, on hearing Delbridge's recommendation, charged up Aiea Heights's macadam drive and asserted himself on Bill Mott's behalf.

"You listen to me, goddammit!" Turner growled at Dr. Delbridge, within an inch or two of his nose. "You show me Mott's most recent tests supporting your goddamn order. If you can find me a goddamn ulcer, you win. If you can't find me an ulcer, I want him released to my command. Period!"

Delbridge replied evenly that it wasn't a matter of the most recent tests, which did indeed indicate that Bill Mott was healed; the problem was with Bill's initial diagnosis, given shipboard before his air evacuation from the Marianas. That diagnosis had indicated a very serious condition, one with the potential—if not the likelihood—for relapse.

When Turner demanded verification, a baffled Dr. Delbridge came up empty-handed. It seemed the paperwork detailing the original diagnosis had gone missing—it couldn't be found anywhere in the hospital.

Bill Mott sat quietly and listened to the two men. Piping up might lead to questions he didn't wish to answer. Fortunately, it never came to that. Turner pressed his position and won the point, if not a friend in Dr. Delbridge. Bill Mott was thus cleared for discharge.

Just as he was preparing to return to *Rocky Mount*, however, another setback almost knocked him back to his hospital cot. The news came in a reluctant call from Benny. At Aiea, Bill had enjoyed weeks of barely concealed optimism about Rosenquist's rescue mission, in which he had placed soaring hope. That dream came to an abrupt end with Benny's call.

If that had been the worst news—that the prisoners had been removed from Davao before Rosenquist could act—it would have been bad enough; but Benny's additional revelation was beyond his imagining. A *US Navy submarine* had torpedoed the Japanese merchant ship carrying the Davao prisoners in its hull? Instead of being rescued by a navy submarine—an image that had animated the sweetest of Bill's dreams—Barton had possibly been *torpedoed* by one?

And their mother knew! Benny delivered this final blow with the greatest reluctance, knowing it would be a dagger to Bill's heart. "My God," was all he could manage. Of all the problems he had anticipated, this was not among them.

Benny assured Bill that he was working tirelessly in Washington to corner the details. He was already in contact with two different branches at the Pentagon to learn all he could. It was not clear that Barton had been among the approximately 680 prisoners killed—it wasn't even certain that he was on that ship. In any case, there were some survivors, he said, and eventually they would be sent to Washington for a thorough debriefing. Maybe he could learn more then.

Meanwhile, Benny had requested the fated ship's roster and a list of the dead from the Captured Personnel and Casualty Branches. He made inquiries with the judge advocate generals' and army provost marshal offices, the International Red Cross, and the State Department, all of which had a keen interest in the circumstances surrounding the *Shinyo Maru* sinking and its survivors. Benny had gone to great lengths to penetrate the bureaucracy and get the facts, but so far he had little to show for it. It was a situation Bill understood all too well.

Benny tried to offer hope, but for Bill there was no solace. The very term "surviving prisoners" brought on waves of nausea. But it was the thought of his mother receiving such news that laid him the lowest. Bill felt sure she would see only this: for all his efforts, he had failed her spectacularly. Again.

34

★　★　★

THROUGH A PRISM:
MACARTHUR'S RETURN

I.

THE PRISONERS AT CABANATUAN knew in their bones that the Americans were closing in. It was just a matter of time. But would that seminal moment come in time to save them? The men alternately rejoiced and lamented as reports of Allied gains vied with rumors of accelerating prisoner shipments to Japan. Camp morale swung from high to low with each version of "the news."

The Davao prisoners had dreaded returning to Cabanatuan, perhaps Charles Armour most of all. His invective-laced complaints filled the scalding boxcar on their train ride north. No doubt Barton shared in the grumbling, but he was emphatically not unhappy at this juncture, still buoyed by the single, cherished letter he received before leaving Davao and by the positive war news at Cebu. He returned to Cabanatuan's rice fields without complaint.

Unlike many of the prisoners, his mind, spirit—even his body, though reduced—were sound. Not only had his center held these three long years, but his trials had undraped a character of steel and an expansive soul. The ragged shrapnel wound from December 1941, which had marked the beginning of his journey to manhood, was now a pigment-free scar in the shape of a lightning bolt. Like a birthmark, it was a constant reminder of where it had all started. Barton's peers revered him for his optimism, selflessness, humor, and—no minor attribute among deprived and desperate men—an innate sense of fairness. If only he could make it home to live out these good lessons. By mid-1944, Barton's prayers had distilled to a single incantation: that they be rescued before it was too late.

"We're going home," he would say to his fellow ensigns, over and over. "We just keep our heads down, and we're all going home." Reflexively, Barton drew from this incorruptible reserve to nudge Charles to his way of thinking. Cabanatuan wasn't nearly as bad as when they left it in 1942, he pointed out. And, anyway, it wouldn't be long now. If he had anything to do with it, Ozark fried pie—Charles's avowed favorite—would be the 1944 Thanksgiving feature at Lilac Hedges. "Its first-ever appearance north of the Mason-Dixon Line, if its last!" Charles surrendered one foul mood after another with a playful swing at the best friend he'd ever had; Barton would raise his hands in mock defense and, as always, throw back his head and laugh.

Barton's optimism aside, Cabanatuan had improved markedly during their absence, if only by prison camp squalor standards. Its cruel former commandant, Lieutenant Colonel "Blood" Mori, had been replaced, an enormous relief to the returnees. While many more had died since their October 1942 departure for Mindanao—nearly three thousand men were interred in acres of shallow graves around the camp—prisoner work teams had made life-saving improvements. They'd built a septic system and irrigation ditches, and obtained permission from the Japanese to douse the latrines with chemicals to reduce contagion. The death toll from infectious disease, particularly dysentery, had dropped dramatically with these changes.

Vegetable gardens also now dotted the compound on every inch of tillable soil, their yields coaxed from tiny seeds pocketed on farming details and variously boasting eggplant, okra, corn, radishes, beans, carrots, peppers, and papaya. That the quantities were small mattered little to famished men desperate to supplement a rice-and-salt diet. In fact, another ritual had been established in the ensigns' absence: *quanning*. "Quan" could be a noun or a verb—even an event—but at its core, it was the repreparation of the miserly rice issue with the day's random harvest, which consisted of any other edibles the men could get their hands on. Garden pickings were prized, but so were ingestible grasses, meat from cats, snakes, and rats, and the occasional purloined egg or chicken.

One thing that had not changed at Cabanatuan was the wary, short-tempered contingent of guards, even with the departure of Commandant Mori. Allied war gains had not improved their disposition, nor had word of the multiple prisoner escapes from Davao, from which these men had just arrived. In fact, the returning draft was initially sequestered, but eventually moved into the main camp. That was a happy day for the ensigns: reuniting with friends not seen in almost two years.

Among such comrades were Barton's former barrack mates Ensigns Andrew Long and George Petritz, and new navy acquaintances too, including fellow Supply Corps officers Chuck Wilkins and Bob Granston. The gaggle of young naval officers found strength in their swelled ranks and for the next several months "stuck together in all things."

In the evenings, they quanned, sang, joked, played cards, and told and retold stories of home and family. The men also indulged in a curiously popular pastime: intense recipe-swapping sessions. While it might seem unusual for perpetually famished men, discussing recipes subliminally conferred the comforts of home-cooked food as well as the promise of someday returning to such pleasures. One evening over tiny servings of okra-dotted rice, the men hilariously debated Charles Armour's Brunswick stew ("sounds awful no matter how much of that shit you put in there"). On such nights, the rise and fall of laughter in the ensigns' barracks was comparable to any revelry floating out of a good New York bar.

The Davao returnees had been back at Cabanatuan about three months when the most restorative moment of their imprisonment occurred. Some would recall it as the most exhilarating moment of their lives. The date was September 21, 1944.

At 0900, the ensigns were already south of camp breaking a sweat in the rice fields. Only clanging caribou tack, trilling birds, and the occasional shrill order broke the Luzon countryside's pastoral quiet. Then, like a stand of alerted deer, one after another of the prisoners looked up from their labors and toward the mountain-rippled horizon. They stood stock-still, hearing something.

The faint hum became a low rumble which grew more insistent by the minute. Planes? The prisoners were familiar with the sound of Japanese planes, but these engines had a different timbre—more finely tuned, yet bolder. Also, the rising growl was coming from the north instead of the west where Japanese airfields were located. Then, suddenly, what started as a hum burst into a roaring crescendo.

The ensigns could only gasp as the guards ran for cover. Despite advances in aeronautic design since their incarceration, the ensigns knew American carrier planes when they saw them. The white stars inside a red-rimmed blue blaze under the wings confirmed the prisoners' fondest hopes. "My God!" blurted Ken Wheeler. "They're ours!"

Over the lush, green peaks of the Sierra Madre Mountains came a thundering series of carrier aircraft formations from Admiral Halsey's Third Fleet, including an air group from USS *Enterprise*. Eight-plane squadrons flew in proud Vs, each flanked by fighter escorts darting protectively in and out of the clouds above them. The versatile aircraft veered variously west toward the Japanese-held airfields and south toward Manila Bay. Minutes after the first flyover, the distant detonation of bombs at Clark Field could be heard.

The ensigns laughed and cried, waving ragged pieces of clothing over their heads and shouting out prayers of thanks. After nearly three years of isolation and brutality, the vaguest encouragement was held dear, but *this*! Pent-up emotions burst their locks as one of the formations passed right over the prisoners' heads. One prisoner pointed skyward, boldly shouting in the direction of the guards peeping from their foxhole, *"Ichibon American hikoki!"* (American plane number one!). Ignoring the risks, the other prisoners picked up the chant, like long-shot underdogs belting out the school cheer. *"Ichibon American! Ichibon! Ichibon!"* (Number one American! Number one! Number one!).

They had barely recovered from the initial euphoria when another wave of planes roared over, like an encore to a wildly appreciative audience. Two pilots dropped down, tipped their wings, and their rear gunners fired in salute to the ecstatic assembly below. Four more planes amused themselves by buzzing the guard towers, driving their occupants down from the nests and up against the inner fence.

Camp administration abruptly called off all work details, but not before the grand finale: a dogfight between one of the American fighters and a Japanese Zero, in plain view of Cabanatuan. Trailing smoke, the US Hellcat dove at its opponent, getting hot on his tail before making good on every round he fired. The Zero's wing blown off, it broke apart and twisted earthward, slamming into a distant hill. A steady plume of smoke rose from the crash site, entertaining the prisoners for hours afterward.

By this time, the guards had emerged from protective ditches and rounded up the field-workers. Bony and barely clothed, the men goose-stepped and sang "God Bless America" all the way back to the stockade. One prisoner recorded the experience in his diary:

"We sat down in the mud and cried . . . just pounding the water . . . We turned to each other with unseeing tear-filled eyes . . . It was the most beautiful sight . . . the first actual proof that our side was winning."

"What a day!" another recalled, "It is impossible to describe the thrill and varied emotions we felt. Gladness, happiness, joy, pride, desire to laugh, cry and shout all at the same time."

Camp administration was badly flustered by the flyovers. In apparent reprisal, the prisoners received no meal that evening—which did nothing to repress their elation. In every barrack, scenes of the day were replayed again and again, bringing alternating tears and incredulous laughter. Better still, damage reports trickled in via clandestine radio: a number of Japanese aircraft and runways at Clark Field had been laid to ruin, and as many as a dozen enemy ships had been sunk in Manila Harbor.

To the last man at Cabanatuan, hopes hit a new high that day. With American airpower in such force over Luzon, they were confident that liberation was near. In any case, they certainly wouldn't be going to Japan now. Unopposed formations flew over the camp again the next day, bolstering that confidence all the more. But the sudden and aggressive show of American force over Luzon had the Japanese revising their own thinking.

The aerial displays had eliminated any lingering doubts that American landings in the Philippines were imminent. As a result, the Japanese decided to accelerate the shipping of their remaining war prisoners to Japan. Their rationales were multiple, but primary among them was that the thousands of American prisoners of war in the Philippines were symbols of their power in East Asia. To relinquish them to victorious American forces would constitute an unacceptable loss of face. Neither did the Imperial Army want liberated prisoners assisting the invading force, nor attesting to criminal mistreatment suffered at their hands. Worker-starved factories in Japan also needed more manpower for war production. For all these reasons, prisoner shipments to the home islands shifted from "as necessary" to "urgent" priority.

In the days and weeks that followed the September air raids, bullish optimism at Cabanatuan began to fade. There were no more flyovers, and the guards insisted that the men would soon be leaving for Japan. Why? *Why?* They tortured themselves with endless speculation. Freedom, which had seemed so tantalizingly close, now seemed to be slipping away.

II.

What the prisoners could not have known was that Central Luzon's guerrilla force—thousands strong and well armed—had been poised for months to break them out of Cabanatuan. One highly respected guerrilla leader, Major Robert Lapham, an unsurrendered American army officer from Davenport, Iowa, desperately wanted to liberate the camp where many of his friends were imprisoned. Lapham was a force majeure: one measure of his effectiveness at thwarting the enemy was the $1M bounty the Japanese had posted for his capture. His Luzon Guerrilla Armed Forces (LGAF), or "Lapham's Raiders," had expanded to more than thirteen thousand well-trained men; by 1944, LGAF controlled the entire northern half of Luzon's great central plain, an area of thousands of square miles.

Lapham had kept Cabanatuan under continuous surveillance since 1942, and had helped smuggle in food, medicine, and even weapons in anticipation of one day freeing the prisoners. But his requests to raid the camp had been rejected repeatedly by Courtney Whitney at SWPA headquarters in Brisbane. "Too risky," came the replies. Some suspected that Whitney kept Lapham's proposals from General MacArthur, whom, they believed, would have supported the plan wholeheartedly.

Lapham felt a renewed urgency to raid Cabanatuan in the fall of 1944. The Japanese had gruesomely executed a group of Filipinos recently caught supplying aid to the prisoners through an elaborate underground network run by two American widows of men who had died at the camp. Margaret

Utinsky and Claire Phillips had avoided detection through a variety of clever means for nearly three years, but their luck ran out that summer. They were captured and tortured within an inch of their lives. The Filipinos caught supporting their efforts were not so lucky.

Lapham was alarmed by the executions as well as obvious Japanese reinforcement of Luzon, but he was also encouraged by a report from the leader of the local guerrilla group that had been shadowing the camp. Captain Juan Pajota rode miles on horseback one night to inform Lapham that there were only about two thousand POWs now interned at Cabanatuan down from a high of some eight thousand after the fall of Corregidor.

To Lapham and Pajota, this presented their best opportunity to raid the camp and liberate those prisoners. The numbers were manageable, and the Japanese were preoccupied with preparations for the imminent American landings. The guerrilla leaders discussed "every imaginable aspect of the rescue operation" that night. A third Luzon guerrilla leader, Lieutenant Colonel Bernard Anderson, concurred enthusiastically that the timing was ideal for a prison break.

So once again, in late September 1944, Major Lapham radioed Brisbane for permission to rescue the prisoners at Cabanatuan. Once freed, Lapham assured, the men would be cared for within a vast network of guerrilla-protected Filipino villages and enclaves. Then they would be rotated to Chick Parsons's and the submarine *Narwhal's* Luzon rendezvous point: secluded Dibut Bay, fifty miles to the east. On *Narwhal's* last trip to Dibut Bay, it had not only surfaced, but docked, and openly unloaded supplies for the guerrillas. To Lapham, sending an empty *Narwhal* back to Australia was a crime. "If we wait much longer," he argued, "we'll be able to rescue what's left in one caribou cart."

But Courtney Whitney turned Lapham down yet again—this time with the slim assurance that prisoner liberation would be given priority once MacArthur's troops arrived on Luzon. And in any case, Whitney said, there were no submarines to spare for this purpose.

★ ★ ★

MORALE AT CABANATUAN FELL to a new low with the sudden October arrival of fifty British and Dutch prisoners. Lee Stiles confided to his diary: "These men are in very bad shape." US Marine lieutenant colonel Curtis Beecher, the camp's senior officer, recorded his own impression. "They were a pitiful sight to behold."

As the resident prisoners scrambled to find clothing and mess kits to share with the gaunt new arrivals—surviving laborers from the Thailand-Burma "Death Railway"—they heard their horrific tale.

In Singapore on July 4, 1,289 of them had been crammed in the hull of a Japan-bound merchant ship, the *Hofuku Maru*. Due to engine trouble, the ship had detoured to Manila, arriving on July 19. They remained in *Hofuku Maru*'s hull in Manila Harbor for *eight* weeks while the ship's engines were dismantled and taken ashore for repair. Stuffed in a dark, crowded hold, they watched in terror for weeks on end as men all around them died of heat prostration, disease, hunger, and thirst.

But that wasn't the worst of it. On September 21, when *Hofuku Maru* finally departed Manila Bay in a ten-ship convoy, it was bombed by the very carrier planes that had brought such jubilation flying over the prisoners at Cabanatuan that same day. More than a thousand Dutch and British prisoners died in the attack.

The dazed, oil-drenched survivors were taken to Bilibid for treatment. The seriously wounded remained at Bilibid, and the remaining fifty were sent to Cabanatuan. "British state that American bombers are too bloody accurate," wrote Lee Stiles after hearing their stories. The existing prisoners now had something new to worry about.

On October 7, with these hellish images in mind, the hopes of the men at Cabanatuan were officially dashed with an announcement by camp administration: except for those unable to travel, they were all going back to Bilibid, now little more than a transfer station for shipment to Japan. Leave the mosquito nets behind, the guards taunted; they would not be needed in the frigid Japanese winter.

Lieutenant Colonel Beecher was ordered to make a list of "able-bodied" prisoners for shipment to Japan. With little to distinguish the weak from the genuinely ill, any man able to walk was put on the list. Armour, Cross, Ferguson, Granston, Long, Petritz, Wheeler, Wilkins, Wuest—all the ensigns. When a dozen trucks pulled up to remove them from Cabanatuan, Juan Pajota's guerrilla scouts could only look on helplessly as more than 1,600 prisoners—including the travel-weary British and Dutch survivors—boarded the truck beds.

Unlike previous journeys, the men were not lashed together or blindfolded, allowing them to observe the frantic Japanese reinforcement of Luzon in anticipation of the American invasion. Truck convoys full of Japanese soldiers were observed all along the road, traveling in both directions. Numerous air transports also passed overhead, with troop-packed gliders in tow, a method of conveyance the long-isolated prisoners had never seen. Droves of *Manileros* clogged the route as well; family after family evacuating the city on foot, their personal belongings balanced on their heads and backs.

With bridges impassable thanks to the recent American bombings, the prisoner convoy had to take a lengthy detour and enter Manila from the northwest, extending the uncomfortable journey by several hours. When they passed through Bilibid's forbidding gates after midnight, they were offered roomier sleeping quarters than before; another draft of 1,800 prisoners had just departed for Japan. The name of their ship was *Arisan Maru*.

III.

Just after midnight on October 20, 1944, an American naval force of 738 ships converged in the Philippine Sea and began filing through the channel leading to Leyte Gulf. The ships carried 160,000 troops, ammunition, equipment, and enough supplies to last months. General MacArthur had spent the evening alternately pacing the bridge of the cruiser, USS *Nash-ville*, and in her wardroom putting final touches on a speech he would soon broadcast through a prepositioned Signal Corps microphone on Leyte's Red Beach.

Devastating preinvasion bombardment rained down death on Leyte the next morning. After watching the display and reminiscing about his young lieutenant days on Leyte as an army surveyor at Tacloban, MacArthur returned to his cabin for an early lunch. When the beachhead was declared secure, the general reappeared in a fresh khaki uniform, sunglasses, and signature corncob pipe. He then descended into an awaiting navy barge, followed by Courtney Whitney (soon to be promoted to general), General Sutherland, and the new Philippine president, Sergio Osmeña, successor to the late Manuel Quezon, who'd died of tuberculosis in August. A phalanx of eager photographers and correspondents followed.

The barge churned through Leyte's busy waters—until it was stopped short by a sandbar. With autonomous authority under such circumstances, the transport's beachmaster told his passengers that they must exit and wade the rest of the way in, interfering with MacArthur's vision of stepping ashore—immaculate and dry—and striding to an awaiting bouquet of microphones.

The skipper pulled the release lever, and the barge's ramp rattled into the shallow surf. After casting him a mordant glare, MacArthur began sloshing toward shore when a cameraman snapped the iconic shot of the wading general and his entourage. In a matter of hours, the famous photograph had flashed around the world. MacArthur's terse expression would settle into the American conscience as a reflection of his grit, determination, and restored honor, not his flash of rage toward an impertinent barge skipper and otherwise all things United States Navy.

On the beach, MacArthur made his way to the microphones. "People of the Philippines," he began, "I have returned!" In the next moment, the heavens opened up, releasing a torrential downpour. MacArthur raised his voice to compete with the pounding rain. "By the grace of Almighty God," he continued, "our forces stand again on Philippine soil—soil consecrated in the blood of our two peoples."

He delivered the rest of his speech against a dueling backdrop of heavy rain and raging combat in the hills behind him, to great dramatic effect and the thrill of an archipelago-wide radio audience. "The hour of your redemption is here . . . *Rally to me!*" he exhorted emotionally. "Let the indomitable spirit of Bataan and Corregidor lead on! As the lines of battle roll forward to bring you within the zone of operations, rise and strike! Strike at every favorable opportunity! For your homes and hearths, strike! For future generations of your sons and daughters, strike! In the name of your sacred dead, strike!"

As General MacArthur delivered his florid oratory, Colonel Whitney stood by wearing a self-satisfied smile. Delivering his prewar client Douglas MacArthur back to the Philippines—where the wealthy Whitney had left behind millions in gold and chromium mining assets—would ensure both men's places in history, and their lifetime financial security as well.

IV.

On October 10, shortly before MacArthur's vaunted Leyte landing, 1,803 prisoners, mostly American, were marched from Bilibid Prison to Manila's Pier 7. When the draft arrived at the docks, they were relieved that the awaiting transport, *Arisan Maru*, was far too small for all of them. They traded bets on who would get to return to Bilibid. But the Japanese were of a different mind, determined to squeeze every last prisoner aboard.

Shivers McCollum was in one of the early boarding groups. The farther into the ship's bowels he and that long line of prisoners were pressed, the more stifling it became. After 600 were loaded and the center hold was full, still more came, and more after them—until all 1,803 men were packed in, standing back to chest and fighting panic. The stygian enclosure was barely large enough for a quarter their number. No sooner were they loaded than the freighter promptly backed away from the pier. An unknown number of prisoners died of suffocation in the first forty-eight hours.

When *Arisan Maru*'s captain was alerted to American carrier pilots patrolling above, he steered into a cove at Palawan Island to wait out the threat. So many men died and were thrown overboard during the layover that some 800 prisoners could be moved to the forward hold, thus relieving severe crowding belowdecks. On October 20, the *Arisan Maru* returned briefly to Manila Bay to replenish supplies. Despite an incoming typhoon, she hastened back out in a twelve-ship northbound convoy the following morning. The prisoners were thrown about in the high seas, coating them in their own vomit and kicked-up coal dust from the hold's previous cargo. Under these conditions, about a third of them had contracted dysentery, resulting in a further coating of fecal filth and the additional torture of swarming flies.

AS THE CONVOY PLIED north, two submarine wolf packs, Banister's Beagles and Blakely's Behemoths, lurked in their path, anticipating attempts by the Japanese navy to foil Allied troop landings at Leyte.

Shortly before midnight on October 23, Commander George Henry Browne of USS *Snook* ordered, "Up periscope!" He cupped his eyes tight to the lens goggle to confirm a beeping surface-radar report. Sure enough, as Browne arced the periscope around, a convoy of Japanese ships hove into view. *Snook* wasted no time firing her first round of torpedoes, and then another and another. In seconds, the dark waters surrounding *Arisan Maru* became a shooting gallery.

After diving deep following the banner kills, the sea wolves climbed from the depths the next morning in search of more prey. They had sunk eight of the convoy's ships the night before, but four others were still afloat and in range. At four thirty in the afternoon USS *Shark* commander Ed Blakely sighted one of them through his periscope. It was barely making seven knots—piece of cake for *Shark*. Blakely radioed his fellow Behemoths: *Shark* was closing on *Arisan Maru*. Since the ship carried no markings or flag indicating its prisoner of war cargo, he could not have known the wholesale slaughter his next command would render.

Three torpedoes roared out of *Shark*'s forward compartments. Blakely lowered his periscope and waited for the explosions to reverberate against the submarine, confirming the kill. Instead, depth charges from two of the other Japanese ships in the convoy came laddering down toward *Shark*. Again and again they came, seventeen crashing explosions in all. Bubbles, oil, clothes, cork, and other debris surfaced shortly. Urgent, repeated calls to Blakely from *Seadragon* and *Blackfish*—"Come in Nan-Zebra-Foxtrot-Oboe!"—brought no response. USS *Shark* was never heard from again.

Aboard *Arisan Maru*, Japanese deck guards watched the bristling wake of the first torpedo race toward the bow of the ship. They made it to the rail just in time to witness a near miss, even as they spotted the rooster tails of a second torpedo hurtling toward the aft section. Spared again, by a hair. The panicked guards then drew their guns and fired at the handful of prisoners on the deck who had been cooking rice for the evening meal, sending the startled men back down into the hold double time.

It was at this moment that *Shark*'s third torpedo ripped into the hull of *Arisan Maru* and exploded amid the prisoners. Hundreds were instantly pulverized. Body parts, bones, and debris flew in every direction, and the hold was coated in blood. At its epicenter, the massive carnage yielded no remains "bigger than a dime," recalled prisoner Calvin Graef.

In the ensuing melee, the guards cut the ladder rope to the forward hold and pounded the rear hatch shut before rowing away in the doomed *Arisan Maru*'s rubber lifeboats. Despite the shock of this additional setback, surviving prisoners acted instinctively to escape. They stacked a pyramid of corpses high enough for them to reach and dislodge the hatch and climb out. Those who made it into the water swam toward the Japanese destroyer that their former guards had just boarded. But when the prisoners heard the splash of bullets and saw Japanese sailors pushing survivors away from the side with long poles, they realized the wisdom of going no closer.

It was nightfall on the South China Sea when the remaining ships in their original convoy disappeared over the horizon. *Arisan Maru* survivors rode the midsea swells on pieces of wreckage or abandoned rubber lifeboats, calling out to one another until only a handful of voices could still be heard. The closest land, Formosa, was 225 miles to the east.

After two days, nine of the original 1,803 draft were still alive. Four were recaptured, but fortune smiled on the other five, who were rescued by a Chinese fishing junk. The Cantonese family operating the boat knew too well what would happen if they were apprehended by the Japanese. They took careful steps to keep the five survivors covered and destroyed all remnants of their raft.

The junk and its surprising catch came ashore at Namyung, Canton. The fishermen fed, bathed, and clothed the grateful men, and then risked their lives to help them evade roving enemy patrols. The mayor of Namyung made contact with Chiang Kai-shek's military leaders and US Army Air Forces, who came to their rescue. The survivors of the *Arisan Maru* disaster were promptly evacuated to Washington for debriefing, even as the final draft of Bilibid prisoners waited in agony for word of their own shipment to Japan.

V.

On October 20, before Helen Cross extinguished her bed lamp for another night of fitful rest, she confided a final thought to her diary:

October 20, 1944

News of MacArthur's Philippine invasion came last night, but I am so cold and numb with the horror of it all that I feel no elation. God be with prisoners everywhere—their position caught between Japs and Americans is of particular terror. I just have a sick feeling that cannot be comforted.

Her only diary entry the following day was, "Sick terror over Barton stops my pen."

35

★ ★ ★

WHAT BENNY KNEW

BEING A RELIGIOUS MAN, Johnny Morrett bent his head in prayer often during the long series of flights from the Pacific to Washington, DC. Two months earlier, his prison ship, the *Shinyo Maru*—carrying 750 prisoners of war—had been sunk off Mindanao by an American submarine. Morrett had been one of the lucky eighty-two survivors, and he just couldn't stop thanking God.

SHINYO MARU'S ALARM WHISTLE was still "screeching like a wounded child" when Morrett jumped into the water and grabbed a pair of floating timbers—two-by-fours, about six feet long. Miraculously, he managed to dodge the spray and splatter of rifle fire from Japanese guards manning the listing vessel's rails, as well as the wrath of enemy scout planes periodically buzzing down and dropping depth charges on the American submarine that had torpedoed the ship.

As Morrett quietly scissor-kicked away from the fast-sinking wreck, he heard another prisoner thrashing in the water nearby. "I can't swim!" the man cried. Paddling over to him, Morrett shouted, "Grab onto the boards!" But no sooner had the man grasped the makeshift raft than a Japanese bullet found its mark, cleaving the man's skull. He slumped forward onto Morrett, who, with a measure of self-loathing, pushed the dead man away with his foot while keeping a watchful eye on Lieutenant Hashimoto, among the cruelest of the Davao guards, directing rifle fire from the bridge.

Staying low in the water, Morrett spotted the head of another prisoner, Major Harry Fischer, drifting with the tide toward shore. Morrett called out to Fischer and urged him to grab onto his makeshift raft.

Together the two survivors kept their heads and bodies as submerged as possible, looking back only once in response to a loud crackling sound—like the crumpling of heavy tinfoil, Morrett would recall. It was the ship's final gasp before thrusting upward and slipping beneath the surface. Five hundred prisoners were still trapped in her hull.

In the evening twilight, Morrett and Fischer saw more bobbing heads scattered across the water's surface: other survivors were either drifting landward with the tide or actively swimming toward shore. Faceless voices called out to one another, and a loose consensus developed: once ashore, they should all make for the heavy foliage fringing the beach. When their feet touched the sandy bottom, Morrett and Fischer—fueled by freedom-induced adrenaline—raced toward the underbrush.

But once in the thicket, they heard a threatening sound. *"Pssst! Pssst!"* Hearts pounding, the two men dropped low before turning toward the source: three grinning, shirtless Filipinos less than five feet away, bolo knives hanging at their sides. Tapping their muscular chests with their thumbs, they called out, "Guerrillas! . . . *Guerrillas!*" Forgetting himself, Morrett sprang to his feet and hugged one of them.

The scenes that followed were the province of dreams. The guerrillas, who moved like cats—noiseless, quick, and efficient—gathered up the first group of survivors on the shoreline and spirited them along a maze of dirt paths to a clearing. There, another group of Filipinos holding candles covered the shivering, mostly naked men with blankets and fed them raw eggs, boiled *camotes*, and bananas. The Filipinos were as gratified to be helping these Americans as the survivors were grateful; this resistance group had been fighting the Japanese for nearly three years.

An armed contingent of guerrillas led the revived men inland along a trail. They walked by the light of the moon, single file, for hours. The shipwrecked prisoners held up admirably despite their injuries and the trauma of the day. While they'd been pressed into many difficult marches in the Philippines, this was their first toward freedom and there would be no slowing or stopping on *their* account.

Those with bullet wounds or fractures were placed on the backs of caribou or, in the case of one man with a broken jaw and several broken ribs, on a mattress carried by four boys. The procession continued through intermittent jungle, tribal areas, tiny villages, and across bodies of water in outrigger canoes, all the while in the guerrillas' protective custody.

On the fifth day, the survivors were met by their old Davao comrade Lieutenant Colonel John McGee, and learned of his daring leap from the prisoner transport that had departed Mindanao before they did. McGee was now working with guerrilla leader Robert Bowler—the same Robert Bowler who had intercepted Harold Rosenquist when he first landed on the wrong side of Mindanao the previous May.

After his escape from *Yashu Maru*, McGee had contacted Wendell Fertig and requested a role in his guerrilla command. Fertig dismissed the request, disparaging McGee as another crazed POW escapee who thought he knew exactly how to win the war. But Colonel Bowler—himself a seasoned army officer—knew better and immediately took McGee under his Mindanao guerrilla wing. Not only had Bowler grown wary of Fertig himself, but he was a prewar colleague of John McGee's, a fellow West Point graduate, and a combat-hardened veteran.

And so when Bowler learned of the *Shinyo Maru* sinking, he did not radio Wendell Fertig as he had on Rosenquist's arrival. Not this time. Here, finally, was Bowler's chance to help the prisoners that had been held on Mindanao. Instead, he summoned like-minded McGee. The two men quickly forged a plan to convey the former prisoners—many of whom needed significant medical attention—off the island.

In the meantime, natives with first aid kits did what they could. They cleaned deep lacerations and bullet wounds with Merthiolate, and then sewed and bandaged them. They applied salves to infected ulcerations and immobilized broken bones, easing them into slings made out of improbable patchworks of cloth. And while a dentist saw to broken teeth, Bowler and McGee divided the able-bodied into three platoons, gave them khakis, shoes, and ammunition, and trained them in the use of the new American carbine. All eighty-two survivors were then moved to a heavily secured guerrilla camp to await the arrival of the USS *Narwhal*—the navy submarine that would take them to Australia.

WHEN HIS FLIGHT FINALLY arrived at Washington's Bolling Field, Morrett and two other survivors traveling with him—USAAF captains Bert Schwarz and Gene Dale—were met by Major Ellis Gray, chief of the army's Captured Personnel Branch. Gray arranged a private car to take the trio to the swank new Statler Hotel at the corner of Sixteenth and K Streets NW, a short walk from the White House. Gray told the men to bill any expenses to the War Department and to get some sleep—Pentagon and other debriefings would be lengthy and tiring, he said, and would take at least a couple of weeks.

At the Statler, Morrett finalized his *Shinyo Maru* casualty list—including branches of service, ranks, and hometowns. These 667 men either had gone down with the ship or were shot flailing in the water following the fatal torpedo blast. Morrett, now the ad hoc adjutant of the survivor group, had readily agreed to prepare the list; these men had been his close friends, and he wanted their fates to be known. Nonetheless, the tabulation had been sad, grim, and slow.

Morrett and the other survivors then assisted the War Department with the heartrending task of notifying the next of kin. Next came the long debriefing sessions with numerous military and other government divisions concerning Philippine airfield conditions, disposition of Japanese troops, guerrilla operations, and many thousands of prisoners still listed as "missing in action."

One of the debriefings was at a location described only as "Box 1142." It was the top secret MIS-X headquarters in Virginia, from which Lieutenant Harold Rosenquist had been dispatched to rescue them nearly a year before. Among other epiphanies at that remarkable compound, the *Shinyo Maru* survivors witnessed a stark contrast between the treatment afforded German POWs being detained there and their own treatment as prisoners of the Japanese.

Japanese atrocities toward Allied prisoners in the Philippines had roiled Washington ever since the Dyess story's first electrifying airing eleven months earlier. Morrett and his fellow escapees were asked to provide actionable examples of Japanese mistreatment of prisoners of war. They proceeded to provide lengthy depositions at the State Department, the Pentagon, and the Offices of the Judge Advocate and Adjutant Generals.

In each case, there were also questions on how the *Shinyo Maru* came to be sunk, which the survivors answered in detail. But even in the context of a global war in which ships were being sunk daily, the escapees were surprised at the low priority given the possibility that this had been a case of Americans firing on Americans. The subject of friendly fire, it seemed, was not a friendly one at the Pentagon.

It was through the Navy Casualty Section that Benny Mott learned of the *Shinyo Maru* survivors' arrival in Washington. Commander Jacobs and his successor, Commander H. B. Atkinson, were complying dutifully with Bill's request to let Benny know of *any* developments that might shed light on Barton's fate. Benny's Ship Characteristics and Fleet Requirements

Office was two long corridors away from Casualty. But despite the Pentagon's size and byzantine layout, "hot dope" traveled fast.

With predictable apprehension, Benny leafed slowly through Johnny Morrett's casualty list. He turned each page carefully, running his index finger down column after column until he reached the last name on the last page.

Another reprieve! Barton was not a *Shinyo Maru* casualty. But where was he now? What could these men tell him about his brother? Benny finally left a note for Morrett at the Statler Hotel, requesting a call. Could they get together?

Days went by before Benny heard back. Between debriefings, Morrett had priority personal matters of his own to attend to, most importantly a reunion with his fiancée, Pat Taylor, who since his capture had joined the Waves. She was now working at the Navy Department in Washington! He had phoned her after landing in San Francisco when he first set foot on American soil. "Pat, darling, I'm home!" he'd said. "I've missed you so much!" While she'd sounded happy to hear his voice, he sensed restraint. Maybe it was just shock, he decided—after all, he'd been listed as missing for nearly three years.

Morrett could barely contain his excitement when Pat arrived for their reunion dinner at the Statler. Trim and athletic, dark haired and beautiful, she looked stunning in her Wave uniform. The engagement ring he'd given her before his deployment still sparkled on her left hand. And in the little spare time he'd had since his return, Morrett had bought her a strand of pearls. The wrapped box bulged from his uniform pocket while they waited to be seated.

But over dinner in the Statler's chandelier-bedecked dining room, Pat broke the bitterest of news. He'd been gone so long, she explained uncomfortably, that she had given him up for dead. She was dating someone else now. She was open to two suitors, she said, incredibly, but the engagement was off.

A devastated Morrett—pearls still in his pocket—returned to his fellow ex-prisoners in their Statler suite. When he opened the door, he got another surprise. In front of him were Calvin Graef and four other friends he hadn't seen since his group of 750 men departed the Davao Penal Colony to work on the Lasang Airfield. Johnny Morrett's merciful God seemed to be playing tricks on him now.

Already unmoored, Morrett was speechless at first. But over the course of the evening, and with the help of a few cold Ballantines, the others caught him up on what seemed incomprehensible to all of them. A month after the *Shinyo Maru* went down, Graef and 1,800 others had boarded another Japanese transport, the *Arisan Maru*, which met an identical fate—torpedoed by an American submarine.

After all their debriefings but before the two survivor groups left Washington—variously for hospital treatment, war bond drives, or home—they were escorted to the White House to meet with a warm and sympathetic President Roosevelt. Following that, they were taken to meet with Secretary of War Stimson and Army Chief of Staff General Marshall.

In his quiet, dignified way, Marshall apologized to the former prisoners for help not arriving before the fall of Bataan and Corregidor. He offered no excuses, just that American forces weren't in a position to rescue them at the time. The men thanked Marshall for his candor and expressed no bitterness. Realizing they were in the company of two historic figures at the crest of a historic war, they apparently only wished to remember the moment that way.

ONE OF THE SURVIVORS' other final meetings in Washington was with Benny Mott. It took place shortly before Christmas 1944, and while its precise location is unknown, most likely it was in the Statler's darkened, smoky bar, where the survivor group often congregated. Benny caught up with three of them—Johnny Morrett, Bert Schwarz, and Calvin Graef, all onetime fellow prisoners of Barton Cross.

Talking with stricken families since their return had taken a toll on the group. So many weeping responses had overwhelmed them. Not only did each conversation rekindle their survivor guilt, but also it extended their grief over hundreds of lost friends. But when meeting with Benny, Morrett, Schwarz, and Graef had relatively good news.

When Morrett's detail departed Davao for Lasang, he assured Benny, Barton was alive and well at the prison camp. And even though there was no *Arisan Maru* casualty list yet, Calvin Graef felt certain that Barton Cross was still at Cabanatuan in early October when he and the first draft of prisoners were trucked from Cabanatuan to Bilibid.

News that Barton was still alive when these men departed the Philippines was good reason for Benny to sponsor a round of drinks. But the news wasn't all good. This was the first that Benny had heard of the *Arisan Maru*—*another* ship loaded with American prisoners sunk by *another* American submarine. Unlike the *Shinyo Maru* incident, the *Arisan Maru* sinking—which would constitute the worst disaster in US naval history— was apparently a taboo topic in senior military circles.

Graef also told Benny about the arrival of British and Dutch prisoners at Cabanatuan after *their* prison ship had been bombed, this one in Manila Bay by US carrier planes. That had come right out of the Brits' mouths, he said. The grim sum of facts shared by these survivors had Benny reeling.

He could tell none of this to his family, he decided—at least not now. News of the *Shinyo Maru* alone had undone Helen Cross. Were she to learn of this apparent cascade of prison ship sinkings off the Philippines, he feared it would finish her.

In any case, Benny would have to get official corroboration of these terrible reports. Yes, that's what he would do: more research was needed before he could assume they were accurate. In the meantime, Benny was determined to rescue his family life.

He was focused on getting his modest new house in suburban Maryland ready for a very special holiday visit from his wife and daughter; they were coming all the way from California. Jeannette was accompanying young Jeanne Marie on a custodial visit to see him, but Benny's fondest wish was that maybe, just maybe, he and Jeannette could put their marriage back together. No better time to do it than Christmas, and lonely Benny had made special plans for the three of them.

When mother and child arrived, however, both were feverish and unwell, probably with the flu. After they opened the Christmas gifts that Benny had lovingly purchased and wrapped, he insisted they take to bed while he went to the store in search of juice, soup, and aspirin. His disappointment was acute, but there was nothing else to be done. After mother and daughter settled into their room, Benny threw the Christmas wrappings into the fireplace and left for the store.

His Packard taillights had barely disappeared around the corner when the discarded wrapping paper went up in a giant whoosh of flames, sending errant sparks onto the carpet. Within minutes, the carpet, drapes, and furniture were consumed in flames. When Benny turned back onto Sleaford Place, three fire trucks blocked the road and fat canvas hoses snaked across his front yard. Firemen trained high arcs of water onto the flames lapping at his roof, a scene that likely reminded him of the devastating fires that killed so many of his gunnery crew at the Battle of Santa Cruz.

Benny threw the car into park and raced toward the house, panicked that his wife and little girl were still inside. But then he saw poor little Jeanne Marie huddled in a blanket next to one of the firemen, shaking and crying. Jeannette was talking to the fire captain; when she spied Benny, she cast an icy glance his way. It was a look he knew too well.

WHILE THE MATTER OF his burned-down house—and divorce—was sorted out, Benny resumed his research on Barton's whereabouts. Bill had been exhorting Benny to check with this officer or that Pentagon branch for updated POW intelligence. MacArthur had claimed to be making great strides in liberating the Philippines. "What of the war prisoners?" Bill wrote Benny.

Benny's last letter to Bill had noted one promising development. Another prisoner, a navy ensign and, he suspected, a prison colleague of Barton's, had just escaped and was being flown from the Philippines to Washington. His name was George Petritz. He had escaped from *another* Japan-bound ship that was sunk, this one in Subic Bay. All Benny knew so far was that he was being evacuated to Washington from the Leyte beachhead. The man needed immediate medical care and would be going to Bethesda Naval Hospital upon his arrival. Benny promised Bill he would visit Petritz as soon as they would let him.

But when Benny finally had his visit with George Petritz, he was so disconsolate over the doomed scenario Petritz described, he could not bring himself to write Bill about it—or at all—for months. This must have been difficult for Benny, but given the choices, reticence seemed preferable to the truth.

36

★ ★ ★

THE *ORYOKO MARU*

FOR THE PRISONERS QUARTERED at Bilibid Prison after the Allies landed at Leyte, the final months of 1944 were an emotional seesaw. Days-long American air raids over Manila in late October seemed to signal imminent liberation; but when the raids paused, prison guards insisted they were going to be shipped to Japan at the next opportunity.

The agony was in knowing that even if they survived a voyage to Japan, it would be months or years before they might be freed, instead of possibly days or weeks. Optimists like Barton Cross believed they would be rescued. Pessimists like Charles Armour believed this was just another case of his being the "fuckee."

The men craned to watch navy carrier planes carry out their attacks on Manila through barred windows on Bilibid's second story. They hooted and cheered every time a plane swooped down at enemy targets all around them; even the weakest hospital cases rose from their cots to thrill at the sight. Another source of satisfaction was the sight of their guards dashing for freshly dug foxholes at the sound of air raid sirens. "The demoralizing effect of inadequate rations is balanced by US Navy bombings [over Manila and Manila Bay]," confided navy prisoner Lieutenant David Nash to his diary. "The raids are spectacular and we watch them regularly . . . They gradually assure us that the Japanese are going to be unable to evacuate us to Japan."

The reigning emotions at Bilibid at that time—hope and apprehension—were perhaps best expressed in a letter to his family written by Ensign Shields Goodman:

> We are presumably awaiting transportation to Japan . . .
> [If so] I shall leave this letter with one of the hospital
> patients because the prisoners here will undoubtedly be
> back in American hands before those sent north to Japan.
> I have great hopes that our forces will come in before the
> Nips can get us out. We hear that Americans have landed 350
> miles to the south of us . . . Our planes have been overhead
> nearly every day since we arrived here. They have bombed
> the airfields and the port area and we hear that there are
> no Nip freighters or any other ships in the harbor . . . We
> feel that our insurance against being sent north becomes
> more concrete with each air raid . . . Happy day it's going
> to be when we are all reunited again. These last . . . years
> will fall away from us like leaves from a tree in fall, and
> it will seem . . . that we have never been apart.

Bilibid was spared any harm thanks to the large "PW" markings on its roof and exterior walls; clearly, the Yanks knew where they were. The prisoners might not have known when their troops would storm the gates, but even the worst skeptics believed it would be soon. Excitement and tensions ran high as they listened to contraband radio broadcasts confirming MacArthur's landing at Leyte. And they knew that MacArthur's troops were going to press north and west toward Luzon, compounding their hopes.

What they did not know was that the Leyte campaign had gotten bogged down, a factor that would alter their fate in ways that could not have been comprehended at the time. Unexpected Japanese reinforcements landing on Leyte's west coast were delivering fierce resistance to the Sixth Army approaching from the east—giving MacArthur his first taste of a fanatical, suicidal defense.

Another factor that helped slow the Leyte campaign was deployment of the enemy's first organized kamikaze force. The term "kamikaze," meaning "divine wind," had evolved into an enduring symbol of Japanese homeland protection after a sudden sea storm thwarted Mongol Kublai Khan's twelfth-century invasion of Japan. In Leyte Gulf, divine wind took the form of squadrons of fuel-bloated, explosive-laden planes flown on one-way suicide missions into Allied ships.

A steady onslaught of kamikazes rained down death on Leyte Gulf. The speed of their descent so confounded antiaircraft defenses that thirty-four ships were sunk and 288 others suffered serious damage. Hundreds of sailors died hideous deaths. The airborne attacks also suspended troopship unloading, which further exacerbated delays ashore.

It would take sixty-seven days to secure Leyte Island, double what MacArthur had confidently predicted for the *entire* campaign to retake the Philippines. The November 20 invasion of his next objective, Mindoro Island—which would also seal off Manila Bay to all Japanese shipping—had to be pushed back. In fact, the Mindoro landings were postponed and postponed again until definitively rescheduled for December 15. Advance carrier air strikes to clear enemy ships of all kinds from local waters would begin at dawn, December 14.

★　　★　　★

ON NOVEMBER 25 A fierce wind blew over Bilibid Prison, and the skies grew dark and ominous. A seaborne typhoon then roared across Manila and southern Luzon, bringing whipping rain and low, heavy clouds— and an abrupt end to six weeks of almost continuous US air raids. After so many weeks of being buoyed by them, the prisoners were dismayed by their sudden halt. Worse, when the storm passed, the planes did not return.

The men fretted and cursed and debated endlessly the possible reasons, even as they strained their eyes and ears for renewed activity. More discouraging was fresh chatter among the guards about the possibility of getting a transport into Manila Bay to ship the prisoners north. "What has happened?" wrote Marine Lieutenant Colonel Curtis Beecher in his journal. "Are we to find out that some serious setback has occurred just when our prospects seem so bright?"

Unaware of the complex revision of the Philippine invasion timeline, the prisoners knew only that the long, reassuring buzz of American aircraft had stopped as abruptly as it had begun. The calendar turned to December under silent skies, and the men grappled with newfound despair. They filled the hours as best they could—trading yet more recipes even as their rations grew impossibly smaller.

One glacial day after another passed this way. To distract from the gathering gloom, detailed instruction in Italian, Greek, French, German, and Polish recipes was added to the usual American gourmandizing. Incipient sommeliers lectured on wine pairings. One memorable presentation was given by Warwick Potter Scott, a navy lieutenant whose pedigreed name and bearing conferred enhanced authority on the subject: the proper sequencing of wine service at a thirteen-course dinner party, such as might be thrown at his home on Philadelphia's Main Line. The room was filled with attentive note takers, and there were a number of earnest follow-up questions. There was little else to do but pace the prison yard, talk longingly of home, and speculate endlessly on what would happen to them next.

On December 12 the uncertainty came to an end in the form of a breathless runner from Manila's Japanese military headquarters. His urgent message was for Bilibid's commandant. Time was of the essence, he told Commandant Nogi Naraji. During the bombing break, a transport ship had made it into Manila Bay. He must prepare a prisoner draft for immediate departure for Japan. Nogi ordered the navy doctors to prepare a manifest of all prisoners capable of travel.

"Our worst fears," wrote Curtis Beecher, "are finally realized."

In a hastily drafted protest letter, a group of senior officers and navy doctors formally objected. The letter forcefully asserted that moving war prisoners through active combat zones was a violation of the Geneva Convention. It also cited recent prison-ship sinkings, indicating that the specific dangers they faced were well understood. But Lieutenant Nogi had the power only to carry out orders, not alter them.

The ensigns shook their heads in dismay as they walked in a circle while coerced medical officers nodded grimly that one after another of them was fit for travel. Charles Armour—who by this time was suffering from beriberi, a painful thiamine deficiency—observed that if you were fit enough to cast a shadow, you were well enough to go.

At *tenko* that evening, a final manifest of 1,619 men was announced—two-thirds of Bilibid's remaining population. The group was primarily composed of officers, chaplains, navy doctors, and corpsmen; they would depart for Japan the following morning. Lieutenant Nogi, a former Seattle physician who had been relatively kind to the prisoners, tried to reassure them in his remarks that evening. There had been no air raids for eighteen days, he said to the sullen assembly; the waters were again safe for travel. David Nash confided in disgust to his diary, "He knew as well as we did it meant suicide."

After nearly three years to the day of hoping and waiting, the indefatigable band of ensigns—Charles Armour, Barton Cross, Earl Ferguson, Bob Glatt, Shields Goodman, Bob Granston, Andrew Long, Ken Wheeler, Chuck Wilkins, Bob Wuest, and George Petritz—scanned the list and gave one another a somber, knowing nod. Every single one of them was on it. They listened numbly to their instructions. They would be mustered at 0400, divided into three boarding groups, and embark on the familiar march to the waterfront. Their destination, once again, was Pier 7, the one-time "Million Dollar Pier."

None of them slept that night. They talked, collected scant possessions, and ate whatever saved Red Cross rations they had set aside.

Some wrote wills and farewell letters to next of kin should they not make it home. These were buried in sealed jars or entrusted to the few hospital corpsmen or patients not designated to depart. Still, throughout the night, a chorus of silent prayer drifted heavenward: *Please, God, let an American air raid cancel the voyage.*

Despite the supplications, they were rousted by the clangorous guardhouse bell at 0400. After a final meal—a teacup of *lugao*—the men organized into their boarding groups. Serial roll calls ensued. Then, inexplicably, the prisoners were ordered back to their quarters, reigniting hope. "Well, we haven't gone yet," said one, bravely. For the next few hours, optimism made a comeback. Bets were placed that their luck would turn, the ever-popular collateral being a steak dinner in Frisco.

At noon, however, the draft was resummoned, recounted, and ordered to fall in. Long columns of four abreast moved out of Bilibid's forbidding gates one last time. Those left behind looked on mournfully, as if witnessing their departure for the guillotine. The pitiful, heavily guarded procession—to the last man, thin, weak, and barely clothed—stretched a quarter of a mile.

With the exception of George Petritz and Shields Goodman, the ensigns were placed under the command of Colonel Curtis Beecher. The forty-seven-year-old marine—a decorated Great War veteran, whose commendations included the Croix de Guerre, the Silver Star, and the Purple Heart—was universally respected, even by the Japanese. The ensigns placed every remaining ounce of faith in him.

But Beecher had his own misgivings. "It was hot in the noon-day sun," he wrote of the march from Bilibid to the docks. "Everyone had lost weight and was in much poorer physical condition since their arrival at Bilibid . . . Many were barely able to walk, and quite a number were picked up along the route after passing out . . . It was a poor start for what at best would be an arduous journey."

The column stumbled past the Metropolitan Theater, across the Pasig Bridge, past the Legislative Building and the Walled City, Intramuros, colonial Manila's historic core, and General MacArthur's prewar headquarters. In every direction, weeds, trash, and abandoned buildings lined cratered streets. Approaching the harbor, they passed the Manila Hotel and then the Army and Navy Club, the latter no doubt evoking bittersweet memories for Barton. The rising sun flew atop its flagpole, and the once-boisterous poolside bar was boarded up. The grounds, trim and verdant in 1941, were vacant and overgrown.

But at each turn, bands of street boys were silhouetted against the ruins, flashing their signature V signs. Inside houses along the route, radio volumes were turned up to blaring as the procession passed, another defiant signal of loyalty to the Americans.

HOT AND EXHAUSTED FROM the four-kilometer march, the ragged columns finally massed at Pier 7 around one thirty in the afternoon. With characteristic optimism, Barton was encouraged when he eyed the awaiting vessel at the dock. Handsome-looking cabins and parlors lined every level. It was large, attractive, and multidecked—more like a luxury travel liner than a troop transport, Barton observed, to a derisive Charles. *Oryoko Maru* was painted on her sides and stern.

Admittedly, the ship did appear considerably more comfortable than any other they had been hosted on so far; with just a little crowding, there might even be room to accommodate all of them in the topside cabins. Barton's initial reaction was shared by a number of the others: this might not be so bad after all.

But there was an ominous retrofit to the civilian liner: antiaircraft gun mounts on the bow, stern, and along the decks in between. The ship bore no flag or markings indicating that it would be carrying Allied prisoners. Nevertheless, some satisfying sights awaited them at the waterfront.

This was their first close-up of the tremendous damage that American naval aircraft had inflicted on the port facilities: sunlight poured through gaping holes in docks and sheds all around the pier. Out in the harbor, masts from dozens of sunken Japanese ships poked through the surface like scattered stubble in a winter cornfield.

When the prisoners arrived at Pier 7, it was already jammed with civilian Japanese carrying bundles of personal belongings. They, too, it seemed, were preparing to board *Oryoko Maru*. The prisoners took heart that this obvious exodus meant the Japanese knew they were about to lose the Philippines. The majority of the civilians were women in brightly colored kimonos, their babies and children in tow. In addition, a large contingent of Japanese troops were preparing to board and a sprinkling of merchant seamen as well, likely former crew of ships sunk in Manila Bay.

While these groups streamed up *Oryoko Maru*'s gangway, the prisoners were held for hours without food or water in a sweltering metal warehouse alongside the pier. They grew increasingly discouraged by the loading: the ship looked crowded already without a single one of the 1,619 of them yet aboard. There was further disappointment when the odious Mr. Wada and his heartless boss, Lieutenant Junsaboro Toshino from Davao Penal Colony, appeared at the dock. Toshino, they learned, would be in charge of the prisoner draft. But the Davao contingent knew all too well that Toshino vested wide-ranging authority in his malevolent interpreter.

Shusuke Wada was new to Colonel Beecher, as he had not left Cabanatuan with the Davao contingent. But the seasoned marine sized up the problem quickly. "Wada was a detestable, gnome-like man, with a screeching, high-pitched voice," Beecher wrote. "I went up to him on the dock to ask a question in connection with the loading and got a snarly, arrogant reply. It was then that I found out that he was going with us, and I felt we were going to have a hard time with him . . . [T]he very fact that all business had to be done through him gave him authority . . . [H]e could refuse to transmit requests and put his own interpretation on orders by his commander."

It was late afternoon by the time all the Japanese passengers were loaded. Then, clearly anxious to weigh anchor and depart while they still could, guards rousted the prisoners to their feet and issued boarding instructions. Three holds belowdeck were assigned to them. The aft hold would be loaded first, the forward hold second, the center last.

It took more than an hour for the first group of seven hundred men, including Petritz, Goodman, and Warwick Potter Scott, to disappear down the long ladder into the aft hold. Guards used various means to hasten the process. At the bottom of the narrow steps stood Sergeant Dau, another Davao guard loathed by the prisoners who knew him. Dau and three Formosan conscripts urged prisoners farther and farther back into the hold's dark reaches—Dau with the aid of a drawn sword, his privates with brooms. With no source of ventilation but the open hatch, those in the rear of the space began to faint well before the loading was complete.

Early cries for air and water from the aft hold were fully audible to the second group climbing the gangway. Barton, Charles, and approximately six hundred others fell in behind Colonel Beecher. They were herded across the hot deck toward the bow, where another hatch revealed a steep, narrow ladder lowering twenty feet into darkness. Their final destination was similar to the one at the rear of the ship: a black and airless space measuring approximately sixty by one-hundred feet, with a four-foot-high wooden shelf extending around the sides.

When the forward cargo space was filled to capacity, with barely room for the men to sit and still 150 to be loaded, Colonel Beecher asked Mr. Wada—standing at the top of the ladder—if the rest of the group could please be redirected to other quarters. The hold was full, Beecher said; men would suffocate if any more were added. But Wada brusquely declined. *"Ippai! Ippai!"* he snarled, which means "chock full."

The loading continued with the help of another familiar Davao sentry: Kazutane Aihara, whose fondness for swatting the men's legs with sharpened lengths of bamboo the Davao prisoners also remembered. Now Aihara used a shovel to press them so deep into the forward hold that men were wedged in the tiny corners of the bulkhead and against the hot side plates of the ship. They sat tight against one another, knees drawn to their chests. Without portholes or vents, their breathing quickly became labored.

On the dock, the temperature was approximately 90 degrees. On the metal-seamed deck, it was closer to 100. Halfway down the ladders, it was hotter still, and in the loaded holds, the temperature quickly reached 120 degrees or more. Having been given no water since their teacup of *lugao* that morning, men along the bulkheads tried to lick the beads of moisture from the rising cloud of perspiration forming on the boards.

The final group of about three hundred descended into the center hold. These were the fortunate ones on *Oryoko Maru*: the center hold had ventilation and, while crowded, it was far from *ippai*.

It was under these conditions that *Oryoko Maru* cast off at sunset. Buckets containing a mixture of seaweed, fish, and rice were lowered into the three holds, but in the dark, distribution was uneven and chaotic; most men managed to grab a handful, but many clawed two, and others got none. Water was lowered as well, but in quantities so small it ran out while being ladled near the hatch openings. The men in the rear got none at all. Panic began to rise.

Oryoko Maru's slow, cautious course through the harbor shipwrecks failed to generate the air circulation the prisoners had hoped for with the movement of the ship. She then halted at the breakwater to await the convoy of freighters and destroyers with which *Oryoko Maru* would travel north. As each hour passed, conditions in the baking, oxygen-deprived holds grew more desperate. In addition to the maddening thirst, overflowing latrine buckets spilled, and their dungeon floors became a shallow bath of human waste.

While the ship awaited the escort vessels, prisoners in the aft hold began begging for air and water. Mr. Wada shouted back, "There is no water for you! You are disturbing the Japanese women and children! If you do not remain quiet I will close the hatch!" This brought no end to their cries. Rising chants of "Air! Water! Air! Water!" continued. Similar pleas came from the forward hold.

Wada responded by slamming shut the aft-hold hatch, its only source of ventilation. This happened around ten o'clock, marking a sharp descent into the most terrifying night in the lives of those who survived it. Colonel Beecher stood watch in the forward hold throughout the night, attempting to keep order—but, as he wrote later, "I have seen death, starvation, brutality, and torture, but have never experienced anything like those 12–14 hours. Men [went] crazy, moaning, groaning, singing or just muttering to themselves . . . It was pitch black, the moaning of the crazed and dying and the shouts of men fighting and killing each other."

During their long imprisonment, all the prisoners had suffered periods of terrible thirst; but that night on *Oryoko Maru*, they experienced the converging mind-altering tortures of extreme thirst and acute oxygen deprivation. The lucky ones suffocated to death before sunrise. Others, increasingly weak and dehydrated, went out of their minds.

Some drank what urine they could drain from their own bodies or from the waste buckets. Others slit open their own veins, or those of their neighbor, with switchblades or broken glass in order to suck the blood. Still others became violent in the hellish dark, beating to death those near them with fists or empty canteens for real or imagined transgressions. Some—including Barton Cross with Earl Ferguson and Robert Granston with Chuck Wilkins—paired up for mutual support and protection. They hung back quietly in the rear recesses of the hold's shelving as madness reigned all around.

At 0300 *Oryoko Maru* again weighed anchor and got under way, this

time in convoy. Turning north into the South China Sea, the convoy hugged
the relative shelter of Bataan's jagged coastline. The date was now December 14.

At first light, a weary Colonel Beecher ascended the ladder and asked
the sentry for a word with Mr. Wada. When the hunchback appeared,
Beecher informed him that men below were dead and dying from suffocation and thirst. The burly marine, who towered over Wada, negotiated
vigorously for water and requested that the prisoners be allowed to rotate
onto the deck for air.

Wada relented on the water request, allowing a detail to come up and
fill buckets from a cabin bathtub. The group worked quickly, managing to
procure enough for one half a canteen cup per man; for men with swelling,
paper-dry tongues, it was better than nothing.

After the water was distributed, Beecher reiterated his request to Wada
that prisoners be allowed brief rotations to the deck, beginning with those
who had lost consciousness. While Beecher waited for Wada to consult
with Lieutenant Toshino on the matter, the lookout in the ship's crow's nest
began calling excitedly, "*Hikoki! Hikoki! Takusan hikoki, American! Kaigoon
hikoki, takusan!*" The ship's air raid alarm followed.

On the deck above, the prisoners heard the drumming of running feet
mixed with deafening bursts of antiaircraft fire. Pleading for calm at regular
intervals, Beecher angled himself onto the ladder, where he could see the
action through the open hatch.

THE AIR SQUADRON BEARING down on the convoy was led by
Commander Robert Riera, Annapolis class of 1935 and a former *Enterprise*
colleague of Benny's. One of her rising star pilots, Riera was awarded the
Navy Cross for his daring sorties from *Enterprise* in the battle at Leyte Gulf.

Now flying missions off *Enterprise*'s sister carrier *Hornet*, Riera's December 14 log noted the targeting of a northbound convoy creeping along
the Bataan coast. At 0710, near the entrance to Subic Bay, Riera gave the

signal, and one Hellcat after another dove down behind him with all they had: bombs, rockets, and relentless sprays of machine gun fire.

Beecher watched from the ladder in suspended disbelief as eight Hellcats peeled into steep dives toward them. Concussive explosions followed, each violently shaking the ship's bulkheads. Not lucky misses, Beecher knew; they were going after the destroyer and freighter escorts first. *Oryoko Maru's* antiaircraft gunners fired furiously at the dive bombers, bringing fierce responses from the planes' rear and wing gunners.

The atmosphere in the hold turned quiet and expectant as guns hammered away and bombs dropped all around them. Over the cacophony, one of the chaplains, Father Duffy, raised his voice in prayer: "Forgive them, Father. They know not what they do."

Commander Frank Bridget, a navy flyer himself, sat atop the aft ladder and, in the words of one witness, "as cool as a tennis match referee, reported the action." Bridget: "Flight of American navy planes headed this way. Two peeling off to attack a freighter . . . another hitting a tanker . . . several burning ships in view. Here they come! Everybody duck!"

The trembling prisoners heeded Bridget's warning as they heard the plane engines accelerate into their dives. The prisoners heeded his every word, but David Nash recalled "hop[ing] to hell they would score and hop[ing] to hell they wouldn't." One by one, the bombs hit the water, each with a violent *thump* before exploding. The ship bounced like a bathtub toy, and the men below were soon covered with dust and rust chips shaken loose by the detonations.

Suddenly light and air poured into the hold; burning shrapnel had ripped a jagged hole in the side of the ship. Dozens were wounded, but the hole brought improved airflow and enabled a better view of the action.

Now they could see their own planes retreat, circle, and roar back for a strafing run. Riera's audacious bombers dropped their bombs from 1,200 feet but strafed at nearly mast height. Bright flashes preceded the rapid chatter of guns firing hundreds of burning rounds down *Oryoko Maru's* throat.

Fifty-caliber machine gun bullets—forged by patriotic factory workers in places such as Elizabethtown, Tulsa, Texarkana, and Ypsilanti—peppered the ship and its human cargo. Scorching bullets and casings ricocheted into the holds. Between attacks, doctors and corpsmen crawled from man to man, dressing fresh wounds with scraps of cloth torn from clothing of the dead.

The worst carnage was above them. Japanese gun crews and their serial replacements had stood and died at their mounts. Pooling blood from the deck dripped down onto the calm, moustachioed Commander Bridget, who continued to interpret the action from his slatted perch. "Not going to Japan, boys. Still right off Subic. Not going to Japan . . ."

In one- and two-hour intervals, Riera's squadron returned to attack the convoy at least nine separate times that day. At nightfall, *Oryoko Maru* was the only ship in the doomed cortege still afloat, and barely at that. With a broken rudder and riddled with holes, she limped into Subic Bay. Doctors were ordered up from the holds to treat wounded Japanese. On return, they confirmed massive casualties throughout the upper decks, cabins, parlors, and dining areas. The topside first-class cabins had been particularly hard hit, they said; chintz window dressing offered no protection from bombs and bullets.

With so many dead and the ship's sides punctured, oxygen supply for the surviving prisoners had improved. But in all other respects, the second night in the hold was as bad or worse than the first. Screams of the insane competed with groans of the wounded, and fights between possessed men could not be stopped.

By dawn on December 15, an eerie quiet hung over the crippled *Oryoko Maru*. The ship was dead in the water about five hundred yards off Olongapo, the onetime US Navy base. Subic's gentle current rippled against her hull as morning light filtered into the hold. Able to see again, doctors began moving about, treating wounds as best they could and gathering up the dead. They worked with dispatch; the bombers were expected to return to resume their work.

When the dazed prisoners gradually came to, they realized that except for a few guards, the Japanese passengers had all been evacuated. Were they being kept aboard intentionally to be sunk by their own navy? The answer came at 0800; the distant grind of airplane engines confirmed the imminent return of Riera's squadron.

Within minutes, unopposed bombs came whistling down. A large explosion convulsed the ship, and she heeled sharply to port. The aft hold had taken the direct hit, instantly killing some 250 prisoners. More died when the guard Aihara emptied his pistol at blast survivors rushing the aft-hold ladder.

In the forward hold, just as listening prisoners began to expect the worst, Mr. Wada spat down new orders: "Abandon ship!" The men were to remove all clothes and shoes and swim ashore. At this, the surviving prisoners seemed to regain a modicum of sanity, even discipline, as they worked together to first hoist up the wounded. Wada ordered Colonel Beecher to depart for shore and organize the incoming prisoners. The imperturbable Commander Bridget took charge on deck.

Bridget reiterated Wada's orders: remove any remaining clothes and shoes, exit the ship from the port side (which faced Olongapo), and swim ashore. The Japanese Naval Landing Party had set up machine guns on the beach and seawall. Orders were to shoot anyone who swam off course. "They mean what they say," Bridget warned.

Ensigns Earl Ferguson and Barton Cross emerged slowly from beneath the wooden shelving in the rear of the hold, weak and shaken, but unharmed. Two other ensigns, Robert Granston and Bob Glatt, did the same. Chuck Wilkins, Granston's best friend and initial *Oryoko* companion, was dead. Like many who had wisely paired up in the hold, faithfully dividing whatever sustenance came their way and keeping watch while the other slept, they had survived the worst of it aboard *Oryoko Maru*.

Separated from Charles since the beginning of the voyage, Barton was no doubt grateful when he saw his tall, gaunt figure stumble across the eerie space. At the ladder, the ensigns tried to assess the losses to their once inseparable band. Word quickly reached them that Ensigns Shields Goodman and Warwick Potter Scott had died in the bomb blast of the aft hold. They could not locate George Petritz, and fretted that he, too, had met the same fate in the aft hold.

Topside, the men gulped the humid air as if it were forbidden fruit. By the time Barton cleared the hatch, the deck was crowded with prisoners, and several had already begun the swim toward shore. Suddenly they heard the drone of airplane engines on the southern horizon; seconds later, four dive bombers descended toward *Oryoko Maru*. Almost in unison, the unmistakably white, bare-assed prisoners, both on deck and in the water, started waving their arms and shouting.

The formation leveled off as if to commence a bombing run when suddenly a plane on the flank waggled its wings and passed low over the scene without dropping its load. The rest of the planes followed suit. They then circled and retreated to the south without firing a shot. Finally, it seemed, they knew.

Charles Armour had never learned to swim. He didn't believe he could make the quarter mile to the beach. Astonishingly, several other prisoners had the same problem. Though weakened, Barton was in relatively decent condition, and years of tackling the Jersey Shore's burly waves had made him a strong and confident swimmer. Once in the water, he beckoned to Charles—who, not surprisingly, had refused to shed his clothes or cap.

In the water, Barton secured Charles under one arm and paddled toward Olongapo with the other. When their feet touched sandy bottom, they waded toward Colonel Beecher, who was standing at the shoreline. Beecher's attention had been drawn to swimmers struggling against the tidal current. Could Barton help them? he asked. Without a word, Barton dove back in and swam toward his floundering fellow prisoners.

Oryoko Maru was nearly empty when David Nash went looking for life jackets for other nonswimmers still on deck. Revived by fresh air and some candy and raw cabbage he found, Nash scavenged further and came across a chest of medical supplies in an aft passageway. Knowing it would prove invaluable ashore, he tried with difficulty to drag it to where it could be lowered onto a raft. In searching for assistance, he saw someone—breathing but unconscious—lying on a high shelf in the aft hold. It was Ensign George Petritz.

Nash approached and shook his friend's foot. "If you're alive you better get the hell out of here," he told Petritz. "Everyone else is just about gone." Disoriented but unhurt, Petritz managed to get to his feet and follow Nash, who had asked him for help getting the medicine chest ashore. "I will help you load it onto the raft," Petritz said, "but I'll never be taken alive by the Japanese again."

After loading the supplies and shoving Nash off, Petritz did some scavenging of his own.

He found Japanese clothing, a life preserver, and a jar of brown sugar and Japanese celery. After gobbling all that he could stomach, he put on the clothes and life preserver and lowered himself over the starboard side. Once in the water, he slipped under a floating wooden crate and waited. When he estimated that the lowering sun's reflected glare on the water would impair the gunners' view from the beach, Petritz slipped off the life preserver— which made him too buoyant in the salt water—and began swimming toward the far shore.

He swam for nearly an hour before coming across a *banca* with two Filipinos aboard: a boy and his grandmother. Seeing that he was American, the boy pulled Petritz aboard, and they took him ashore. Giving him his first taste of freedom in nearly three years, local villagers and guerrillas fed and protected Petritz as they might a family member. In time, they arranged for his conveyance to the Leyte beachhead in a navy PT boat. From there, he was evacuated stateside and eventually to Bethesda Naval Hospital outside Washington, DC.

37

★ ★ ★

END GAME IN THE PACIFIC

PLANNING THE SEQUENTIAL AMPHIBIOUS invasions of Iwo Jima and Okinawa was a months-long undertaking and the most complicated of the Pacific War. Where invasion rehearsals were staged was a minor logistic in the epic context. But when Leyte Island in the Philippines was selected for the Okinawa rehearsals, the earth moved under Bill's feet. He hoped only that it wouldn't be too late.

His long-sought goal of reaching Barton finally seemed at hand, and Admiral Turner knew it. Late on the evening of the Okinawa rehearsals decision, a wound-up Turner telephoned his groggy flag secretary to discuss a matter to which he'd given considerable thought: Bill should take liberty on their arrival at Leyte, Turner told his startled aide.

The Philippines should be firmly in hand by their scheduled arrival in March, the admiral continued. He wanted Bill to take the earliest possible opportunity to search for his brother. With the sequential D-days for Iwo Jima and Okinawa—code-named Detachment and Iceberg, respectively—set sequentially for February 19 and April 1, the flagship might be conducting rehearsals in the Philippines for as long as three weeks between the two invasions. This would give Bill ample time to go ashore and investigate.

Bill listened quietly at first, too stunned to respond. But when Turner finally paused for breath, he gratefully accepted the admiral's offer; this was no time for forced selflessness.

Turner said he hoped to meet Barton after all the good things he'd heard—maybe even aboard the flagship, if it could be arranged. After a pause that gave them both a moment to savor the scenario, Turner returned to the mechanics of his proposal. First, he indicated that the planners' five-day estimate to secure Iwo Jima might be overly optimistic. But even a week's delay would still have them at Leyte by early March, he hoped. Either way, Bill would have time to go ashore. By that time, the Philippines would almost certainly be in Allied hands, and there would be some system in place for locating prisoners.

If his penchant for alcohol had been a factor in Turner's unusual late-night call, that concern was vacated when the energetic amphibian commander reiterated his overture the next morning, and even made recommendations on where Bill might make inquiries. As though to counterbalance his sanguine proposals, Turner also cautioned Bill to prepare for what he might or might not find.

His boss's interest struck a deep chord, especially since Bill's quest to find out about Barton had become an increasingly lonely and discouraging enterprise. Recent communications from his mother and Arthur devolved into diatribes against the president, the Joint Chiefs of Staff, and—not least—the United States Navy. Nothing less than Barton's safe return home would assuage them now.

More disturbing was that Bill's latest entreaties to Benny seemed to be falling on deaf ears. It had been weeks since his last letter inquiring about the latest dope from the Casualty Branch and escaped prisoners now in

Washington. Why had Benny not responded? In the meantime, Bill had done his own sleuthing, but it brought scant comfort.

Captain Mac McCollum, back in Australia with the Seventh Fleet, confirmed that prisoners had been aboard some of the recent enemy ships sunk off the Philippines. All had been quartered on Japanese merchant vessels traveling north toward Japan. None had been flagged as carrying prisoners of war. Maddeningly, no manifests were available, but Bill had faith that McCollum was motivated to get his hands on them; he was as anxious about his cousin Shivers as Bill was about Barton.

Next came the news of a prisoner massacre on the Philippine island of Palawan. Survivor affidavits stated that on December 14, upon hearing US planes approaching Palawan, Japanese guards at Puerto Princesa herded 150 prisoners into air raid shelters—wood-lined, subterranean enclosures recently constructed by the prisoners themselves on orders by their captors. When the prisoners were loaded, the guards poured gasoline through shelter air slats and tossed in flaming grenades. The pits exploded into raging infernos.

Engulfed in flames, screaming prisoners rushed the exits only to be met by guards with machine guns, bayonets, and clubs. Miraculously, eleven of the 150 prisoners escaped in the melee, though all badly burned. They survived thanks to their quick interception by Filipino civilians and transport to the Leyte beachhead by yet another guerrilla band. Palawan survivors were on their way to Washington, where they would be treated and debriefed. Such reports threatened to reulcerate Bill's stomach.

One encouraging rumor made its way to Bill just before he shoved off for Iwo Jima. Another prisoner rescue plan was in the works: this time from a prison camp on Luzon. The plan seemed to be gaining traction thanks to the advocacy of one particular American guerrilla on Luzon, Major Robert Lapham. Convinced that more prisoner slaughter was in store, Lapham had persisted in his call to liberate prisoners from a place called Cabanatuan before it was too late. Most of the camp's population had been removed in October, but apparently hundreds of prisoners were still there.

Bill's pulse shot up and down with every report, each one maddeningly devoid of details that might hint at how Barton fit into it all. Which prisoners had been massacred? Which had gone down with their ships? Which were candidates to be rescued? Did the escaped naval ensign, George Petritz, have any of these answers—or news of Barton? As the amphibians set sail for Iwo Jima in January 1945, Bill sent Benny one last letter, summarizing his findings.

Hinting at recently garnered intelligence, he listed unanswered questions and offered Benny guidance on where he might find answers. What, for example, was the status of the Palawan survivors and this Ensign Petritz—all, presumably, in Washington now? Why hadn't he heard back? Was Benny too beset by his own troubles? Or did he know something too dreadful to share?

NEW OBSTACLES LOOMED AHEAD of the amphibians' departure for Iwo Jima. It might have been Bill's obdurate navy perspective, but one way or another, they all seemed to lead back to Douglas MacArthur. The general's consecutive setbacks in retaking the Philippines had now seriously thrown off the schedules for Operations Detachment and Iceberg.

MacArthur had assured the Joint Chiefs—and President Roosevelt—that he would take Leyte with four divisions in thirty to forty-five days and begin air strikes on Luzon shortly thereafter. But with nine divisions and in twice that time, the job still wasn't done. Since six weeks' spacing between MacArthur's Philippine and Nimitz's Iwo Jima invasion was necessary—as they were using the same combatant ships for their respective operations—Detachment had to be postponed from January 20 to February 3, and then again to February 19.

The April 1 invasion date for Okinawa (Iceberg) could *not* be postponed, due to the predictable onset of the pernicious spring typhoon season. MacArthur's every delay in retaking the Philippines therefore shortened the amphibians' rehearsal hiatus in the Philippines—and Bill's window to search for Barton.

Admiral Turner and his planners had little time to grouse about MacArthur or his slipping timetable. They had more immediate problems. Amphibious warfare techniques were evolving so rapidly that fresh lessons from recent invasions had rendered many of their planning labors obsolete. From hydrography and underwater demolition to the loading and unloading of mammoth amounts of supplies to beachhead organization and gunfire support, amphibian invasion "best practices" were in a constant state of change. More than once, they had to scrap entire planning sections and start over.

Such were the challenges facing Admiral Turner and his strategists as they labored through eighteen-hour days over a four-month period, from October 1944 to January 1945, to choreograph the invasions of Iwo Jima and Okinawa. Comparable in size and scope to the amphibious landings at Normandy—itself years in the planning—the Iwo Jima and Okinawa campaigns would pull thousands of ships and nearly a million men from every branch of service.

A primary difference between these operations and their European counterpart was supply-line logistics: the supply line across the English Channel in support of the Normandy invasion was approximately ninety nautical miles. The supply line for Iwo Jima and Okinawa would stretch an incomprehensible four thousand miles.

ON JANUARY 10, 1945, staff and crew saluted as Admiral Turner's colors soared up the yardarm of his brand-new flagship, the USS *Eldorado*. Weeks of shakedown followed before she nosed out of the Pearl Harbor channel bound for Iwo Jima, but by all accounts, it wasn't much of a sight. Like her predecessor the USS *Rocky Mount*, *Eldorado* resembled a drab cargo vessel barely able to navigate an inland waterway—a crafty disguise for the electronic nerve center of the amphibian fleet and most powerful communications and operations center ever set afloat.

From her state-of-the-art CIC deep within the armor of the ship's hull, staff could monitor and direct shore and air battles as never before. The control room was outfitted with a dizzying alphabet soup of the latest in radar and sonar equipment: SP, SG, PPI, DRT, CASCU, CAP, TBS.

Together these various devices facilitated real-time communications among all sectors of the amphibious machine: from weather updates, to troop interaction ashore, to detection and defense against enemy threats, be they planes, ships, mines, or submarines. Updates on all the above were applied continuously to illuminated Lucite boards lining the CIC. Shipborne technology had traveled light-years since the morning of December 7, 1941, when the USS *Enterprise*'s Jack Baumeister had puzzled behind a black curtain over a radar report on his single, low-resolution screen.

When *Eldorado* hove into Iwo Jima's waters in mid-February, an assault force of some nine hundred ships came into view. Extending to every horizon was an anchorage of aircraft carriers, destroyers, transports, hospital ships, landing vessels, and scores of smaller vessels taxiing among them. Each was poised to play its specific role in the painstakingly choreographed invasion of Iwo Jima.

Also known as "Sulphur Island," the objective was a putrid, eight-square-mile heap of scrub, volcanic ash, and razor-sharp kunai grass, which crawled with biting, typhus-carrying insects. The terrain resembled a Hollywood moonscape. The island was a treeless, cratered, inhospitable piece of ground yielded from boiling magma vomited forth in prehistory through an errant crack in the earth's crust. Reeking gasses hissed from ubiquitous rock fissures, its beaches were black as death, and Mount Suribachi, Iwo's 550-foot volcanic high ground, menaced over its general wretchedness. But to war planners, Iwo Jima was solid gold.

Reverently labeled "the unsinkable aircraft carrier," it boasted a trio of airstrips half the flight distance to Japan from the current B-29 bases in the

Marianas. It was also valued for its powerful symbolism in Japan. As a Japanese infantry officer wrote in his diary in June 1944, long before the Iwo Jima assault was planned, "Iwo Jima is the doorkeeper to the Imperial capital."

On February 16, war correspondents crowded into Admiral Turner's wardroom for a final prebattle briefing. With his usual powder-keg intensity, Kelly Turner studied Bill's fresh supply of intelligence communiqués, memorizing which facts could be publicized ahead of battle and which could not. Press censorship had relaxed considerably since the war's dismal early going. The powers in Washington had learned—to their collective surprise following the seismic response to the Davao escapees' atrocity reports—that strong media coverage actually galvanized public support, which in turn boosted faltering war bond sales.

As a result, the gathering correspondents would be reporting more about the battle for Iwo Jima than would ever have been allowed three years earlier. And with *Eldorado*'s broadcast capacity rivaling that of Radio Honolulu, their stories of valor and heartbreak would be received stateside before any spilled blood had dried—rather than the days, via ship or floatplane, that it had taken to sound the horrors of Guadalcanal.

Readying their notepads and pencils that morning were some of the world's best-known journalists. A handful of them had covered the Pacific War since the first scrappy hit-and-run carrier raids, as well as Turner's own baptism by fire at Guadalcanal—the Battle of Savo Island.

Bob Sherrod of *Time* and *Life* and Keith Wheeler of the *Chicago Sun-Times* were there, along with Walter Davenport of *Collier's*, John Marquand of *Harper's*, Hamilton Freon and Clark Lee of the Associated Press, and John Lardner of the *New Yorker*. With heavy straps and loaded with equipment, photographers Lou Lowery of *Leatherneck* magazine and Joe Rosenthal of AP also jostled for position, along with a pool of radio broadcasters that included NBC's popular Bud Foster.

Bill greeted the correspondents as they filed into Admiral Turner's inner sanctum. As the ship's censor, he was already acquainted with a number of them from the long days and nights aboard *Rocky Mount* during the battles for Saipan, Tinian, and Guam. That was when he'd met Sherrod and Wheeler, who had regaled him with tales of riding along in *Enterprise* Sky Control with Benny Mott during the 1942 carrier raids. "You must be little Benny!" Wheeler had crowed at their first meeting.

Bemused to hear a nickname he hadn't heard since plebe year, Bill nodded in cautious assent. The warm and garrulous Wheeler moved on to a geyser of Benny stories, making Bill happy and sad at the same time. These were stories about Benny in Benny's World of the USS *Enterprise*. In two short years, it seemed this veteran correspondent had pocketed more priceless anecdotes about his older brother than Bill had accumulated in a lifetime.

Hearing such tales from these new acquaintances felt like watching his brother through a hidden camera with his *other* family, in his *other* home—constellations away from their proprietary, Garden State–rooted, three-decade fraternal past. It felt good having big-shot reporters like Wheeler and Sherrod laud Benny, but it made Bill homesick for his brother's companionship. Perhaps the reverse had been felt aboard *Enterprise* in those dark days of 1942. Otherwise Wheeler might never have heard of "Little Benny."

THE ROOM CAME TO a hush when Admiral Turner moved to the microphone. He assembled his papers and cleared his throat like a maestro tapping his music stand. The briefing had been his idea, and for good reason. Counteracting MacArthur's widely publicized criticism of the navy's amphibious campaigns as "unnecessary slaughter" had been a principal motivator. A 1944 *Time* cover story featuring "Terrible Turner" wearing his best sneer had also had its effect.

Turner had long put the demands of his job over tending to his public image. He had belatedly come to appreciate that this neglect had contributed to a distorted public perception of the navy's amphibious campaigns in the Pacific. MacArthur's anti-navy diatribes had gained him an edge in the interservice public relations war, and Turner considered it a point of honor to set the record straight.

Life magazine's Robert Sherrod recalled the February 16 press conference aboard *Eldorado* vividly: "[It] was a rather emotional affair—there was the sort of pit-of-the-stomach emotion one feels when he knows many men who love life are about to die. Kelly Turner, peering over his spectacles and looking like Grant Wood's *American Gothic* farmer, ran the conference."

"The primary objective," Turner began, "is to capture Iwo Jima for fighters which can accompany B-29 bombers in their raids on Japan . . . We expect losses, of ships, and of troops," he continued solemnly. Turner's entire demeanor—including the full back brace he wore daily—reflected the leaden weight of that burden.

"They will be considerable."

He paused and looked into the faces around the room, as though to allow a moment for that unavoidable reality to be absorbed.

"But we are taking steps to keep them as low as possible . . . Iwo Jima is as well defended as any other fixed position in the world today. *Gibraltar* would be a setup by comparison . . . We are going to have losses, but we expect to take the position."

He continued at length on the details of the upcoming operation, finishing his remarks by explaining that *Eldorado* would have to leave Iwo Jima "after a few days, to prepare for future operations."

"Everyone knew he was talking about Okinawa," Sherrod recalled, "but he did not name it."

The next to take the microphone was USMC General Holland "Howlin' Mad" Smith who would be in charge of the tens of thousands of US Marines fighting ashore. The gathered assembly needed no introduction to Smith; he had already led a number of hard-won Pacific campaigns in the Gilberts, Marshalls, and Marianas. The general's delivery was punctuated by deep, collecting breaths.

"There is very little I can add," he began haltingly. "The stage is set.

There has been a tremendous amount of preparation by a large number of officers and men. Everything that can be done has been done . . .

"This is not set up," Smith then said abruptly, wagging his finger as though he'd heard a rumor. "Anybody who indulges in such wild flights of fancy has had no experience against these Japs. Every cook and baker will be on the beach with some kind of weapon . . . Aerial photographs show that the number of pillboxes has increased since October and especially since December, and the Japs on Iwo have no barracks aboveground. We have got to dig them out . . . There is no maneuver ground. This is a frontal attack."

Smith paused.

"The proper way to do it is as quickly as possible," he resumed, stressing the One and Only Marine Way. "We are not accustomed to defensive positions. There is nothing more detrimental to [Marine] morale than to be stabilized. Almost every weapon the Japs have got can reach us on the beaches. We may have to take high casualties—maybe forty percent of the assault troops."

Here he paused again.

"In Admiral Turner we have full confidence—we would rather go to sea with him in command than any other admiral under whom we have served. The navy brought us out here, and we have never yet had to swim ashore . . . though sometimes it has been close."

He allowed a smirk at the jab, which referred to the abrupt pullback of navy ships during the first landings on Guadalcanal. There were reports that by the end of his remarks, the tough-as-nails, foul-mouthed, cigar-chomping "Howlin' Mad" Smith was misty-eyed. He concluded by saying, simply, "We have never failed, and I don't believe we shall fail here."

There was universal surprise when Admiral Turner introduced the next speaker: Secretary of the Navy James Forrestal. He had traveled all the way from Washington to observe firsthand the battle for Iwo Jima.

"It has just been said," Forrestal began, "that you are honored to have me here . . . Quite the reverse is true. It is a high privilege to see in action the quality of leadership America has produced. I have seen Admiral Turner before, in the summer of 1942. His job was to take Guadalcanal with the US Marines. It was a tough job—a very tough job. But that was his mission, and he did it. The American people still do not realize the narrow margin of that pivot point of the Pacific War.

"I am also impressed," he continued, "by the meticulous precision of these operations; the amount and extent of planning that is required. This is a different kind of war that must be fought out here. These assaults on limited land areas present a tough task . . . Iwo Jima, like Tarawa, leaves very little choice except to take it by force of arms, by character, and courage."

Secretary Forrestal ended by giving generous due credit. "My hat is off to the marines. I think my feeling about them is best expressed by a letter written by a major general to his wife after Tarawa. He said, 'I can never again see a United States Marine without experiencing a feeling of reverence.'"

THREE DAYS OF THE most intense naval bombardment of the Pacific War immediately got under way. The ships' pounding of Iwo Jima came after seventy-four straight days of *aerial* bombardment, the longest ever ahead of a Pacific invasion. In all, 7,500 tons of bombs were dropped, and 22,000 shells were lobbed at the tiny atoll, mostly—the marines would soon find out—for naught.

The Japanese had tunneled down seventy-five feet beneath Iwo's barren landscape and constructed a vast, impregnable bulwark, which the long cannonade barely scratched. Miles of tunnels linked subterranean command posts, living quarters, ammunition dumps, and hundreds of concealed pillboxes with forty-inch-thick walls. Mount Suribachi alone had seven levels of passageways connecting a thousand individual chambers. There were multiple entrances, exits, stairwells, and interconnecting corridors, all lined with an ultrahard concrete made from plentiful indigenous volcanic ash.

Iwo Jima's D-day—February 19—began at 0830 with Admiral Turner's customary bellow through the ships' speakers, "Land the landing force!" Waves of marine-loaded landing craft and amtracs cranked away from the anchorage toward the beaches at the signal.

At the shoreline, however, they were stopped in their tracks by soft, black volcanic ash, exposing men and machines to torrents of fire coming from concealed subterranean hideouts. By the end of Day One, two thousand casualties littered the beaches and barely beyond.

CINCPAC's After Action Report detailed the unfolding horror:

```
With each wave, boats would be picked up and thrown broad-
side onto the beach, where succeeding waves swamped and
wrecked them and dug them deeply into the sand, beyond hope
of salvage . . . [They] . . . could not be dragged up even when
assisted by caterpillars. The coarse volcanic sand had no
cohesive consistency . . . Troops debouched from the landing
crafts struggled up the slopes under heavy fire, ankle deep
in it. Wheeled vehicles bogged to their frames, tanks stalled
in the surf, and the 40% grade of the cinder slope brought
amphibious tractors to a halt. As vehicles left the LST ramps,
they immediately sank down, their spinning treads banking
the sand back under the ramps, making it harder for each
succeeding vehicle.
```

In his first Iwo dispatch from *Eldorado*, Robert Sherrod summarized the early landings with astounding understatement: "The Jap plan of defense was plain. Only a few men would defend the beaches. The mortars and machine guns from the hillside caves . . . would stop the landing."

Up on deck, Turner, Smith, Forrestal, and rotating flag staff watched through binoculars with jaws clenched. Rising smoke and ash obscured their view, but beachhead reports confirmed quickly what their collective gut already had: the landings had emphatically not gone according to plan.

Little ground had been gained, and bullet-riddled bodies were strewn along miles of beach.

Bill barely saw his bunk in the grim early going of Iwo Jima. He spent most of that time shuttling between Admiral Turner's quarters and the CIC. He also monitored relays among the Navajo code talkers; the admiral demanded every decoded transmission as soon as it was available. Tensions ran high as Navajo receivers in *Eldorado*'s CIC transcribed each gruesome transmission ("Catching all hell from the quarry"; "Taking heavy casualties and can't move. Mortars killing us"), and Bill delivered them dutifully to Admiral Turner.

By February 21—D-day Plus 2—Holland Smith's dreaded estimates had already become reality: casualties on the beach were running 40 percent. "[The beach] is a two-mile stretch of death . . . all of it ours," reported Staff Sergeant David Dempsey. "An officer in charge of a tank landing boat received a direct shell hit while trying to free his boat from the sand. He was blown in half. A life preserver supports the trunk of his body in the water."

That evening brought another rude surprise. The hundreds of warships at anchor themselves came under siege. Fifty planes, thirty-two of them kamikazes, dropped from a low cloud ceiling just before nightfall— the witching hour for such raids, nerve-frayed crews would learn—and thrust themselves with savage ferocity at ships in the anchorage. The carrier *Bismarck Sea* was hit by two planes and sank in ninety minutes. Attempts to rescue the hundreds of sailors left foundering in dark and heavy seas continued through the night, but more than three hundred were lost. Several other ships were damaged; a mere foretaste of what was to come.

To protect the ship's battle command center, not to mention the secretary of the navy, *Eldorado* briefly withdrew to a protected position that night. From that point forward, a raw fear hung over the seven-mile-wide flotilla. Kamikazes seemed to select targets at random and were nearly impossible to defend against.

There was much discussion of this terrifying new threat in the 0400

CIC briefing on D-day Plus 3. Among the decisions made was that the press would not be allowed to report on this disturbing new enemy tactic. Recently returned from the beachhead, a shaken Robert Sherrod handed Bill his draft copy for review. Its opening line was: "Iwo Jima can only be described as a nightmare in hell."

Sherrod then dropped a bomb of his own. "Wheeler's been hit. He got it right through the neck when he stood up in the shell hole." Bill's dismay at the loss registered before Sherrod could add that his foxhole companion at Attu, Tarawa, Kwajalein, Saipan, and Tinian "was lucky, actually—he fell into the arms of two doctors and less than ten feet from a box of plasma. On his way to Aiea Heights by now."

Otherwise the day began much as the previous two had: with high casualty reports and gained ground measured in yards. On the other side of the command center, a glum Secretary Forrestal studied aerial photographs of the thoroughly pocked objective. "The planes just can't do it on an island like this," he said. Forrestal had hoped to go ashore to observe the operation, but Holland Smith would not allow it.

D-day Plus 4 began rainy and gray, reflecting the mood inside the smoky nerve center. Clacking teletype and the pinging, buzzing, and beeping of electronics were interrupted less by conversation than by the percussive snap of metal cigarette lighters. Next to the Navajo transmission operators—perhaps the busiest of all—were the men directing evacuation of the wounded to hospital ships already overflowing with casualties.

Around midmorning, the somber din was broken by an unusually excited transmission over the Navajo radio net. It was from code talker Teddy Draper to Holland Smith's command post on the beach. Bill stood impatiently over the translator as he methodically transcribed this message: "Asdla-ma-as-tso-si tse-nihl gah tkin nesh-chee dzeh Ashihi, Tkin Ts-a Ma-e A-Kha: Belasana Be Moasi. Bi-tsan-dehnah-jad-ah n-kih tseebii Dzeh Nakia, taa has-clish-nih Besh-legai-a-lah-ih Lin Klizzie . . . nihl neeznaa n-kih nos-bas."

When he finished, the translator handed Bill the piece of paper. Bill blinked his bloodshot eyes and studied the document:

```
To: 5th Marine Division Info: ADC
From: LT 28 E Company, 3rd Platoon:


Sergeant Ernest Thomas [USMCR] platoon raised US flag and
secured Mt. Suribachi at 1020.
```

A tremendous chorus of cheers and ships' horns reverberated throughout the anchorage as Bill clutched the message and loped in the direction of Admiral Turner. He found his boss standing on the flag bridge in the mist, already training his field glasses to Iwo Jima's highest elevation where Old Glory was rippling in the breeze.

ON MARCH 9 *ELDORADO* hastened out of Iwo Jima waters, even though the battle would rage on for two more weeks. The five-day estimate to secure the island had been weeks short of the mark; their delayed departure further shrank the flagship's planned rehearsal hiatus in the Philippines. That delay was exacerbated by a seven-hundred-mile detour to Guam to collect a surprise addition to the Okinawa leadership team.

In a dispatch straight from Washington, US Army Lieutenant General Simon Bolivar Buckner had been ordered to replace USMC General Holland Smith as commander of all landed forces at Okinawa. Grounded in spite, the decision was a direct result of Holland Smith's controversial demand for the replacement of Army General Ralph Smith at Saipan in the heat of battle.

Senior army brass all the way up to General Marshall had seethed over the incident ever since, and this would be their revenge. The revered Holland Smith thus became the highest-ranking victim of an interservice power struggle that had plagued the Pacific War from its inception. Not only would he not lead the invasion at Okinawa, the ground force charged with taking the next objective would be army infantry this time, not marines; a first for Admiral Turner and the amphibians. Moreover, neither Buckner nor his infantry had any previous amphibious assault experience.

It was an inauspicious beginning. Admiral Turner and General Buckner had only one thing in common: neither had ever landed a field army—another immense bait-and-switch for the planners. Moreover, this newlywed amphibian team now had less than half the allotted time to rehearse landing an untested force on a land mass fifty-six times the size of Iwo Jima and maniacally defended by 120,000 Japanese. Despite these escalating pressures, Admiral Turner insisted that Bill go ashore at Leyte as planned.

On the evening of March 15, *Eldorado* finally led the amphibian task force into Leyte Gulf and Bill took the launch to the beachhead the next morning. He hurried from Quonset hut to Quonset hut making inquiries to harried staff at each stop. It took half that first day to learn he was on the wrong island. Evacuating prisoners were being processed at a place called San Fernando la Union, and the central repository for prisoner records was Bilibid Prison in Manila. Both places were on Luzon.

The next morning, March 17, Bill's Irish luck was with him. He caught a transport to Luzon's Poro Point on Lingayen Gulf, also now a bustling Allied beachhead. Bill hitched a ride into San Fernando la Union with an army sergeant. They chatted amiably as the jeep lurched along a sandy road lined with mango groves and into the ruins of San Fernando. Bill walked toward a shrapnel-pocked train station, next to which stood a temporary structure with a "Replacement Center" sign over the door. This was where he'd been told that ex-prisoners were being processed. Was his search for Barton about to come to an abrupt end?

He found the enclosure mostly empty. One hundred twenty-five US Navy prisoners had just been put on a ship in Lingayen Gulf and evacuated to the States, a sympathetic army nurse told him; would he like to see the list? The manifest was of prisoners recently liberated from Bilibid. In his initial split-second review, Bill's heart made the wildest of leaps. He thought he'd caught the prize: "Cross, USNR, Cavite Navy Yard." Could it be? He had to steady himself before tracing his finger back to the spot, for a careful rereading. "Cross, Cornelius, USNR, Cavite Navy Yard." The crush of disappointment lengthened with the discovery that there were no other Crosses on either the "liberated" or subsequent "rescued" lists supplied by the nurse.

That didn't mean Barton hadn't survived, she assured an obviously disappointed Bill. Too little was known at this point. And yes, she added, he *should* go to Manila. Thousands of prisoner records were at Bilibid; tens of thousands, actually.

Back at Poro Point, Bill boarded one of the many PT boats traveling back and forth between Lingayen Gulf and Manila Bay. A call at Manila during his midshipman cruise had dimmed in Bill's memory, but he remembered the general layout of the city. Given the reported condition of Manila's roads and likely difficulty finding transportation, he might have to make his way to Bilibid on foot. The Lingayen nurse had warned that GIs working at the prison had only just started to make sense of the jumble of records, grave registrations, and other documents left in total disarray by the fleeing Japanese.

Reports of Manila's final ravaging had prepared Bill for a city radically altered from what he remembered. But what came into focus during the slow putter toward Pier 7 was beyond his bleakest imaginings. The sheer volume of floating wreckage—bodies drifting past scores of overturned hulks, masts poking up like dead trees from a swamp. The bay was nearly unnavigable. The stench of rotting flesh in the tropical heat forced Bill to pick his way up the bomb-pocked pier with his nose covered with a handkerchief.

US troops had stormed Manila in early February, but there had been another month of vicious street-by-street, building-by-building, and floor-by-floor combat before the city was declared secure. MacArthur himself had only entered Manila's smoldering remains on March 4, and not along a cheering parade route feting his sixty-fifth birthday as he had once envisioned. Between the rubble from blasted buildings and the bomb-cratered, body-strewn pavement, the streets were barely passable—even for General MacArthur. An estimated hundred thousand civilians had died in the final struggle, many first brutally raped or mutilated. The bodies of countless *Manileros*—men, women, and children—were covered with pieces of corrugated tin or other debris to preserve some tiny measure of dignity.

Bill walked north past the wreckage, his destination the intersection of Azcarraga and Quezon. The prison was circled on a map that the kindly Replacement Center nurse had given him—though most of the places and streets it marked had long since been destroyed. Homeless dogs roamed, sniffing mounds of trash and other leavings of a citizenry caught between warring armies: a child's shoe, a broken doll, a cane, a smashed baby stroller.

Along the way, Bill checked himself against unrealistic hopes and girded for bad news. Who could possibly have survived this devastation? With little time left, he hoped to find critical clues on Barton's whereabouts—before all the information was shipped out and dispersed among the Pentagon's harried bureaus.

When he finally arrived at Bilibid, he found a letter appended to the heavy entrance gate. It had been posted by fleeing Japanese guards:

```
                          The Bilibid Hospital
                          Manila P.I.


                          February 4, 1945
                          11:30 A.M. (Tokyo)


1.   The Japanese Army is now going to release all the
     prisoners of war and internees here on its own accord.
```

2. We are assigned to another duty and will be here no
    more;

3. You are at liberty to act and live as free persons;

4. We shall leave here foodstuffs, medicines and other
    necessities of which you may avail yourselves for the
    time being.

Another sign read simply:

Lawfully released prisoners of war and internees are quartered here. Please do not molest them unless they make positive resistance.

                              Imperial Japanese Army

At the prison office, Bill described his quest to the GI on duty. He responded, as the nurse on Lingayen had, that army officials had only just
begun to sift through the thousands of records and grave registrations the
Japanese had left behind. And more were arriving, daily, from several other
prison compounds. He would do what he could to help, but recommended
that Bill first review the batch of grave-registration lists. It might save them
both a lot of time.

Even with the clerk's assistance, this task alone took Bill the better part
of the day; the thousands of names were neither alphabetized nor divided
by service. At the start of each list, Bill braced himself for what he might
find. But when he came to the last page of the last one, he allowed a measure of relief. While he knew these lists were hardly an exhaustive account-
ing of prisoner dead, A. Barton Cross Jr., USNR, was not on any of them.

He then turned to the dozens of other rosters stuffed in various files,
few of which had been reviewed—or even translated. "Bilibid—1942,
1943, 1944, 1945." "Cabanatuan—Camp 1, Camp 2, and Camp 3."

"DAPECOL; O'Donnell." "Puerto Princesa." And on and on. There were also dozens of recovered jars that prisoners had buried containing messages, sketches, letters, and diaries. It was overwhelming, and Bill came to the rueful conclusion that he'd arrived too late to rescue Barton but too early to grasp what had happened to him.

As he pored over prison camp rosters, the clerk pulled another stack of lists from a box on the floor. These were prisoner transport manifests, he explained; maybe Bill should go through these next. This was when Bill began to fully comprehend the extent of the massive prisoner transfers from the Philippines to Japan—aboard ships named *Shinyo Maru*, *Hofuku Maru*, *Yashu Maru*, *Rakuyo Maru*, and *Oryoko Maru*. It was here he learned that Mac McCollum's cousin Shivers had been aboard the fated *Arisan Maru*.

The final manifest was of the last prison ship to depart Manila Bay before the Allies sealed it off to enemy traffic. The ship had departed December 13, almost exactly twelve weeks earlier. Bill was momentarily stunned. After all this time, *Oryoko Maru* manifest in hand, here it was, finally: Cross, Arthur Barton Jr., Ensign, USNR. He peppered the clerk with questions on what was known of this ship and its destination, then rose wearily and thanked him. He would be back, he said, but it might be awhile; he was shoving off for Okinawa shortly.

While the PT commander negotiated his way out of the shipwreck-ridden Manila Bay, Bill was quiet. But when it came time for them to turn south toward *Eldorado*'s Leyte anchorage, he made an impulsive request. Might they detour briefly north—to Subic Bay?

The sympathetic helmsman, who by now knew the story, pushed up the throttle and made a graceful northward arc into the South China Sea. But no clues of past disasters awaited Bill at Subic Bay—it had been under refurbishment by army engineers for weeks.

"The ones that could swim made out better than the ones that couldn't, that much I can tell you," the Bilibid clerk had said. He didn't have much more information than that, just that the survivors that did make it ashore needed clothing and other supplies. And he knew that only because the navy doctors who were being evacuated from Bilibid when he arrived told him that they had been ordered to assemble supplies for the prisoners who had just shipped out on *Oryoko Maru*. The ship had been bombed not long after exiting Manila Bay, they were told. But there *had* been a large number of survivors.

"Where did it go down?" Bill had asked, with out-of-body composure.

"Subic Bay, off Olongapo. Survivors came ashore by the old navy base. I mean, damn, the last ship the Japs got out, and it gets sunk. "

It was nightfall before the PT boat pulled into Leyte Gulf. After expressing heartfelt thanks to the PT commander and the promise of a steak dinner after the war, Bill boarded *Eldorado*, saluted the officer of the deck, and went straight to his cabin. He wanted to write Benny about the day's events while they were fresh in his mind. He hadn't found Barton, but he hadn't found him dead, either.

With *Eldorado*'s imminent departure, there was no more time to run down the details of Barton's doomed ship—or the survivors. It would have to wait until their return to Manila, after Okinawa.

38

★ ★ ★

A SAILOR'S NIGHTMARE

APRIL 13, 1945, EAST longitude time, dawned sunny and warm off Okinawa, but it would soon become the blackest Friday the thirteenth Bill Mott would ever remember. At 0700 he was in *Eldorado*'s CIC poring over two final drafts on the same critical subject. One was the first-ever press communiqué on the Kamikaze Corps. The other, stamped "S-E-C-R-E-T," was a directive from Admiral Turner to all hands. Entitled "Information and Means for Combating Suicide Plane Attacks—Revision 1," the memo had been hastily drafted the previous evening at the conclusion of another massive kamikaze raid on the ships standing off Okinawa—the second since the invasion of the island began.

Just 340 miles from Kyushu, Japan's southernmost island, Okinawa was prized by the Allies for its proximate air base potential for a final assault on mainland Japan. For this same reason, preventing Okinawa's fall was crucial to the Japanese. A fight to the finish had been expected.

The Easter Sunday landings of tens of thousands of army troops had gone eerily unopposed—unlike the furious and bloody start at Iwo Jima. Kelly Turner was so amazed, he radioed Admiral Nimitz at his CINCPAC headquarters on Guam: "I may be crazy," Turner said, "but it looks like the Japs have quit the war." Having seen intercepts indicating the enemy was lying in wait farther inland, Admiral Nimitz flashed back, "Delete all after 'crazy.'" By the end of Okinawa's first week, that intelligence proved brutally correct. Only after Allied troops moved inland did the enemy bare itself— both on the island and over the 1,418-ship anchorage.

Despite ongoing pleas by Robert Sherrod, war correspondents had been forbidden to report on the intensifying kamikaze menace since its debut at Leyte Gulf the previous October. The months-long news embargo had been intended to protect soldier and sailor morale, among other reasons. But the carnage from these last two attacks—by rapid, sequential waves of kamikaze bands called *kikusui*—changed all that.

Hundreds of planes at a time had screamed over the horizon at random intervals and hurled themselves at the anchorage. The first of these airborne banzai charges began at dusk on April 6. Like swarms of angry bees, hundreds of aircraft at a time dropped through the low cloud ceiling, fanned out, and roared toward target ships. Of all the scenarios anticipated in the thousands of pages of Iceberg planning documents, this one had not even been dreamed of.

Stunned fleet defenses were quickly overwhelmed in the first attack. Three destroyers, two ammunition ships, and one landing vessel were sunk. Ten other ships were damaged so severely that they were forced to withdraw. But *kikusui* number one was far from over. At dusk the next day, hundreds more planes lit up radar screens across the fleet.

Flyers from Admiral Mitscher's fast carrier group shot down a number of them, but 116 hell-bent suiciders punched through the protective air perimeter. The next line of defense was Combat Air Patrol (CAP)—made up of Hellcats and "whistling death" Corsairs—which splashed 55 more. But

61 kamikazes still managed to pierce both air defense rings and strike at the fleet's 1,200 ships. The rest was up to the ships' antiaircraft batteries.

Literally shooting in the dark, gunners sent up thousands of tracer shells, leaving a mad scribble of red lines through the Southern Cross. They shot down 39 of the attackers, but 22 were able to complete their deadly missions. A cacophony of distress signals erupted, jamming circuits. Fire and rescue triage began immediately—in rolling seas, billowing smoke, and stygian darkness.

The second twenty-four-hour *kikusui* had ended the previous evening, April 12. Eighteen more ships, including *Enterprise*, were crippled in the onslaught. A five-hundred-kilogram bomb exploded at the turn of her bilge, causing severe shock damage. An hour later, a second "Yokosuka Judy" just missed *Enterprise*'s starboard bow, but its bomb detonated, puncturing the carrier below the waterline.

Frantic control parties miraculously sealed the breach, even as water gushed through with the force of a colossal fire hose. Their heroics prevented *Enterprise*'s capsize, but the mighty carrier was also forced to withdraw for major repairs. It was one action by that gallant crew that Bill was grateful Benny had missed.

By the morning of the thirteenth, the number of navy casualties in the waters off Okinawa competed with those ashore, and the injuries weren't just physical. The suggestive crackling of ships' loudspeakers alone had become cause for emotional breakdowns among crews. Across the flotilla, officers and men were inching toward nervous exhaustion from the perennial state of high alert.

For the antiaircraft gunners, the worst part was a *kamikaze* pilot's deep maniacal stare as he bore down—even if hit and aflame—through a barrage of bullets. For others, it was the sight of fellow crewmen ejected high into the air and blown apart. Back down they inevitably came, like so many broken pieces of a toy soldier: a helmeted head, a booted foot, a flaming torso. Such images wedged deeply into survivors' psyches, and nervous breakdowns had become as numerous as the climbing fatalities.

And the previous night, as if in celebratory finale to *kikusui* number two, the Japanese also launched their first *oka*: a rocket-boosted suicide glider that could dive at speeds of five hundred miles per hour. The debut *oka* hit destroyer USS *Mannert L. Abele* with such force that she broke apart and sank in five minutes.

Admiral Nimitz had thus far resisted making the kamikaze threat public, partly for morale reasons but also to deny the Japanese confirmation of their successes. He finally relented the previous evening. The American people, he decided, needed to know about these "witches on broomsticks" and the increasingly diabolical mental state of the enemy. Bill proofed the final release before transmitting:

```
CINCPOA PRESS RELEASE #72, APRIL 13, 1945
The Commander in Chief, U.S. Pacific Fleet and Pacific Ocean
Areas, has authorized the following statement:
     For some months the Japanese have been employing aircraft
on a gradually increasing scale in suicidal attacks upon our
forces in the Western Pacific. These aircraft were initially
piloted by a group of pilots who were known as the "Kamikaze
Corps" by the Japanese. The enemy has made much in his propa-
ganda of this "sure-death-sure-hit" suicide technique which is
simply an attempt to crash planes on the decks of our ships.
     The "suicide attack" and the so called "Kamikaze Corps"
are the products of an enemy trapped in an increasingly des-
perate situation. Pushed back upon their own inner defenses
the Japanese have resorted to fanatical methods which, from
a purely military viewpoint, are of doubtful value.
     The "Kamikaze Corps" is apparently being used not only
to attempt to damage our ships but also to stir the lagging
spirits of the Japanese people. Although these "sure-death-
sure-hit" pilots are reported to be volunteers, many have very
```

willingly become survivors of "suicide" missions and are now
[our] prisoners of war.

The "suicide" technique is continuing at the present time.
Although it is always considered and prepared for as a factor in estimating the enemy's capabilities, it cannot prevent
our continuing success in the war in the Pacific.

The press release was directed as much at the Japanese as it was at the
American public.

THE SECOND DOCUMENT WAS Admiral Turner's amended guide-
lines for combating the suicide attacks. Reflecting very recent intelligence
from the previous evening, this latest All Hands Tips-for-Survival primer
had updated guidelines on radar, CAP vectoring and tactics, communications among ships, and revised directives on radical maneuvering, antiaircraft defense, damage control, rescue, repair, and salvage. It began with a
simple restatement of the problem:

The principal difference between suicide plane attacks by
the Japanese on a large scale and conventional airplane attacks are as follows:

(a) The range of enemy attack is greater because no return
     trip is necessary;

(b) Percentage of hits is higher because the missile is
     aimable right up to the point of impact;

(c) Suicide pilots are more determined and daring and are
     not deterred by actual or psychological obstacles;

(d) The suicide plane, with or without a bomb, is an extremely
     effective incendiary agent because of the gasoline car-
     ried;

(e) No standard pattern of attack is apparent and to date no
     cure-all solution has been found.

Bill understood the primal fear a kamikaze attack inspired. On Easter Saturday—twenty-four hours ahead of the paschal invasion of Okinawa— he had just left USS *Indianapolis*'s mess, where he'd thought to catch a quick breakfast following the final pre-invasion briefing on Admiral Spruance's flagship. But a recalcitrant stomach shortened his meal, and he quickly exited the mess to catch the launch back to *Eldorado*. The time was 0710.

On his way up to the quarterdeck, he paused at the shrill report of the boson's whistle. Before he could comprehend its meaning, Bill was knocked off his feet by a rocking explosion from below. Sure as hell, the ship had been struck by a torpedo, he thought, scrambling to his feet.

Only after fire and rescue teams emerged from the *Indianapolis* mess carrying the charred remains of his fellow breakfasters did Bill learn it had been the work of a kamikaze. One fast-acting gunner had deflected the aim of the suicider, whose plane sank off the fantail. But its bomb had released just before crashing, penetrating the port quarter's deck armor and tearing through the mess, a berthing compartment, and fuel tanks before exploding under the hull.

The wounded *Indianapolis* was forced to withdraw to a California shipyard for repairs—the start of a tragic odyssey for the famed cruiser. Admiral Spruance reluctantly shifted his flag to the USS *New Mexico*.

Bill's timely departure from the mess left him shaken. It was the first of many deeply unsettling blows off miserable Okinawa. Another took place a few minutes later as he labored over the twin kamikaze missives.

The duty radioman alerted him to an urgent message that was starting to click through: "To All Hands: From Secnav to All Nav." Navy Secretary Forrestal was not one to send routine messages in the heat of battle. Bill hovered over the teletype, as was his habit, reading each new line as it hammered out Secnav's message. The first sentence stunned him no less than had it reported a death in his own family. Forrestal wrote:

I have the sad duty of announcing to the naval service
the death of Franklin Delano Roosevelt, the President of the
United States, which occurred on twelve April.

The world has lost a champion of democracy who can ill be
spared by our country and the Allied cause. The Navy which
he so dearly loved can pay no better tribute to his memory
than to carry on in the tradition of which he was so proud.

Colors shall be displayed at half mast for thirty days
beginning 0800 thirteen April West Longitude Date insofar as
war operations permit. Memorial services shall be held on the
day of the funeral to be announced later at all yards and
stations and on board all vessels of the navy, war operations
permitting.

Wearing of mourning badges and firing of salutes will be
dispensed within view of war conditions.

The president had died suddenly of a cerebral hemorrhage at "the little White House" in Warm Springs, Georgia, near the healing mineral waters that had long soothed his polio-withered legs. Vice President Harry S. Truman had taken the Oath of Office within hours of FDR's death. A new president! Choked with sadness and deeply preoccupied, Bill made for Admiral Turner's cabin just as ships' loudspeakers sounded the report across the fleet. The announcers' voices were thick with emotion:

"Attention! Attention! All hands! President Roosevelt is dead! Repeat, our supreme commander, President Roosevelt, is dead."

A typhoon roaring over the horizon could not have struck with greater impact an audience with scant memory of any other sitting president. Roosevelt had led the country for twelve turbulent years—a majority of the sailors' young lives. They mourned all the more because Roosevelt had been the navy's president, a sailor at heart.

As Bill carried Forrestal's memo to Admiral Turner's cabin, he replayed his last Oval Office conversation with Roosevelt. *"Mr. President, I hate to leave, but you may be sure I'll be back for the peace conference."* Roosevelt had met his gaze and then looked away. *"Well, son, I'm not sure there will ever be one."*

He pondered anew what the late president had meant. Had Roosevelt sensed his imminent death? Or had he hinted at some other terrible meaning beyond Bill's comprehension? Bill paused at the forecastle rail and watched with an aching heart as hundreds of national ensigns fluttered to half-mast.

A memorial service on *Eldorado*'s fantail was scheduled for the following morning, April 14. Rites would begin at 1000 hours to coincide with the late president's state funeral in Washington, DC. They had learned by radio that Mrs. Roosevelt wanted Dewitt Moore—a popular American soloist and, coincidentally, *Eldorado*'s radar intelligence officer—to sing two of the Anglophile president's favorite hymns at the ship's service, both by British composers. One was "Faith of Our Fathers"; the other, not surprisingly, was "Eternal Father Strong to Save," or simply the "Navy Hymn," known and cherished for a century by sailors of the American and British navies.

The next morning, a throng of war correspondents looked on as Chaplain Valentine Junker, Admiral Turner, and hundreds of officers and sailors in their crisp dress whites lined up in arrow-straight rows on the *Eldorado*'s aft deck. But Chaplain Junker barely got off his opening line of prayer when the familiar wail of sirens and nerve-shattering general quarters signaled the approach of another horde of kamikazes.

Kikusui number three had begun.

The tidy assembly burst apart like so much spilled milk, and the fantail emptied in seconds. Every crew member dashed to battle stations—above, below, fore, and aft—to defend against the onslaught. They all knew that triangulation of *Eldorado*'s steady radio beacon made her a prime and constant target.

Admiral Turner himself—onetime fleet gunnery officer—took over the ship's voice command circuit and began directing fire. He took this unusual step increasingly at Okinawa, to provide an extra measure of reassurance to a thoroughly rattled crew.

Officers and crew made a determined trek back to the fantail after the wave of assailants was repelled. The enemy would not cancel *Eldorado*'s tribute to their beloved late president. Waiting on the aft deck were radio correspondents who had lashed together a bouquet of microphones so that all Americans might hear Moore's sonorous rendering of the "Navy Hymn"—from the heart of the fleet in the heat of battle—sung in dirge for their president:

> *Eternal Father, strong to save*
> *Whose arm hath bound the restless wave,*
> *Oh hear us when we cry to thee,*
> *For those in peril on the sea.*

Admiral Turner seemed in a trance during the service, likely reflecting on his own experiences with his late commander in chief. His most memorable had been in the tension-laden spring of 1939. Roosevelt had personally requested that Turner lead a goodwill mission to Tokyo, ostensibly to escort the late Japanese ambassador Saito's ashes to home soil.

Not one to be tapped for diplomatic anything, a flattered Turner executed the ceremonial mission flawlessly. In Tokyo Bay, throngs of Japanese had toured his ship, the USS *Astoria*, and Imperial poets and musicians dedicated verses and lyrics to the vessel that had brought Saito's ashes home. A special Japanese "Welcome Astoria March" was composed and formally performed before the ship's company. Turner's mission helped measurably in thawing diplomatic relations with Japan at the time, but the sentiments were short-lived—demonstrated not least by *Astoria*'s sinking at Guadalcanal three years later.

Returned from his musings, Admiral Turner spoke briefly before Chaplain Junker's benediction:

"The president's death is a great loss to our country, and especially it is a loss to the war effort of which he was our firm and unquestioned leader. Undoubtedly, the fact that President Roosevelt personally spent himself so freely in this struggle was the underlying cause of his death. Thus he is a battle casualty in exactly the same sense as those who give their lives in battle out here."

BY MID-MAY 1945, PRESIDENT Truman's burdens had shifted, if not lightened. Nazi Germany had surrendered, but in the Pacific, the US Army's struggle to claim Okinawa had ground to a halt. Lines had barely advanced in the face of savage Japanese resistance on ambush-ridden terrain, all the more treacherous from eleven inches of rainfall. Unabating kamikaze attacks continued to pummel the sentinel Fifth Fleet; casualties both on and off shore were running sky high.

Navy losses at Okinawa had already surpassed all records for a single campaign. "I doubt if the army's slow, methodical [approach to] fighting really saves lives in the long run," Spruance grumbled to his chief of staff. In late April, Admiral Nimitz told General Buckner that the stalemate was losing him "a ship and a half a day." Nimitz proposed that the marines make an amphibious landing behind enemy lines to break the impasse. Buckner objected vigorously: this was a ground battle under US Army command, and the navy should not interfere.

Nimitz was also concerned about the toll that the vicious, protracted engagement was taking on his three top Okinawa commanders, Admirals Spruance, Mitscher, and Turner. To Bill and the rest of *Eldorado*'s flag staff, Kelly Turner seemed to be suffering the most. The continuous high alert and murderous destruction of his amphibious vessels and crews afforded Turner little rest and exacerbated his chronic back pain.

At Okinawa, Terrible Turner was as irascible and foulmouthed as any of them had ever seen him, itself a milestone. Things got worse in May with the introduction of kamikaze speedboats, or *kaiten*, which took aim at ships' hulls in the dark of night. At each *kaiten* alert, Bill reluctantly awoke Turner to make the call on whether a "smoke" order should be issued to enshroud the ships for protection. The procedure had become a critical defense tool by spoiling the aim and navigation of these seaborne assailants.

On May 17, well after Turner had retired to his quarters, the alert came once again: *kaiten* were on the prowl. Reluctantly, Bill knocked on his exhausted boss's cabin door. Getting no response after several tries, he turned the handle and peeked inside. Admiral Turner was in a deep slumber—*very* deep. The scent rising from a nearby glass told the story.

A mix of pineapple juice and grain alcohol—the latter procured from Sick Bay—was the suspected somnolent. Unable to arouse Turner, Bill quietly closed the admiral's door and made for the deck. He first advised Commander Paul S. Theiss, Turner's chief of staff, to evaluate the need for a smoke order. Then he visited the ship's doctor, who needed no introduction to Turner's condition. The doctor, an unsmiling New Hampshire reservist, got defensive.

"He said it was for a sore on his foot, and, to be honest, I didn't follow that story," the doctor said without a trace of empathy. "I just want you to know that I can't be taking this responsibility," he continued. "I'm going to have to put something in it that will make him throw it up. It won't kill him, of course, but it will make him violently ill."

Of all the crises Bill had come to anticipate at Okinawa, this was one he hadn't seen coming. He quietly asked the doctor to forbear until he took the matter under advisement. He then called a meeting of the *Eldorado* flag staff. After much deliberation, the higher-ups made a decision: Bill should make his way over to Spruance's flagship *New Mexico* and report the problem to the Fifth Fleet's head surgeon.

Incredulous, Bill reminded them of his relatively junior status on the flag staff and recommended that someone more senior be elected to ferry their collective concerns over to the *New Mexico*. But Bill was the only *reserve* officer among them, they reasoned. The rest of them were on a promising career trajectory in the regular navy. In their view, he could afford the certain career disembowelment that would result from reporting one's commanding officer for drinking on the job in the middle of the largest amphibious campaign of the Pacific War.

As the specter of Bill's cancelled naval career played out in his head, he proceeded to Admiral Spruance's flagship with the same enthusiasm he might feel for being a *kaiten*'s next victim. He paced *New Mexico*'s quarterdeck for an hour, discussing the problem with the fleet surgeon and Admiral Spruance's own flag secretary, Chuck Barber. When they finished, the fleet surgeon indicated he would take the matter from there. Not at all sure what that meant, Bill returned to *Eldorado* with a heavy heart.

The following morning, Admiral Turner was advised that Admiral Harry Hill, his second in command, was taking over for him at Okinawa. Turner was to report to Admiral Nimitz at his forward headquarters on Guam. A contagious glumness spread across *Eldorado* en route to Guam. It affected everyone except, curiously, Admiral Turner. For the duration of the trip, he rested, read, and sipped orange juice without additives from the granite-faced ship's doctor.

At Guam, Turner received a desultory flag staff salute as he debarked *Eldorado*. Smartly returning the salute, Kelly Turner appeared fully restored—confident, self-possessed, and impatient as ever. He charged up Guam's Fonte Plateau, nicknamed "Nimitz Hill." It was the eve of his sixtieth birthday.

Chester Nimitz greeted Turner with a broad smile. In fact, he had decided to order a respite from battle for all three of his Okinawa commanders—Admirals Spruance, Mitscher, *and* Turner—out of a growing concern that the prolonged, high-stress nature of that campaign would diminish their effectiveness, not to mention their mental and physical health. All three men had been in continuous combat since the start of pre-bombardment at Iwo Jima, a record three months straight.

When Admiral Halsey and his new flagship the USS *Missouri* arrived at Okinawa to take over command from Admiral Spruance, the Japanese were confused anew. Once again, it seemed, the Third Fleet had overnight "replaced" the Fifth Fleet.

KELLY TURNER EMERGED FROM his meeting in Guam with a promotion to full admiral. Nimitz had chosen to mark the occasion by giving credit where it was due, pineapple-juice additives notwithstanding. Turner had brilliantly conceived, executed, and prevailed in every Pacific campaign he had undertaken. Nimitz would say later that he knew of no other navy admiral who could have performed that feat.

Along with his prized fourth star, Turner carried new orders back to *Eldorado*. They were to make sail for Manila immediately. Their mission was to coordinate Operation Olympic—the Allies' long-anticipated assault on Japan's home islands—with General MacArthur. The objective was to seize the island of Kyushu and secure its airfields and ports for Operation Coronet, the subsequent invasion of the island of Honshu and its capital, Tokyo. The sequential operations were code-named Downfall.

Of all *Eldorado*'s celebrants, Bill Mott was perhaps the most electrified by Admiral Turner's reversal of fortune. Not only did it seem that both their once-careening naval aspirations were back on course, but also they were returning to Manila! Bill's best and last chance to reach Barton had just fallen into his lap.

Spirits were well restored aboard *Eldorado* en route to Manila. Admiral Turner, too, was pleased by the turn of events, particularly over the other options, but he was deeply skeptical about Olympic and Coronet. With the stratospheric losses at Okinawa top of mind, he knew the death toll from a mainland Japan invasion would be exponentially higher.

Turner's naval superiors agreed. They believed that a greatly weakened Japan could be finished off (with far fewer casualties) by adopting a dual strategy of aerial bombing and imposition of a naval blockade. Admirals Nimitz, Spruance, and King had all made this case. But the Joint Chiefs of

Staff had proceeded instead with MacArthur's preference: a heroic, decisive, and dramatic ground invasion of Japan.

With the war in Europe concluded, Americans—including President Truman—had turned their full attention to the shocking slaughter at Okinawa. Its soaring cost in human life was attracting greater and greater public scrutiny. Hundreds of thousands—including Americans, Japanese, civilians, and Okinawan conscripts—had already died, and the battle continued to rage.

Okinawa headlines coincided with those announcing the doubling of mandatory Selective Service call-ups and mass troop redeployments from Europe to the Pacific. The impact of these sobering reports was exacerbated by the belated and brutal physical evidence of the Pacific War pouring into mainland US hospitals. Aiea Heights Naval Hospital had long since filled to overcapacity. The Pacific wounded were now overwhelming stateside medical facilities. It was against this grim backdrop that President Truman became increasingly uncomfortable with the potential for calamitous casualties from an amphibious invasion of mainland Japan.

Truman made clear to a war-weary public and his Joint Chiefs that he intended to end the Pacific War with as few additional American casualties as possible. In his two short months as president, preventing "another Okinawa from one end of Japan to the other" had become a paramount objective. In mid-June 1945 he decided to give Olympic and Coronet another hard look.

Meanwhile, with Admiral Turner's repeated blessing, Bill debarked *Eldorado* as soon as she made anchor in Manila Bay. Olympic's scheduled invasion date was at least four months away, allowing him enough of a reprieve to complete his investigation into Barton's whereabouts. Finding prisoner files at Bilibid much better organized, he was able to get right to work. He was only a few hours into poring over manifests and prison population lists when he came across an electrifying new document. It was a tally of the dead and missing from the fated *Oryoko Maru*.

During his March visit to Bilibid, Bill learned that Barton had boarded *Oryoko Maru* on December 13. He also learned that that ship was sunk in Subic Bay two days later. This newly discovered document confirmed both those findings, and now that Barton had survived the *Oryoko Maru*, his name was not on the official casualty list.

With renewed optimism, Bill peppered Bilibid office staff with questions on what else was known about the prisoners who swam from the wreck and made it ashore. At the end of the day, he thanked them and made his way back to *Eldorado*. These new discoveries—and the range of possible scenarios for survival that they offered—left room for hope. Back in his quarters, he wrote of the day's findings to his sister Rosemary instead of Benny, despairing of his brother's continued noncommunication.

```
                        Office of the Commander

                        Amphibious Forces,

                        US Pacific Fleet

                        Lieutenant Rosemary Cross

                        Office of the Commandant

                        Brooklyn Navy Yard

                        Brooklyn, New York


                        July 3, 1945


              CONFIDENTIAL


Dear Muff,


    I have delayed writing you or any of the family as I

wanted to first investigate further into Barton's status.

Every time I started a letter, he was always uppermost in my

mind, and I found it difficult to speak of anything else.
```

Before departing for Okinawa, I spent some time in the
Philippines and naturally did everything humanly possible
to run down concrete news of Barton. At that time, I wrote
rather completely of my findings to Benny and asked him to
investigate further in Washington. I enclose copies of those
two letters, to which, incidentally, I have not yet received
an answer.

Perhaps, there was no answer. At any rate, I can now
take up where I left off in my letter of March 24th. Most
of the information is negative, but is of the most reliable
kind. I have pursued an exhaustive investigation of the
rumor in the attached letter that the ship Barton boarded
was sunk. I am now able to report the following with fair
assurance of accuracy:

(a) Barton survived the sinking of December 13 in Subic
     Bay. I learned this from a list of the dead and missing
     from this sinking that the Japanese left behind at
     Bilibid Prison.

(b) He was evacuated to Japan or Korea on a ship which left
     the Philippines on December 27th.

(c) It is not known whether this ship ever reached port
     nor is it known, on the other hand, that it did not. The
     presumption is that it did.

(d) People out here are expecting that Japan will notify
     Washington through Geneva of the prisoners which were
     taken to Japan or Korea in that ship.

Of course I shall continue to do everything I can from
this end. I am trying desperately, with every available
minute, to turn every stone where there might be a clue.

I am going to visit in the near future several of the places
where Barton was held, in hopes that someone will remember
him, for whatever small comfort that may be. In this I am
somewhat handicapped by not having with me a picture of
him. Could you forward a snapshot by return mail?

Much of the information which I have given you is
confidential and its disclosure in the wrong places could
get me in very serious trouble; therefore I beg of you to see
to it that it stays within the family. My request is that
you talk it over with Arthur and, above all, keep it away
from crack pot [POW] organizations like that one in North
Dakota or Texas. Please ask Arthur--and whatever you decide
to tell Mother--not to disclose any of the information I
have given.

What if anything, Benny has done to contact Ensign
Petritz (see enclosed letters), I do not know. It seems to me
that a talk with him might be fruitful, especially since
[Petritz] knew Barton. You can find out where [Petritz] is
by going to, or calling, Washington and asking George Elsey
at the White House to get the information on his present
whereabouts from the Bureau for you. If George is not there,
Lt. Marian Enright in the Navy Bureau of Personnel, or her
boss who is a classmate of mine named MacDonald, will help
you I'm sure.

There is also in the Bureau a section which deals
exclusively with prisoner of war problems. It used to be
headed by a Commander Jacobs (now a Captain and still
there), but I am sure he has been superseded by now. All of
these places should be visited, but I can't be both places
at once. Please don't disclose to them the source of your
information and I implore you to keep Mother from writing

letters to Senators and the Navy Department. They will do
no good and would very probably handicap me in further
investigation. Also, don't jump down Benny's throat till you
know what he's accomplished. He may have done everything
possible. I have some hope of being in Washington later this
month, and there is much more I will be able to tell you
then. In the meantime, please let me know what you find
out, if anything. I feel as though my other two letters on
this matter were dropped down the drain. I know Benny has
his troubles and is terribly busy, but the uncertainty of
not knowing what he was doing and not hearing from him
prompted me to put the facts in your hands. Please handle
them circumspectly.

I have been working terribly hard for the last six
months with very little respite. I am looking forward to the
day when I arrive in New York and my big little sister can
take me out and pour civilization all over me.

Devotedly,

Bill

He reread the letter before sending it off, making minor edits here and
there. He'd done the best he could and hoped at least that providing this update, such as it was, would bring relief from the anxiety of knowing *nothing*.

His disappointment that Barton was no longer in the Philippines was
acute, and now the Allied plan to invade mainland Japan brought new anxiety. The Palawan massacre of 150 prisoners was ordered by a camp commander who'd believed the island was under imminent Allied attack. In the
Gilbert Islands, a group of prisoners was beheaded, another group at Bal-
lale bayoneted to death, and another on Wake Island executed by machine
gun—all following Allied bombing raids. Given this pattern of retributive

intent, the incipient Japanese home-island invasions would place the 168,000 Allied prisoners still in Japanese hands in their gravest danger yet.

Yet Bill still found reason for hope, both because Barton's name was not on the *Oryoko Maru's* casualty list and because of the relatively high number of fellow survivors of the sinking: 1,300 out of 1,619. With luck—if one could call it that—Barton might have been shipped to Korea instead of to Japan. In any case, Barton had, by all available accounts, survived three years of bestial enemy treatment. Bill prayed this meant his brother had developed both resilience and survival skills, just as he had at the Citadel and Annapolis. If only those instincts might serve him a few more months.

39

★ ★ ★

IN THE END, A QUESTION OF CASUALTIES—AND SEA POWER

PRESIDENT TRUMAN WAS STILL on a steep learning curve in the summer of 1945. It seemed that Roosevelt had shared relatively little with his last vice president, including the very existence of the White House Map Room and the fact that the world war was being run out of it. Nor had Truman been told that enemy codes had been cracked and were supplying crucial intelligence to the Allies.

To the surprise of his top military advisors, however, the new president, a onetime respected army colonel, took quick grasp of strategic options in the Pacific and their relative stakes in American blood and treasure. Daily "gloves off" Map Room briefings expedited the process, and it wasn't long before Harry Truman had two seminal concerns.

The first was Okinawa, by far the bloodiest battle of the Pacific War, which was still not won. The second was a looming shortage of combat-ready troops for a final assault on Japan—this despite a hundred thousand men a month being called up, double the rate twelve months earlier. Truman's twin dilemmas weren't Map Room secrets; they were front-page news across the war-weary country. By mid-June, these concerns—compounded by a growing fear of unprecedented casualties from an invasion of Japan proper—prompted him to make new inquiries. He started with his chief of staff, Admiral William Leahy.

Fleet Admiral Leahy's opinion mattered. He was a senior military strategist who had served in the Roosevelt White House since the dark days of 1942. He knew every aspect of this world conflict, and he was no advocate of a ground invasion of Japan. Admiral Leahy also favored the "bomb and blockade" option; to him the statistics seemed to prove the point.

The air campaign was causing withering destruction: six hundred thousand tons of enemy shipping had been sunk in June alone. The strategic naval blockade was not only limiting the ability of resource-dependent Japan to wage war but also severely curtailing its ability to feed seventy-two million citizens. In a desperate act, Japan had begun to organize schoolchildren to gather a million tons of acorns to be ground for flour due to drastically declined stocks of rice and wheat.

To Leahy, the collective evidence weighed heavily in favor of continuing this strategy. He believed it would force Japan's capitulation and save countless American lives. This was the strategy preferred by most navy brass, and it was a hard-won point of view.

After increasingly deadly amphibious campaigns to capture enemy-held islands across the Pacific, the navy had become well acquainted with Japan's fighting spirit. Surrender was unthinkable, and in every Pacific campaign, they had fought nearly to the last man. The relative few still standing had shown a strong preference for *hara-kiri* over the shame of being taken prisoner.

The navy knew that Japan would defend her home soil even more fanatically—to the last woman and child. Ever-rising casualties on Okinawa, with the largest toll among civilians, reinforced that view. And Admiral Leahy—in whose experience, honesty, and intellect President Truman placed great faith—firmly agreed.

★   ★   ★

AT THE ABRUPT START of his presidency, Truman had vowed to carry on "the legacies of [his] illustrious predecessor." One such legacy was a decision made in September 1944 at Octagon, the second Allied conference held in Quebec. At that meeting, Roosevelt and Churchill agreed that an invasion of mainland Japan must follow Germany's capitulation.

By June 1945, however, Truman's misgivings about this preordained course were too powerful to ignore. On June 17 he confided to his diary, "I have to decide Japanese strategy—shall we invade Japan proper or shall we bomb and blockade? This is my hardest decision to date . . . I'll make it when I have all the facts."

The next day, he asked Admiral Leahy to call a meeting of the Joint Chiefs of Staff. The topic would be the singular matter of casualties that might result from a ground invasion of Japan versus alternative solutions for ending the Pacific War. Leahy promptly dispatched a top secret memorandum:

```
The White House
Washington


                              14, June 1945


            URGENT--IMMEDIATE ACTION

    MEMORANDUM FOR THE JOINT CHIEFS OF STAFF:


The President today directed me to inform the Joint Chiefs

of Staff that he wishes to meet . . . in the afternoon

of [June] 18th, in his office, to discuss details of our

campaign against Japan.

    He expects at this meeting to be thoroughly informed

of our intentions and prospects in preparation for his

discussions with Churchill and Stalin.
```

He will want information as to the number of men of the army
and ships of the navy that will be necessary to defeat Japan.

He wants an estimate of the time required and an
estimate of the losses in killed and wounded that will
result from an invasion of Japan proper.

He wants an estimate of the time and the losses required
and the losses that will result from an effort to defeat
Japan by isolation, blockade, and bombardment by sea and
air forces . . .

It is his intention to make his decision on the campaign
with the purpose of economizing to the maximum extent
possible the loss of American lives.

Economy in the use of time and money is comparatively
unimportant.

I suggest that a memorandum discussion of the above
noted points be prepared in advance for delivery to the
president at the time of the meeting.

                              William D. Leahy

The memorandum took the JCS and their war-planning staffs by surprise. The memo's phrase, "it is his intention to make his decision on the
campaign," was especially unwelcome to army planners. As General George
Lincoln put it, the army viewed Operation Olympic as "a matter of fact."

Olympic was to be the army's—and Douglas MacArthur's—glorious
and climactic hour in the Pacific War. It would be the largest military assault
in history: MacArthur was to lead as many as fourteen divisions against
the Japanese, as opposed to Eisenhower's nine at Normandy. Moreover,
the invasion had *already* been approved by one commander in chief (and
Churchill, too) and was deep into the planning phase.

And regarding Leahy's specific request on behalf of the president for prospective casualty estimates, there was a unity of reluctance. Quantifying casualty estimates to a sitting president ahead of an invasion? This would set a dangerous precedent, they feared, even though the army had already developed those numbers.

Army planners had obtained casualty estimates from their surgeon general in order to assess invasion requirements for battlefield medical needs: corpsmen, morphine, plasma, bandages, scalpels, body bags. But army brass feared that disclosing even that relatively low casualty projection (135,000) might persuade Truman to alter or cancel Olympic—not to mention their recent order of an additional 500,000 Purple Heart medals.

In the end, the army declined to comply with the request by their commander in chief. When the Joint Chiefs gathered in the Oval Office four days after receiving Leahy's directive, they instead presented the president with more palatable ratios of Allied versus Japanese losses from *previous* campaigns. General Marshall presented the chart. It indicated that the Leyte campaign had resulted in the lowest Allied versus enemy losses (1:4.6) and the final days at Iwo Jima the highest (1:1.25). Okinawa, which was still going on, was a close second, 1:2.

Taking exception, Admiral Leahy reminded the group that the president had asked for *actual* loss *projections*, and suggested US casualties resulting from an invasion of Kyushu (Olympic) would most likely resemble losses at Okinawa, currently running at 35 percent of total forces. Since the upcoming Olympic assault force size was known to meeting attendees—766,700—simple arithmetic would have yielded Olympic's potential for loss of life. That number, 268,345 casualties—equal roughly to total American losses over the entire three and a half years on the European Front—would certainly have raised eyebrows. Curiously, however, that percentage was not converted into a casualty estimate at the June 18 JCS meeting.

Truman asked instead whether *more* Japanese defenders at Kyushu than currently projected for Olympic—which Marshall estimated at 350,000—might be transported from other Japanese islands, thereby pushing the ratio of American casualties even higher. General Marshall confidently replied in the negative; daily air raids were preventing the Japanese from reinforcing the area. Marshall then read aloud from a telegram he had just received from General MacArthur:

"I believe the [Olympic] operation presents less [sic] hazards of excessive loss than any other that has been suggested . . . and its *decisive effect* will eventually save lives." General Marshall said he agreed with MacArthur's stated position and a unanimous JCS vote to proceed with Olympic followed.

After the vote, President Truman reluctantly assented to Olympic despite the fact he had been denied the requested casualty projections by his most senior military advisors. But he withheld approval of Coronet, the follow-on invasion of Honshu, saying he would revisit that decision at a later date.

Admiral King voted with the majority at the Joint Chiefs meeting that day, but not because his position had changed on the wisdom of a mainland invasion. He simply understood the need to proceed with its *planning*. The chief of naval operations was as shrewd as he was cantankerous. He was merely postponing withdrawal of his support for Olympic until later in the summer. He knew his defection would result in a titanic army-navy clash over final Pacific strategy—and, denied unanimity among his military chiefs, would likely void Truman's support for the invasion.

Admiral King did, however, fire off a complaint-riddled memo to his fellow chiefs after the June 18 meeting. His first objection was that the army's antiseptic casualty ratio presentation had omitted all of the navy's casualty projections provided by Admiral Nimitz. Given the real-time horrors taking place on Okinawa, this was a particular irritant to King. He further stated that the overall casualty data presented to Truman was "not satisfactory." "[I]t appears to me the Chiefs of Staff will [eventually] have to give an estimate of casualties expected in the operation," King admonished.

In response, General Marshall assured King that naval losses should and would be included in a revised casualty brief for the president. But there is no archival evidence that a revised brief was ever submitted to Truman—the man on whose shoulders the fate of those lives ultimately rested.

On July 6, three weeks after the Oval Office casualty estimate meeting, President Truman, Admiral Leahy, and a contingent of White House staff boarded the USS *Augusta* for a transatlantic sail to Germany. Their final destination was Potsdam, for the thirteenth Allied war conference. During the twenty-two days it took for *Augusta* to reach its first port at Plymouth, England, Truman's June 18 query regarding Japan's potential to bolster its Kyushu defenses had become a reality. The developing scenario of massive new enemy reinforcements now mooted earlier troop strength estimates.

But it was the arrival of a different piece of highly classified news that commanded the greater of President Truman's attention: an urgent report confirming the success of an atomic bomb test in New Mexico's Alamogordo desert. An astoundingly powerful new weapon, the president learned, had just been added to the US arsenal. It was, to borrow from MacArthur, a weapon of *decisive effect*—minus the potential for stratospheric American casualties.

IRONICALLY, THE JAPANESE INTERCEPTS confirming skyrocketing enemy troop buildup on Kyushu had come from MacArthur's own G-2 at Manila. Specifically, they had been provided by Central Bureau, his persistently autonomous intelligence operation, which had grown from dozens of cryptanalysts to thousands since its humble 1942 beginnings in Melbourne, Australia.

Despite serial efforts by the War Department to bring Central Bureau under its control, MacArthur had resisted all attempts to tether it to Washington intelligence gathering. While similar intercepts suggesting the buildup on Kyushu may have been netted at the War Department's listening posts, those analysts were not the ones to sound the alarm; it was MacArthur's own intelligence chief, General Willoughby.

In his July 29 analysis summarizing decrypted intercepts of the previous two weeks—distributed "locally" to senior Olympic planners in Manila—Willoughby made his dismay official: a full twelve weeks ahead of X-day (Olympic's November 1 invasion date), enemy garrisons on Kyushu had *already* reached previously predicted invasion maximums— "with," Willoughby wrote, "no end in sight."

Also confirmed was a vast arsenal of suicide weapons under development at Kyushu, as well as the training of a "Patriotic Citizens Fighting Corps," a millions-strong civilian combatant force. In addition, all schools would be closed in order to mobilize thousands of children for the defense. "There are no civilians in Japan," read one decrypted message. In all, the Japanese were preparing for a "no withdrawal" water's-edge defense—a marked shift from Okinawa, where defenders had lain in wait for Allied troops to move inland before pouncing.

As July progressed, intercepts revealed more and more alarming data. The breadth and size of the suicide arsenal was as troubling as the massing of additional enemy troops. Admiral Turner's landing craft, charged with ferrying hundreds of troops at a time to Kyushu's beaches, were named as primary kamikaze targets. Also targeted would be Turner's 1,500-ship amphibian-support force, expected to be anchored just beyond Kyushu's breakers.

At least ten thousand kamikaze planes were hidden across the island— in mines, under viaducts and railway tunnels, even department store basements. A large number of them were of such balsa-light construction that they would not be detectable by ships' radar, rendering useless the crucial kamikaze detection and defense tactics developed at Okinawa. Thousands of suicide pilots were said to be in training, with emphasis on night operations.

An assortment of other suicide weapons were also verified. There would be thousands of flying bombs (*oka*), human-manned torpedoes and suicide attack boats (*kaiten* and *koryo*), midget suicide submarines (*kairyu*), and navy swimmers transformed into human mines (*fukuryu*). These, too, would be capable of evading radar detection. The size and strength of the incipient suicide force at Kyushu already exceeded what had been hurled at the Fifth Fleet over three months at Okinawa. And X-day was still twelve weeks away.

When the intelligence summaries on metastasizing troop and kamikaze strength landed on Admiral Turner's desk, they hit Olympic's amphibian commander like a one-two punch. Much the wiser following his three years of planning and executing ever-larger amphibious campaigns, Turner had developed a powerful acumen for applying raw intelligence to invasion realities.

To Kelly Turner, the revised intelligence boiled down to this: a recipe for American slaughter on an epic scale. He quickly calculated casualty estimates based on the new intelligence. The math was grim; he estimated at least 600,000 American casualties—more than quadruple the army estimate of one month earlier (which had not included potential navy losses). And with Leyte, Luzon, Saipan, Iwo Jima, and Okinawa all as guides, Japanese casualties would run much higher, undoubtedly into seven figures.

Turner sent for Bill Mott and got right to the point. Manila intelligence summaries were not routinely forwarded to Washington, and President Truman needed to see these numbers. As a former White House naval aide, could Bill get this new intelligence to the attention of the president? Turner believed that with these new battle ratios and casualty projections in hand, Truman would cancel Olympic in favor of options less costly in American blood and treasure.

Bill replied that he was confident he could get the materials to the attention of the president. Turner told him to pack. Bill's first stop would be Guam, where he would provide Admirals Spruance and Nimitz's aides with the data; from there he would proceed to Washington.

"Temporary Additional Orders, as orally assigned" were promptly drawn up:

```
Upon receipt of these orders you will proceed aboard first
available government transportation to the port in which
the Commander of the Fifth Fleet may be [Guam]. Upon ar-
rival at this port, report to the Commander Fifth Fleet for
```

such temporary additional duty as has been orally assigned
to you . . . Upon completion of this temporary duty you will
further proceed and report to the following named places for
such temporary additional duty as has been orally assigned
to you in Washington, DC . . . Upon completion thereof, you
will return to your present station.

At Guam, Bill was greeted by his old friend Chuck Barber, Admiral
Spruance's flag secretary. The two men had not seen each other since their
late-night meeting with the Fifth Fleet's chief surgeon aboard the USS *New
Mexico*. After discussing Bill's classified delivery, he was off to Washington, DC.

THE OPPORTUNITY TO RETURN to Washington should have provided a happy, if brief, family reunion for Bill and his wife and children.
But Romie and the children were in Nova Scotia, and Benny was away on
a multiplant inspection tour. Pressing questions regarding Barton that Bill
had hoped to resolve would have to wait.

His family's absence may have felt like a reprieve, if an uncomfortable
one. Bill had changed since going to sea, and not just in terms of new gray
hairs, the doubling of his Lucky Strike habit, or even the new lines creeping
across his forehead from a constantly furrowed brow. Between ill health, a
frustrating struggle to find Barton, and sequential, increasingly violent amphibious campaigns, Bill's time-honored optimism was flagging. Perhaps he
wasn't ready for that to be detected by those who knew him best. Like Larry
Darrell in Maugham's *The Razor's Edge*, Bill had been altered by war in ways
he was only beginning to understand himself.

"Sixteen hundred Pennsylvania Avenue," Bill instructed the driver as
they pulled away from hot, dusty Bolling Field.

Returning here for the first time in two years, Bill indulged a deferred
moment of grief. The absence of President Roosevelt struck first, but also
missing was Mrs. Roosevelt's warm greeting and concerned inquiries about

his family. As he turned corner after corner in the familiar manse, he absorbed the absence of one White House colleague after another—all departed following FDR's death in April and the abrupt arrival of the Truman administration.

Gone were the old reliables who had taught him his White House knots—Grace Tully, Steve Early, Admiral Brown—along with so many other ghosts of Roosevelt's tight-knit White House staff. Despite the warm hero's welcome Bill received from butler Alonzo Fields and switchboard operator Hacky Hackmeister, there were few other familiar faces. As his footsteps echoed along the black-and-white harlequin hallways, he belatedly mourned the passing era.

Bill understood his delivery had to travel via the most secure of conduits, an important consideration when Admiral Turner assigned him the task. The materials he carried had a higher classification than "Most Secret." The term "Ultra" was rarely spoken aloud, and documents carrying that designation were usually destroyed following eyes-only reviews by select officials. His rigorous White House training in the absolute primacy of their security made him the ideal delivery boy.

But what were President Truman's habits for receiving classified enemy intercepts? Admiral Leahy's method for getting these to President Roosevelt was to have Map Room naval aides personally present them twice a day. On many a morning, Bill had been the presenter while Roosevelt shaved in his bathroom. He would simply close the toilet seat, sit down, and read the secret digests aloud.

The afternoon briefings had been held either in the Map Room or down the hall in Admiral McIntire's office. There Roosevelt either read or was read the material while McIntire massaged his withered legs or packed his chronically congested sinuses with a cocaine-based antihistamine. Regardless of where he was, Roosevelt was always keenly interested in these briefings, sometimes even asking to read the individual decryptions on which they were based.

The intelligence value of these intercepts was so high that Bill had no reason to suspect Admiral Leahy had discontinued sharing them with President Truman. But with Leahy and Truman both now at Potsdam, there were only two secure methods for getting them the sensitive materials. The first was via the White House Map Room encoding machine (ECM), which transmitted to a receiving unit in the traveling map room that accompanied the president. The second was via a locked, specially keyed mail pouch, in which pressing documents were assembled daily at the White House and dispatched by air to President Truman and Admiral Leahy.

Using the Map Room ECM presented at least two drawbacks: not only were the documents of the most sensitive nature, but also they were likely too lengthy to be encoded verbatim. Map Room watch-officer procedure for conveying the import of long documents was to distill them to a page or less, which in this case Bill feared might result in critical omissions. That concern was exacerbated by the fact that a very new trainee was currently manning the Map Room: Bill's former watch officers, the seasoned George Elsey and Frank Graham, and Truman's new naval aide, James Vardaman Jr., had all gone to Potsdam.

Vardaman, a Missouri banker and political operative with a brief wartime reserve commission, inspired little confidence as an intelligence officer. Moreover, just before departing for Potsdam, he had hastily recruited a St. Louis confidant, an attorney named Clark Clifford, to cover the Map Room in his absence. While Bill had no specific objections to the initiate Clifford, this was a far cry from the exacting recruitment protocols of 1942 that he had painstakingly put in place. In any case, this was not a mission to risk entrusting to a novice trainee with scant military background.

So he decided on the air dispatch option and addressed it to Admiral Leahy's attention. It would be in his hands at Potsdam by the next morning. Regardless of who logged the pouch at the other end, Bill knew that Admiral Leahy would find this intelligence of seminal interest and that he had the final say on what—and in what order—was placed before the president.

Bill then delivered his final copy to the Pentagon, presumably to Admiral King's attention, and headed back to the airfield.

WHILE BILL NODDED ON and off on his long return journey to Manila, confirmation of the altered Kyushu defense picture was already shaking things up on the ground. At the Pentagon, a memorandum was prepared by the Joint War Planning Committee—the staff arm of the Joint Chiefs—suggesting alternative recommendations:

[T]he possible effect upon the Olympic operations of this build-up and concentration is such that . . . commanders in the field should review their estimates of the situation, reexamine objectives in Japan as possible alternates to Olympic, and prepare plans for operations against such alternate objectives.

MacArthur was furious, particularly given the source of the information: his *own* intelligence operation. In an attempt to discredit his intelligence chief General Willoughby, MacArthur replied:

I am certain . . . that the Japanese potential reported to you . . . is greatly exaggerated . . . I do not, repeat do not, credit the heavy strengths reported to you in southern Kyushu. There should not, repeat not, be the slightest thought of changing the Olympic operation. The plan is sound and will succeed. Throughout the Southwest Pacific, intelligence has pointed to greatly increased enemy forces. Without exception this buildup has been found to be erroneous.

With all evidence so irrefutably to the contrary, MacArthur's emphatic statement gave even his supporters pause, some already aware of

MacArthur's potential for mendacity. General Marshall had recently confided to War Secretary Stimson that MacArthur "is so prone to exaggerate
and so influenced by his own desires, that it is difficult to trust his judgment." But none ever said so publicly, so enormous was MacArthur's popularity and perceived importance to American morale in wartime.

Bill's first return leg concluded at an Oakland airfield on Monday evening, August 6. His next flight wasn't scheduled to depart until August 8.
Before making for the officers' quarters on the Presidio, he telephoned a
few friends in the area, hoping to avoid spending the next two days alone.
With luck, he reached a law school classmate who invited him to lunch in
downtown San Francisco the next day. Bill would be very impressed by
their fellow diner, the friend said, and gave him directions to the Bohemian
Club at the northeast corner of Post and Taylor Streets. They certainly had
plenty to discuss, didn't they?

The reference was lost on Bill, who had been in the air during the White
House's climactic announcement on the Pacific War's climactic event. And
due to the three-hour time difference, the report was in none of that day's
West Coast papers. But by the time Bill reached the assigned San Francisco
street corner for lunch on August 7, he was up to speed on the biggest war
news since Pearl Harbor.

President Truman himself had issued the statement: that on August 6
the United States had exploded an atomic bomb over a city named Hiroshima, "a major quartermaster depot and port of embarkation for the Japanese. In addition to large military supply depots, it manufactured ordnance,
mainly large guns and tanks, and machine tools, and aircraft-ordnance parts."

Like the rest of the country, Bill was surprised. He could only make
educated guesses as to this bomb's impact on the war or its relationship to
his very recent mission to the White House. At first reading, it was hard to
imagine a weapon of exponentially greater power than those he witnessed
in the withering bombardment of Saipan, Iwo Jima, and Okinawa. But one
of the West Coast accounts claimed that this single bomb was "equal to the

load of 2,000 B-29s and more than 2,000 times the blast power of what previously was the world's most devastating bomb."

He also learned that President Roosevelt had appointed a commission back in 1939 to investigate use of atomic energy for military purposes. Suddenly Bill wondered anew: Could *this* have been the meaning behind Roosevelt's parting comment to him regarding a peace conference? *"Well, son, I'm not sure there will ever be one."*

Bill combed the morning newspapers for details ahead of his luncheon. The August 7, 1945, *San Francisco Chronicle* could only speculate on its impact:

```
JAPAN HIT BY ATOM BOMB--MIGHTIEST WEAPON
  IN HISTORY! TOKYO ADMITS HEAVY DAMAGE

    Associated Press WASHINGTON, August 6--
The most terrible destructive force ever harnessed by
man--atomic energy--is now being used against Japan
by the United States. The Japanese face a threat
of utter destruction and their capitulation may be
greatly speeded up . . . The existence of this great
new weapon was announced personally in a statement
by President Truman, released by the White House at
11:15 Eastern Standard Time.
```

With newspapers tucked under his arm, Bill entered the Bohemian Club beneath its Shakespeare-inspired motto, "Weaving Spiders Come Not Here"—intended to discourage business or political conversation. He located his luncheon party in a wood-paneled dining room adorned with blinking mahogany owls. It turned out Bill recognized both men; the surprise addition was former president Herbert Hoover—an apparent fellow Bohemian. Here, finally, was a bit of news he could share with his mother that would meet unequivocal approval.

Given the august company and the day's headlines, the diners' conversation was lively from the start, if strictly out of compliance with the club's motto. Prognostications on the bomb's power and impact on Hiroshima led the way, followed by guesses as to its impact on the war. Could an invasion of Japan now be avoided? Hoover surprised the table with his remarkably detailed understanding of homeland invasion logistics as well as its potential casualty yield. How this one-term, extremely unpopular Republican president was so thoroughly well informed on the topic was a mystery to his luncheon companions.

Conversation then turned to conjecture on the new weapon's chemical properties. Hoover, who had something of a science background, pulled out his engraved gold pen and began scratching out periodic table configurations and isotopic ratios for uranium on a "BC" engraved napkin. He also hazarded a few guesses on the chain of reactions necessary for nuclear fission. The busy calculations ran over onto the linen tablecloth, which visibly irritated their waiter. In any case, by the arrival of coffee, the diners agreed on one thing: if this terrible new weapon could expedite the end of the war, it would be well worth the reported devastation.

ON THE AFTERNOON OF August 8, another uncomfortable air transport lumbered off an Oakland runway bearing Bill on the next-to-last leg of his five-day odyssey; a distance of 5,800 miles. The mid-Pacific dot that was Guam was growing fatter and greener as they lowered toward the island's airfield—when something unusual caught Bill's attention. Against Apra Harbor's deep blue waters, otherwise stocked with gunmetal-gray warships, a zinc-white vessel drew the eye like a splash of paint on dress blacks. A hospital ship was making anchor.

A phalanx of nurses and hundreds of sailors hovered near the mooring, and a long queue of stocky ambulances with red crosses on their roofs stretched beyond the bend in the road. Bill looked on with a sense of dread as the USS *Tranquility*'s crew secured her lines. With no Pacific battles raging at the moment, what could this spectacle mean?

He was soon to learn that the line of stretchers being handed down *Tranquility*'s gangway carried surviving *Indianapolis* crew members. Out of a crew of 1,199, these were the 316 lucky survivors of four days in shark-infested waters.

After its top secret delivery of the first atomic bomb to awaiting pilots on Tinian Island, *Indianapolis* had sailed south, stopped briefly at Guam, then set out for Leyte, another 1,350 miles. Traveling without escorts or shipboard sonar, the storied cruiser was defenseless against a Japanese submarine lurking halfway between the Philippines and Guam. In the dead of night, it had fired two torpedoes into *Indianapolis*, cutting the ship in half. She sank almost immediately. CINCPAC's forward headquarters at Guam was in a collective state of shock that the one-time Fifth Fleet flagship could have gone missing, unreported, for so long. Bill drew no closer to the scene after he landed. His threshold for absorbing the death of friends had long since been reached.

By the time he completed his seventeen-thousand-mile odyssey and reported back to Admiral Turner in Manila, alternatives to Olympic were already under consideration, despite General MacArthur's vigorous objections. Bill's delivery to Washington had, he believed, helped bring about the desired result.

Yet next steps in the Pacific were anything but clear. Despite the dropping of a second atomic bomb on August 9—on Mitsubishi Steel and Arms Works at Nagasaki on the island of Kyushu—Allied firebombing of mainland Japan had continued apace. And reluctantly redeployed troops from the European theater were still arriving by the thousands in Manila for retraining against a very different enemy.

Even after the stunning devastation conferred by two atomic bombs, Japan had not communicated any intention to surrender. It was the Japanese military, not her emperor or diplomats, who were running the war, and they had shown no inclination for retreat. Accordingly, General Marshall made no change to his imminent vacation plans, evidence alone that Japan's capitulation was not expected.

But before the second week of August 1945 was out—a week that included Russia's declaration of war against Japan and the Red Army's entry into Manchuria—Japanese military leaders were finally brought to their knees by their own emperor. On August 14, Prime Minister Kantaro Suzuki notified the Allies of Emperor Hirohito's issuance of an Imperial rescript accepting the unconditional surrender terms laid out in the Potsdam Declaration. The next day, Hirohito made a rare radio address to a weeping nation, announcing his decision.

Developments proceeded at a sprint after that. Truman named General MacArthur supreme commander for Allied Powers (SCAP), in which capacity he would lead postwar occupation of a vanquished Japan. Not surprisingly, MacArthur's crowning rankled navy feathers. But when Admiral Nimitz learned that MacArthur was also chosen to accept Japan's surrender, he displayed a rare flash of anger. He growled that this appeared to give the army credit for winning the Pacific War and resolved not to attend the ceremony. Only when Navy Secretary Forrestal stepped in was the day saved for both Admiral Nimitz and navy posterity.

Forrestal suggested that the surrender ceremony be held aboard a US Navy battleship, USS *Missouri*, in Tokyo Bay. Secretary Forrestal also ensured that the Pacific Fleet commander would cosign the surrender document with MacArthur. Thus assuaged, Nimitz flew to Tokyo Bay, arriving a day ahead of MacArthur. In this, deservedly, the commander in chief of the Pacific Fleet was the first to witness the most formidable display of naval power ever assembled in a single anchorage.

Admiral Nimitz settled into temporary quarters aboard the USS *South Dakota* and promptly convened a large group of war correspondents. He had a few things to say for—and on—the record. On the evening of August 29, Nimitz reminded the press of the pivotal role the US Navy had played throughout the Pacific conflict. Japan's surrender came before any invasion was necessary, he said, because of "sea power, spearheaded by carrier-borne aircraft and an excellent . . . submarine force."

Nimitz said that US naval sea power had made the use of the atomic bomb possible by its seizing of mid-Pacific atolls from which planes could carry it to Japan. "Without sea power," said Nimitz, "we could not have advanced at all."

AS THE WAR'S CLOSING events swirled around Manila, one in particular stood out for Bill Mott: the order to immediately free all prisoners of war. Better yet, Operation Swift Mercy decreed that prisoners being held in Japan must be transported to and processed in Manila before their repatriation to the United States. After enduring weeks of wildly fluctuating assumptions, Bill felt a shiver of expectation.

Admiral Halsey promptly dispatched hospital ships and a special task force to Japan to retrieve Allied prisoners from camps previously located by aerial reconnaissance. Most were suffering from severe malnutrition and other illnesses, ranging from serious to critical. In late August, navy photos of the first ecstatic group of liberated prisoners—from Omori, a camp near Tokyo— appeared on the front page of nearly every major American newspaper.

Preparations were under way in Manila to receive the tens of thousands of emaciated ex-POWs, with first arrivals expected by the third or fourth of September. Offices were set up to evaluate hospital and troopship rosters against uncorroborated grave-registration lists and lists of the missing. Infirmaries, dispensaries, and reception centers—and thousands of cots—were requisitioned and set up all over Manila.

On September 1, just as the first prisoner-loaded hospital ships prepared to depart Japan, Admiral Turner and his flag staff departed Manila for a particular battleship in Tokyo Bay. The formal Japanese surrender would be held at 0900 the next day on the USS *Missouri*, which was still Admiral Halsey's flagship.

After the ceremony, while a grand display of a thousand naval aircraft roared over Tokyo Bay, Admiral Turner asked Admiral Hall, freshly minted commander of the Tokyo Naval Force, if a sedan might be made available to take him and his staff into Tokyo. Hall referred the request to General Robert Eichelberger, the army area commander. Eichelberger hedged, saying that the army had not yet established patrols in Tokyo and could not ensure Turner's safety. But he did not say no, and in a manner unknown, a sedan was procured.

Admiral Turner and his entourage thus drove off, stopping first at a police station to get directions to the shrine of Admiral Tōgō, victor of the Tsushima Strait Battle in the 1904–05 Russo-Japanese War. Turner had been greatly impressed by the Tōgō shrine during his 1939 diplomatic mission to Japan aboard *Astoria*.

"We went into the police station to get a road map," recalled one staffer. "The police were very polite to us, and we were very polite to them. When we came out of the police station, Admiral Turner said, 'When they surrendered, they really surrendered.'"

Standing before the Tōgō shrine, Admiral Turner made this prescient observation: "If we play our cards well, the Japanese will become our best and most worthwhile friends. They have certain fundamental virtues in their character, which in time, I hope, will be appreciated by all worthwhile Americans. We should be most careful to respect their Gods and their traditions, and I hope they will come in time to respect ours."

Here again Turner was his usual thoughtful and brilliant, and the moment left an indelible print on his flag staff. But Bill was still privately roiled by persistent rumors of post-surrender reprisals against Allied war prisoners. As stunning and memorable as the day's events had been, he could think only of getting back to Manila. Once there, he would dissect every single roster of ships returning prisoners from Japan and search the faces of debarking men for Barton.

40

★ ★ ★

NO PEACE AT LILAC HEDGES

SEPTEMBER 1945 BEGAN AT Lilac Hedges as it had for decades. Despite the ecstasy of Japan's surrender and the subsequent agony of waiting to hear from or about Barton, Helen had her autumn gardening schedule to keep. Without a conventional job, she battled corrosive anxiety by working her seeds and soil as hard as any man labored at the office. Arthur had his textile business to keep him from going mad with the waiting.

They had relished the joyful news of Japan's unexpected surrender, toasting each other with highballs. "To Barton!" Then came the ongoing news of Allied prisoner liberations from such alien place names as Omori, Sian, Kyuryu, Sham Shui Po, Kanchanaburi, Mukden, Karenko, Nong Pladuck, Konan; after which came gleeful media reports of POWs reuniting with their jubilant families. Their nerves frayed as the days grew shorter and the list of liberated places longer, with no news of their son.

As the month wore on, Bill's regular but increasingly anxious assurances from Manila had yielded little. So preoccupied was Helen that she barely sniffed at Bill's own good news: that the Pacific admirals had formally recommended his transfer from the reserves to the regular navy, a long-sought goal.

With little else to distract her each morning after seeing Arthur off for the train, Helen took to the garden before the sun cleared the oak canopy on the east lawn. She would first drag a heavy brick across the porch to wedge open the door so as not to miss the much-awaited telephone call. Then, after fastening her bandana and donning her dirt-smudged apron, she gathered up her tulip, tiger, and rockery trowels, a mattock, hoe, and shrub rake, and went to work.

There were endless spent blooms to pinch, rosebushes to corset, and arbors to tie up. And with so much of her landscaping ripped away in last year's hurricane, there was the planting of new hemlocks, dogwoods, and Japanese maples to oversee. And then she must turn to the rigors of mulching, using the rich nutrient yield of fallen leaves already flecking her lawn. Ticking off tasks on these to-do lists became Helen's units of measure for marking time in September 1945.

As each day progressed, she kept a vigilant ear above autumn birdsong and honking geese for the mailman's footsteps and the particular pace of passing cars. Any day now, the mailman might bring joyful, if belated, tidings—and if no car slowed to a stop in front of her house, no uniformed officer could emerge with news she could not bear to hear.

How she missed Sable! For years, he had accompanied her morning garden rounds, courting her moods and patiently listening to her musings. But the graying spaniel had suddenly passed away in late January. Helen was convinced Barton's beloved dog finally died of a broken heart.

So she forged ahead alone that September, mapping out a gardening regimen that would take her through October, she calculated, what with putting in the young saplings, tulip and crocus bulb planting and transplanting, raking, composting, and mulching. Soon enough would come the job of spreading that black gold over her sleeping beauties in carefully delineated quadrants. This alone would take days.

But Helen did not follow her scripted plan to the letter that autumn. Early in the month, she declined to pull up the summer annuals on schedule—why void the lovely mounds of white impatiens lighting up the lilacs' understory before Barton's return? The same occurred the day she had scheduled cutting back her hydrangea. They still had good color, she reasoned, some deepened to a purplish garnet, others a sun-kissed bronze. Wouldn't he love to drive up after so long and see her garden "just so"?

She had loved it more than she ever let on when Barton would say, "Everything looks swell, Ma!" He had always complimented her horticultural flair. While she rarely spoke of it, his gift of noticing even the most mundane garden adjustment made her feel uniquely appreciated.

That September, it seemed that every one of Helen's gardening decisions had a Barton counterpart. She coaxed Lilac Hedges's summer glory to hang on so that Barton could see it before the garden faded to browns and grays.

THE FIRST FREED WAR prisoners in Japan had been from a camp called Omori. The September 7 article said they were actually liberated at the end of August, before the surrender was formally signed. Helen was trembling by the time she finished reading the front-page piece in the *New York Times*. With the help of a magnifying glass, she scrutinized the accompanying photo: a dirty band of gaunt, shirtless, exhilarated men. It caught them in a state of sheer exuberance, midshout, midlaugh, some with fingers fixed in Vs, others waving British and American flags.

"What of Barton?" she groaned. She asked this again and again, to her diary and out loud, but no longer to Sable, whose reliable attention and empathy she particularly missed now.

Besides her various trowels, Helen's only other weapons for taming anxiety were her fountain pen and typewriter. Since Japan's mid-August surrender announcement, she had repeatedly written both the army and navy. The war was over! Prisoners were being released all over Asia! Where was her son? September dragged into the double digits, and the gardening and letters continued apace, but replies from Washington never varied: "At last report to this Department, Ensign Cross was interned as a prisoner of war in the Philippines."

News of a darker nature had also begun to agitate Helen. Following each camp's liberation came a fresh round of press accounts—no longer subject to a war censor's pen—on Japanese treatment of their onetime captives. Front pages were crammed with one chilling ex-prisoner interview after another. The stock tales were of starvation, beatings, and beheadings, but another, more troubling, theme was also emerging.

The men told repeatedly of being shipped to Japan from conquered territories, shoved deep in the bowels of unmarked Japanese transports. So frequent were these stories that the press dubbed these vessels "hell ships." Drastic conditions and stunning cruelty aboard these ships spilled out daily in black and white. Worse, went the stories, as many as a dozen of these vessels had been attacked en route by the United States Navy.

If these accumulating newspaper reports were accurate, prisoner transports exiting the Philippines received particular attention by the US Navy. According to one survivor account, hundreds died from a single air squadron strike on his prison ship in Subic Bay at the end of 1944. Subsequent air strikes killed hundreds more prisoners before their voyage was done.

Carrier pilots' orders had been to "eliminate" all enemy shipping except hospital ships or those transporting prisoners of war, but none of the latter were marked as such. This was a flagrant violation of the Geneva Convention, but Japan had not been a signatory to those global rules of conduct. Helen simmered. *Hadn't the navy learned by that point that the Japanese were not marking their prisoner transports? She had written Roosevelt on this subject over a year earlier!*

The fall equinox came and went at Lilac Hedges with still no word from Ensign Cross. Helen was certain she knew the name of every Japanese prison camp in Asia by this time. They sounded unbidden in her head, in sync with the mourning meter of autumn crickets or to the rhythm of her shoes sloshing through wet grass, like a bad tune that cannot be banished: Saitami, Hokkaido, Shikoku, Ofuna, Shinagawa, Kawasaki . . . She spat out the names on the ever-lengthening list of liberated prison camps.

With each report, Arthur's forced optimism grew less convincing, even as he assured his fretting wife that there were still camps in Korea yet to be liberated. She just needed to be patient.

And so September dragged on, day in and day out.

On Tuesday, September 25, various morning headlines held little interest for Helen or Arthur. That the 1945 World Series would pit the Detroit Tigers against the Chicago Cubs was a disappointment to any self-respecting baseball fan. One sportswriter dubbed it the "World's Worst Series." Another quipped that he didn't think either team could win. Though they could have used the distraction, Helen and Arthur couldn't muster their usual enthusiasm for America's final baseball contest of the season.

Then there was the bit about Secretary of War Henry Stimson and his "deserving" retirement from public service. As far as Helen and Arthur were concerned, Stimson had neither protected their son at the start of the war nor done anything to bring him home at the end of it.

Arthur made for the train a little after eight, and Helen set out for the garden. When dark skies and wind gusts threatened rain in late morning, she headed back toward the house. But as she started up the porch steps, the mailman's distinctive gait stopped her in her tracks. Having sent off so many inquiries, she could only hope that today he brought a glimmer of news.

After placing her clippers and cuttings on the step and pulling off her garden gloves, she gratefully accepted the short stack of mail. With the dexterity of a card shark, she leafed through the mix of bills and letters. She stopped at the prize card—finally, a letter from the navy! With a mix of anticipation and nervousness, she sat down on the step and ripped open the envelope. Inside was a one-page letter, folded in thirds and neatly typed.

Dear Mr. and Mrs. Cross:

It is with deep regret that this Bureau informs you that it is in receipt of a cablegram from the International Red Cross in Tokyo, dated 19, September, 1945, stating that your son died of acute enteritis on 30 January 1945 while aboard a Japanese transport ship apparently en route to a prisoner of war camp in Japan.

The delay in the arrival of this information is a result of the slowness with which the Japanese Government has cooperated in the handling of the information concerning prisoners of war.

The Bureau deeply regrets its inability to supply further information at this time. The cablegram from the International Red Cross was brief and did not state the place of burial, type of ceremony, or medical attention administered. Now that the Japanese have surrendered, additional information is becoming available daily. Should further details be received concerning your son, they will be forwarded to you from the Navy Department.

The various agencies of the government having jurisdiction over settlement of death benefits in cases involving deceased naval personnel have been informed. These agencies will forward to you the necessary forms to be used in order to file a claim for any benefits to which you may be entitled.

The Navy Department extends sincere sympathy to you in

your great sorrow and hopes that you may find comfort in
the knowledge that your son gave his life in the service of
his country.

                              By direction of the Chief of

                              Naval Personnel.

                              Sincerely Yours,

                              H. B. Atkinson

                              Commander, USNR

                              Officer in Charge

                              Casualty Section

How long did it take for this news to sink in—that her son had been dead already *eight months*? How long for Helen to begin sobbing and rocking back and forth on that porch stair, for her bandana to slide off, for the strands of gray mingled with defiant red to mat her face, the tear-soaked letter still in hand? Had she already known on some unconscious level—felt that ominous, marrow-deep inkling that only a mother can decrypt?

At some point, Helen must have managed her way back into the house, past her War Mother's Flag still boasting a proud quartet of blue stars. It had adorned the front window for nearly four years now. Soon enough, a fellow War Mother would arrive, discreetly, and sew gold thread over the third one down to announce the incomprehensible loss of a dear child to a distant war.

There were no uniformed officers at her door to thank for their kindness in her moment of great anguish, no body to weep over, no forehead to stroke one last time, and, without a body, no funeral to plan. All conventional palliatives for a mother's grief were denied her. Helen had only this letter from the Navy Department to respond to—and respond she would. Her heart would bleed with purpose, she determined, through the nib of her pen.

That they had declined to notify her in person was perhaps the greatest insult. Her four children all naval officers and the navy too busy to come to her home, even with the war concluded? And her dear one's death due to "acute enteritis"? After everything she had read in the previous three weeks, she rejected this with every fiber of her being. Years of incompetence, and now lies!

Arthur mourned as any well-trained son of the British Empire might—silently and stoically. He reeled from the death of his namesake, but spoke little of it and cried less. While Helen announced her grief with vehemence, Arthur's only solace was work, to which he returned in too few days following the terrible news.

Helen abandoned her gardening for the rest of 1945—anguish and rage had snuffed out the joy it had once brought her. But she did not sit idle. As autumn leaves fell unanswered on tufting grass and spiking weeds and chill winds blew them about neglected beds, stacks of letters weighed down the mailman in his daily retreat from Lilac Hedges.

Her first round of salvos—to the army, the navy, and President Truman—demanded the names and addresses of surviving prisoners who had known her son. If Pentagon and White House powers couldn't or wouldn't help her learn the truth, she resolved to get the answers elsewhere. Once she received the contact information, she would solicit Barton's prison comrades for answers.

In the meantime, she gathered as much information as she could on the much-publicized hellships, easily confirming that her son had died after seven weeks of incarceration in the rusted, boiling-then-freezing hulls of three such vessels. The first two, *Oryoko Maru* in Subic Bay and *Enoura Maru* at Takao Harbor, Formosa, had been laid to waste by exploding bombs dropped by navy carrier planes, each time killing and wounding hundreds more American prisoners.

Surviving prisoners of the second prison ship bombing at Takao Harbor, including Barton, were transferred to the hull of a third ship, *Brazil Maru*. This last crumbling, stinking hulk then set course for Japan—into the teeth of its coldest winter in decades. All were starving, ill, and emaciated, and many had untreated shrapnel wounds from the previous bombings.

Prisoners in the horse manure–laden hull of the *Brazil Maru* died by the hour. The death rate on this final, bitter leg to the enemy's homeland reached forty men a day, their purpling corpses stacked like cordwood together with the men in the hull.

With every new revelation, Helen absorbed fresh shock and grief. Then she gathered herself up and fired off a fresh barrage of accusations and questions to Washington. As postwar press scrutiny of these doomed prisoner voyages intensified, Helen became increasingly convinced that Barton was a victim of friendly fire. Official replies never satisfied.

Even as the navy resisted her building rationale that Barton was killed by one of his own, Helen reasserted her mounting evidence against them. Article after article, all drawn from survivor accounts, continued for months after the war. Without wartime censorship, the military was powerless to stem the rising tide of damning information.

One brutally candid fourteen-part series, based on some of the first press interviews after surrender, left Helen shattered. Barton had been on every one of the ships described in the cruel forty-nine-day odyssey.

In the syndicated "Cruise of Death," Pulitzer Prize–winning correspondent George Weller of the *Chicago Daily News* spared no detail. The series ran in December 1945 and was carried by major newspapers across the country:

SEVEN WEEKS IN JAP-MADE HELL
Story of Cruise of Death of 1600 American
Prisoners Told by the 300 Who Lived

George Weller Pieces Together the Record
of Bombs, Suffocation, Starvation,
Murder on Voyage from Manila.

This is the story of a cruise of death. It is the
story of 49 days of savagery and tragedy unequaled

in the war in the Pacific, of a Jap-made hell from
which approximately 300 Americans from more than
1600 emerged, alive . . .

Survivors were interviewed in prison and rest
camps in the Pacific.

It is the story of a twisting, tortuous journey
on prison ships from Manila to southern Japan during which men died from Japanese bullets, American
bombs, suffocation, starvation and murder. Some went
insane . . . Its accuracy is unquestionable.

The story begins in Manila. December 13, 1944 . . .

DOWN AT THE NAVY Department's Casualty Section, a perspiring
Commander Atkinson doggedly responded to each of Helen Cross's salvos,
but he never wavered from the navy's original claim of Barton's cause of death:

Dear Mrs. Cross:

Receipt is acknowledged of your letters addressed to
President Truman and referred to this Bureau for reply
concerning your son, the late Ensign Arthur Barton Cross, Jr.

Although you state your son died as a result of
Allied bombing attacks on a Japanese prison ship, the
records available to this Bureau indicate he died of acute
enteritis. There is no evidence available in the Navy
Department to substantiate your belief that your son died
as a result of Allied bombings.

After the war was over with Japan in August, 1945,
the captured enemy records were carefully translated

and scrutinized for clues as to the fate of Army and Navy
personnel who had fallen into the hands of the enemy.

In some instances, it was learned that naval personnel
who had survived Japanese attacks had subsequently been
taken into custody and killed by the Japanese. Other
prisoners died of disease due to malnutrition, among whom
was listed your son.

Your anxiety to learn the details of your son's death
is appreciated and it is regretted there are no additional
facts known in his case.

Sincere sympathy is again extended to you in the loss
of your son.

> By direction of the Chief of
> Naval Personnel.
> Sincerely Yours,
> Commander H. B. Atkinson
> Officer in Charge
> Casualty Section
> Bureau of Naval Personnel
> Washington 25, DC

Yet Atkinson had a mother, too, and he did what he could to assuage the
aggrieved Helen Cross. He sent a warm personal note with Barton's Purple
Heart medal, awarded posthumously for wounds he received in the December 1941 bombings at Cavite. He thought she might also like to know that
Barton had been promoted to Lieutenant (jg) while a prisoner, something
he expected would make her very proud. But Atkinson's efforts were unrequited. She replied to his every missive (with courtesy copies to members
of Congress and President Truman) with withering scorn:

Dear Sir:

Answering your last letter I was for a moment confused—it had been so long since I had addressed the President and then only when the Navy seemed quite unconcerned.

As to your Purple Heart, its late arrival was not mentioned to me by my family who intercepted it in fear of further anguish being brought me. However since the story of [sic] a Major General receiving one for a broken leg received when he fell drunk from a second story—this medal leaves me quite indifferent.

If that is all the Navy has to offer those poor devils whom it bombed and killed after three years of horrible imprisonment by the Japs, you may have your Purple Heart back.

As to my son's death, he was bombed by Navy fliers in Subic Bay and again by Navy hands off of Formosa, and after such sufferings reportedly died of exhaustion and pneumonia which might be blamed on the Japs.

This was not the work of Army fliers, mind you—thank God that their branch was not guilty of so terrible a mistake!

And then, what does the Navy do? Does it send one ranking surviving officer who might have been with our dear one in his last hours? No, you killed our son, not even in fair battle either, and never has there been such callous disregard of heart-broken relatives as the Navy has shown in this instance.

Furthermore, though my son has been gone from this earth for approaching a year, and the Red Cross has notified me of his insurance and back pay, not any of this has reached me. Not that ten times the amount would atone for one of my son's fingers, it just further confirms dilatory Navy procedure.

Don't take this personally. It is the Navy we despise, "Bull" Halsey who gave orders to those fliers and the brass hats in safe places who *didn't care. Only Congressional investigations will cure Navy arrogance and stupidity.*

The public is awake to it—witness how few officers of the Reserve care to remain in such an organization.

Very sincerely,
Helen C. Cross

cc: President Harry S. Truman
Senator Albert Hawkes (R-NJ)

More-satisfying responses to Helen's missives were trickling in from Barton's comrades who had survived the ordeal. Most were written from beds at military hospitals across the country and arrived over a period of several weeks. Helen hungrily read and reread each moving fellow-prisoner testimonial. They were her sole consolation, providing a montage of Barton's world over the past three years and filling dozens of blanks she had long agonized over.

The letters were also full of anecdotes and unabashed declarations of respect and affection for their lost friend. She and Arthur both were amazed—and taken aback—by the picture that emerged of their son, who had been transformed in his bondage. The letters attested to the courage, strength, honor, and persistent optimism Barton had to the last—none easy traits to retain under such conditions. They described at length the difference "Bart" had made in their respective lives, which, they attested variously, had been critical to their own survival.

Who was this person these fellow prisoners described? Could her son really have left home such a boy and in captivity become such a *man*?

"In all those three years, under humiliating and weakening conditions, Bart was ever the gentleman, a true inspiration to all who knew him!" wrote one.

Another said: "I was with Bart under all kinds of conditions, and I can truthfully say he was one of the finest men I have ever known. He never complained. He was cheerful and courageous until the end." And another: "He organized a Sunday choir, concerts, a glee club, and baseball games— and even a baseball team that played against the Jap guards. His courage was unbelievable, and his morale building efforts were continuous among officers and men in both the prison camps and aboard the prison ships."

Each treasured account added its own texture, depth, and color to a portrait of the man this grieving mother's boy had become beyond her care. The correspondence was mostly from naval ensigns and young lieutenants. Some had been quartered with Barton since the Philippines fell; others had known him only at one camp or another. One man said he didn't really get to know Barton until they were thrust together on the last of the three hellships, but under such conditions, he wrote, they formed a sure and fast bond.

Their precise recounting of Barton's final moments varied to a degree, doubtless due to their own drastically diminished conditions. One fellow prisoner claimed Barton had succumbed to wounds incurred when a navy bomb struck their ship at Takao, Formosa. Another said Barton had died from starvation and exposure. One said dysentery had claimed him; another said it was pneumonia, of which so many had died on that final, frigid voyage. Try though she did, Helen was unable to reconcile these accounts. Perhaps, she mused, he had fallen victim to all of them.

Barton's fellow prisoners all stressed that by the end of the forty-nine-day trip, those still alive were barely so. They unanimously declared it a miracle that any of them had survived. The final numbers were grim. Of the 1,619 prisoners that departed Manila on December 13, 1944, 450 arrived alive in Japan on January 30, 1945. Of those, 161 died in Japanese labor camps shortly thereafter.

Describing the details of Barton's last days and hours was painful for Barton's fellow prisoners, but tell they did, perhaps believing that the only possible salve for his family was the truth.

41

★ ★ ★

FINAL HOURS

Dear Mrs. Cross,

I have been in the hospital for several weeks and just received your letter. I am very sorry that I have not written you sooner--but then too, I didn't want to merely write a letter and let it go at that . . .

Bart and I were captured in Manila on January 1, 1942. He and I were together all the time until his death. We were in camps on Luzon, moved to Davao, Mindanao, and then back to Cabanatuan on Luzon in the summer of 1944. We were returned to Bilibid Prison in Manila that October and left there on December 13, 1944, on a Japanese ship bound for Japan. This ship was sunk . . .

> Charles W. Armour to Helen Cross, dated November 2,
> 1945, from a naval hospital in Memphis, Tennessee

My Dear Mrs. Cross,

I am so glad that you have written me. I do appreciate
the many unanswered questions that must be in the minds of
Bart's family. I know he would wish that I be as truthful
and frank as possible with his family. With that in mind,
I shall do my very best to accurately recall the important
things.

I met Bart at Bilibid Prison after the fall of Bataan.
From that time on, we were in the same camps and became
close friends . . .

> Kenneth R. Wheeler, dated November 3, 1945, from
> a naval hospital at Oak Knoll, California

Dear Mrs. Cross,

Yes, I did know your son. I only wish I could talk with
you about him in person rather than set the facts down
in an impersonal letter, but I will do the best I can. I'm
awfully sorry I didn't know how close I was to you when
I traveled to Philadelphia to see Captain and Mrs. Wuest.
Their son Bob was also a close friend of ours, and I wanted
to give them his U. of Penn ring I managed to bring back. He
died on the trip from Manila to Moji, Kyushu, and, like you,
they had little or no information about his death . . .

Bart and I met after the surrender [at Corregidor]
and were sent to Cabanatuan, where we ensigns all lived in
one barrack. In the fall of 1942, Bart and quite a number
of other naval personnel were sent to Davao on Mindanao.
About July 1944, I believe, the Davao detail returned to

Cabanatuan, and we were all together again. We ensigns
had quite a bit of fun at Cabanatuan. We stuck together
in all things and that in itself made life a lot easier.
That October, we were all sent down to Bilibid to await
transportation to Japan.

Because of American raids on Manila, we were kept at
Bilibid until December 13th. Then a typhoon gave the Nips
the break they were waiting for. We were loaded onto the
"Oryoko Maru" that same afternoon and sailed within several
hours. American planes began bombing the ship on the
14th and sank her on the 15th. Bart and most of the other
ensigns made it ashore. We were kept there at Subic for 5
days . . .

Andrew Long Jr., dated November 6, 1945, from a
military hospital in Springfield, Missouri

DECEMBER 15, 1944

IT WAS LATE AFTERNOON by the time surviving *Oryoko Maru* prisoners were herded together on the beach and marched to an improbable new
enclosure: a tennis court on the former US Naval Base at Olongapo. It was
only about five hundred yards away, but the men staggered the distance from
the combined trauma of shock, exhaustion, hunger, and thirst. They also
struggled to carry their two hundred wounded, some at the point of death.

A scowling Mr. Wada greeted Colonel Beecher—still damp and attired
only in socks and boxer shorts—at the tennis court gate. Waving the ship's
manifest, the interpreter demanded a survivor count. Beecher agreed, but
insisted wisely that he be allowed a confirming second count before certi-
fying it. A miscount in the chaos could falsely indicate escape, triggering a
fresh round of Japanese reprisals; this he wished to avoid at all costs.

Beecher's method was to send a hundred prisoners through the court gate at a time, but so many passed back and forth carrying in the wounded that he quickly lost track. The process took hours, with no certain count at the end of it.

The following morning, Beecher began a second count after mustering a burial detail to inter the three men who died in the night. He then dragged the tall referee's chair to the court's center and began calling roll. It went badly from the start. Beecher recalled,

[W]hen a man didn't answer to his name, it had to be repeated several times in order to be sure the man who . . . was actually missing. The doctors and corpsmen had to nudge patients to respond, as many were in such condition as to be unable to recognize their names when called . . . When there was no answer, I asked, "Well, does anyone know what happened to him?" A voice might say "I think he passed out last night" or "I believe I saw him with the dead on the deck of the ship." Then there would be contradictions. "The hell you did! He was in the bay next to me. A bomb fragment got him." Another might respond, "How could a bomb have got him when I saw him swimming away from the ship?"

The sun was low on the horizon on December 16 by the time a survivor count of 1,320 prisoners was submitted. Beecher calculated that some 50 of the 300 casualties had occurred during the two horrific nights aboard *Oryoko Maru*; the rest died during the aerial attacks or at the hands of guards gunning from the seawall. They had shot any prisoner deemed to be swimming off course.

By dusk the second day, an order of sorts had emerged on the Olongapo tennis court. So, too, had the prisoners' realization that they had survived the *Oryoko Maru* only to endure a bizarre new phase of suffering. On the ship, they had endured suffocating heat, maddening thirst, random acts of murder, and a vicious—if unwitting—attack by their own navy. Those fortunate enough to make it ashore now questioned how lucky they really were.

The tennis court measured sixty feet by eighty feet, barely larger than the ship's hold. To fit, they were packed into eleven lines of a hundred men each, their legs either drawn knees to chest or scissored around the man in front of them.

The wounded were housed in the court "hospital," a sand-and-gravel width behind the faded baseline shaded by a piece of torn sheeting. Surviving doctors, themselves depleted and barely clothed, did what they could to dress wounds while calculating which men's hours were numbered and beyond care.

There was a water source at the court—a significant relief. But accessing the single, trickling spigot was no small effort. The men queued up at all hours, and guards were posted by the spigot around the clock. A lucky few still had a cup or canteen to fill for their effort, but most had to hold their mouths to the water for as long a draught as the guards would allow.

Despite their unpleasant new circumstances, the prisoners were relieved to no longer be heading to Japan. Every hour they remained in the Philippines, went the thinking, their chances for rescue by the fast-approaching Allies improved.

BARTON AND CHARLES CONDUCTED a survivor count of their own on the tennis court. Two members of their tight ensign fraternity—George Petritz and Shields Goodman—had not been seen since the order to abandon ship. Nor had Ensigns Chuck Wilkins and Warwick Potter Scott. They mourned quietly, remembering their late comrades with anecdotes drawn from three years of shared misery and privation.

Small sacrifices had made big differences. Charles reluctantly shared his old navy cap for an hour or so at a time so that the others could get temporary relief from the head-scorching sun. Before doing so, he re-moved a tiny address book from the inside flap in which he'd painstakingly recorded dozens of recipes over the years. The significance of the miserly Charles's hat loan was not lost on the others. His accumulated recipes had become almost as important to him as food itself. That hat had safeguarded them as much as it did his head.

Somehow Barton had hung on to his strapped canteen, despite the lengthy amount of time he'd spent in the water. He traveled back and forth to the spigot line at all hours, each time returning to pass the canteen around to the ensigns. When it was empty, he got back in the water queue. Barton engaged in his usual self-deprecating banter to deflect their gratitude, but his colleagues knew the man better by now.

In this manner, water was plentiful on the tennis court, but food was not. Their first food was finally tossed through the court gate on the second day, but in the form of two seventy-pound sacks of uncooked rice. Without cooking facilities, two level tablespoons of hard rice kernels were meted out to each prisoner. To supplement the meal, several reached through small openings in the fence perimeter and pulled up grass. A forearm's width of bare ground soon surrounded the enclosure.

As the prisoners chewed their stony rations, Admiral Halsey's planes returned in full view of the tennis court. Against a brilliant azure sky, one bomb load after another found their marks on the listing *Oryoko Maru*. Prisoner cheers went up with each direct hit, with the biggest whoop re-served for when the hated vessel burst into flames and slipped beneath the surface.

An apprehensive silence followed when Commander Riera and his air group made a circle and flew directly toward them. The planes circled and dove, circled and dove, striking fuel depots and other targets all around the prisoners. They seemed to be taking pains to avoid the court itself, ignit-ing fresh hope among the prisoners. This must mean the flyers knew that these were the abandoned soldiers and sailors of Bataan, Cavite, and Corregidor. Surely they would hasten to send help. But yet another cruel spike in optimism ended in disappointment. There was no rescue, and no planes returned after December 16.

As the calendar pages turned, misery on the tennis court compounded. By noon each day, tropical heat pushed the concrete slab to over 100 degrees. The barely clad men baked and blistered on the black, unshaded surface. When afternoon mercifully faded to dusk, the relief was brief. Chill evening breezes transformed the court into a cold, hard torture rack. At night, protruding hips and ribs were marked by purpling welts and bruises. The men huddled together for warmth.

The evening winds also brought clouds of biting flies and mosquitoes. The insects feasted on open wounds, and sunburned skin turned to gooseflesh. Of those long nights on the tennis court, Manny Lawton recalled that the prisoners were "cold, hurting, and hungry. Few slept." By the third day, cases of gangrene had set in.

Removal of a gangrenous arm with a mess kit knife was the first surgical procedure in the court hospital. The patient was Marine Corporal Eugene L. Specht. The arm had taken a bullet that guards fired into the ship's hold on December 15. After hearing his options, Specht agreed with the medics: his only chance at survival was removal of the arm.

Poor Specht screamed in agony and had to be held down for the procedure. Afterward, the surgeon wrapped the bloody stump in a dirty towel, and, mercifully, the patient fell asleep. The next day, Specht was buried by the seawall alongside the accumulating prisoner dead.

> On the fifth day, a convoy drew up to the tennis courts
> and we were ordered to load.
>
> Kenneth Wheeler to Helen Cross

★   ★   ★

THE NINETEEN TRUCKS THAT lumbered up on December 20 felt like a celestial vision. The prisoners had begun to wonder how much longer they could endure brutal exposure and a diet of 55 calories a day. After Lieutenant Toshino loaded the trucks to overcapacity, the convoy snaked out of sight. The six hundred prisoners that remained on the tennis court—Barton and Charles among them—were left to mull their fates.

There were benefits for those left behind, however. That night, they received a triple ration of rice from their unpredictable captors—six level spoonfuls of dry grain instead of two, plus a spoonful each of salt and dried fish. There was also more room to spread out on the court. With that and the extra food in their bellies, they slept a little better that night.

They were nonetheless relieved when told to prepare for their own move. Following a generous breakfast of *ten* spoonfuls of raw rice and more dried fish, Mr. Wada ordered the ensigns to clean the tennis court. Barton's mordant quips over the absurdity of this task elicited laughter—good and ancient medicine—even as the men labored to comply. Humor was their sole remaining antidote for misery, and it could not be taken away.

While the ensigns swabbed the blood- and feces-splattered tennis court, guards drew their swords and cut large tree branches to camouflage the trucks. A familiar mix of dread and anticipation returned when the prisoners learned why. The truck drivers reported that American pilots were actively patrolling above the main roads.

The truck ride was an uncomfortable zigzag over roadbeds rutted by weather, neglect, and war. At the intermittent buzz of approaching planes, the convoy lurched into ravines or under roadside tree canopies for cover. But when the trucks pressed northeast across the Zambales Mountains and away from the sea, the prisoners found cause for encouragement.

Could there be no more enemy ships to remove them from Luzon? With every hairpin turn, morale rose again with the prospect they might be liberated. But ominous signs mixed with positive ones. A steady stream of Japanese soldiers passed their convoy, variously hauling weapons, food, large guns, and ammunition. Recalled Colonel Beecher, "We felt . . . that the Japs were moving into position somewhere . . . We hoped . . . we would still be in the Philippines when [the final battle] took place."

The thirty-seven-mile truck ride ended at San Fernando, Pampanga, a town deep in Luzon's central plains. The last tennis court draft was marched along the town's vacant main street to a deserted cinema. After entering under the bullet-ridden marquee, the men groped in the dark. When their eyes finally adjusted, they saw that the theater's seats had been pulled up and tossed into an orchestra pit. Its singular water source was a spigot outside a barbed wire fence surrounding the theater. That spigot, and the latrines— slit trenches dug behind the rear of the building—could be accessed only by climbing through a small window. Still, the abandoned cinema was pro-tected from the sun by day and from biting wind and insects by night.

They felt a spark of jealousy, however, when they learned that the ear-lier prisoner draft was being held at the town jail, which had plumbing and cooking facilities—even cots. But when their first cooked meal in a week appeared shortly after their arrival, all was forgiven. It had been prepared— unbidden—by their colleagues at the jail. The meal of steaming rice, sea-weed, and *camotes* arrived on a sheet of corrugated roofing, and the men gratefully wolfed it down.

On the second evening in San Fernando, Mr. Wada called Colonel Beecher to the entrance of the cinema. Eventually they would resume their trip to Japan, Wada told a disappointed Beecher. He then directed the colonel to select fifteen sick and wounded—those least able to make a sea journey—so they could be sent to a hospital. Beecher was elated but also conflicted, for hundreds of prisoners easily met the criteria.

Fifteen men were finally culled from among the most extreme cases at the jail and theater. When the patients were loaded onto the two truck beds, Beecher recalled thinking, *Well, there go at least fifteen prisoners who in spite of their wounds are pretty lucky. They'll get back to Bilibid and probably pull through; certainly better off than us left behind.*

But Beecher was tragically mistaken, unaware that Lieutenant Urabe at Manila POW headquarters had ordered Toshino to exterminate any POWs unable to withstand further movement. A shallow grave had been prepared before the trucks arrived at a cemetery south of town. When Lieutenant Toshino and Sergeant Tanoue Suketoshi reached the darkened site, the patients were bound and dragged to the grave's long border. Sergeant Tanoue then drew his sword and decapitated the first seven men. When their heads and bodies failed to fall cleanly into the grave, an irritated Toshino ordered the guard detail to bayonet the remaining patients.

ON THE FOLLOWING DAY, Christmas Eve, the prisoners' stooped and thinning frames converged on San Fernando's vacant main street for a dubious yuletide march. Their destination was the San Fernando train station. The men were upbeat, buoyed by rumors that they were heading back to Bilibid. But at the bomb-cratered train platform, a short line of hot, windowless boxcars awaited. The prisoners grew quiet with dread when Mr. Wada announced that 185 men must board each car.

Even the sadistic Wada could not overcome simple physics: there was not enough space on the train for all the prisoners, crammed in or not. Only when air raid sirens signaled the approach of American bombers did Wada order the remaining prisoners on the platform to mount the cars' rickety ladders and take seats on the rooftops. Two guards were posted with each group of roof riders; they numbered twenty and thirty a car. Bandaged prisoners were instructed to wave their arms and shout if the planes zeroed in on the train.

Despite obvious danger and discomfort, Charles, Barton, and Jack Ferguson felt nothing but gratitude to have won spots on top. Engine smoke and soot blew on them throughout, and it was a cold, hazardous ride, but that was far preferable to another long trip inside the suffocating boxcars.

There were other upsides, too. One was the excellent view of dogfights between American and Japanese planes as the train pulled out of San Fernando, and of the bombing of Clark Field against a magnificent sunset. Smoke plumes from downed Japanese planes wafted skyward in the distance.

The train chugged deep into the night, passing through one darkened barrio after another. Despite the advancing hour on Christmas Eve, local Filipinos gathered and called to them from each train platform: "Merry Chrees-mass, Joe!" As the train rolled through, they tossed bananas, eggs, sugarcane, and mangoes up to the ragged roof riders, and groups of children broke into spontaneous caroling. The prisoners waved and wept, grateful beyond words for the moral support and life-saving offerings.

His body was cold, dirty, and depleted, but his fellow prisoners all recalled that Barton's spirits soared on this particular night. He felt free as air, and his mass of curly, unkempt hair whipped in the wind just as it had when he stuck his head out the Packard window on family drives to the Jersey Shore. His quick, glancing green eyes took in every detail. My God, he said to Charles and Jack, what stories they would have to tell when they got home! This Christmas train, their long camaraderie, the big-hearted Filipinos—still defiant, loyal, and generous to the Americans despite their own privations and long struggle—would make for grand tales in their old age. Tales of faith, sacrifice, generosity, and persistence in the face of seemingly hopeless odds.

This night threw the qualities of a transformed Barton Cross into high relief. His eager fellowship and routine sacrifices had earned him deep respect among his prisoner peers. But Barton believed he had survived the long ordeal only *because* of those sacrifices, not in spite of them—and that's if he ever admitted to sacrificing at all.

His strongest conviction had been the most infectious: that their iron-clad fellowship was their best defense against the worst the Japanese could throw at them. It fortified them all, mentally, physically, and emotionally.

The strength of this indivisible bond had become religion for Barton the prisoner. On this Christmas Eve, the shallow vanities of Barton's former self—that insulated youth of 1941—had long since faded away.

THE ENGINE LURCHED NORTH at the first track switch, away from Manila. If not to Bilibid, then where? They were desperate enough to pray for the despised Cabanatuan, as the train approached the last possible switch that could take them there.

But when the conductor did not oblige at that final split, a new apprehension seized the prisoners. They all knew their Luzon geography by now. Lingayen Gulf, the last remaining Luzon port still in enemy hands, had suddenly become the only possible terminus, which almost certainly meant shipment to Japan.

After seventeen hours and a final belch of choking smoke, the wood-burning engine jerked to a halt at 0400 Christmas morning. For the men on top, the platform sign confirmed their arrival at another town named San Fernando, this one a small coastal village in the La Union Province. The salty report of sea air filled Barton's nostrils—and his memory. For countless summers, detecting that first briny scent through that open Packard window had stirred anticipation of the Jersey Shore's many delights. This morning it brought a dread so great it threatened nausea.

Barton followed his comrades down the boxcar ladder to join gasping prisoners pouring out of the interiors. Discouraged, famished, and chilled to the bone, the reassembled ensigns said little. There was no need to parry over the meaning of this destination. Instead, they reflexively huddled together when ordered to lie down on the cold and crowded platform. A prescient few first snapped up scraps of dried coconut littering the landing and crammed them into their mouths. It was a Christmas morning none who survived would ever forget.

They were rousted at dawn and marched a few kilometers to the perimeter grounds of an abandoned trade school outside the town. Memories of savage thirst always present, the search for water began immediately. All they could locate was a muddy, hand-dug well by the latrine pit. One after another prisoner gorged from the fouled supply after "purifying" it with iodine drops. Potable or not, fear of water deprivation overwhelmed even the most cautious by this point. Without pots or a heat source to boil the water, the revised wisdom was that one might just as well die from typhoid or dysentery as thirst.

One rice ball per man was meted out for Christmas dinner, after which the prisoners surrendered to sleep on the trade school grounds. But no sooner had they dozed off than a Japanese sentry appeared with new orders. They must rise and march to the shore of Lingayen Gulf and await their ship. The sudden, unhappy news was met in turns with shock and angry objections, followed by a flash of violence near the rice supplies. A small but determined group of prisoners overpowered their own colleagues guarding the food and clawed what they could, spilling precious supplies before being brought under control. Military discipline within the prisoner ranks had disintegrated once again. It was no match for the primal powers of hunger and fear.

After the melee, the overweary prisoners formed up in customary columns of four and stumbled onto the shore road. It was a breezy, pastoral hike, in stark contrast to their demoralized state. As they walked past moonlit hedges of flowering hibiscus and mango trees, they snatched what they could, gobbling down fruit, flowers, and leaves alike.

Evidence of the looming peril grew with every step.

"The march was about two miles," Major John Wright recalled, "over a rough road with bare feet . . . Oil storage tanks had been blasted to bits, buildings knocked down, and there were many bomb craters . . . Japanese . . . beach defenses—pillboxes, barbed wire, foxholes—all indicated they expected an invasion any hour. We wondered anew whether it would come soon enough to save us."

★   ★   ★

THE PRISONERS WERE HALTED at a windblown spit of sand and ordered to sit. A menacing Lingayen Gulf churned before them. It was just past midnight, and the moon over the water illuminated as many anchored Japanese vessels as it did ruined masts and sunken ship stacks breaking the surface. The men burrowed into the sand to protect from the stiff gulf winds as trucks, horses, ammunition carts, and troops hurried past on the road behind them.

Manny Lawton wrote: "With our bony frames molded into the soft sand . . . it was more comfortable than . . . the cement tennis court. Still, we shivered and shook . . . Two men died that night . . . By midmorning [the heat] was intense. Nothing stood up to the sun but a thin growth of stunted brown grass."

As on the tennis court, no sooner did the night's cold give way to daybreak than they were tormented by tropical sun beating down from every angle. There was the added agony of their bare skin on blistering-hot sand, and thirst again reached crisis proportions. Colonel Beecher implored Mr. Wada for water, to no avail.

However, Wada did relent to Beecher's suggestion that the prisoners be allowed to rotate into the gulf to bathe blisters and allow the salt water to absorb into thirsty pores. The system worked until one water-crazed officer dashed in and began gulping seawater. Just as the guards lifted their rifles and took aim, the man's fellow POWs dragged him back onto the beach.

When the equatorial sun slipped behind a pink-and-purple reef of clouds on the horizon, its majesty was no doubt lost on the prisoners. To them, sunset meant only one thing: the imminent arrival of the night winds. In this manner—searing by day and freezing by night—the prisoners spent forty-eight hours on the sands of Lingayen Gulf.

On December 27 the moon and Orion were high in the night sky when the prisoners were rousted and led across a narrow strip of land to a wooden pier. The transition went relatively smoothly until Mr. Wada ordered the men to board two barges alongside the pier, knocking hard against the pilings. Both vessels were fifteen feet below, and there were no ladders. The prisoners hung back in fear.

"*Speedo! Speedo!*" exhorted Lieutenant Toshino. At this, Wada ordered the guards to employ their rifle butts and push the prisoners off the dock. The result was a fresh round of sprains, broken bones, and bruises. Several missed the barges entirely. One officer was pulled lifeless from the tossing waters. The guards laughed.

At first light, the packed barges finally inched out into Lingayen Gulf toward two Japanese freighters. *Enoura Maru* was lettered on one, *Brazil Maru* on the other. The ships' captains seemed as anxious as Lieutenant Toshino to join the departing convoy before the inevitable return of American planes. "*Speedo! Speedo! Speedo!*" The guards waved clubs and rifles to expedite boarding. Neither ship bore Red Cross or other protective markings.

Colonel Beecher led the larger draft of 1,070 prisoners—including most of the ensigns—onto *Enoura Maru*. Barton and Charles were grateful that Beecher had remained in charge of their group and not diverted to the other freighter. If the Japanese respected any of them, they respected Curtis Beecher.

They filed past hundreds of wounded Japanese soldiers on *Enoura Maru*'s upper decks before the long prisoner queue began another cautious descent into a deep cargo hold. This time a pungent wave of ammonia fumes stopped them in their tracks. The hold was covered in fresh horse manure.

Major John Wright wrote: "[T]he filth was disgusting. The ship had brought cavalry [horses] to Luzon and we loaded into the hold [right after] . . . Scattered in with the manure was millet and oats . . . This was picked out grain by grain and eaten."

Some men shoveled the manure aside, others, beyond such a task, simply lay down in the dung. Large flies covered their mouths, faces, and eyes. But soon the prisoners were distracted from the present misery by a bigger problem: explosions rocked the ship's starboard side. *One. Two. Three.*

"Navy submarine torpedoes," said Lieutenant David Nash. The seasoned naval officer recognized the tenor of the blasts, which narrowly missed them. The convoy quickly hastened out of harbor and pointed north, hugging the Philippine coastline for protection for as long as possible.

On *Enoura Maru*, the prisoners slipped further into degradation. "We were dirty, bearded, and full of diarrhea," Carl Engelhart wrote. "We ate from our hats, from pieces of cloth, from our hands . . . A handful of rice clutched against a sweaty naked chest, so the flies could not get it, eating like an animal with befouled hands."

"Starving men forget discipline, forget honor, and forget self-respect," wrote John Wright.

Manny Lawton put it more bluntly: "Only survival mattered."

On New Year's Eve—day five of the voyage—a riot broke out in the hold. Servers were suddenly punched and thrown aside while distributing food in the semidarkness. The mob of hunger-crazed prisoners bit and slapped their way to the buckets, and then clawed at their contents. Tubs of precious soup and tea—the most sustenance offered since departing Leyte—were spilled in the melee. The raiders got their fill, while others got nothing. By the time *Enoura Maru* made anchor at Takao, Formosa, later that night, twenty-one more prisoners had died.

WITHOUT EXPLANATION, THE PAIR of prison ships lay at anchor for several days in Takao Harbor. Fervent hopes that their arrival at Formosa would mean fresh sustenance from imagined shore supplies faded quickly. Mr. Wada repeatedly denied prisoner pleas for additional food and water. "American submarines sink Japanese supply ships. No food for you," he replied.

The prisoners wallowed and despaired in the fetid hold; four or five more men died each day. They barely stirred at the intermittent buzz of planes overhead. Would American planes strike this ship, too? More than a few prayed they would. The men's growing desperation for food and water mattered far more than the rat-a-tat of antiaircraft fire from the deck.

Not only had swearing, fighting, and incredible filth become the norm, but disease was now sharply on the rise. Dysentery patients were moved in increasing numbers to "the hospital area," a planked platform directly above the hold. The helpless patients' uncontrollable diarrhea dripped through the floorboards onto the prisoners in "the pit" below. On January 5 John Wright wrote: "Two more deaths last night, two more today. Just waiting, wondering, and praying."

In the second week of January, it finally seemed the ship was being readied for departure. The number of deaths on both ships allowed for consolidation, and the *Brazil Maru* prisoners were moved to *Enoura Maru*. The Japanese also laid in new supplies, including several burlap sacks of sugar. A large tanker was brought alongside them as well, signaling the assembly of a convoy. But the new arrangements brought new troubles.

Stored sugar within feet of starving men was too great a temptation for Charles Armour and others. Despite stern Japanese warnings, Charles broke open one of the bags and gobbled down handful after handful. A stubble of sugar crystals covered the lower half of his face. Emboldened, other prisoners followed suit. Either too honorable or too fearful of reprisal, Barton withdrew from the scene.

After spying loose sugar at the foot of the hold's ladder, a passing guard called out to his superiors in urgent staccato. Seconds later, an angry Mr. Wada appeared at the top of the ladder. "You will surrender the thieves!" he demanded. No food or water until this was done, he warned. The silence that ensued surprised no one. Experience had taught them that deliverance of anyone under such circumstances meant certain torture and likely execution.

Colonel Beecher made a plea for volunteers to step forward on behalf of the whole, promising extra rations. After a weighted silence, a tired but resolute voice called out. "I'll go." A sea of bodies parted with deference as a man named Hannenkrant, an army medic, headed for the ladder. Then another voice rang out. All eyes settled on a young British sergeant named

Trapp. A pall of shame hung over the rest of them as the two brave men disappeared up the ladder.

Miraculously, the pair returned within an hour after only being cuffed and slapped. The prisoners speculated that their captors had spared them out of respect for their raw, and by now rare, courage.

At 0930 on January 9, a relative calm prevailed in the hold as breakfast was distributed. The prisoners were settling into their meal just as a loud whine of diving aircraft shattered the quiet. There was a burst of running and shouting above them, then the rapid *ack-ack* from the antiaircraft guns.

ON THIS SAME MORNING, General MacArthur's ground troops came ashore in full force at Luzon's Lingayen Gulf. As with MacArthur's mid-December Mindoro landings, Admiral Halsey's Task Force 38 was summoned for air support and the beachhead was secured before the day was through. Halsey's carrier pilots began their sorties early that morning, targeting multiple sites from which the enemy might attack Allied ships unloading in Lingayen Gulf. Airfields in southern Formosa were their primary objectives, but the airmen also prized any shipping in Formosan harbors, particularly tankers.

At 0915 on January 9, target coordinator Commander Robert Riera—and his same Air Group Eleven that had decimated *Oryoko Maru* in December—sortied from the USS *Hornet* in a tidy line. Carrying 250- and 500-pound bombs, the twelve fighter planes rounded the tip of southern Formosa in as many minutes. After climbing through tier after tier of scattered clouds, they broke into the clear at 6,500 feet. Takao Harbor spread out like an aerial photograph beneath them. It was "the only spot so favored on the coast," Riera noted in his after-action report. "Twenty-five ships were counted in Takao's inner harbor, more in its outer perimeter, a bomber's dream. Some [ships] were moored in pairs, presenting unusually attractive targets."

One after another, each plane went into a 5,000-foot dive and dropped its load onto the oil tanker and the *Enoura Maru* next to it. "Four good hits were observed, with others probable . . . antiaircraft [fire] moderate. The most successful antishipping strike flown by this squadron to date," Riera boasted.

THE FORWARD HOLD AND engine room received direct hits. The bomb intended for the second hold—where most of the prisoners were eating breakfast—exploded alongside the ship, shredding the starboard hull. Beams and hatch covers crashed down, and torrents of steel splinters and shrapnel sprayed into the hold.

The result was a smoke-filled hell pit of ripped flesh, severed limbs, and crushed skulls. David Nash recalled the horror: "Before it could register in our minds, we were being jarred by falling bombs . . . All around us were killed and wounded . . . A near miss had made a sieve of the side of the ship. One sight haunted me for days. That was a man whose skull was laid wide open and yet he breathed for hours. About that time, I discovered that my leg was bleeding from a deep gouge. I don't know when I received it."

Ken Wheeler also recounted the scene: "When the dust and fire cleared away, I was stunned [by] the carnage . . . Over 300 in our group were killed outright. Almost everyone was wounded . . . The hatches, hatch covers, and massive plank . . . had been blown into the hold on top of us."

Those not crushed to death were pinned beneath the fallen beams.

There was a stunned silence in the hold after the attack, as dazed survivors took stock. After the initial trauma, those able to move started toward their wounded comrades. Barton was in shock following the blast, and his head ached, but his injuries were nothing compared with those around him. The macabre scene unfolded like a soundless nightmare. Ensigns Bob Wuest and Jack Ferguson were both mortally wounded and covered in blood. Without immediate assistance from the Japanese, they—and hundreds of other wounded—would surely die. Barton joined the other able-bodied who were crafting crude tourniquets and splints while they waited for medics.

Nothing was heard from the Japanese for hours after the blast, and the situation rapidly deteriorated. Finally, Colonel Olson, with his forearm blown off and a rag tied above the elbow, mounted the ladder and called out for Mr. Wada. He appeared after several long minutes and glared down at Olson like an angry chimera. "I ask nothing for myself," Olson began boldly, "but these men are dying. In . . . the name of the Gods that you believe in, can't you do something for them? They will die without bandages or medicine or food and water."

Mr. Wada curled his lips, baring a mouthful of yellow, protruding teeth. "They were your planes that bombed ship," he sneered. "They were your planes, and they have killed our men too. We don't care if you die." With that, he disappeared.

At Wada's departure, the only sound below was the weeping and moaning of grown men who had lost every last hope. But then another voice called out—urgent, steady, and clear. Every man recognized the speaker. "Listen to me, men! You must listen to me!" It was the deep, resonant voice of Father Cummings, the Catholic chaplain who had earned universal authority the hard way: by going through every inch of the agony with them. Some had been with "Father Bill" since Bataan; others gratefully remembered his prayers and counsel at various prison camps, and all of them during the *Oryoko Maru* ordeal. The hold went silent as men of all faiths strained to listen.

The beloved priest who at Bataan had declared, "There are no atheists in foxholes," did not follow with a plea for faith. Instead, Father Cummings simply began praying aloud in his comfortingly familiar tone: "Our Father, who art in Heaven, hallowed be thy name . . ." Some men murmured the Lord's Prayer along with him; others followed with closed eyes and clasped hands. They listened as never before.

"Father Cummings's prayer," wrote Sidney Stewart, "floated like a benediction . . . caressing every one of us."

"It penetrated our very souls," wrote David Nash.

As if by celestial intervention, Japanese guards shortly thereafter began lowering bandages, bottles of iodine, mercurochrome, and buckets of water into the hold. Encouraged, survivors started to reorganize and function; some dressed wounds with the new supplies, while others cleared away debris and began the grisly task of stacking bodies by the hatch.

Two more days would pass before the Japanese sent down working parties to remove the dead; an excruciating process that itself took another two days. Thirty bodies at a time were loaded onto cargo nets attached to a cable, and then winched out of the hold and deposited onto an awaiting barge. The bodies jumped grotesquely as the crane operator jerked the cable for amusement, laughing as bloody pieces of flesh and body parts splattered and slid on the barge's cambered surface.

"So passed an additional four hundred," Beecher lamented. "For the eight hundred or so men [remaining], though more dead than alive, the ordeal was far from over."

IT WAS DURING THIS postbombing grimness at Takao, Formosa, that Barton Cross—separated from his closest comrades either by death, incapacitation, or unknown shipboard circumstances—teamed up with another ensign, one he only came to know after returning to Cabanatuan from Davao Penal Colony. Like Barton, "Bob" Granston was reeling from loss. Chuck Wilkins had died aboard *Oryoko Maru*. The two Washington natives had been best friends at the University of Seattle and signed up for the Navy Supply Corps together. Barton and Bob forged a bond through a paradoxical combination of need, shared grief, inborn optimism, and the will to survive.

Granston wrote Helen Cross of their survival pact aboard *Enoura Maru*: "It was from this point forward that Bart and I joined forces and shared our fortunes. And we did, in every respect. We slept when we could sleep together to keep one another warm, we evenly divided every morsel of our food and every drop of our water. I am sure you can see why Bart meant so much to me."

All prisoners knew that "buddying" greatly improved survival odds. It had become protocol by this point. Prisoners who withdrew from others, whether due to exhaustion, delirium, or irreversible misery, did not last long.

Over the next twenty days, there would be no secrets between Bart Cross and Bob Granston. The two men came to know as much about each other as any of their respective friends, lovers, or family members had ever known. Indulging in the continuum of stories that had shaped their young lives up to those frigid, dark hours was the only remaining salve that could not be wrested away. With their tacit pact sealed, they moved together to the final ship that would carry them to Japan.

> Barton was a very close friend of mine, and I shall
> always cherish that friendship born in a common struggle.

> Robert Granston to Helen Cross

ON JANUARY 14, THE shrunken prisoner band—shivering, filthy, bandaged, and emaciated—moved from the crippled *Enoura Maru* back to the *Brazil Maru*, which had not been damaged in the American air attack. Those who died in the difficult transfer were thrown overboard. The *Brazil Maru* then weighed anchor and pressed north in a twelve-ship convoy. Inconceivably, on this voyage, the men suffered their greatest hardship since departing Manila.

> During this last trip, food and water were almost non-
> existent. We all became weaker every day. Many went to sleep
> at night and never woke up the next morning. They were
> just simply too weak from cold and lack of food and water to
> carry on.

> Charles Armour to Helen Cross

★   ★   ★

THE SHIP SAILED INTO the coldest Asian winter in forty years. Icy drafts whooshed through the hold as they reached cruising speed—a cruel harbinger of what lay ahead. On the first night out of Takao, twenty men died. *Brazil Maru's* daily death rate rose unabated after that.

Through a winter scrum each morning, just enough light slanted belowdecks to permit a body count of those who had passed away overnight. The dead were first stripped of desperately needed clothing and then piled in a passageway. After each morning count, they were removed to the deck and buried at sea. Only in this manner was initial overcrowding on the third ship relieved. Day and night, chaplains murmured last rites to the point of monotony.

Barton's resilience slowly ebbed aboard the *Brazil Maru*. Less than a day after Bob Wuest's wounded, wasted corpse was cinched and spiraled out of the hold, Jack Ferguson followed in the same manner. One after another, the haunting remains of the dearest friends Barton had ever known—the men he'd bolstered and who had bolstered him—twisted naked and lifeless out of sight.

Until Father Cummings himself died, the good chaplain asked for a moment of silence every evening so that he might offer a brief prayer. His voice grew progressively fainter and weaker until he could no longer speak his comforting refrain: "Eternal rest grant unto them, O Lord, and let perpetual light shine upon them. May the souls of the faithful departed, through the mercy of God, rest in peace. Amen."

Despite the increasingly nightmarish environs, "Bart" and "Bob" always retreated to the transformative refuge of conversation. They moved through the annals of their respective lives—stories large and small, successes and failures, love interests, and their families and homes. Even as hollowed-out men all around scrambled like rodents for the tiniest edible or spoonful of water, even as the ship dodged submarine fire and pitched in the high seas, even as they wallowed in a hold slick with filth and disease and shivered in subfreezing temperatures, the two men indulged in the simple joy of story-telling, sourced entirely from their pasts.

> I came to know all of you, intimately, for Bart
> introduced each of you to me. We swapped endless yarns and
> family stories. Bart described you all in detail and never
> once gave up hope he would see you again . . . In turn, I
> paraded my family life before his eyes. He was fascinated
> by my family, certainly less prominent than the Crosses,
> but it is a warm, close family. There were so many stories
> he wanted to hear over and over again . . . By so doing we
> passed many long hours and forgot for long stretches of
> time the hopelessness of our situation.
>
>   Robert Granston to Helen Cross

THERE WAS A CADENCE to their yarn swappings. One would start with a story about a time, a place, or a life episode. A corresponding chronicle from the other would follow, related in some way to the initial story. Characters from their respective pasts burst out of dusty sterling frames and old leather albums they'd long since left behind. One elaborately rendered scene after another hovered above them like guardian spirits.

Granston's childhood vignettes were in stark relief to Barton's. His renderings were of an alluring world of rural western life on a small farm outside Seattle, Washington. Barton was mesmerized. With all its formalities and unvoiced tensions, Lilac Hedges was galaxies away from the open and affectionate traditions of the Granston family farm. His heart swelled with vicarious pleasure over freedoms he had never even dreamed of.

The simple abundance of a boisterous Granston dinner was a Barton favorite. With each sentence, Bob filled out the dreamscape of an unadorned farm kitchen full of heavenly smells and happy faces, a weathered, wide-board table groaning with freshly harvested delights—all enjoyed amid lively conversation, pea-shooting, and frequent laughter. Barton sat rapt, knees to chest, like a child. He salivated over the menu, but also the textured riches of a raucous, informal, and intensely loving home.

Barton's stories centered on growing up in New Jersey, but also described ventures into New York City, the stuff of dreamy escapes for Bob Granston. Barton waxed on his early taste of independence at Christ School, and his surprising and enduring epiphanies there.

He also told, with a weakening smile, of his truncated baseball and singing careers, both of which reached their zenith in prison camp. Then there was the almost–love of his life, a girl named Eve that he'd met at Pearl Harbor before setting sail for Manila.

Bob Granston was a keen observer, even in his own fragile state. He saw that all Barton's childhood and teen recollections had a similar subtext: of being prodded to become something he was not. Nor did it take Granston long to figure out that the Cross clan hailed from a higher social order than his own, or to grasp that material wealth was no guarantee of happiness.

But despite their differences, or perhaps because of them, the two men bonded like alloyed steel. They talked to exhaustion each evening. The power of such unburdening was surely a comfort to Barton. The simple exercise of seeing his brief life through the compassionate eyes of another both resolved its disappointments and affirmed its value. Only when the final half-light withdrew from the hold each evening and their wasting brethren grew indistinct did Bart and Bob draw close for warmth and doze off.

IN THE LAST FRIGID week of January, Barton reached the limits of human endurance. Snow swirling into the hold could neither revive him nor cool his burning forehead. Granston urged him on by the hour, but a triple assault of dysentery, pneumonia, and infection springing from a hidden head wound—likely obscured by a wild mat of filthy hair—joined forces with exposure, starvation, and thirst to immobilize him.

Barton now depended upon Granston like an infant, and Granston did not disappoint. He divided whatever sustenance came his way—every sip of water and infinitesimal issue of rice was split and shared. He would raise Barton's head, open his mouth, and spoon it in, dose by tiny dose. But by the time they arrived at Moji Port in Japan on January 28, Barton was drifting in and out of consciousness.

> I know I have not spared you much--I have gone into
> great detail that might well have been kept from the Cross
> family. But your letter was a plea for information (good or
> bad) about Bart. It is in answer to that plea and my own
> love for Bart that I have written of all the conditioning
> circumstances that led directly and indirectly to his
> death.
>
>   Robert Granston to Helen Cross

WHEN *BRAZIL MARU* DOCKED at Moji on January 29, a contingent of Japanese military personnel boarded the ship and peered into the hold. At the sight of the five-foot-high corpse pile, they turned and departed in shock. Hours later, the prisoners were instructed to organize in alphabetical order to receive an issue of clothing.

At the call of their name, each prisoner went up to the deck to receive an issue of green flannel Japanese military uniforms, shoes, and woolen overcoats. With Barton unable to sit up, much less stand or talk, Bob Granston made for the ladder when "Cross" was called. He returned to the hold with the chilly garb, damp to the touch and smelling vaguely of mildew and cigarette smoke. He proceeded to dress his friend, still clinging to life but in a feverish stupor.

In due course, Bob's own name was called and he again scaled the ladder to the deck. But when he reached for his clothing issue, Mr. Wada squinted hard at him, then whipped into a fury. Believing he had caught Granston attempting to hoard clothing, Wada barked an unintelligible order, prompting the nearby guard to pummel and punch Bob until he stumbled backward into the hold, where he lay stunned and bleeding as the clothing muster droned on.

On January 30, 500 survivors of the original 1,619 prisoner draft that had departed Manila forty-nine days earlier queued up to debark onto Japanese soil. After the final indignities of head-to-toe disinfectant dousing and the insertion of glass rods up their rectums to test for dysentery, they exited the ship.

Scores of incapacitated were carried off first and laid on the dock. It will never be known if Barton was aware that, in his case, the task was performed by Charles Armour. Stooped and grunting under the weight, a determined Charles gently placed Barton on the dock and then crumbled to a seated position next to him.

Japanese medical examiners, visibly shocked by the group's condition, began their assessments, moving with their clipboards quietly among the men on the cold wooden platform. Their superiors, meanwhile, deliberated over what to do with these diseased and emaciated prisoners of war.

Charles sat glum and silent next to his incognizant friend, waiting his turn to be examined. He had aged dramatically over his imprisonment. The distinctive lope had turned to a halting gait, thanks to beriberi and other assaults on Charles's body. A receding veil of thin blond strands bared a pate dark with freckles, and his once-strong Saxonesque face was hollow, lined, and expressionless. All fierceness and resistance were gone. Back when there was energy and cause for laughter, Charles would joke that for every hair he lost, Barton seemed to gain ten; even now, Barton's resting head was an unruly mass of brown waves.

Remorse rolled over Charles, or perhaps it was regret that he had taken this good and true friend too much for granted for too long. He watched his friend's chest rise and fall, rise and fall, grateful now for every breath Barton drew. He closed the top button on the Japanese overcoat that Bob Granston had put on him, and pulled the collar up around Barton's ears.

How Barton would have laughed at the sight of himself wearing a Japanese uniform, Charles thought. "Over my dead body!" He would have laughed that big, ironic, endearing laugh and thrown his head back the way he always did. As if in response to Charles's musings, Barton inhaled deeply and released an encouraging sigh. But following that exhale, there were no more.

Charles looked on in disbelief, choking back tears. Here was Charles Armour—so willing to take his own life three years earlier, placing others' lives at risk in the process—still alive. And here lay Barton Cross, who had protected him at every turn—not only from the Japanese, but also from himself—dead.

With a spark of the old Charles, he gritted his teeth at the approaching Japanese medical technician. But he did not resist when the gloved examiner crouched down to feel for Barton's pulse, first on his wrist, then on his neck. Detecting none, the examiner unbuttoned the overcoat and turned Barton's body over for a closer look, showing particular interest in the back of his head. After scrawling a few notes on a pad, he moved on to the next case.

It would be fifty-four years before that Japanese medical examiner's findings—slipped untranslated into Barton Cross's long-archived naval personnel file—would be discovered, translated, and the dual causes of his demise revealed.

Beside the date January 30, 1945, was written: "Acute enteritis and death from bomb wound to the head."

EPILOGUE

IN 2009 I REOPENED the long-closed inquiry into my Uncle Barton's death. I requested all documents bearing his name from the International Committee of the Red Cross in Geneva—still the reigning global authority on *prisonniers de guerre*. A year later and after a payment of 100 Swiss francs, the documents arrived. I also procured Barton's naval personnel file from the military records archive in St. Louis.

Both sets of records contained an official copy of Barton's death certificate. It was dated September 14, 1945, curiously, nearly two weeks after the formal Japanese surrender and more than seven months after his passing. The given cause of death was "acute enteritis" (dysentery). But this same ailment, I discovered, was cited as the killer of hundreds of other expired prisoners pulled from *Brazil Maru* on its January 30, 1945, arrival at Moji, Japan. How did they know how these men died so long after the fact? Virtually all their death certificates were created that September, seven months later, and most by the same bilingual Japanese scribe. His name was

"Huryojohokyoku," a very recent hire at General MacArthur's occupation headquarters in Tokyo.

It was impossible to discern on what medical basis this postmortem diagnosis was made. But after reviewing volumes of archives, it appears to have been generic shorthand for a presumptive mix of dysentery, starvation, dehydration, exposure, and unimaginable cruelty. Barton's personnel file, however, contained an additional clue; there was one Japanese document that, unlike every other in his file, had no companion translation. Locating a bilingual Japanese national willing to translate that wartime document was challenging. But I succeeded thanks to the assistance of a family member who works with a team of young Japanese professionals at Patagonia.

The document was a routine prisoner tracking record maintained by Barton's captors. Its first entry was the date Barton was seized from Sternberg Hospital in Manila. The last entry was dated January 30, 1945; the place, Moji, Japan. Between the two, every ailment, medical treatment, and prison camp relocation had been dated and entered with chilling Japanese efficiency. So startling was the translation's final entry, however, that I sought a second translation from an independent source: this time by linguists at the Tokyo office of a prominent US law firm.

The second translation corroborated the first. Entitled "Other Information," the ailment acute enteritis was indeed cited, presumably by the Japanese medic examining prisoners on the Moji dock—both dead and alive. But it was written in a sequence that altered its import entirely: "Acute enteritis, and death from bomb wound to head." Helen Cross had been right all along.

Was this significant omission simply a military snafu, or was it a case of intentional deception intended to hide a friendly fire incident? How is it that this never-translated prisoner record had not been discovered until now? Why hadn't my father, who had pursued the case for four years after the war, found it?

First of all, postwar mishandling of prisoner records and other wartime documents, both by the Japanese in the weeks before their surrender and by Allied occupiers in the months and years afterward, has been uniformly described as deplorable. Thousands of records were destroyed, misfiled, or lost by one party or the other. Secondly, it was not until after 1952, which marked the end of the Allied occupation of Japan, that thousands of war-record-stuffed file cabinets began to be repatriated to the United States. My own conclusion is that Bill Mott's search, which lasted until 1949, ended before the document surfaced in Barton's long-archived personnel file—which probably occurred sometime in the 1950s.

That scenario notwithstanding, the following statistic has never been formally acknowledged by the US government: of the 21,039 POW deaths that occurred aboard Japanese transports during World War II, most were the result of unwitting attacks by either Allied submarines or war planes.

FOR MORE THAN THREE years after the war ended, my grandmother Helen continued to fire off inquiries to political and military powers in Washington, demanding more information about Barton's death. Over time, however, responses to her letters ebbed. Just as fighter aircraft were dumped into the sea, tanks were left to rust on distant Pacific islands, and warships were cut up for scrap, Helen's fierce salvos were quietly filed away.

While waiting for answers that never came, she traveled to Barton's alma mater, Christ School in Arden, North Carolina, to establish the Barton Cross Memorial Scholarship. Deprived of her son's adult years, she chose to memorialize Barton's adolescence by honoring individuals who "best ex-emplified his qualities of character, citizenship, and leadership." Barton had developed these attributes during his time at Christ School, and it helped him—and helped him help others—endure a long and harsh imprison-ment.

Every spring thereafter, until her passing in 1967, Helen made the 750-mile drive to Arden to announce the scholarship winner at the commencement-eve banquet. The recipient was always a member of the junior class whose senior year tuition was to be paid with the award. Helen was known to approach the lectern quietly and make eye contact with each boy as she recalled her son before the hushed assembly.

"Shortly before leaving for the Philippines," she would begin, "Barton spoke lovingly of Christ School, saying that his most cherished ideals were forged through his training and associations there. He also asked that, if he did not return, a cross bearing his name be placed in the school's chapel yard." While that final request has not been fulfilled, a granite memorial was erected in 2011 near the campus chapel bearing his name, along with other alumni killed in foreign wars.

BENNY—OR UNCLE BERT, our own affectionate name for him— met and married Helen Lacey after the war. Over five decades of marital bliss followed. But Benny had another postwar love: preservation of the USS *Enterprise*, both the ship itself and its historic and heroic naval legacy. While most soldiers and sailors who fought in World War II wanted nothing more than to bury those memories and get on with their lives, Benny wanted just the opposite.

He published numerous postwar essays on Pacific naval warfare and firsthand accounts of iconic *Enterprise* battles, both critical sources for this book. He was also instrumental in setting up the USS *Enterprise* (CV-6) Association and helped lead the effort to establish the carrier as a floating museum. It was to be located on the Potomac River near the Washington Monument.

The vision had an auspicious beginning. The most decorated warship in American naval history received a celebrity homecoming in October 1945. One hundred and one fighter planes kicked off the biggest Navy Day celebration on record as they escorted *Enterprise* up the Hudson River at sunrise and into New York Harbor. The thundering flyover had awakened an entire city by the time she tied up at Pier 26.

New York headlines competed to memorialize the occasion: "The

Pride of the Navy Comes Home in Dawn's Early Light"; "The Unsinkable *Enterprise* Enters Harbor as Bands Play"; "Hunter, Home from the Kill"; and "The Big E, Fightin-est Carrier—In!"

Fireboats sprayed gushers, bands played, military units marched down the avenues, and huge crowds of navy Waves and Red Cross girls gathered to cheer the *Enterprise* crew—who obligingly lined the rails and cheered back. Long queues of patriots and their children snaked up her gangplank in good and bad weather, all wanting to board the famous carrier they had been reading about since 1941. They climbed into her turrets, ran their hands along her gun barrels, and toured her cavernous hangars, messes, and wardrooms. Before exiting the ship, they invariably crouched down to touch the grooved Douglas fir planking of her revered flight deck.

On Navy Day proper, the crew traded grateful salutes with President Harry Truman. I can only imagine Benny's pride when *Enterprise*'s night fighter group growled up the Hudson at dusk and put on a show for some four to six million spectators, including an estimated 1.5 million from New Jersey, who lined the opposite banks for miles. The planes roared over the anchored ships in salute formation and then circled back with lights blazing in a V-for-victory formation. Their finale was greeted with deafening cheers—a third and final flyover was in a glorious "E" formation in honor of their mother ship.

Following Navy Day festivities, Truman promptly approved Navy Secretary James Forrestal's request that the *Enterprise* be "permanently enshrined in an appropriate location as a visible symbol of American valor and tenacity in war, and of our will to fight all enemies who assail us."

The president's approval seemed to ensure the carrier's preservation, but over time, budget concerns grew and private fundraising foundered. In 1958, after languishing twelve years at a Bayonne, New Jersey, shipyard, the *Enterprise* was slated for the scrap heap. Benny was devastated.

Several symbolic features of the ship, however, were preserved for posterity. The *Enterprise* bell rests at the entrance to the Naval Academy's

Bancroft Hall and is rung only after midshipmen victories over West Point. The battle flag flown from her tripod mast during the harrowing Battle of Santa Cruz is on permanent display at the Aviation Museum in Pensacola, Florida. Her sixteen-foot-long stern plate, a massive steel work bearing the ship's name in raised letters, greets visitors to Veterans' Memorial Park in River Vale, New Jersey, and her two-story-high anchor marks the entrance to the Washington Navy Yard.

Unfortunately, the plan to crown the new Annapolis football stadium with *Enterprise*'s Sky Control tower was cancelled due to maintenance estimates on its outdated steel construction. But happily, the promised honor was upheld. A cement replica, named *Enterprise* Tower, was erected there instead.

IN 2012, I TRAVELED to England to meet Benny's daughter, Jeanne Marie. I had never met my cousin (who had taken on the nickname Mara) because she moved to England when I was very young. Over scones and a pot of Earl Grey tea, Mara shared difficult wartime memories that still pained, even in her late seventies. She remembered Benny's long absences, and then his homecoming, shortly after which their home in Bethesda burned down. "Sleaford Place," she shuddered. "Terrible."

An accomplished equestrian, Mara said she left home in her late teens and made a living exercising horses owned by a series of wealthy patrons. One of these, a British doctor, became her husband. Dr. and Mrs. Hodgson had no children, but instead dedicated their lives to British dressage and their beloved thoroughbreds. Benny visited Mara and Dr. Hodgson often at their home in Surrey, renewing their bond and healing old scars. Their visits were long, warm, and conversation filled. This, of course, was the joyful and hoped-for outcome that had populated Benny's dreams aboard the wartime *Enterprise*.

Last Christmas, I received a package bearing a British postmark. Inside was a small wrapped gift: Benny's 1930 Annapolis class ring. Mara's enclosed note thanked me again for my visit, saying it had been an important catharsis. Now widowed, she had sold her home in Surrey, she said, and was planning to travel abroad for an indefinite period. She asked that the ring remain in our family forever.

MY FATHER WAS IN Manila in September 1945 when he learned that Barton would not be returning. He contacted the Navy Casualty Branch at the Pentagon to notify them that he would travel immediately to Lilac Hedges to break the difficult news himself—per his 1942 instructions to that office. When he learned that the Casualty Branch had already notified the family by letter, he cancelled his travel plan. Instead of returning home to crushing sadness and certain anger, Bill stayed put and began the long and complicated investigation into Barton's death and the search for his remains.

Four years later, the search yielded results. An army recovery team had discovered a mass grave near Moji Harbor in 1946. These unknowns had been removed to another site, and then to a third location in 1949, at which point they were positively identified. The long-awaited news reached Bill via a cryptic memorandum from the US Army quartermaster at Tokyo after a lengthy stopover at the Bureau of Naval Personnel in Washington.

```
Subject: Cross, Arthur B., Jr., Ens., Identification of
remains


The remains of Unknowns X-385 through X-444, cremated
in a communal urn, British Commonwealth War Cemetery,
Yokohama, Japan, formerly interred at the USAF Mausoleum
#1, Honshu, Japan, have been identified as the recoverable
remains of 302 Allied personnel, one of whom is the subject
named decedent.
```

It is unclear how X-385 through X-444—which would seem to denote 59 Unknowns—came to equal 302 individuals, but at least after four years of searching, Barton's final resting place had been confirmed. Helen and Arthur declined to travel to Japan to view the site; this was left to my father, who promised to take photographs, in what must have been an awkward exchange. In May 1949, he boarded a military transport for the long trans-Pacific flight.

There were a number of familiar stops along the way, likely in connection with his official duties at the time. The itinerary included Midway, Guam, Saipan, Okinawa, and Manila, all postwar American military bases. I frequently imagine him on this somber mission—reflecting back on the amphibians' tear across the Pacific—as his plane lowered through the clouds toward those once hotly contested atolls.

In Tokyo, MacArthur's SCAP headquarters provided a car and driver that took him the twenty-five miles to Yokohama, a journey replete with scenes of a rebuilding country and a populace bent on erasing its belligerent war personality from national memory. When he arrived at the cherry-blossom-adorned British Commonwealth Cemetery of the Allied War Dead, Bill retrieved his camera and looped the brown leather strap around his neck.

The dreaded destination was visible from hundreds of yards away: a large, square, marble columbarium flanked by fields of graves on three sides and topped with a towering white cross. He walked past saluting sentries and line after line of headstones bearing familiar American, English, and Australian surnames. Inside the shrine, he faced a single interior adornment: a polished metal urn anchored in a rectangular marble pedestal.

Above it was etched:

In the urn below rest the ashes of 333 sailors, soldiers and airmen of the British Commonwealth, the United States of America and the Kingdom of the Netherlands who died as prisoners of war in Japan. The names of 232 are inscribed on these walls. The identity of their 51 comrades is unknown. There be of them that have left their name behind that their praises might be reported, and some there be which have no memorial. But their righteousness hath not been forgotten and their glory shall not be blotted out.

Long rows of names were engraved on the facing walls—some very recently. Since the listings were organized by service and country rather than alphabetically, Bill had to first locate the US Navy insignia, beneath which he read through lengthy columns of surnames. Peterson, Church, Goodpaster, Conover, Weeks, Magnusan, Murchison, Austin, Gardner, Butler, McGee, Baker . . . And then, finally, there it was: Arthur Barton Cross Jr., Ensign, USN, age 25.

Did he reach up and run his fingers along the sharply etched letters before surrendering to overwhelming guilt and sorrow? Whatever the answer to that question, my father took advantage of several opportunities in his life to redeem that loss. In many respects, both his professional and personal postwar lives were parallel progressions toward honoring his brother's sacrifice and ensuring that he had not died in vain.

IN 1946, COMMANDER BILL Mott became chief of the navy's International Law Branch and Foreign Claims Office. In this capacity, he served as a delegate to the International Red Cross Conference in Stockholm. I cannot imagine any more productive an outlet for a grieving brother of a perished prisoner of war. In Bill's work as a conference delegate, he played a direct hand in reforming the 1929 Geneva Convention regarding the treatment of war prisoners. Working to ensure that future POWs would not suffer as Barton and his colleagues had—and would live to come home—was both redemptive and a powerful palliative.

Any signatory to the revised and greatly expanded Articles would be bound by their strengthened protections, including proscriptions against torture, acts of violence, and other inhumane treatment. It also required that prisoners be provided adequate housing, food, and clothing, and that medical care be provided. And just as important, it required that any ships carrying sick or wounded prisoners be explicitly marked. The Convention's new Article III—which put in place the strongest protections in history for prisoners of war—was adopted by the Swiss Federal Council in 1949. To date, 196 countries have committed to obey them, including Japan.

CAPTAIN BILL MOTT'S ORDERS to Pearl Harbor had been to serve as legal advisor to the new commander in chief of the Pacific Fleet, Admiral Arthur Radford, a rising star in the constellation of navy admirals. Admiral Radford's and my father's worldviews were identical, especially regarding their postwar commitment to "peace through strength." A veteran of both world wars, Admiral Radford was an ardent and controversial advocate of expanded investment in ship strength and carrier aviation in an era of shrinking military budgets and a civilian-minded Congress. But it was also an era of rising global instability, Radford argued relentlessly, and my father became a lifelong disciple of his fierce opposition to any policy or budget designed to contract American naval strength or readiness, both with respect to ships and personnel. A strong navy, he believed, was also the best protection for crews posted to dangerous places. It would keep future Bartons out of harm's way.

In October 1950, President Truman made a stopover at Oahu en route to his Wake Island meeting on the expanding Korean crisis with General MacArthur. One of my father's most pleasant duties was to accompany the president on his early-morning walks. As the two made their way around the Makalapa Crater one of those mornings, the president and my father got into a conversation on the complicated geopolitics resulting from America's use of the atomic bomb. At some point, Truman shook his cane and said, "Aren't you the young man who brought back the estimates of six hundred thousand American casualties if we invaded mainland Japan?" Bill was prompt with his reply. "Yes, sir, I am."

That, the president said, is why it was the right thing to do.

"As commander in chief, I would never approve an operation where there was an estimate of six hundred thousand American casualties. I had no credible evidence that Emperor Hirohito or the Japanese military had any intention of suing for peace. And that is why I authorized the dropping of the atomic bomb."

This oft-repeated story brought my father both pride and solace. It affirmed his part, however large or small, in preventing a ground invasion of Japan, which saved hundreds of thousands of lives, including his own, if not his brother's. And it had spared their families as well—from a grief he knew too well.

Admiral Mott's last set of active duty orders came at the start of John F. Kennedy's presidency. The 1960 appointment was to serve as the navy's twenty-first judge advocate general. He had in that position another opportunity to keep young men out of harm's way—and also to help bring an end to a tense and dangerous nuclear standoff with Russia.

In the fall of 1962, my father proposed an alternative to mounting Pentagon support for a military strike against Russian-backed, nuclear-armed Cuba. The alternative was for the US Navy to repel approaching arms-laden Russian vessels by establishing a perimeter of American warships around the island nation, cordoning off its seaborne approaches. He had first proposed the idea of a naval "quarantine" (also called a shipping interdiction or defensive maritime zone), to President Eisenhower in 1955. That Oval Office meeting had been convened to evaluate nonbelligerent options for protecting Formosa (now Taiwan) from incursions by Communist-controlled mainland China via the Formosa Strait.

The Cuban Missile Crisis had intensified by the day in October 1962. Finally, after reviewing all his options, President Kennedy, himself a former naval officer and PT boat commander, chose the naval quarantine over the others. After announcing his decision, the president turned to CNO admiral George Anderson and said, "Well, Admiral, it looks as though this is up to the navy." Anderson replied, "Mr. President, the navy will not let you down."

And it didn't. The quarantine was put in place immediately and was an unqualified success. One after another Russian vessel reversed course at the five-hundred-mile arc of American warships arrayed off the coast of Cuba. The standoff ended without a single shot being fired.

This historic action is frequently referred to as a naval blockade, but blockades can be imposed only in times of war, which is why such terminology was carefully avoided, at least at the time. War was precisely what the quarantine sought to prevent. Having been through one war and lost so much, my father saw high value in the tactic of brandishing American naval strength without having to use it. The role he played in helping to end the Cuban Missile Crisis was one of his proudest accomplishments.

It was as a parent, however, that he faced perhaps his best opportunity to compensate for Barton's death. During the Vietnam War, my brother Adam was a US Air Force officer flying intelligence missions over combat zones in the North. From his post in Saigon, he contacted our father at his office in Washington, DC.

Adam had a favor to ask: Could Dad arrange for his temporary detail to the USS *Forrestal*, out in the Gulf of Tonkin? In Adam's mind, "that was where the action was." Our father replied that he could easily arrange it; his good friend and Annapolis classmate Admiral James Reedy was commander of the Seventh Fleet and as such had oversight of the carriers in the Tonkin Gulf. But his response to Adam was an unequivocal "No." Years ago, he told Adam, he had, with the best of intentions, used his influence to arrange another family member's military orders: his brother Barton's.

"That," he said, "is why I no longer play God with orders." It was after my father denied Adam's request that a freak Zuni rocket exploded on the flight deck of the USS *Forrestal*, still in the Gulf of Tonkin, and set off a chain of explosions that sparked a devastating fire; 134 of her crew were killed and another 161 severely injured.

MY SIBLINGS AND I all remember another particular story, just the way my father told it. He gave many speeches throughout his career, as a high-ranking officer in the navy and later as an executive in the private sector, as head of two legal nonprofits he founded, and on behalf of the American Bar Association. After one of these speeches, the story went, a man approached him and introduced himself as a fellow prisoner of Barton's. The man was reportedly near tears and spoke haltingly. "I escaped from that camp where we were imprisoned together," the man told Dad. "But it wasn't supposed to be me—it was Barton they wanted with them. I was the alternate. Only your brother refused to go for fear the Japanese would make good on their threat to execute ten prisoners for every escapee. So I was selected to take his place."

The man said his guilt over this matter had worsened over the years, and when he heard that Dad would be speaking locally, he decided to come and confess to him what had happened. I do not remember what my father replied, only that he thanked the man for his courage and candor, and told him that he, for his own reasons, also struggled with the memory of Barton.

My father told this story infrequently, but often enough and so emotionally that it is etched in my memory and that of my siblings. Before I typed this just now, I called and asked them to tell me again what they remembered of it, and it had not changed. Perhaps we remember this story so well, and other similar ones, because they all seemed to awaken a rarely exposed emotional side of Bill Mott.

We could not get enough of these stories—in part because of how animated he became when he told them. But we also loved them because of their personalized historical content. We heard about Churchill's Map Room code name ("Former Naval Person"), his jumpsuit and drinking habits after midnight, the rakish angle of FDR's cigarette holder, and Madame Chiang's soft southern contralto yet unpopularity with White House domestic staff for the way she clapped her hands when she wanted something. They riveted, always.

Madame Chiang was one of my father's favorite White House visitors, in part, perhaps, because of Helen's Wellesley connection. But he spoke of her often, and when he visited Taiwan during his JAG tenure (1960), he saw her again, and wrote about it in a letter home. "Our visit to the presidential palace was the highlight of the trip. Suffice it to say . . . I felt Madame Chiang stole the show. She is as I remember her from my White House days—a gracious, charming woman. She doesn't look a day older, in fact she has grown more beautiful with age." Madame Chiang apparently remembered him warmly as well; he brought home a sleeve of her paintings she had given him, and also two beautiful painted vases. The letter from which I just quoted lives inside one of them.

The stories were especially seductive because they unmasked a rarely seen side to a deeply emotional man, one that we knew more for his exhortations on parsimony, ladylike behavior, and school performance, and his own mental discipline. They were the one window we had on what lay beneath that tough exterior.

BILL AND ROMIE'S MARRIAGE disintegrated soon after his return from the Pacific. Many factors led to the divorce, not least of which was the corrosive mix of Bill's postwar grief and Romie's own emotional struggles, which had worsened over the lonely two years her husband had been half a world away with Admiral Turner and the amphibians. But even out of this personal defeat, an opportunity for love and family emerged.

A year after the divorce, Bill met Edith Grace, a Boston native and wartime analyst for the Manhattan Project at the Massachusetts Institute of Technology. Shortly after their nuptials in 1947, the newlyweds moved to Pearl Harbor, where the first of four more Mott children was born. Not only did my father find love, but he built the large, boisterous, and loving family that had eluded him in his own childhood. We all went on to have families of our own, and restored that cousin joy interrupted one summer evening, decades earlier, by the argument on our grandmother's porch.

PART OF MY QUEST to repair that broken day was not just to learn our Uncle Barton's story but also to track down the men who had witnessed it.

I wanted to know how his fellow POWs had gotten on with their lives, and whether part of Barton had remained with them. Some were simply lost after coming home, but others had moved on just as I had imagined Barton would have.

Charles Armour's mother also received a letter from the navy in September 1945, but hers relayed that Charles was alive and would be returning stateside—to a naval hospital in Memphis, 125 miles from their home in Little Rock. Charles would need time to recuperate, the letter said, and discouraged the family from visiting him in the hospital. Finally, one day in October 1945, a taxi pulled up to the curb at 501 Holly Street, and Charles Armour stepped out. His sister Jane had an indelible memory of that moment.

Jubilant when she looked out the window and saw her brother emerge from the taxi, she raced out the front door to greet him. But Charles was oddly quiet and standoffish. "On the surface he was home, but he . . . looked at me like I was a stranger," she recalled. Charles later told the family about his beriberi, which had damaged his heart. He was also being treated for dysentery and scurvy, and the scars on his face and hands were from multiple skin cancer surgeries he'd undergone at the Memphis hospital.

Charles's ailments were not all physical. He frequently sat at home by himself, staring at nothing in particular. "I guess he was just remembering things," Jane said. In the afternoons, he would dress in his naval uniform and go to the town movie theater to watch newsreels and movies about the war. Sometimes he would sit through the same show two or three times. "He didn't know anything about what had gone on, what happened in the war, what it all looked like," Jane said.

Charles married a nurse that he'd met at the Memphis Naval Hospital. Following a simple ceremony, Charles and Millie had a celebratory dinner at the Peabody Hotel and danced to Al Jolson. Charles died of a heart attack in 1953.

Widow Millie recalled years later that Charles never could seem to get enough to eat, especially rice. Ironically, he had insisted she cook it the way the Japanese did, steamed and served in balls. He told her that the prisoners whittled away the hours trading favorite home recipes. They had sustained themselves on the memory of the tastes and smells of home-cooked food. They would get into fights over whose mother was the best cook, he'd told her, and showed her his faded navy cap where he had stored the recipes away. "Sad," Millie recalled.

When he talked about his time as a prisoner, which was infrequent, it was usually late at night while they were lying in bed. He talked a lot about that tennis court, she remembered, and the long voyage to Japan. But he got uncomfortable talking about the latter because he said it reflected badly on our own. "If someone died on the prison ship," he said, "others would scratch at them and drink their blood." Asked if Charles had done that, Millie replied she didn't know, he never said, but that he frequently woke up at night screaming and sitting bolt upright. At one point, he warned her: "If I start fighting you, if I start touching you and screaming, don't fight back."

In an interview shortly after his 1945 release, one unidentified officer who survived the forty-nine-day journey from Manila to Moji told a newsman, "Yes, the Japs are as bad as you say. But we, the three hundred or so [that survived], we are devils, too. If we had not been devils, we could not have survived. When you speak of the good and the heroic, don't talk about us. The generous men, the unselfish men, are the men we left behind."

WITH ONLY A LETTER to Helen Cross postmarked November 1945 and a long-defunct return address to go on, I searched endlessly for Robert Granston, the other man who was with Barton at the end. Finding no obituary, I looked in every veteran database, directory, and archive. After two years of searching, my persistence finally paid off. I came across a transcript of an "oral history" interview he had given in 2002—at a tiny public library in Palm Coast, Florida. With that, I went to the electronic White Pages for Palm Coast and located a telephone number. When I dialed it, Bob Granston answered on the second ring.

His first reaction to my stumbling introduction was shock—then tears. Bob said he had just been thinking about Barton the other day, remembering their final hours together. He was eighty-nine years old. I flew to Florida to see him the following week. When I pulled my rental car up to his house and saw a pair of matching Japanese-made Lexuses in the driveway, I suspected this was a man who had forgiven his former enemies and gotten on with his life.

Unlike Charles Armour, Bob Granston had survived the war with body, mind, heart, and soul intact. He told me he weighed 102 pounds at his release, but once returned to a hearty diet of Granston farm food, he was up to 190 pounds in no time. He credited his survival of tropical diseases and harsh treatment to the powerful immunities he gained from a childhood full of farm dirt, germs, and love.

One month and a day after his release, Bob married his high school sweetheart, Norma, the girl he had described in detail to Barton in those final dark and frigid hours aboard the *Brazil Maru*. Two children, Jeff and Sharon, soon followed. After earning a Stanford MBA, he moved his family to Washington, DC, where Bob continued his navy career for thirty more years. After retiring as a captain, he moved to Florida.

PERHAPS THE MOST REWARDING connection I made in my commemorative search for Uncle Barton was with his namesake, my cousin Barton Cross-Tierney, Aunt Rosemary's son. This was the young cousin with whom we had been playing badminton when loud voices on the porch broke the peace at Lilac Hedges back in the 1960s.

The announcement that her brother would not be returning began Aunt Rosemary's long descent from life of the party to angry, depressed, and increasingly alcohol dependent. She married briefly after the war, but reportedly only to sire a son to "replace" her brother. She succeeded in this—and named that one son Barton Cross-Tierney—and then promptly divorced the father. It would not be her last divorce.

As children, we were always cautious around Aunt Rosemary. She had a penchant for sudden and terrifying outbursts—at the navy, at my father, at young Barton, and even at our grandmother Helen, whom we called Kiki. Rosemary's impaired ability to parent, however, provided Kiki a special opportunity: she played a dominant role raising our Cousin Barton, who bears a striking resemblance to his namesake.

Careers, family, and Cousin Barton's move to the West Coast in his twenties resulted in our losing touch for decades. But after another determined search, and with the help of my sister Diane Mott Davidson, I located him. He had moved back to New Jersey and lived within minutes of where this story began. I made that eerily familiar drive from Washington, DC up to Monmouth County a week later. It was a long-deferred and happy reunion.

On some level, we all knew that Rosemary had started the row on the porch, but we knew nothing of the unresolved sadness at the heart of it. The impact that confusing and painful experience had on me did not diminish with time. I couldn't solve it as an eight-year-old, but in researching and writing this account as an adult—and connecting with the characters who had shaped it—I found a measure of peace and a way to honor my uncle's surprising legacy. His was the big heart that had bestowed on fellow prisoners a will to get to the next day, a love born in the twilight games of three Jersey brothers. From Barton came the brotherhood that, even after his death, helped forge our family and its deeds.

On that unforgettable return to New Jersey, my cousin produced a dust-covered cardboard box with no markings on the outside. We sat cross-legged on the floor and opened it together. Inside were the numerous letters from fellow prisoners, Uncle Barton's posthumously awarded Purple Heart, and a cache of old family photographs, letters, and other archives crucial to this story. Cousin Barton had stored that box for nearly twenty years before my visit. He had never opened it.

Afterword

I thought it would take a year or two to excavate and reconstruct this story. It took me ten years. I started by sorting through documents at my dining room table, which back then fit into a single box. I now rent an office, and my archival cache has expanded to fill two file cabinets and the surfaces of two large tables. They are crammed and stacked with timelines, maps, documents, letters, and unpublished and privately published recollections, memoirs, and letters from men imprisoned with Barton in the Philippines; men who served on the USS *Enterprise*, the USS *Rocky Mount*, and the USS *Eldorado*; and men who served in the White House Map Room from 1942 to 1945. I have two ceiling-height bookcases as well, filled with volumes on the above subjects, many long-out-of-print primary sources procured from antique booksellers after lengthy waits.

My inquiry took me from the National Prisoner of War Museum and Archives on the grounds of the notorious Confederate prison camp in Andersonville, Georgia, to navy bases, hospitals, and former prison camps in the Philippines, to the homes of onetime war prisoners and colleagues of Barton Cross and to that of my father's first White House Map Room hire, the late George Elsey. Interlibrary loans allowed me access to reels of microfiched articles from long-defunct New Jersey newspapers. I interviewed dozens of individuals who collectively knew the three brothers, both in peace and in war.

My interviews with these old colleagues, as well as Helen's diary entries, penned recollections, and letters to the Cross family, helped me flesh out their actions and comprehend the depth of their relationships, particularly those formed among the ensigns and other prisoners. I was surprised at the number of human details—the gestures, the mannerisms, the dialogue and expressions—that these men recalled, and how vivid the moments remained. For my immediate family members, I also drew from my own memories of their habits—Benny pinching his nose constantly, and my father always clearing his throat before speaking, or raising his finger to make a point.

Other key resources were the Roosevelt Presidential Library in Hyde Park, New York; the MacArthur Memorial Archives in Norfolk, Virginia; the Truman Presidential Library in Independence, Missouri; the Naval Historical Center at the Washington Navy Yard; the National Personnel Records Center in St. Louis; the National Archives; the International Red Cross in Geneva; Ateneo University in Manila; the US Naval Institute in Annapolis, Maryland; and student archives at the US Naval Academy, Wellesley College, Christ School for Boys, the Citadel, and the University of North Carolina at Chapel Hill.

In the digitized Japanese war crime tribunal records located online, I discovered that Charles Armour's nearly lifelong home was the house of his parents, built at 501 Holly Street, Little Rock, Arkansas. I learned that long after the Armour clan departed, it was purchased by nonfiction author and editor James Morgan, who wrote a fascinating book about the unique home and all its prior occupants. Jim provided incredibly valuable insight on Charles Armour, and later, excellent input on this entire story. I am proud to call him my friend.

I wrote hundreds of letters over the course of my research, and to my delight and surprise, I received a number of long and informative replies, many of which led to unforgettable meetings and telephone calls.

In January 2005 I traveled to the Philippines with a group of former veterans and prisoners who had fought there, and their families. Our group was feted by Filipino dignitaries throughout Manila—all the way up to Malacanang Palace—in celebration of the sixtieth anniversary of that city's liberation from the Japanese. We stayed at the Manila Hotel, across from the Army and Navy Club of Manila, and from there traveled to every prison camp on Luzon.

The trip to the Philippines took place very early in my quest. At the time, I understood that Barton had been wounded and was treated at Sternberg

Hospital, but I still did not know where he was taken after January 1, 1942. He was not rostered at Cabanatuan until late spring of that year. While the Philippines trip filled critical blanks, it did not solve that mystery. Where were the hospital patients in that intervening period? While inquiries wended their way to one possible source after another, I delved into other parts of the story.

Fortunately, my father gave several interviews about his time at Naval Intelligence, in the White House, and with Admiral Turner, and his accounts are also found in a number of history books. I found his Naval Intelligence and White House correspondence files, ordered chronologically from 1940 to 1943, after he passed away in 1997. These were a fascinating and potent primary source for this book.

Benny's first-person perspective is reflected throughout this story. Fortunately, he wrote eyewitness accounts of many of his *Enterprise* experiences— including the Wake Island bomber delivery in November 1941, the attack on Pearl Harbor, the carrier's early hit-and-run raids, the Doolittle Raid, and the seminal sea battles at Midway and Santa Cruz. Some were published in USNA's *Shipmate* magazine, but my father also had a complete file of his brother's letters and war essays, virtually all written from "the perspective of the antiaircraft officer." Benny's camaraderie with war correspondents resulted in personal anecdotes recalled in the books they wrote about their experiences on the *Enterprise*, especially their early coverage of the Pacific Front.

All the while, I continued to search for clues on what happened to the Sternberg navy patients after the fall of Manila. I regularly checked for new entries in the Veterans History Project database of interviews being conducted around the country. It was here, in 2007, that I got my first big break. In one such interview, a nurse who had served at Sternberg Hospital early in the war described the chaotic New Year's Eve when the army patients were removed to the Manila docks for evacuation. The interviewer asked, "What happened to the navy patients?" She replied, "I don't know, I was sent to Corregidor after that. They just stayed there, I guess."

That interview had been conducted under the auspices of the navy's medical branch, the Bureau of Medicine and Surgery (BUMED). I promptly contacted BUMED, and after several referrals around a very large bureaucracy, I was connected to its historian in Washington, DC. The gentleman gave me some useful leads, and almost as an afterthought added an astounding additional piece of information: the Philippines had closed most of its American military facilities (airfields, bases, hospitals) in the mid-1990s, and had been boxing and returning American files to the respective military units stateside over a period of years. It seemed that a large number of medical files from the 1940s had been discovered in a storage area at the former Cavite Naval Station, since renamed Sangley Point Naval Station. Apparently they had been overlooked in the file repatriation process and were very recently shipped to BUMED, he told me. They were in storage right there, on-site.

At the time of this discovery, BUMED was headquartered on "Navy Hill," a historic campus of buildings, including the old naval observatory, located across the street from the State Department in Washington, DC—a thirty-minute drive from my home. When I arrived, the gentleman on the phone led me to an unheated storage area filled with brown file boxes. They were not labeled, much less alphabetized, so I just sat down on the floor and went through each and every one.

Box after box contained daily records kept by the navy doctors, pharmacist's mates, and corpsmen of the men they treated after the Japanese bombing of the Cavite Navy Yard. This medical staff moved with and continued to care for these patients at Sternberg Hospital and beyond—until they and their patients together became prisoners of the Japanese. Not only did I now know where Barton Cross had been during that missing period and what his condition was, in astounding detail, I had actually toured these intervening prison holds—Santa Scholastica Women's College and Pasay School—during my trip to the Philippines, so I knew exactly where they were and what they looked like.

When my *cousin* Barton came to my mother's funeral at Arlington National Cemetery in January 2008, he brought with him our grandmother Helen's diaries from the 1940s, which had been in another box he saved from Lilac Hedges after the house was sold. Helen's entries were so powerful, unique, and relevant, I knew I had to incorporate her diarist voice. In this same time frame, I arranged for the translation of an all-important Japanese document in Barton's personnel file, the only one lacking a companion English translation.

Slowly, from this accumulating trove, I assembled the story of *The Jersey Brothers*. It took longer than I had planned, but it was worth the wait.

—SALLY MOTT FREEMAN

Acknowledgments

When I stumbled upon my father's White House correspondence files shortly after his death, I was shocked and thrilled in equal measure. How long, I wondered, had this historic cache—found stacked behind a cabinet in the rear of my parents' attic—been up there? That discovery, along with a curled black-and-white photograph of the three brothers with "Christ School" written on the back, marked the beginning of this long journey. But this effort was emphatically not a solo quest; scores of people helped me along the way.

For their love, patience, and faith in this project, I am deeply grateful to the following people: my husband, John Freeman, who provided insightful commentary on more drafts than he may care to recall; my two sons, Christopher and Bobby Lawrence, for their early reads and unwavering support, and also my stepson Alexander Freeman for his uncanny ability to produce file cabinets out of thin air; to my siblings, Janie Mott Fritz, Adam Sutherland Mott, Diane Mott Davidson, Lucy Mott Faison, and Bill Mott Jr., and my cousins, Barton Cross-Tierney and Mara Mott Hodgson, for sharing their own memories and family archives; to my late brother-in-law, beloved Captain Tom Fritz, for his early feedback and accumulated trove of stories told him by my father and, as a former chief of staff at the Office of Naval Intelligence, his expert ability to interpret their high relevance; and to Bremen Schmeltz of Patagonia, Inc., attorneys Bob Lawrence and Mark Weeks, and translators Kayoko Morimitsu and Jennifer Connelly of the Tokyo office of Orrick, Herrington & Sutcliff LLP, for their invaluable assistance in translating Japanese documents.

Thanks also to my many-decade friend and Sweet Briar classmate, Megan Morgan, for her persistent faith, insightful comments, reliable wit and humor, and technical expertise in readying this manuscript for submission; to Major General Matthew Caulfield, USMC (Ret.), I offer a smart salute for his generous military review of an early draft, which greatly improved key sections on the US Marines and the amphibious campaign, and to both he and his wife, Patricia, for all those delightful and encouraging dinners at the Army Navy Club on Farragut Square. I am also indebted to the late Heno Hutson, Citadel graduate, US Marine, Christ School graduate and, later, its headmaster, for opening Christ School's door to me and making key introductions—to Denis Stokes, director of Christ School's External Affairs, and Paul Krieger, headmaster. These gentlemen, together with Mary Pope Maybank Hutson and Claire Dennison Griffith, provided valuable insight into Christ School's history and culture.

Thanks, too, to the following individuals, who gave of their knowledge, resources, moral support, and time in so many different ways: Ron Parsons, USMC (Ret.), Grace Lourence Brunner, Ted and Diane Cadwaller, Elsie Zamora, Mike Rawl, Kathleen Kernisan, Ann Brinsmead, Leigh and Rick Leverrier, Liz Haile Hayes, Barbara Kafka, Al Leonard, Betty Jo Dominick, John Duff, Tad Tharp, Lynn O'Roarke Hayes, Anita McBride, former Chief of Staff to First Lady Laura Bush and board member, White House Historical Association, and to family friend Kevin Kinsella, at whose San Diego home I typed "The End" in front of a window overlooking the mighty Pacific.

My deep respect and gratitude are also due to PhD historians and Mott family history experts Cousin Margaret "Peg" Steneck and her husband, Nicholas Steneck; Judith and the late Duane Heisinger for sharing their painstaking research regarding the movement of navy prisoners of war in the Philippines; to Robert Granston, for filling in so many blanks, and to both he and his wife, Iris, for their gracious hospitality; to John Lukacs, for his superb research and book, *Escape from Davao*, and for introducing me to the late Colonel Jack Hawkins, USMC, a Davao escapee; to Dee Grashio, widow of another escapee, Sam Grashio; to the late Roger Mansell, preeminent archivist of Pacific POW databases; to archivist James Zobel, MacArthur Memorial Archives, as well as the archivists at the Citadel, Wellesley College, USNA, UNC Chapel Hill, the *Asbury Park Press*, and Bernadine at the Morris County Clerk's Office; to Washington Navy Yard historian Jack Green, archivists Randy Sowell, Truman Presidential Library, and Bob Parks, FDR Presidential Library, and Don Pettijohn, Andersonville, GA, National Prisoner of War Museum; to Sandra Rosenquist, daughter of Harold Rosenquist, for sharing her recollections and a copy of her father's wartime diary; to author Barrett Tillman, for his canon of excellent books and articles on the USS *Enterprise*, and for sharing his early interviews with Benny Mott. I am also grateful to the heroes who make up the USS *Enterprise* Association, and Benny's *Enterprise* shipmates, Barney Barnhill and Bernard Peterson.

On the craft of writing a book of this nature, there is another group of friends and mentors to whom I am deeply grateful: the marvelous instructors, my fellow board members, and the strong literary community at the Writer's Center, with particular thanks to Barbara Esstman, Jim Mathews, Tom Young, Catherine Mayo, and Ken Ackerman; and the professors and classmates at the Iowa Summer Writing Festival, where during a transformative few weeks the structure for telling this story emerged. And last but not least, I am endlessly grateful to my all-star ICM literary agent, Binky Urban, and her colleague Molly Atlas, for their enthusiastic embrace of this life project, as well as to my all-star team at Simon & Schuster: Executive Editor extraordinaire Priscilla Painton, president and publisher Jon Karp, assistant editors Megan Hogan and Sophia Jimenez; just the best!

Notes

1: APRIL 1942, LUZON, THE PHILIPPINES

6–7   At approximately 1100 hours: Details of December 8–10 Japanese attacks on Cavite Naval Base and Manila: Clay Blair Jr., *Silent Victory: The U.S. Submarine War Against Japan* (Annapolis, MD: Naval Institute Press, 1975), 129–35.

9   Barton missing from USS *Otus*, December 10, 1941: *Otus* Ship's Log, December 10, 1941, National Archives (NARA), College Park, MD.

10   US Navy patients left behind at Sternberg Hospital:

- Recollections of Captain Ann Bernatitus, USN (nurse): Oral history dated January 25, 1994. Bernatitus recalled the shock of navy nurse Bertha Evans: "The Army got their patients down [to the docks] and put them on a hospital ship. Bertha said, 'What about the Navy patients? What's supposed to happen to them?' Nothing. They just sat there." Historian, Bureau of Medicine and Surgery (BUMED), Washington, DC.

- *Pass in Review* (newsletter of the Idaho Military Historical Society and Museum) interview with Dorothy Danner, nurse, USN: "On December 31, they were really jolted when the army patients were rushed down to the port area to be taken aboard an inter-island ship bearing a huge red cross. They wondered, why not our navy patients? They thought they would be evacuated any minute."

11   Charles Armour's fragile mental state and attempted suicide prior to the outbreak of war was disclosed in a letter written to Canacao Hospital personnel by the USS *Louisville* ship's doctor. Armour's file, National Personnel Records Center, St. Louis.

11   "A total of 224 officers and enlisted men:" George Korson, *At His Side: The Story of the American Red Cross Overseas in World War II* (New York, Coward-McCann Inc., 1945), 22.

12   Over the next several months: Re Prisoner movement from Canacao to Sternberg, Santa Scholastica, Pasay, and Cabanatuan:

  • Captain L. B. Sartin (Medical Corps, USN) kept a journal of the movements of all medical personnel and patients (later prisoners) that had been on the original Canacao hospital patient roster (BUMED).

  • Pharmacist's Mate Robert Kentner recorded medical personnel and patient movement from outbreak of hostilities until February 5, 1945. Entries included descriptions of the patient marches and boxcar ordeals. "Kentner's Journal" was recovered from Sangley Point, Philippines, in September 1960. Source: BUMED, Washington, DC.

  • Letters to Cross family from surviving prisoners, and UNC/Chapel Hill alumni newsletter obituary on A. Barton Cross.

  • Chi Phi *Chuckett* article on Cross, November 1945 issue.

13   The Kempeitai eyed the navy patients and:

  • "We were the only American unit left behind in Manila": Captain Robert G. Davis (Medical Corps, USN), Journal, 1941–1945.

  • "Dr. Kentner's Journal" also confirms the capture of USN medical personnel and their navy patients from Sternberg Hospital on January 1–2, 1942.

15   He didn't want his family to know: Barton Cross "Happy Christmas" telegram sent from Army and Navy Club, and MacArthur radiogram (original, printed on heavy card stock) re wounded patient evacuation from Manila to Australia aboard SS *Mactan*: William C. Mott, official correspondence file, 1940–1943.

2: BENNY

30 "Battle Order Number One": Captain E. Bertram Mott (USN, ret.), *Shipmate*, May 1985.

32 *Enterprise* return to Pearl Harbor following Japanese attack: Edward P. Stafford, *The Big E: The Story of the USS* Enterprise (New York: Ballantine Books, 1962), 14–60.

38 "Hundreds of thousands of pounds": Ibid., *Big E*, 33.

38 "It's up to you carrier boys now": Eugene Burns, *Then There Was One: The* USS *Enterprise and the First Year of War* (New York: Harcourt Brace & Co., 1944), 18.

3: HELEN

47 Barton Cross was born prematurely (Fall River, MA), while Helen and Arthur were touring textile plants for Arthur's company. Fall River was a strong northeastern textile center at the time.

49 "One eleven-year-old neighbor": Interview with Bill and Benny's childhood friend Al Leonard, March, 2006.

4: BILL

52 Merchant ship sinkings by U-boats along US East Coast: David Kennedy, *Freedom from Fear: The American People in Depression and War, 1925–1945* (New York: Oxford University Press, 1999), 488.

52 District of Columbia's transition to wartime footing: David Brinkley, *Washington Goes to War* (Thorndike, ME: Thorndike Press, 1988), 215–20.

54 "I have my eye on a chap named Mott": John McCrea, Oral History, *Setting Up Map Room in White House and Other Incidents in Connection with Service There*, March 1973, FDR Presidential Library, Hyde Park, New York, 4.

54 "Fix up a room for me like Churchill's": George Elsey, *An Unplanned Life: A Memoir* (Columbia: University of Missouri Press, 2005), 18.

55 USNA induction protocols in the 1930s: Kendall Banning, *Annapolis Today* (New York: Funk & Wagnalls Company, 1938), 65–79.

56 Snellen vision tester used at USNA: Ibid., 7–12.

61 "Dear Benny, My new job is quite interesting": WCM official correspondence file, April 1942.

61 WCM Republican background, working for a Democratic president: from
    the John Toland interviews:

    The first time the President came into the Map Room when I was
    there—I hadn't been there very long—the Secret Service announced,
    "The President of the United States." The Secret Service was not allowed
    to remain in the room, so I took over the president's wheelchair. Now, we
    had a lot of equipment in there, and we put ramp-coverings over all the
    wires so you could wheel his chair over them. First I took him around and
    showed him the disposition of the fleet. We had a file cabinet in the corner
    and somehow I got the wheelchair stuck in the corner between the map of
    North Africa and the file cabinet. And the damn thing wouldn't come out.
    You know how the little wheel in the back goes cross wise? The sweat began
    to pour down my back, and I thought of all the places they sent naval of-
    ficers who got presidents stuck in corners. Like Iceland. And the President
    looked up at me and said, "Young man, are you trying to file me?" Well, this
    kind of broke the ice and I had sense enough to straighten the wheel and
    got him out of there.

    Well, my grandfather was chairman of the New Jersey State Republican
    Committee. So was my uncle, after him. The President eventually found
    me out and kidded me about it. But anyway my grandfather considered the
    family disgraced because I went to work for "that man." I tried to explain to
    him, you know, naval officers follow orders. These were my orders. When I
    finally got leave to visit Rockaway [NJ] my grandfather was still upset about
    this—he wouldn't even listen to the fireside chats—and my grandmother
    said, "Why don't you go in and tell Grandfather that story. It's a good
    story." So I went into his study, and he was sitting at his roll top desk. He
    listened very quietly while I told the story, kind of rapidly. When I repeated
    the punch line, "Young man, are you trying to file me?" in a heartbeat, my
    grandfather said, "Young man, you have just missed the opportunity of the
    century."

62 "Every task force, every convoy": War Secretary Stimson's diary entry, April
    12, 1942.

63 Map Room procedures and personnel memoranda: Boxes 194 and 195,
    Roosevelt Presidential Library, Hyde Park, NY.

63 Map Room cables: Robert Sherwood, *Roosevelt and Hopkins: An Intimate History* (New York: Harper & Brothers, 1948), 498–510.

64 Map Room initiate process and annotated "Three Monkeys" cartoon vignette: George Elsey, *An Unplanned Life*, 20–48.

65 In penning Mott's promotion, Captain McCrea wrote:

> "The Situation Room at the White House, which is now administered by Lieutenant Mott, is a receiving room for all military matters of interest to President Roosevelt. It is the function of Lieutenant Mott to collect and organize all military intelligence of interest to the President.
>
> Mott must have many contacts with high ranking officers of our own military as well as officers of the British Chiefs of Staff. [H]e is entrusted with specific directives dealing with most secret matters by the President, Mr. Harry Hopkins, Admiral Leahy, myself and others. Also, in my frequent absence, Lieutenant Mott is the Senior Naval officer present in the White House to carry out naval matters.
>
> In view of these responsibilities as well as his outstanding performance of his duties and furtherance of the prestige of the navy, his promotion to the rank of Lieutenant Commander is recommended."

5: CABANATUAN, SPRING 1942

72 Prisoner work details, rising incidence of disease and death, and other insights and observations on life at Cabanatuan: Lieutenant Colonel William E. Dyess, *The Dyess Story* (New York: G.P. Putnam's Sons, 1944), 120–37; Duane Heisinger, *Father Found: Life and Death as a Prisoner of the Japanese in World War II* (Maitland, FL: Xulon Press, 2003), 237–64; Kenneth Wheeler, "Friends," in . . . *For My Children* (unpublished memoir); Donald Wills, *The Sea Was My Last Chance* (London: McFarland and Co., 1992), 26–35; Bob Wodnik, *Captured Honor: POW Survival in the Philippines and Japan* (Washington State University Press, 2003), 59–68.

6: WHITE HOUSE MAP ROOM, APRIL 1942

74 WCM routine in Map Room, examining incoming cables, adjusting grease pencil markings on maps: Elsey, *Unplanned Life*, 19–25.

76 MacArthur press releases from Philippines: Richard Connaughton, *MacArthur and Defeat in the Philippines* (New York: Overlook Press, 2001), 223–28.

77 Personnel losses at Pearl Harbor: National Park Service Historical Statistics, USS *Arizona* Memorial, Hawaii.

80 Note: the navy's Bureau of Navigation was responsible for all naval personnel issues in early 1942. It was renamed Bureau of Personnel (BUPERS) later that year.

7: "THIS FORCE IS BOUND FOR TOKYO"

83 Re Admiral Halsey: "perfect willingness" to divide the Pacific Ocean with the Japanese. We'll take the top half, they can have the bottom": James Hornfischer, *Neptune's Inferno: The US Navy at Guadalcanal* (New York: Bantam Books, 2011), 210.

85 Re Task Force 16 and Doolittle Raid mission recollections: Bertram Mott, "Memories of the Tokyo Raid," *Shipmate*, 1961; Bernard Peterson, telephone interview with author (November 2007); *Briney to the Blue*, Petersen's self-published battle recollections, 48–49; James Barnhill, telephone interview with author (November 2007); Barnhill's privately published battle recollections, *My Enterprise Battles*.

89 "The Dauntless pilot had spotted an enemy patrol vessel fifty miles ahead": Stafford, *Big E*, 78.

89–90 Additional details on Task Force 16 formation and Doolittle Raid: Ibid., 74–79.

8: BARTON, 1930–1941

97 Hazing that Barton endured at the Citadel is detailed in letter from Helen Cross to USNA commandant.

97 A detailed description of plebe hazing at the Citadel: Pat Conroy, *My Losing Season* (New York: Bantam Books, 2002), 100–107.

99–107 Details of Barton's abbreviated tenure at USNA: Midshipman A. B. Cross Jr. USNA student file, Nimitz Library, USNA Archives, Annapolis, MD.

9: THE PERILS OF ESCAPE—AND A LITTLE BASEBALL

116 Ten-and-one squads and execution of Staunton Ross Betts: Tarleton E. Woods, *March of Death: An American Soldier's 1,216 Days as a POW of the Japanese* (Spartanburg, SC: Honoribis Press, 2006), 37–38.

117–118 William Wordsworth, "Lines Composed a Few Miles Above Tintern Abbey on Revisiting the Banks of the Wye During a Tour," July 13, 1798.

119–20 Description of Charles Armour's house in Little Rock, AR, perspectives on his childhood and family relationships: James Morgan, *If These Walls Had Ears: The Biography of a House* (New York: Warner Books, 1996), 43–90.

121–22 Barton Cross formed a prisoner baseball team and arranged a game with the Japanese guards: "In Memoriam on Brother Cross," Chi Phi *Chuckett*, November 1945; included stories about his imprisonment, informed by interviews with fellow prisoners.

10: A BROTHER'S BURDEN: THE SEARCH

124–25 Newspaper article and photograph of Ensign A. B. Cross noting his status as missing in action: *Red Bank (NJ) Register*, March 12, 1942, Rutgers University Archives, microfiche obtained via interlibrary loan with Montgomery County Library, Rockville, MD.

133–34 Captain Newsom's letter from Darwin, Australia, to Bill Mott: WCM correspondence file. Same letter also found in Barton Cross's USN personnel file.

11: MIDWAY

142 Admiral King's perspective, judgment, and personality: Andrew Roberts, *Masters and Commanders: How Four Titans Won the War in the West, 1941–1945* (New York: HarperCollins, 2009), 195, 404–8.

145–49 Eyewitness recollections of Midway battle: Benny Mott essay and letters to Bill Mott; Peterson, Midway chap., *Briney to the Blue*, and author interview; Barnhill, *My Enterprise Battles*, and telephone interview with author; Stafford, *Big E*, 82–106.

146 "a wiry, energetic man": Ibid., 91.

146 "From stem to stern": Ibid., 93.

146 "On the flank of the enemy's anticipated thrust": Arnold Olsen, Midway, USS *Enterprise* CV-6 Association Public Affairs Issue.

147 B. Barnhill filming battle: James "Barney" Barnhill, self-published battle recollections, *Galloping Ghost.*

150 "On the way back to Pearl the radio was busy": Stafford, *Big E*, 117.

12: UNDER SIEGE: JN-25

152 "Dear Bill, I haven't had much time to write, as you might imagine": WCM official correspondence file, June 1942.

155–58 *Chicago Tribune* leak that US had broken Japanese naval code (JN-25) and WCM White House meeting with Captain Larry Safford: transcript of WCM interview with John Toland obtained from Franklin D. Roosevelt Presidential Library, Hyde Park, NY; and Clay Blair Jr., *Silent Victory: The U.S. Submarine War against Japan* (Annapolis MD: Naval Institute Press, 1975), "The Midway Security Leak," 256–60.

13: TO DAVAO: *EN AVANT!*

160 "There was one overriding thought on every prisoner's mind: would [Davao] be better than Cabanatuan?" *Life* magazine interview with Mellnik and McCoy, published February 7, 1944, following their escape, return to the United States, and lifting of gag order.

163–65 Journey from Cabanatuan to Davao Penal Colony: Kenneth R. Wheeler, "For My Children" chapter: "Davao Penal Colony"; Heisinger, *Father Found*, 329–39; Davao references in letters to Mott/Cross family from Barton Cross's fellow prisoners.

14: AND THEN THERE WAS ONE: USS *ENTERPRISE* VERSUS JAPAN

169 "Dear Benny, The suspense I have gone through since hearing from you last": WCM correspondence file, October 1942.

173–75 MacArthur claimed Nimitz had violated the divided command structure: James P. Drew, LCDR, USN, "Tarnished Victory: Divided Command in the Pacific and Its Consequences, et al." (Thesis, Fort Leavenworth, KS, 2009).

173–75 Dispute between MacArthur and Nimitz regarding Guadalcanal and for scarce military resources in Pacific: Blair, *Silent Victory*, 295; Winston Groom, *1942: The Year That Tried Men's Souls* (New York: Atlantic Monthly Press, 2005), 260–61.

173–75   Harm caused by divided military command structure at Guadalcanal and beyond: James P. Drew, LCDR, USN, "Tarnished Victory: Divided Command in the Pacific and Its Consequences, et al." (Thesis, Fort Leavenworth, KS, 2009).

176–83   Benny's viewpoint: Captain E. Bertram Mott, undated Santa Cruz battle retrospective essay, "The Battle of Santa Cruz and Guadalcanal from the Anti-Aircraft Viewpoint."

178–81   Battle sequence, Santa Cruz: Stafford, *Big E*, 192–211.

179   Reporters' observations during and after Battle of Santa Cruz: Richard Tregaskis, *Guadalcanal Diary* (New York: Random House, 1943), 62–70.

15: THE OTHER WAR: ARMY-NAVY FOOTBALL

184–85   Condition of USS *Enterprise* at Nouméa following Santa Cruz battle: Stafford, *Big E*, 241–43.

190   "Parsons was only sworn in to the United States Navy when a fellow Philippine reserve officer awakened him in the middle of the night on December 8, informing him that the entire personnel and equipment of the Luzon Stevedoring Company had been taken into the United States Navy. He was then sworn in by Admiral Hart as a lieutenant, senior grade." Travis Ingham, *Rendezvous by Submarine* (New York: Doubleday Doran, 1945), 23–24.

190–92   Background and lead-up to 1942 army-navy football game and game statistics: http://forwhattheygave.com/category/army-navy-football; Gene Schoor, *100 Years of Army Navy Football: A Pictorial History of America's Most Colorful and Competitive Sports Rivalry* (New York: Henry Holt, 1989), 112–14.

16: HAPPY DAYS AT THE PENAL COLONY

193–200   Details of prisoner life at Davao as observed by local Filipinos who worked at or near the colony: Mari Virginia Yap Morales, *Diary of the War: WW II Memoirs of Anastacio Campo* (Quezon City, PI: Ateneo University Press, 2006), 51–131.

193–200   The following diaries and memoirs also contributed to author insight into the prisoner experience at Davao: David Nash, Nash Diary; Hugh McGee, *Rice and Salt* (San Antonio: Naylor, 1962); Stephen Mellnik, *Philippine Diary 1939–1945* (New York: Van Nostrand Rheinhold, 1969); Carl S. Nordin, *We Were Next to Nothing: An American POW's Account of Japanese Prison Camps and Deliverance in World War II* (Jefferson, NC: McFarland & Company, 2004), 73–82.

197–200   Davao Christmas celebration: Morales, *Diary of the War*, 51–131; Kenneth Wheeler, "Christmas at DAPECOL," chapter, in "For My Children"; Red Cross packages to prisoners: Wheeler, "For My Children"; John M. Wright Jr., *Captured on Corregidor: Diary of an American P.O.W. in World War II* (Jefferson, NC: McFarland & Co., 2009), 66–69; Heisinger, *Father Found*, 327–28.

18: ESCAPE: CRIME AND PUNISHMENT

211–14   Primary and secondary sources consulted on Davao prisoner escape and aftermath: John D. Lukacs, *Escape from Davao: The Forgotten Story of the Most Daring Prison Break of the Pacific War* (New York: Simon & Schuster, 2010); Mellnik, *Philippine Diary*; Melvin McCoy, *Ten Escape from Tojo*; Dyess, *Dyess Story*; Samuel Grashio and Bernard Norling, *Return to Freedom* (Spokane, WA: University Press, 1982); 2010 author interview with the late Jack Hawkins at his home near Quantico, VA (arranged thanks to the kind assistance of John Lukacs).

212–14   The morning of April 4, 1943: The escape from Davao Penal Colony and effect on prisoners left behind: Heisinger, Father Found, 333–39; Wheeler, "No Escape," in "For My Children."

212–14   After the escape from Davao Penal Colony, effect on prisoners left behind: Heisinger, *Father Found*, 333–39; Wheeler, "No Escape," in "For My Children."

213–14   Punishment of prisoners in Barracks 5 to 8: Wheeler, "No Escape," in "For My Children"; Nash, Nash Diary; McGee, *Rice and Salt*, 103–8.

19: FAREWELL TO THE WHITE HOUSE

219   "You know I have been trying for some time to get some kind of sea duty": Excerpt of letter from Bill to Benny, WCM correspondence file, May 1943.

225 William C. Mott new orders: personal correspondence file, 1940–1943; WCM's USN personnel file; WCM Navy Orders file.

20: A TALE OF ATROCITIES

232–38 Debriefing of Dyess, Mellnik, and McCoy in Australia: Colonel Allison W. Ind, *Allied Intelligence Bureau: Our Secret Weapon in the War Against Japan* (New York: David McKay, 1958), 180–82; Mellnik, *Philippine Diary*, 279–316.

233 The guerillas fed and clothed them: William Wise, *Secret Mission to the Philippines: The Story of "Spyron" & the American-Filipino Guerrillas of World War II* (New York: E. P. Dutton, 1968), 112.

233 Improving state of guerrilla resistance movement in the Philippines: Ibid.

234 Guerrilla radiograms sent from PI to MacArthur HQ in Brisbane regarding prisoners in Philippines: Paul P. Rogers, *The Bitter Years: MacArthur and Sutherland* (New York: Praeger Publishers, 1990), 4.

236 "This is superb": A very good index of Whitney's habitual dealings with MacArthur: Paul P. Rogers, *The Good Years: MacArthur and Sutherland* (New York: Praeger, 1990), 296.

237–38 The GHQ audience showed intensified interest: William Wise, *Secret Mission to the Philippines: The Story of "Spyron" & the American-Filipino Guerrillas of World War II* (New York: E. P. Dutton, 1968), 112.

237 Training of guerrillas in the Philippines during World War II: Larry Schmidt, USMC, "American Involvement in the Filipino Resistance Movement on Mindanao During the Japanese Occupation, 1942–1945" (academic paper, Fort Leavenworth, KS, 1982). Excellent background on training protocols and intelligence transmission between Australia and guerrillas.

21: AUGUST 1943: ALLIED WAR SUMMIT, QUEBEC, CANADA

239–40 Preparation for and references to Quadrant conference: Elsey, *Unplanned Life*, 36–40.

239–44 Quebec Conference attendees, vignettes, and general tenor of conference: Doris Kearns Goodwin, *No Ordinary Time: Franklin & Eleanor Roosevelt: The Home Front in World War II* (New York: Simon & Schuster, 1994),

459–62; John Costello, *The Pacific War 1941–1945* (New York: Harper-Collins, 1981), 416–17.

240–42 Admiral King and Quadrant: Roberts, *Masters and Commanders*, 195, 407; John Byrne Cooke, *Reporting the War: Freedom of the Press from the American Revolution to the War on Terrorism* (New York: St. Martin's Press, 2007).

241 Quadrant Conference outcomes: Robert H. Ferrell, ed., *The Eisenhower Diaries* (New York: Norton, 1981), 48, 50.

243 Reading of Dyess affidavit excerpts at Quadrant: Monday, August 23, 1943, Minutes of Combined Chiefs of Staff meeting, Château Frontenac, Quebec. Source: Franklin D. Roosevelt Presidential Library, Hyde Park, NY.

244–45 FDR's ritual before dictation: Grace Tully, *Franklin Delano Roosevelt: My Boss* (Chicago: Peoples Book Club, 1949), 80–82.

245 FDR and Helen Cross correspondence: Cover memo to FDR on Helen Cross's incoming from Miss Grace Tully: "Letter from Mrs. A Barton Cross Lilac Hedges, Oceanport, New Jersey. Her son is Lt. Com. Mott. Source: Roosevelt Presidential Library, Hyde Park, NY.

245 Excerpt of 1943 MacArthur letter to FDR: Lukacs, *Escape From Davao*, 284.

22: REVENGE ON THE INNOCENT AND A COVERT PLAN

249–50 After crouching for thirty days in feces-strewn wire hutches: Heisinger, *Father Found*, 333–39; Wheeler, "No Escape," in "For My Children."

252–57 Secret MIS-X plan to spring Davao prisoners and description of Claro Lauretta's guerrilla resources: Mellnik, *Philippine Diary*, 280–86.

253–57 Mellnik's recall of his first conversation with Harold Rosenquist and later General Sutherland in Washington is entered here nearly verbatim: Ibid., 299–305.

255–56 Captain Lauretta's reference to doctors and hospitals operating in the hills of Mindanao: Ingham, *Rendezvous by Submarine*, 153.

255 A note on MacArthur's political and financial aspirations and their effect on policy and war theater decisions: In 1943, General Sutherland traveled to Washington for war planning conferences and also to promote General MacArthur's candidacy for the presidency. Himself the son of a senator and

wise to the ways of Washington, Sutherland worked with Senator Arthur Vandenberg of Michigan to get the War Department to rescind the order preventing MacArthur from seeking or accepting political office. Source: http://www.arlingtoncemetery.net/rksuther.htm.

Roosevelt felt pressured to keep MacArthur happy because he was a Republican, a household name, and potential future presidential candidate, depending on the course of the war. He did not interfere when, in February 1942, MacArthur accepted a payment of $500,000 ($7.5 million in current value) from Philippine president Manuel Quezon. MacArthur's staff members also received payments: $75,000 for Sutherland, $45,000 for Richard Marshall, and $20,000 for another low-level aide, Sidney Huff. Eisenhower, after being appointed Supreme Commander Allied Expeditionary Force, was also offered money by Quezon, but Eisenhower declined the offer. These revelations were made public by historian Carol Petillo in 1979 after she uncovered correspondence and archived bank deposits and later by Rogers, *MacArthur and Sutherland: The Good Years* and *The Bitter Years* (2 vols.), 1990, 1991.

23: SECRETS INSIDE THE OXYGEN TENT

259 Oxygen tent operation: Margeurite Klein, "Nursing Care in Pneumonia," *American Journal of Nursing* (October 1941).

260–61 Standard procedures for evacuating Americans caught behind enemy lines in the PI: Americans were routinely evacuated from prearranged rendezvous points after USS *Narwhal* and USS *Nautilus* had delivered their cargo to the guerrillas. Four hundred seventy-two Americans boarded the emptied submarines in the Philippines between 1943 and 1945 in this manner: Wise, *Secret Mission to the Philippines*, 141–43; Edward Dissette and H. C. Adamson, *Guerrilla Submarines* (New York: Ballantine Books, 1972), 236; Mellnik, *Philippine Diary*, 288.

261 "[T]hey had been working intensely on a plan to extract the prisoners at Davao Penal Colony—well ahead of Rosenquist's departure for Brisbane. Stories of MIS-X success facilitating escape and evasion in Europe, well behind enemy lines—in areas crawling with Germans—were legion. Let this be the answer to a thousand prayers. And now Rosenquist, MIS-X plan in

hand—approved by Sutherland—was in Australia." Willoughby, *Guerrilla Resistance Movement in the Philippines*, 175–77.

261 Captain McCollum's concern for his cousin Shivers: "I was trying very hard to get these people saved. I had a personal interest in it because my favorite first cousin was a prisoner there. He was an army officer, Shivers McCollum." Rear Admiral Arthur McCollum's Oral History, Source: USNI, Annapolis, MD.

262 General Sutherland and decision-making at GHQ: Rogers, *Good Years: MacArthur and Sutherland*, 230–35.

262 Courtney Whitney biographical background: RG-16 "Biographical Sketch," Papers of Major General Courtney Whitney, 1942–1947, MacArthur Memorial Archives, Norfolk, VA.

262 Courtney Whitney's long-standing mercantile interests in the Philippines: Peggy Seagrave, *Gold Warriors* (London: Verso Press, 2002), 93–94.

262 Whitney was more MacArthur loyalist than military professional: RG-16 "Biographical Sketch," Papers of Major General Courtney Whitney, 1942–1947, MacArthur Memorial Archives, Norfolk, VA.

263 Eleanor Roosevelt's telephone call to Newport hospital per WCM interview with John Toland:

WCM: "I came down with double pneumonia and nearly died, they later told me. They didn't have penicillin readily available in those days, and I was in the infirmary, then the hospital in Newport, Rhode Island. This was while I was at the Naval War College. I was in an oxygen tent, and Mrs. Roosevelt found out about it, and she called the hospital and got the night nurse and said, 'This is Mrs. Roosevelt, and I'd like to inquire about Billy Mott.' And she only got that far when the nurse snapped, 'Yes? Well, this is your Aunt Fanny,' and hung up. She reported it the next morning and there was an investigation.

"But that's the way she was, a very warm person. Here's another interesting example of how they cared about the White House staff. We burned coal to heat our home in those days, and we had an automatic device—I forget what you call them—that fed coal into the firebox. A part broke on it, and consequently we had no heat. We had a small child, and my wife was pregnant at the time, as I recall. I was wondering how I was going to keep my family from freezing when the telephone rang. They said, 'We understand you have a problem; that you need some heating. Mrs. Roosevelt has some electric heaters in the White House attic, and you can borrow them.' Then the Secret Service arranged to fly the coal feeder part in from Cleveland. By the way, I also realized that this meant that the home telephones of those of us that worked in the Map Room were tapped. I had told nobody at the White House about this problem."

24: HERO OF BATAAN VERSUS THE WAR DEPARTMENT

264–67   A censored William Dyess's frustrated attempts to publicize details of Japanese treatment of its prisoners in the Philippines: Lukacs, *Escape from Davao*, 277–336, and Dyess, *Dyess Story*.

25: BAD TIDINGS

270   "The exterior was bare and boxy": Christopher Gray, "Streetscapes: The Henry Hudson Hotel, 353 West 57th Street; From Women's Clubhouse to WNET to $75 a Night," *New York Times*, January 4, 1998.

276   Japanese atrocities revealed to an outraged American public: *New York Times*, January 28, 1944, A1, and other newspapers, e.g., *Los Angeles Examiner*, "Yanks Starved, Beheaded, Buried Alive By Captors"; and in following days, *NYT* headline, "Ruin Japan! Is Cry of Aroused Nation."

26: POLITICS IN BRISBANE

278–81   Courtney Whitney's role in the fate of prisoners at Davao Penal Colony: A lengthy description of the Rosenquist mission and its failure provides strong support of the view that Courtney Whitney and, to a slightly lesser degree, R. J. Marshall (deputy chief of staff) were responsible for the intentional detainment of Rosenquist at Brisbane for the purpose of dooming the rescue plan: Major General Charles A. Willoughby, *The Guerrilla Resistance Movement in the Philippines* (New York: Vantage Press, 1972), 56–63.

280–81   Mellnik and Rosenquist run into difficulties with Courtney Whitney at Brisbane GHQ: Mellnik, *Philippine Diary*, 386–92.

280–81   But from the moment Courtney Whitney got word: Courtney

Whitney's role in the fate of prisoners at Davao Penal Colony; Major General Charles A. Willoughby, *The Guerrilla Resistance Movement in the Philippines* (New York: Vantage Press, 1972), 56–63.

281 "I'm staying out of this G-2 brawl": Memorandum from Acting Chief of Staff General Richard Marshall, February 1944, MacArthur Memorial Museum and Archives, Norfolk, VA.

281 Original documents, radiograms, and memoranda between staff at MacArthur's GHQ and between GHQ and guerrillas in the Philippines: MacArthur Memorial Museum and Archives, Norfolk, VA.

27: "PROCEED TO KWAJALEIN"

282–83 Bill Mott Orders to Pacific: WCM interviews with John Toland, September, October, and December 1979; WCM Navy Orders file.

282–83 Kelly Turner biographical data: Fifth Amphibious Fleet database, NARA, College Park, MD.

286 Size of Joint Expeditionary Force: T. D. Stamps and V. J. Esposito, *A Military History of World War II: Operations in the Mediterranean and Pacific Theaters* (West Point, NY: United States Military Academy, 1953), 382.

28: THE BEST-LAID PLANS

291–92 Colonel Whitney's improvement of nascent guerrilla operations in the Philippines and training of new recruits: Mellnik, *Philippine Diary*, 279–86.

291–93 Courtney Whitney's block of rescue plan: Mellnik's and Willoughby's memoranda and, later, their books, all finger Whitney in crafting the serial delays of the Rosenquist rescue mission.

292 "Whitney's influence too strong." Harold Rosenquist diary entry. Sandra Rosenquist Kahn.

293 Sutherland influence at GHQ: Rogers, *Good Years: MacArthur and Sutherland*, 230–35.

296–302 Interaction between Rosenquist and Fertig on Mindanao: In his ghostwritten memoir, Fertig admits to disobeying GHQ prisoner rescue order Rosenquist handed him. Wendell Fertig, *They Fought Alone* (New York: Lippincott Company, 1963), 383–89.

In "A Critical Review of *They Fought Alone*," Captain Clyde Childress criticizes Fertig's military disobedience. Childress, who reported to Fertig, stated that Fertig was vain and self-absorbed—and routinely disdainful of General MacArthur and GHQ's oversight of the guerrillas. "Had Fertig . . . engaged in better communication with his superiors in Australia and his guerrilla commanders on Mindanao, this fiasco could have been avoided . . . There were guerrillas already in place that were perfectly capable of performing the task that Rosenquist was sent in to do. Had the guerrillas been directed to keep the Penal Colony under surveillance, this failed mission and the loss of the POWs might have been prevented."

29: INITIATION AT SAIPAN

310 "By mid-1944, the United States Navy was about to surpass all the world's navies combined": History International Documentary: *Imperial Sunset at Saipan.*

311 "Peace at War" poem, WCM, 1944, WCM poetry file.

315 Coastwatcher Chapman's sighting of the Japanese fleet in San Bernardino Strait and Stahl's assistance in relaying his message to Fifth Fleet: Robert Stahl, "The Turkey Shoot," chap. 9 in *You're No Good to Me Dead: Behind Japanese Lines in the Philippines* (Naval Institute Press Special Warfare Series, Annapolis, MD: Naval Institute Press, 1995), 100–102.

321–23 Smith vs. Smith: From WCM interview with John Toland: "I was right in the middle of that one . . . It was just the difference in the way the marines and the army operated. The army believes in artillery barrages, etc. . . . and the Marines say, 'Oh Christ. Go in and take your losses.' The same thing happened on Okinawa. The marines had their part of the island cleaned up in no time. Of course, the army will say they didn't have the same kind of opposition, but this was the marine way. Wherever you put a marine division alongside an army division, you're going to have trouble!"

323–24 Source for Manila casualties in final Japanese rampage: Daws, *Prisoners of the Japanese*, 534.

30: DECAMPMENT

328–32 First-person accounts of the DAPECOL prisoners' journey from Mindanao to Bilibid, a three-week ordeal: In addition to surviving prisoner letters sent to the Cross family, accounts by the following were excellent resources: Manny Lawton, *Some Survived* (Chapel Hill, NC: Algonquin Books of Chapel Hill, 2004), 138–48; McGee, *Rice and Salt*, 126–45; Alan McCracken, *Very Soon Now, Joe* (New York: The Hobson Book Press, 1947), 130–64.

331 "His morale was sky high": Postwar letter from Ensign Andrew Long Jr. to Helen Cross regarding Barton Cross's outlook in late 1944.

31: SEPTEMBER 1944, LILAC HEDGES

337 Under an unrehearsed divided command between the army and the navy, such incidents: James P. Drew, LCDR, USN, "Tarnished Victory: Divided Command in the Pacific and Its Consequences, et al." (Thesis, Fort Leavenworth, KS, 2009).

338–31 Benny's munitions factory speech: Source: *Rockaway (NJ) Record*, October 6, 1944. Benny delivered similar awards and stateside speeches to numerous converted munitions plants around the country. These factories variously made bomb sites, pistols, rifle receivers, and torpedoes.

341–42 Helen Cross letter to President Roosevelt regarding the *Shinyo Maru* POW transport sinking: A. Barton Cross Jr. Naval Personnel File, National Personnel Records Center, St. Louis.

32: HOPES DASHED

344 Major Harold Rosenquist told me he was here to: Sworn statement by escapee Jim McClure, MacArthur Memorial Museum and Archives, Norfolk, VA.

344–45 Several sworn testimonials from both guerrillas and escaped prisoners working with the Mindanao guerrillas averred that Rosenquist's plan to rescue the prisoners from the Davao Penal Colony would have succeeded if Rosenquist had been allowed to depart Australia even one month earlier than he did. MacArthur Memorial Archives, Norfolk, VA.

344–45   With mounting resentment toward Courtney Whitney: A lengthy description of the Rosenquist mission and its failure provides strong support of the view that Courtney Whitney and, to a slightly lesser degree, R. J. Marshall (deputy chief of staff) were responsible for the intentional detainment of Rosenquist at Brisbane for the purpose of dooming the rescue plan: Major General Charles A. Willoughby, *The Guerrilla Resistance Movement in the Philippines* (New York: Vantage Press, 1972), 56–63.

345   This message is written with a prayer to God that it: Letter from Harold Rosenquist to Lieutenant Colonel Rogers, POW, MacArthur Memorial Museum and Archives, Norfolk, VA.

345–46   Letter from Harold Rosenquist to Colonel Rogers at Lincayan Airfield (Lasang): Source: MacArthur Memorial Archives, Norfolk, VA.

348   Re Coastwatcher LeCouvre's urgent POW ship change message to army GHQ at Brisbane and its failure to forward it to US Navy submarines monitoring enemy shipping in the area: Virginia Hansen Holmes, *Guerrilla Daughter* (Kent, Ohio: Kent State University Press, 2009), 149.

348   As required by the divided command structure: James P. Drew, LCDR, USN, "Tarnished Victory: Divided Command in the Pacific and Its Consequences, et al." (Thesis, Fort Leavenworth, KS, 2009).

349   Official Japanese order to kill all POWs: Doc 2701, Exhibit "O" Source: NARA, War Crimes, Japan, RG 24, Box 2015.

349–50   Re *Shinyo Maru* survivor accounts: Heisinger, *Father Found*, 394–95; John Morrett, *Soldier Priest* (Roswell, GA: Old Rugged Cross Press, 1993), 110–14.

350   This is a headache: Penciled a note on the radiogram regarding a submarine rescue of the surviving *Shinyo Maru* prisoners, MacArthur Memorial Museum and Archives, Norfolk, VA.

33: SETBACKS

352–53   Medical air transport insight, description: Keith Wheeler, *The Pacific Is My Beat* (New York: E. P. Dutton, 1943).

355–57   Background and details regarding 1944 Pearl Harbor summit, July 27, 1944: Costello, *Pacific War*, 491–96.

356–57   Re MacArthur guarantee that Luzon campaign would be completed in thirty days to six weeks: George Dyer, *The Amphibians Came to Conquer: The Story of Admiral Richmond Kelly Turner* (US Marine Corps, 1991), 975.

357   "Give me an aspirin . . . In fact, give me another aspirin to take in the morning": William Manchester, *American Caesar: Douglas MacArthur 1880–1964* (Boston: Little, Brown and Company, 1978), 369.

357–59   Submarine warfare effectiveness: Blair, *Silent Victory: True*, 17–20 and 87–88; Larry Bond, *Crash Dive: Stories of Submarine Combat* (New York: Tom Doherty, 2010), 234–37.

359   Re Halsey's orders under divided command scenario: E. B. Potter, *Nimitz* (Annapolis, MD: Naval Institute Press, 2008), 325.

359–61   Divided command insight: "MacArthur's Navy—Admiral Kinkaid and the Seventh Fleet and Admiral Halsey and the Third Fleet . . . a divided command creating a very dangerous situation indeed in the face of a brave and determined enemy." Edwin P. Hoyt, *How They Won the War in the Pacific: Nimitz and His Admirals* (New York: Lyons Press, 2000), 422.

360–61   Additional divided command insight: Lieutenant Commander Thomas J. Cutler, "MacArthur, FDR, and the Politics of Leyte Gulf," *Naval History* 23 No. 5 (October 2009).

360–61   Re MacArthur's tight control over communications between the Seventh Fleet and Halsey's Third Fleet attack forces: "MacArthur was so damned insistent on having his own fleet and his own people that he wouldn't let, would not have, any direct channel of communication between Halsey [Third Fleet] and the Seventh Fleet. There were no radio channels set up. Halsey was working for Nimitz, and so MacArthur would not include him in any of the operations plans. They had this long, complicated communications plan for the Seventh Fleet . . . There was no setup for that outfit to communicate directly with Halsey. It was part of MacArthur's hatred of the navy or craving for power or something—I don't know which, but he insisted on it being that way." From oral history of Admiral George Van Deurs: USNI, 487.

34: THROUGH A PRISM: MACARTHUR'S RETURN

367–70   First-person accounts of USN flyers over Luzon, September 21, 1944: Wheeler, "For My Children," 78–80; Heisinger, *Father Found*, 407–9 (including diary entries by Manny Lawton and Lee Stiles); Lawton, *Some Survived*, 108–110; Thomas Hayes, "Bilibid Journal," 149–53.

367–68   After *Enterprise's* Air Group 20 (led by Commander Robert Riera) supported the September 1944 Peleliu invasion, they struck Japanese airfields and shipping in and around the Philippines: http://www.cv6.org/1944/1944.htm.

367–68   Admiral King's Second Report to the Secretary of the Navy, Combat Operations March 1944–March 1945.

370–71   Major Robert Lapham overtures to Courtney Whitney at GHQ for permission to conduct a Cabanatuan rescue mission: William Breuer, *The Great Raid*, 141–42; Charles W. Sasser, *Raider*, 119; Ray Hunt and Bernard Norling, *Behind Japanese Lines: An American Guerrilla in the Philippines*, 196–98; Robert Lapham and Bernard Norling, *Lapham's Raiders: Guerrilla Raiders in the Philippines, 1942–1945*, 177–78.

372   Sinking of *Hofuku Maru*: "British state the American bombers are too bloody accurate": Heisinger, *Father Found*, 410 (quoting from Lee Stiles's diary); "They were a pitiful sight to behold": Recollection of Curtis Beecher when he first saw *Hofuku Maru* survivors arriving at Bilibid. Unpublished recollection entitled "A Survivor's Account of Americans Who Were Prisoners of the Japanese in the Philippine Islands April, May 1942–December 1944," Brigadier General Curtis Beecher, USMC, Douglas County Museum, Roseburg, OR; *Hofuku Maru* survivors taken to either Bilibid or Cabanatuan: Sources: Cecil Peart, Peart's Journal; Heisinger, *Father Found*; and McCracken, *Very Soon Now, Joe*.

375   Delivering his prewar client Douglas MacArthur back to the Philippines: RG-16 "Biographical Sketch," Papers of Major General Courtney Whitney, 1942–1947, MacArthur Memorial Archives, Norfolk, VA., Peggy Seagrave, *Gold Warriors* (London: Verso Press, 2002), 93–94.

375   Courtney Whitney's prewar activities and investments in the Philippines: Whitney worked for the top Manila law firm, Dewitt, Perkins & Enrile (as did the father of MacArthur's G-2 assistant chief, Joseph McMicking).

The firm handled all MacArthur's investments and financial affairs in the Philippines. Another major client was Benguet Consolidated Mines, the country's largest gold mining operation, in which MacArthur had a considerable investment. In 1936 Courtney Whitney was president of Benguet Consolidated Mines, either concurrent with his law partnership or immediately prior to it. Source—July 1936 American Chamber of Commerce of Manila—quoted below:

[Benguet] Consolidated Mines recently reported good results from its development work . . . of the vast chromite mine in Masinloc, Zambales. Courtney Whitney, Benguet's President, is in the United States working on the sale of this ore. [Benguet's] gold production has also improved steadily; gold output for the period under discussion is much higher than in 1935.

Total gold production in the five years preceding WWII was 37 tons per year, the Philippines' most lucrative export.

375 MacArthur's Philippine-derived wealth: General MacArthur sold his shares in Benguet after the war for more than $1 million.

377 Re *Arisan Maru* sinking: Calvin Graef, Official Statement to the War Department, December 5, 1944, www.rockawaymemories.com/JosephAngelone01.htm; William Bowen, *The Arisan Maru Tragedy*; Gavan Daws, *Prisoners of the Japanese: POWs of World War II in the Pacific* (New York: William Morrow, 1994); "no bigger than a dime": Calvin Graef and Melissa Masterson, *Ride the Waves to Freedom* (Kearney, NE: Morris, 1999), 73, telling of Graef's imprisonment and survival following the sinking of the *Arisan Maru*.

36: THE *ORYOKO MARU*

391 Shields Goodman's letter: "A letter from Bilibid Prison," *Shipmate*, November 1989, 13–14.

393–94 Curtis Beecher observations: Curtis T. Beecher memoir, unpublished.

394–95 Bilibid Prison, December 1944: Pharmacist's Mate Robert W. Kentner, diary entries on rostered patients and naval medical personnel.

398–404 Recollections of *Oryoko Maru*: Lawton, *Some Survived*, 145–54.

398–406 Prisoner experiences described in this chapter: family letters, diaries, unpublished memoir, as well as author interviews with survivors.

401 "Hikoki! Hikoki!": Wheeler, "For My Children," 83.

401 Robert Riera log entries: USS *Hornet* log and USS *Enterprise* ship's muster, November, December 1944, and January 1945, www.cv6.org/company /muster/display_ag.asp?page=VB-20 and usshornet.org.

402 Description of Commander Frank Bridget's announcements of American planes attacking the prison ship: "as cool as a tennis match referee, called the action": Lawton, *some survived*, 160.

402 The men "hoped to hell they would score and hoped to hell they wouldn't," according to David Nash: Heisinger, *Father Found*, 456.

37: END GAME IN THE PACIFIC

415–17   Iwo Jima press conference: Robert Sherrod, *On to Westward: The Battles of Saipan and Iwo Jima* (New York: Duell Sloan and Pearce, 1945), 154–61.

417–18   Iwo Jima statistics: Ronald H. Spector, *Eagle Against the Sun: The American War with Japan* (New York: Macmillan, 1985), 495, and Sherrod, *On to Westward*, 163.

417–20   D-Day and D-Days Plus 1, 2, 3 at Iwo Jima: CINPAC Monthly Operations Report, February 1945, noted in Dyer, *Amphibians Came to Conquer*, vol. 2, 1027.

420 Text of Navajo message on Iwo Jima flag raising: *"Ashdla-ma...nos-bas...":* Sally McClain, *Navajo Weapon: The Navajo Code Talkers* (Tucson, AZ: Rio Nuevo, 1944), 179–81.

38: A SAILOR'S NIGHTMARE

429 *Kikusui:* Literal translation is "floating chrysanthemums," the longtime symbol of Imperial Japan. Operation Kikusui at Okinawa consisted of more than 1,500 army and navy suicide-bent aircraft. Operation Kikusui was launched in ten waves between April and June 1945: http://ww2db .com/battle_spec.php?battle_id=15.

429 Correspondent Robert Sherrod's recollection of early censorship of kamikaze attacks: Sherrod, *On to Westward*, 292–93.

429–30   Note on kamikazes at Okinawa: The rate of early ship losses to the kamikaze threat was stemmed by the establishment of an outer defense perimeter of radar picket ships. These vessels bore the greatest burden. Of the 206 ships that served on radar picket duty, nearly 30 percent were sunk or damaged by kamikazes, making theirs the most hazardous naval surface duty in World War II. Toward the end of the battle, the radar picket ships became the prime kamikaze targets as Japanese pilots despaired of getting through the "big blue blanket"—the constant presence of the blue-painted Hellcats and Corsairs over the fleet at all hours—to reach larger prey.

431–433   Admiral Turner All Hands memo re Kamikaze Corps and April 13, 1945, and RKT Statement on Roosevelt's death: RKT general file, Navy Yard, Washington, DC.

433   USS *Indianapolis* kamikaze attack, March 31, 1945: Thomas B. Buell, *The Quiet Warrior: A Biography of Admiral Raymond A. Spruance* (Annapolis, MD: USNI Press, 1987), 378; William C. Mott oral history; www.ussindianapolis .org.

434–40   The ships of the Third Fleet also formed the basis of the Fifth Fleet. When the Pacific Fleet sailed under Admiral Halsey's flag, the force was named the Third Fleet. The ships were redesignated as the Fifth Fleet when sailing under the command of Admiral Spruance. Halsey and Spruance would alternate command of the fleet for major operations, allowing the other admiral and his executive staff time to prepare for the subsequent campaign. A secondary benefit was that this system (due to the flag changes) confused the Japanese into thinking that they were actually two separate fleets—and that our naval capacity was twice its actual size.

436   Refrain of hymn, "Eternal Father Strong to Save," Rev. William Whiting (1825–1878).

437   "I doubt if the slow, methodical Army approach": Spruance letter to Carl Moore: Buell, *Quiet Warrior*, 387.

437   Exchange between Nimitz and Buckner on bringing in marines behind enemy lines: Costello, *Pacific War*, 565.

438–40   Admiral Turner drinking incident: Transcript and tapes of WCM interviews with John Toland, November 30, 1979; December 6, 1967, and WCM letters to VADM George Dyer during his research for *Amphibians Came to Conquer*. These letters and memoranda, other personal stories re amphibians, are part of a research cache in papers of VADM

Dyer, located in Manuscript and Division, Library of Congress, Washington, DC.

440–41   Admiral Spruance on Turner's drinking habits: "I always felt I could handle Kelly and his drinking . . . I never saw him tight during working hours, except once on Guam after he had finished up at Okinawa. His breath would knock you down at fifteen feet. His head was clear as a bell." Dyer, *Amphibians Came to Conquer*, vol. 2, 1161; Admiral Turner's statement on FDR's death, Ibid., p. 965.

441   June–July 1945 casualties pouring into US hospitals from all theaters of war: McKitterick Clarence Smith, *U.S Army Medical Department: Hospitalization and Evacuation in World War II* (Office of the Chief of Military History, USA, 1956), 200–213.

441   Truman hoped "that there was a possibility of preventing an Okinawa from one end of Japan to another": D. M. Giangreco, *Hell to Pay: Operation Downfall and the Invasion of Japan* (Annapolis, MD: United States Naval Institute Press, 2009), 60, and footnote, 303.

445–46   Likelihood of retributive action against prisoners in Japan: Frank, *Downfall*, 161.

451   Okinawa battle and nonbattle casualty estimates: There are a range of Okinawa casualty estimates in military literature. Historian and author Richard Frank's statistics are widely acknowledged as the most reliable: Richard Frank, "The Pacific War's Biggest Battle," *USNI Naval History* 24, no. 2 (April 2010):

  US Army and Marine casualties (killed and wounded) at Okinawa numbered 82,229. For the navy, 1,465 kamikaze sorties sank 36 ships and damaged 368. The carnage among naval personnel was the highest ever suffered in a single naval campaign, mostly from kamikazes. 4,907 sailors died, with a nearly equal number wounded—a ship casualty rate of one in four. Japanese casualties at Okinawa were far greater: 107,539 soldiers were killed—23,764 of them presumed to have died sealed in caves. The highest death toll of all was among Okinawans: 142,058, more than a third of the island's civilian population.

451   If Operation Olympic had been launched and carried to completion it would have dwarfed "into insignificance" any other amphibious assault

attempted in history. USN (Ret) Vice Admiral Daniel E. Barbey, *MacArthur's Amphibious Navy: Seventh Amphibious Force Operations 1943–1945* (Annapolis, MD: United States Naval Institute Press, 1969), 321.

39: IN THE END, A QUESTION OF
CASUALTIES—AND SEA POWER

449–50   Admiral Leahy's June 1945 memo to Joint Chiefs regarding Operation Olympic: Memo SM-2141, US Department of Defense.

451   Army Surgeon General's casualty estimates: Richard B. Frank, *Downfall: The End of the Imperial Japanese Empire* (New York: Random House, 1999), 135–36.

451   Olympic casualty estimates as of June 18, 1945: General HQs, US Army Forces in the Pacific (USAFPAC) Staff Study: Operation Olympic, 32.

451   Re Truman denied the casualty data he requested: Frank, *Downfall*, 144–45.

452   General Marshall's estimates of MacArthur's overall battle ratio of 22.6:1 was later revised to 5:1.

453–55   Excerpts from Willoughby memos on Kyushu buildup stressed gravity of new intelligence, per his Amendment 1 to G-2 Estimate of the Enemy Situation with Respect to Kyushu:

"The rate and probable continuity of Japanese reinforcements into the Kyushu area are changing that tactical and strategic situation sharply . . . [T]here is a strong likelihood that additional major units will enter the area before target date; we are engaged in a race against time by which the ratio of attack effort vis-à-vis defense capacity is [now] perilously balanced . . . If this deployment is not checked, it may grow to a point where we attack on a ratio of one (1) to one (1), which is not the recipe for victory."

453–54   Autonomy of SWPA's Central Bureau, MacArthur's intelligence gathering operation: Edward J. Drea, *MacArthur's ULTRA: Codebreaking and the War Against Japan, 1942–1945* (Lawrence: University Press of Kansas, 1992), 28–29.

453–55   Additional sources on chronology of Japanese buildup on Kyushu: Douglas A. MacAeachin, Joint Report by CIA's Center for the Study of Intelligence and the Harvard University program for Studies of Intelligence and Policy: "The Final Months of the War with Japan: Signals Intelligence,

US Invasion Planning, and the A-Bomb Decision"; Giangreco, *Hell to Pay*; Frank, *Downfall*.

454 "suicide weapons being developed on Kyushu": Ibid., 212.

454 Ten thousand planes hidden in "mines, railway tunnels": James Martin Davis, "Operation Olympic: An Invasion Not Found in History Books," *Quan*, September 2003.

455–63 WCM to Washington, Summer 1945: WCM's Naval Orders show RKT dispatched him to Washington with latest report on spiking enemy troop strength on Kyushu. Story retold in lengthy WCM interview in *Daily Progress*, Charlottesville, Virginia's, main newspaper, on August 6, 1995 (fiftieth anniversary of Hiroshima).

A second source is an undated "joint letter of criticism" from both my parents sent to the *Daily Progress* editor, responding to a previously published editorial dated April 25, 1995, which had suggested the US apologize to Japan for dropping the atomic bombs. The letter was joint because my mother had worked as a data analyst on Project Manhattan at MIT in Boston (though its employees did not know the precise objective of their work until after the fact). The letter objected to "factual misstatements" in a previous LTE in the *Daily Progress*. After a brief discussion of my mother's role came the relevant passage from my father:

> I, the other half of our household, had been through three costly amphibious assaults on the Marianas, Iwo Jima, and Okinawa, where casualties grew with each invasion and the coming of the kamikazes. In the final weeks before the bomb was dropped, I was in Manila Bay helping to coordinate the planning for our amphibious invasion of mainland Japan. At that time, the estimate was that we would suffer 600,000 casualties in the invasion.
>
> When that estimate reached the invasion commander, Admiral R. K. Turner, he sent for me and asked whether as a former White House aide to President Roosevelt I might be able to bring this intelligence to the attention of President Truman. When I responded in the affirmative, I was ordered back to Washington on the next plane, and I did get the estimate to the attention of the President.

457–58   Bill orally summarized important enemy intercepts to Roosevelt, frequently in his bathroom while (the president) shaved: David Kahn, "Roosevelt Magic and Ultra," *Cryptologia* 16, no. 4 (1992).

458   Communications traffic and Leahy and Truman receipt of documents from Washington at Potsdam: Elsey, *Unplanned Life*, 86–87.

458   Official Log of the president's trip to "Berlin Conference," July 6–August 7, 1945, www.trumanlibrary.org.

458   Clark Clifford: James Vardaman hired Clifford for Map Room duty shortly before the conference at Potsdam as a "stand-in" watch officer so that Vardaman could travel to the conference. Matthew Connelly and William Rigdon Oral Histories, Harry S. Truman Library, Independence, MO.

460   Mott further disclosed in the August 6, 1995, *Daily Progress* article: "I was having lunch at that exclusive men's club in San Francisco with former president of the United States Herbert Hoover. A mutual friend had invited both of us to lunch. The bomb had been dropped, and Hoover was drawing formulas on napkins and the tablecloth, which was annoying the hell out of our waiter. Hoover had a scientific background and was trying to figure out the formula for the bomb. At the time, he said he thought that dropping the bomb was a good idea."

460   MacArthur was "so prone to exaggerate": From War Secretary Henry Stimson's diary, December 27, 1944, per footnote on page 419 in Frank's *Downfall*. Frank also noted a March 30, 1945, diary entry by Stimson along similar lines, when MacArthur's fitness to command the final invasion of Japan was being debated in Washington.

462   President Hoover had provided the Roosevelt Administration with casualty estimates for a final assault on Japan: D. M. Giangreco, "Casualty Projections for the US Invasions of Japan, 1945–1946; Planning and Policy," *Journal of Military History* 61 (July 1997): 521–82.

464–65   Admiral Nimitz opinion on importance of sea power to Pacific victory: Walter R. Borneman, *The Admirals: Nimitz, Halsey, Leahy, and King— The Five-Star Admirals Who Won the War at Sea* (New York: Little, Brown, 2012), 453–54.

465   Processing freed prisoners via Manila: Reports of General MacArthur:

MacArthur in Japan: The Occupation Military Phase, vol. 1, supp., 1966, Library of Congress Catalog Card Number: 66-60006.

465–66   Admiral Turner and flag staff at Tojo Shrine, Tokyo, September 2, 1945: Dyer, *Amphibians Came to Conquer*, 1114–15.

40: NO PEACE AT LILAC HEDGES

475   Excerpt from "Cruise of Death," by George Weller, *Chicago Daily News*, December 8, 1945.

41: FINAL HOURS

493   "The march was about two miles": Wright, *Captured on Corregidor*, 111.

494   "With our bony frames": Lawton, *Some Survived*, 180.

495–96   Torpedo explosions that missed *Enoura Maru* at Lingayen Gulf: David Nash later confirmed that the torpedoes that missed their ship were fired by the USS *Blenny*, commanded by Lieutenant Commander William Hazzard, who—along with Air Group Commander Robert Riera—was a 1935 Annapolis classmate of Nash's.

496   "We were dirty, bearded": Unpublished memoir, E. Carl Engelhart, 162.

496   "Only survival mattered": Lawton, *Some Survived*, 186.

497–98   Sugar theft incident: Wheeler, "For My Children," 93–94.

498–501   Bombing of *Enoura Maru* and removal of the dead: Wright, *Captured on Corregidor*, 122–24.

499–500   Colonel Olson's bravery and Father Cummings's prayers aboard *Enoura Maru*: Sidney Stewart, *Give Us This Day* (New York: W. W. Norton, 1956), 211–13.

501–07   Barton Cross and Robert Granston aboard *Brazil Maru*: Two-day SMF interview with Granston in Palm Coast, Florida, and Granston's November 1945 letter to Helen Cross.

511   More than 126,000 Allied prisoners were transported in 156 voyages on 134 Japanese merchant ships. More than 21,000 Americans were killed or injured from "friendly fire from American submarines or planes": Gregory F. Michno, *Death on the Hellships: Prisoners at Sea in the Pacific War* (Annapolis, MD: United States Naval Institute Press, 2001), Appendix, 317.

Select Bibliography

MAJOR INTERVIEWS BY AUTHOR

Barney Barnhill (USS *Enterprise*), by telephone, January 2006.

Warren Elder, former POW, Luzon, Philippines, January 2005.

George Elsey, Irvine, CA, March 2007.

Robert Granston, Palm Coast, FL, February 2006 and several later interviews by phone.

Dee Grashio, widow of Davao escapee Samuel Grashio, by telephone, Spring 2005.

Jack Hawkins (USMC, retired), Quantico, VA, 2010.

Judith Heisinger, widow of Duane Heisinger (son of former POW Samuel Laurence Heisinger, USN and author of *Father Found*), Northern VA, 2008 and 2010.

Al Leonard, childhood friend of Bill and Benny Mott, by telephone, March 2006.

Roger Mansell, Center for Japanese Prisoner of War Research, Palo Alto, CA, January 2005.

Senator John McCain, US Senate, Washington, DC, 2006.

Bernard Peterson (USS *Enterprise*), by telephone, January 2006.

Sandra Kahn Rosenquist, daughter of Harold A. Rosenquist, by telephone, May 2007 and October 2008.

Mac Showers (Naval Intelligence), by telephone, June 2007.

Robert Wolfensky, former POW, Luzon, Philippines, January 2005.

RESEARCH VENUES

Ateneo University, Manila, Philippines.

Cabanatuan, Bilibid, O'Donnell, and Pasay prison camps, Santa Scholastica
Womens College, Philippines.

Center for Research, POWs Under the Japanese, Palo Alto, CA.

Churchill Map and War Rooms, London, England.

Citadel, Charleston, SC.

Citadel, Le Château Frontenac, Quebec, Canada.

Embassy of the Philippines, Washington, DC.

Library of Congress Manuscript Div., Washington, DC.

MacArthur Memorial Archives, Norfolk, VA.

National Archives (NARA), College Park, MD, and Washington, DC.

National Personnel Records Center, St. Louis, MO.

Naval Historical Library, Navy Yard, Washington, DC.

Prisoner of War Museum and Library, Andersonville, GA.

Roosevelt Presidential Library and Archives, Hyde Park, NY.

Rutgers University Library and Archives, New Brunswick, NJ.

US Naval Academy (USNA) Archives and Library, Annapolis, MD.

US Naval Institute (USNI), Annapolis, MD.

US Navy (USN) Bureau of Medicine and Surgery (BUMED), Washington, DC.

USS *Hornet*, San Francisco, CA.

USS *Yorktown*, Charleston, SC.

PARTIAL LIST OF REFERENCES

Andrew, Christopher. *For the President's Eyes Only.* New York: Harper Perennial,
1996.

Andrews, Robert. *Masters and Commanders: How Four Titans Won the War in the
West, 1941–1945.* New York: HarperCollins, 2009.

Arnold-Forester, Mark. *The World at War.* New York: Stein and Day, 1973.

Banning, Kendall. *Annapolis Today.* New York: Funk and Wagnalls, 1938.

Barbey, Daniel E. *MacArthur's Amphibious Navy, Seventh Amphibious Force*

Operations 1943–1945. Annapolis, MD: United States Naval Institute Press, 1969.

Barnhill, James C. *The Galloping Ghost*. Self-published, March 1987.

Bartsch, William H. *December 8, 1941: MacArthur's Pearl Harbor*. College Station: Texas A&M University Press, 2003.

Bishop, Gordon. *Gems of New Jersey, Written for the Star-Ledger*. Englewood Cliffs, NJ: Prentice-Hall, 1985.

Bliven, Bruce, Jr. *From Pearl Harbor to Okinawa: The War in the Pacific, 1941–1945*. New York: Random House, 1960.

Bocksel, Arnold A. *Rice, Men and Barbed Wire: A True Epic of Americans as Japanese POWs*. Hempstead, NY: Michael B. Glass, 1991.

Bond, Larry. *Crash Dive: True Stories of Submarine Combat*. New York: Tom Doherty, 2010.

Borneman, Walter R. *The Admirals: Nimitz, Halsey, Leahy, and King—The Five-Star Admirals Who Won the War at Sea*. New York: Little, Brown, 2012.

Brands, H. W. *Traitor to His Class: The Privileged Life and Radical Presidency of Franklin Delano Roosevelt*. New York: Anchor Books, 2008.

Breuer, William B. *MacArthur's Undercover War: Spies, Saboteurs, Guerrillas, and Secret Missions*. New York: John Wiley and Sons, 1995.

Brinkley, David. *Washington Goes to War*. Thorndike, ME: Thorndike Press, 1988.

Buell, Thomas B. *The Quiet Warrior: A Biography of Admiral Raymond A. Spruance*. Annapolis, MD: USNI Press, 1987.

Bureau of Naval Personnel. *The Gunnery Officer*. Navpers, 1955.

Camus, José S. *Rice in the Philippines*. Manila: Bureau of Printing, 1921.

Caraccilo, Dominic J., ed. *Surviving Bataan and Beyond: Colonel Irvin Alexander's Odyssey as a Japanese Prisoner of War*. Mechanicsburg, PA: Stackpole Books, 1999.

Childress, Clyde (USA, retired). A Critical Review of *They Fought Alone*." *Bulletin of the American Historical Collection* 31, no. 1 (January 2003). AHC consists of some thousands of books, articles, and photographs related to the American experience in the Philippines and to the relationship of the two countries.

Churchill, Winston S. *The Grand Alliance: The Second World War*. Boston: Houghton Mifflin, 1950.

Connaughton, Richard. *MacArthur and Defeat in the Philippines*. New York: Overlook Press, 2001.

Costello, John. *The Pacific War: 1941–1945*. New York: HarperCollins, 1981.

Cross, Helen Chamberlain. Wartime diaries and letters, 1940–1946.

Davis, R. G., Captain, MC, USN, MOIC. *Canacao Journal: A Report and a Journal, 1941–1945*, PI (Hospital Corps Archives, Bureau of Medicine and Surgery, June 1946.

Daws, Gavan. *Prisoners of the Japanese: POWs of World War II in the Pacific*. New York: William Morrow, 1994.

Difford, Floramund Fellmeth. *An Angel's Illustrated Journal: It Has Taken Sixty Years to Explain Why She Was on the* Mactan *and Not a Prisoner*. Toledo, WA: Chapters of Life, 2005.

Dissette, Edward, and H. C. Adamson. *Guerrilla Submarines*. New York: Ballantine Books, 1972.

Dower, John W. *War Without Mercy: Race and Power in the Pacific War*. New York: Pantheon Books, 1986.

Dyer, George C. *The Amphibians Came to Conquer: The Story of Admiral Richmond Kelly Turner*. 2 vols. Washington, DC: Department of the Navy, 1991.

Dyess, William E. *The Dyess Story*. New York: G. P. Putnam's Sons, 1944.

Elsey, George M. *An Unplanned Life: A Memoir*. Columbia: University of Missouri Press, 2005.

Erickson, Commander George E., Jr., JAGC, USNR. *Transcript of Oral History Interview of Rear Admiral William C. Mott, USN, retired*. Charlottesville, VA, 1991.

Frank, Richard B. *Downfall: The End of the Japanese Imperial Empire*. New York: Penguin, 1999.

Giangreco, D. M. *Hell to Pay: Operation Downfall and the Invasion of Japan*. Annapolis, MD: United States Naval Institute Press, 2009.

Glines, Carroll V. *Doolittle's Tokyo Raiders*. New York: Van Nostrand Reinhold, 1981.

Goodwin, Doris Kearns. *No Ordinary Time: Franklin & Eleanor Roosevelt: The Home Front in World War II*. New York: Simon & Schuster, 1994.

Gordon, John Steele. *An Empire of Wealth: The Epic History of American Economic Power*. New York: HarperCollins, 2004.

Gordon, Richard M., and Benjamin S. Llamzon, PhD. *Horyo: Memoirs of an American POW.* St. Paul, MN: Paragon House, 1991.

Grashio, Samuel, and Bernard Norling. *Return to Freedom.* Spokane, WA: University Press, 1982.

Groom, Winston. *1942: The Year That Tried Men's Souls.* New York: Atlantic Monthly Press, 2005.

Grove, Martin, and Martin Stephen. *Sea Battles in Close-Up: World War 2.* Annapolis, MD: United States Naval Institute Press, 1998.

Heisinger, Duane. *Father Found: Life and Death as a Prisoner of the Japanese in World War II.* Maitland, FL: Xulon Press, 2003.

Hoyt, Edwin P. *How They Won the War in the Pacific: Nimitz and His Admirals.* New York: Lyons Press, 2000.

Ind, Colonel Allison W. *Allied Intelligence Bureau: Our Secret Weapon in the War Against Japan.* New York: David McKay, 1958.

Irwin, Richard T. *A History of Randolph Township, Morris County, New Jersey.* Hicksville, NY: Exposition Press, 1976.

Kennedy, David. *Freedom from Fear: The American People in Depression and War, 1925–1945.* New York: Oxford University Press, 1999.

Kennedy, Robert S., Pedro C. Gonzales, Edward C. Dickinson, Hector C. Miranda Jr., and Timothy H. Fisher. *A Guide to the Birds of the Philippines.* New York: Oxford University Press, 2000.

Kentner, Robert W. *War Diary: Canacao Naval Hospital.* Unpublished, located at Bureau of Medicine and Surgery, Washington, DC.

Kuykendall, Ralph S., and A. Grove Day. *Hawaii: A History, from Polynesian Kingdom to American Commonwealth.* New York: Prentice-Hall, 1948.

Levie, H. *Documents on Prisoners of War.* Newport, RI: Naval War College Press, 1979.

Levie, H. *Prisoners of War in International Armed Conflict.* Newport, RI: Naval War College Press, 1979.

Life. December 23, 1940.

Life. March 31, 1941.

The Lucky Bag. Naval Academy Yearbooks, Years 1930, 1933.

MacArthur, Douglas. *Reminiscences: General of the Army.* New York: McGraw-Hill, 1964.

Map Room Letters, Background Reading Files, Watch Officer Instructions, Memos, Telegrams (Boxes 13, 14, 15, 194, 195). Roosevelt Presidential Library, Hyde Park, NY, Map Room Files.

Masterson, Melissa. *Ride the Waves to Freedom: Calvin Graef's Survival Story.* Kearney, NE: Morris, 1999.

McClain, Sally. *Navajo Weapon: The Navajo Code Talkers.* Tucson, AZ: Rio Nuevo, 1994.

McCullough, David W. *Three Score and Ten: A History of Christ School, Arden, North Carolina, 1900–1970.* Alexander, NC: WorldComm, 1996.

McGee, John Hugh. *Rice and Salt.* San Antonio: Naylor, 1962.

Meacham, Jon. *Franklin and Winston: An Intimate Portrait of an Epic Friendship.* New York: Random House, 2003.

Mellnik, Stephen M. *Philippine Diary, 1939–1945.* New York: Van Nostrand Reinhold, 1969.

Meredith, Lee. *Grey Ghost: The Story of the Aircraft Carrier Hornet.* Sunnyvale, CA: Rocklin Press, 2001.

Michno, Gregory F. *Death on the Hellships: Prisoners at Sea in the Pacific War.* Annapolis, MD: United States Naval Institute Press, 2001.

Miller, Donald L. *The Story of World War II.* New York: Simon & Schuster, 2001.

Miller, Francis Trevelyan. *History of World War II.* Philadelphia: John C. Winston, 1945.

Monohan, Evelyn M., and Rosemary Neidel-Greenlee. *All This Hell: U.S. Nurses Imprisoned by the Japanese.* Lexington: University Press of Kentucky, 2003.

Morgan, James. *If These Walls Had Ears: The Biography of a House.* New York: Warner Books, 1996.

Morton, Louis. *The Fall of the Philippines.* U.S. Army in World War II: The War in the Pacific. Washington, DC: Office of the Chief of Military History, Department of the Army, 1953.

Mott, Captain Bertram E. *Memoirs of World War II Sea Engagements.* Orange County, CA.

Mott, Lieutenant Commander William C. Personal Correspondence, White House Files, 1940–1943.

National Park Service Historical Statistics, USS *Arizona* Memorial, Hawaii.

Navy Department, *Ordnance and Gunnery Instructions for Naval Armed Guards on*

Merchant Ships, 1944. 4th ed. Washington, DC: United States Government Printing Office, 1944.

Official Gazette. Manila, the Philippines, January 1942–1944, vols. 1–44.

Olson, Colonel John E. *O'Donnell: Andersonville of the Pacific, Extermination Camp of American Hostages in the Philippines.* Lake Quivra, KS: J. E. Olson, 1985.

Oral history dated January 25, 1994, provided courtesy of the Historian, Bureau of Medicine and Surgery: Recollections of Captain Ann Bernatitus, USN. Washington, DC: Naval Historic Center, Washington Navy Yard.

Paul, Doris A. *The Navajo Code Talkers.* Pittsburgh: Dorrance, 1973.

Pearson, Judith L. *Belly of the Beast: A POW's Inspiring True Story of Faith, Courage, and Survival Aboard the Infamous WWII Japanese Hell Ship* Oryoku Maru. New York: New American Library, 2001.

Peart, Cecil Jesse. Pharmacist's Mate, USN, *Daily Journal 1944–1945.* Unpublished, located at Bureau of Medicine and Surgery, Washington, DC.

Peterson, Bernard. *Briney to the Blue: Memoirs of WWII.* Self-published, 1992.

Pictet, J. *Commentary on the Geneva Convention Relative to the Treatment of Prisoners of War.* Geneva: International Committee of the Red Cross, 1960.

Potter, E. B. *Bull Halsey.* Annapolis, MD: United States Naval Institute Press, 1985.

Potter, E. B., and Chester W. Nimitz. *The Great Sea War: The Story of Naval Action in World War II.* Englewood Cliffs, NJ: Prentice Hall, 1960.

POW. *The Fight Continues After the Battle.* Washington, DC: United States Government Printing Office, 1955.

Prange, Gordon W. *At Dawn We Slept: The Untold Story of Pearl Harbor.* New York: McGraw-Hill, 1981.

Prisoners of War Bulletins. Washington, DC: American National Red Cross. Issues dating from June 1942 to May 1945.

Red Book Register. Red Book, New Jersey, Princeton, NJ: New Jersey State Archive, Microfiche Division 1941–1945.

Redmond, Lieutenant Juanita. *I Served on Bataan.* New York: J. B. Lippincott, 1943.

Report on American Prisoners of War Interned by the Japanese in the Philippines. Office of the Provost Marshall, Washington, DC: November 1945.

RG-16 Biographical Sketch. Papers of Major General Courtney Whitney, 1942–1947. MacArthur Memorial Archives, Norfolk, VA.

Rhea, Milton A. *War Is Hell.* Victoria, Can.: Trafford, 2003.

Rockaway (NJ) Record. Princeton, NJ: New Jersey State Archive, Microfiche Division, 1941–1945.

Rogers, Paul P. *The Good Years: MacArthur and Sutherland; The Bitter Years: MacArthur and Sutherland.* 2 vols. New York: Praeger, 1990, 1991.

Romulo, Brigadier General Carlos P. *My Brother Americans.* Garden City, NY: Doubleday, Doran, 1945.

Roscoe, Theodore. *United States Submarine Operations in World War II.* Annapolis, MD: United States Naval Institute Press, 1949.

Rothberg, Abraham. *Eyewitness History of World War II.* Vol. 4, *Victory.* New York: Bantam Books, 1962.

Sartin, L. B. (Captain), Med Corps USN, Journal, PI, 1941–1945.

Schmidt, Larry, USMC. "American Involvement in the Filipino Resistance Movement on Mindanao During the Japanese Occupation, 1942–1945." Academic paper, Fort Leavenworth, KS, 1982. (General background on birth of aid and intelligence between guerrillas and Australia.)

Seagrave, Peggy. *Gold Warriors.* London: Verso Press, 2002. (Background on Courtney Whitney.)

Sears, David. *At War with the Wind: The Epic Struggle with Japan's World War II Suicide Bombers.* New York: Citadel Press, 2008.

Sherrod, Robert. *On to Westward: The Battles of Saipan and Iwo Jima.* New York: Duell Sloan and Pearce, 1945.

Sherwood, Robert E. *Roosevelt and Hopkins: An Intimate History.* New York: Harper & Brothers, 1948.

Shoemaker, Lloyd R. *The Escape Factory: The Story of MIS-X, America's Ultra Secret Masterminds of World War II's Greatest Escapes.* New York: St. Martin's Press, 1990.

Shofner, Austin Conner, USMC. Diary, 1941–1943. Tennessee State Library, Microfilm.

Sperber, A. M. *Murrow: His Life and Times.* New York: Fordham University Press, 1998.

Stafford, Commander Edward P., USN. *The Big E: The Story of the USS* Enterprise. New York: Ballantine Books, 1962.

Stahl, Robert. *You're No Good to Me Dead: Behind Japanese Lines in the Philippines.* Annapolis MD: United States Naval Institute Press, 1995.

Stevenson, William. *A Man Called Intrepid.* Guilford, CT: Lyons Press, 1976.

Stewart, Sidney. *Give Us This Day.* New York: W. W. Norton, 1956.

Sulzberger, C. L. *World War II.* New York: American Heritage Press, 1985.

Sun Tzu. *The Art of War.* Translated by Samuel B. Griffith. New York: Oxford University Press, 1963.

Tenney, Lester I. *My Hitch in Hell: The Bataan Death March.* Washington, DC: Brassey's, 1995.

Tillman, Barrett. *Clash of the Carriers: The True Story of the Marianas Turkey Shoot.* New York: Penguin Group, 2005.

Tillman, Barrett. *Enterprise: America's Fightingest Ship and the Men Who Helped Win World War II.* New York: Simon & Schuster, 2012.

Toland, John. *Infamy: Pearl Harbor and Its Aftermath.* New York: Berkley Books, 1982.

——. *The Last 100 Days.* New York: Random House, 1966.

Toland, John. Transcript of Toland's 1982 series of interviews with William C. Mott regarding Naval Intelligence operations leading up to Pearl Harbor and Mott's subsequent service in the White House Map Room. Acquired from Roosevelt Presidential Library, Hyde Park, NY.

Tregaskis, Richard. *Guadalcanal Diary.* New York: Random House, 1943.

Truman, Harry S. *Memoirs.* Vol. 1, *Year of Decisions.* Garden City, NY: Doubleday, 1955.

Tunny, Noel. *Winning from Down Under.* Brisbane: Boolarong Press, 2010.

US Army. *The Fall of the Philippines.* U.S. Army in World War II: The War in the Pacific. Washington, DC: Center of Military History, United States Army, 1989.

U.S. Division of Naval History. *History of Ships Named Enterprise.*

United States Navy. *The Bluejackets' Manual.* Annapolis, MD: United States Naval Institute, 1943.

USNI Oral Histories: Chick Parsons, Admiral John McCrea, Admiral A. H.

McCollum, Admiral Stuart Murray, Admiral George Dyer, Admiral Van Deurs, Captain Joseph Rochefort, Admiral Arthur S. Carpender, Admiral Ernest Eller, Captain Slade Cutter, Admiral Gerald Bogan, Admiral Raymond D. Tarbuck, and Admiral Bernard Bieri.

USS *Otus* Ship's Log. Obtained from National Archives, College Park, MD.

van der Vat, Dan. *The Pacific Campaign: World War II—The U.S.-Japanese Naval War 1941–1945*. New York: Simon & Schuster, 1991.

Veronico, Nicholas A., and Armand H. Veronico. *Battlestations! American Warships of WWII*. St. Paul, MN: MBI, 2001.

Waggener, Nelson. *Memories of World War II While in the Southwest Pacific*. Self-published, 1979.

Wheeler, Keith. *The Pacific Is My Beat*. New York: E. P. Dutton, 1943.

Wheeler, Kenneth R. *For My Children*. Unpublished manuscript, no date.

Wiest, Andrew, and Gregory Louis Mattson. *The Pacific War: The Campaigns of World War II*. St. Paul, MN: MBI, 2001.

Willoughby, Major General Charles A. *The Guerrilla Resistance Movement in the Philippines*. New York: Vantage Press, 1972.

Wills, Donald. *The Sea Was My Last Chance*. London: McFarland, 1992.

Willson, Captain Russell. *Watch Officer's Guide: United States Navy*. Annapolis, MD: United States Naval Institute, 1941.

Wodnik, Bob. *Captured Honor: POW Survival in the Philippines and Japan*. Pullman: Washington State University Press, 2003.

Woods, Tarleton E. *March of Death: An American Soldier's 1,216 Days as a POW of the Japanese*. Spartanburg, SC: Honoribis Press, 2006.

Wordsworth, William. "Lines Composed a Few Miles Above Tintern Abbey on Revisiting the Banks of the Wye During a Tour, July 13, 1798."

Zich, Arthur. *The Rising Sun*. Alexandria, VA: Time-Life Books, 1977. (Japan's policies in conquered territories, 148–49.)

Image Credits

Index

About the Author

SALLY MOTT FREEMAN is serving her fourth term as board chair of the Writer's Center (TWC) in Bethesda, MD. The Writer's Center hosts hundreds of writing workshops annually and over seventy literary events a year, featuring authors of local, national, and international renown. Freeman previously served as a media and public relations executive in both the public and private sectors.

She was a speechwriter at the Federal Communications Commission and later the agency's News Media Division Chief, as well as Director of Legislative and Public Affairs for FmHA, the finance arm of USDA. In the private sector, she was a vice president in the telecom practice at Fleishman Hillard, Inc., and later ran corporate communications for two technology trade associations.

Freeman graduated with a degree in English literature from Sweet Briar College, which awarded her its 2016 Distinguished Alumna award, and spent a year studying Renaissance literature at the University of Exeter, England. She and her husband, John Freeman, have four adult children and live in Bethesda, Maryland.